Gift to the Church and World

Global Perspectives on the New Evangelization

Volume 3

Series Introduction

> Then he sat down and taught the crowds from the boat. After he had finished speaking, he said to Simon, "Put out into deep water and lower your nets for a catch." Simon said in reply, "Master, we have worked hard all night and have caught nothing, but at your command I will lower the nets." When they had done this, they caught a great number of fish and their nets were tearing.
>
> —Luke 5:3–6

"How beautiful upon the mountains are the feet of the one bringing good news, announcing peace, bearing good news, announcing salvation, saying to Zion, 'Your God is King!'" (Isaiah 52:7). Evangelization is something beautiful. Derived from the Greek word, *euaggelion*, evangelization means to bear a "happy/blessed message." It is safe to say that every human being longs for good news, and the entire drama of salvation history, as revealed especially in Scripture and Tradition, hinges on a claim to the best news there is. In a word, salvation through divine intimacy—Emmanuel, God with us (see Isaiah 7:14; Matthew 1:23). And as for the essence of this salvation? Isaiah's witness makes it clear: a return to goodness, peace, and the lordship of God.

The bridge of meaning between Isaiah's text and the life and teachings of Jesus of Nazareth is unmistakable: "After John had been arrested, Jesus came to Galilee proclaiming the gospel (*euaggelion*) of God: 'This is the time of fulfillment. The kingdom of God is at hand. Repent, and believe in the gospel'" (Mark 1:14–15). Jesus not only proclaims the good news indicated by Isaiah—"Your God is King!"—he manifests and embodies it. Jesus is the good news of God in person: "And the Word became flesh and made his dwelling among us" (John 1:14). In Jesus's humanity united with his divinity, the good news of God becomes sacrament through the perpetual liturgy of incarnation. Yet the totality of God's revelation in Jesus is laced with paradox. He is a servant king. His royal garments are stark nakedness. His crown is woven of thorns. His ministry is unconcerned with the accumulation of material wealth but, to the contrary, is about giving all away. His queen is a vestal virgin, the Church, *in persona Mariae*, and he reigns from a wooden throne of suffering.

In the twenty-first century, the paradoxical message of the Gospel is no less shocking than it was two thousand years ago. If anything, it is even more riveting to scientific sensibilities and to a surging expansion of secularism taking root in virtually every cultural setting of the world. As Pope Paul VI put it in his 1975 apostolic exhortation, *Evangelii nuntiandi*, we have entered definitively "a new period of evangelization (*feliciora evangelizationis tempora*)" (2). In other words, today we find ourselves in a happy and profitable season to evangelize.

This book series, *Global Perspectives on the New Evangelization*, aims to contribute to the mission field of this "New Evangelization." By offering fresh voices from a diversity of perspectives, these books put Catholic theology into dialogue with a host of conversation partners around a variety of themes. Through the principle of inculturation, rooted in that of incarnation, this series seeks to reawaken those facets of truth found in the beautiful complementarity of cultural voices as harmonized in the one, holy, catholic, and apostolic Church.

John C. Cavadini and **Donald Wallenfang**, *Series editors*

"Joseph Ratzinger's demanding and original *Introduction to Christianity* deserves a set of interlocutors able to rise to its own high level. It has found them in the studies collected here, ranging as they do from close-up snapshots of the work in its place and time to confrontations with a choice of theologians, culture-critics, filmmakers, and visual artists closer either to now or to home."

—**Aidan Nichols**, OP, author of *The Thought of Pope Benedict XVI: An Introduction to the Theology of Joseph Ratzinger*

"This collection provides sixteen precious vignettes into Ratzinger's celebrated classic *Introduction to Christianity*. These eminently scholarly perspectives celebrate a book that presents in 1968 divine-human relationality as *the* concrete Vatican II watershed. The authors convincingly argue that this christocentric shift grounds the believer in the life and charity of the Blessed Trinity, which in turn permits genuine interhuman charity to flourish. This volume is indispensable for understanding deeper Ratzinger. Most welcome and highly recommended!"

—**Fr. Emery de Gaál**, Chairperson of Dogmatic Theology at Mundelein Seminary

"This book identifies a classic that has never received the notice it's due. Ratzinger's *Introduction* is so much more than a book; it's a pedagogy, a way of teaching. This fact shines through every contribution here, but especially in the pages that compare Ratzinger's masterpiece with C. S. Lewis's *Mere Christianity*. Ratzinger did not simply introduce people to Christianity; he invited them into communion, where the mysteries lead to a living faith. *Gift* is the rare book that acknowledges the deeply mystical element in the theological task and a person's intellectual life."

—**Scott Hahn**, founder and president of the St. Paul Center of Biblical Theology

"Is there a theology worthy of the name that does not introduce its readers to the One who 'introduces' the Father through the Spirit? If in this sense all true theology is an introduction to Christianity, then Joseph Ratzinger's corpus—of which his *Introduction to Christianity* is an exemplification—focuses always on introducing us to the person of Jesus Christ in the face of the difficulties that threaten to block him from our mind and heart. Thus Ratzinger's *Introduction* has an enduring place in teaching modern theologians how and why to do theology. With its deft elucidations of Ratzinger's approach, the present volume should lay the foundations not only for the future of Ratzingerian studies but for the future of Catholic theology as a discipline."

—**Matthew Levering**, James N. and Mary D. Perry Jr. Chair of Theology, Mundelein Seminary

Gift to the Church and World

Fifty Years of Joseph Ratzinger's *Introduction to Christianity*

EDITED BY
John C. Cavadini
AND
Donald Wallenfang

GLOBAL PERSPECTIVES ON THE
NEW EVANGELIZATION

☙PICKWICK *Publications* · Eugene, Oregon

GIFT TO THE CHURCH AND WORLD
Fifty Years of Joseph Ratzinger's *Introduction to Christianity*

Global Perspectives on the New Evangelization 3

Copyright © 2021 Wipf and Stock Publishers. All rights reserved. Except for brief quotations in critical publications or reviews, no part of this book may be reproduced in any manner without prior written permission from the publisher. Write: Permissions, Wipf and Stock Publishers, 199 W. 8th Ave., Suite 3, Eugene, OR 97401.

Pickwick Publications
An Imprint of Wipf and Stock Publishers
199 W. 8th Ave., Suite 3
Eugene, OR 97401

www.wipfandstock.com

PAPERBACK ISBN: 978-1-7252-8646-7
HARDCOVER ISBN: 978-1-7252-8647-4
EBOOK ISBN: 978-1-7252-8648-1

Cataloguing-in-Publication data:

Names: Cavadini, John C., editor. | Wallenfang, Donald, editor.

Title: Gift to the church and world : fifty years of Joseph Ratzinger's *Introduction to Christianity* / edited by John C. Cavadini and Donald Wallenfang.

Description: Eugene, OR : Pickwick Publications, 2021 | Series: Global Perspectives on the New Evangelization 3 | Includes bibliographical references and index.

Identifiers: ISBN 978-1-7252-8646-7 (paperback) | ISBN 978-1-7252-8647-4 (hardcover) | ISBN 978-1-7252-8648-1 (ebook)

Subjects: LCSH: Ratzinger, Joseph. Introduction to Christianity. | Apologetics. | Apostles' Creed. | Theology, Doctrinal.

Classification: BT993.2 .G54 2021 (print) | BT993.2 .G54 (ebook)

03/16/21

The editors would like to dedicate this volume
to Pope Emeritus Benedict XVI—

"(a) man who seeks a view of the whole"
(*Introduction to Christianity*, 155).

Contents

List of Contributors | xi

Acknowledgments | xiii

Introduction by John C. Cavadini | xv

I. Overview and Context

CHAPTER 1: Integral Faith Formation in the Spirit of the Second Vatican Council: Joseph Ratzinger's *Introduction to Christianity* (1968) | 3

—*Most Rev. Rudolf Voderholzer*

CHAPTER 2: The Articulation of Faith Between Memory and Recollection | 24

—*Rev. Richard Schenk, OP*

CHAPTER 3: The Reception of *Einführung in das Christentum* among the Reviewers | 44

—*Tracey Rowland*

II. Fundamental Theology

CHAPTER 4: The *Introduction to Christianity* in Light of *Principles of Catholic Theology* | 67

—*Cyril O'Regan*

CHAPTER 5: Ratzinger on Lessing's "Ugly Broad Ditch": Augustinian *Ressourcement* and Modern Rationalism | 89

—*Rev. Aaron Pidel, SJ*

CHAPTER 6: An Introduction to Tradition in Ratzinger's *Introduction to Christianity* | 109
—Catherine R. Cavadini

CHAPTER 7: An Introduction to Scripture in Ratzinger's *Introduction to Christianity* | 129
—Anthony J. Pagliarini

III. Philosophical Theology

CHAPTER 8: *Nein und doch:* Ratzinger's Philosophy of Renunciation in an Augustinian Key | 143
—Donald Wallenfang, OCDS

CHAPTER 9: "Being for" and Normativity in a Post-Durkheimian Age | 168
—Anthony C. Sciglitano, Jr.

IV. Dogmatic Theology

CHAPTER 10: Joseph Ratzinger's "Spiritual Christology" | 189
—Rev. Robert P. Imbelli

CHAPTER 11: Touching the Void: Ratzinger's Soteriology | 213
—Francesca Murphy

CHAPTER 12: The Homelessness of Pneumatology: Ratzinger on the Spirit and the Church in the Modern World | 225
—Patrick X. Gardner

CHAPTER 13: Hide and Seek: The Eschatology of *Introduction to Christianity* | 241
—Leonard J. DeLorenzo

CHAPTER 14: The Liturgical Metaphysics of Gift in *Introduction to Christianity* | 255
—Timothy P. O'Malley

V. Spiritual Theology

CHAPTER 15: On Christian Structures | 275

—*Clemens Sedmak*

CHAPTER 16: On the Absenting of Christ: Cruciform Beauty in Ratzinger's *Introduction to Christianity* | 294

—*Jennifer Newsome Martin*

Epilogue: "The Pedagogy of Introducing," by John C. Cavadini | 317

Index | 327

Contributors

Catherine R. Cavadini, Associate Teaching Professor of Theology at the University of Notre Dame

John C. Cavadini, Professor of Theology and Director of the McGrath Institute for Church Life at the University of Notre Dame

Leonard J. DeLorenzo, Academic Director of Vision in the McGrath Institute for Church Life at the University of Notre Dame

Patrick X. Gardner, Assistant Professor of Philosophy and Religion at Christopher Newport University

Rev. Robert P. Imbelli, Associate Professor Emeritus of Theology at Boston College

Jennifer Newsome Martin, Assistant Professor in the Program of Liberal Studies at the University of Notre Dame

Francesca Murphy, Professor of Theology at the University of Notre Dame

Timothy P. O'Malley, Academic Director of Notre Dame Center for Liturgy in the McGrath Institute for Church Life at the University of Notre Dame

Cyril O'Regan, Catherine F. Huisking Professor of Theology at the University of Notre Dame

Anthony J. Pagliarini, Assistant Teaching Professor of Theology at the University of Notre Dame

Rev. Aaron Pidel, SJ, Assistant Professor of Theology, Marquette University

Tracey Rowland, St. John Paul II Chair of Theology at the University of Notre Dame, Australia

Rev. Richard Schenk, OP, Honorary Professor of Theology at Albert-Ludwigs University, Freiburg im Breisgau

Anthony C. Sciglitano, Jr., Associate Professor of Religion, Seton Hall University

Clemens Sedmak, Professor of Social Ethics in the Keough School of Global Affairs at the University of Notre Dame

Most Rev. Rudolf Voderholzer, Bishop of Regensburg

Donald Wallenfang, OCDS, Professor of Theology and Philosophy at Sacred Heart Major Seminary

Acknowledgments

It is an occasion of joy to recognize those whose support has made this book possible. First, the editors would like to acknowledge the McGrath Institute for Church Life at the University of Notre Dame, and, especially, the self-giving vision of Robert and Joan McGrath. The McGrath Institute for Church Life sponsored and hosted the "Ratzinger's *Introduction to Christianity* at 50" Conference in November of 2018 and endowed the compilation of this book project that is the fruit of the conference proceedings. Second, we owe Mark Therrien a great amount of gratitude for his dexterous editorial work across all of the essays of the volume. Third, we thank Wipf and Stock Publishers, especially Charlie Collier and Matt Wimer, for giving the *Global Perspectives on the New Evangelization* book series a lasting home. Fourth, we thank the William G. Congdon Foundation of Buccinasco, Italy, for granting permission to reprint the following images within Dr. Jennifer Newsome Martin's essay, "On the Absenting of Christ":

> William Congdon
> *Crocefisso No. 2* (1960)
> oil on masonite—35x23 in
> © The William G. Congdon Foundation, Milan
>
> William Congdon
> *Crocefisso No. 46* (1969)
> oil on panel—23 7/8 x 19 3/4 in
> © The William G. Congdon Foundation, Milan
>
> William Congdon
> *Bombay No. 19* (1973)
> oil on panel—23 5/8 x 19 3/4 in
> © The William G. Congdon Foundation, Milan

William Congdon
Crocefisso No. 90 (1974)
oil on panel—47 1/4 x 39 3/8 in
© The William G. Congdon Foundation, Milan

William Congdon
Crocefisso No. 91 (1974)
oil on panel—41 x 31 1/2 in
© The William G. Congdon Foundation, Milan

And finally, we thank all of the contributors to this volume for their careful scholarship and communal spirit circulating around the life and legacy of Pope Emeritus Benedict XVI. May this book validate all of its contributors as *cooperatores veritatis* ("cooperators of the truth").

Introduction

John C. Cavadini

Prologue

On the occasion of the fiftieth anniversary of the publication of *Einführung in das Christentum* in 1968, released in 1969 in the English Translation of J. R. Foster as *Introduction to Christianity*, the contributors present this collection of essays intended to honor the remarkable achievement of a book that has been continuously in print since its publication, still in use up to the present day in courses both undergraduate and graduate, and translated into twenty-two languages in addition to the English. The papers in this volume were presented at an international conference sponsored by the McGrath Institute for Church Life at the University of Notre Dame in October, 2018, to mark the anniversary of publication. They have been revised for inclusion here.

    Why has this book managed to capture the attention of so many teachers and scholars of theology for so long? What is the secret of its appeal? Perhaps it is only after the passing of time that this question can be answered. Perhaps it is only now that we have sufficient perspective to notice what the singular genius of this book is that has caused it to outlast many similar efforts at "introducing" Christianity to various audiences.

    Perhaps it is the act of "introducing" itself that shines forth as a theological activity worthy of consideration in its own right as a perpetual task that is, again perhaps, mostly overlooked as something "preliminary" or "elementary," and therefore merely propaedeutic to theology proper. Perhaps in this book "introducing" is itself "introduced" as an element proper to all theology, at least if its message is to be taken seriously, unlike that of the circus clown in the famous story Ratzinger cites.[1]

---

1. Ratzinger, *Introduction to Christianity*, 39–40.

Perhaps as the default temperament of our age has grown more and more secular since the publication of the *Introduction*, we can see even more clearly the importance of beginning, as this text does in so many instances, with the difficulty of believing, with the obstacles to faith, with all of the ways it seems implausible, outdated, and irrelevant to life today. Even we believers can wonder if we have actually "outgrown" the faith once and for all, along with the rest of our scientific age. "In a situation like this," Ratzinger comments, "what is in question is not the sort of thing that one perhaps quarrels about otherwise—the dogma of the Assumption, the proper use of confession—all this becomes absolutely secondary. What is at stake is the whole structure; it is a question of all or nothing."[2] A theology which holds ever before itself the difficulty of believing, the seeming implausibility of the Christian message and its irrelevance to an age of scientific maturity, to which is added "the petty spectacle of those who, with their claim to administer official Christianity, seem to stand most in the way of the true spirit of Christianity"[3]—such a theology will always be "introducing" Christianity, not as an attempt to re-package it and enclose it in a new "structure" or system, but as part and parcel of a re-proposal of the very invitation of "God," from the "fullness of his love" that, in revelation, "addresses men and women as his friends, and lives among them, in order to invite them into his own company."[4] Ratzinger realizes that no one can accept an invitation they are not able to "hear" spiritually. A theology that is always aware of itself as "introducing" will always operate from the awareness of the difficulties people have in "hearing." But since faith comes through hearing, it will be one that tries to make this invitation audible, even if it is finally left to the work of the Spirit to convert the heart.

All of the contributors to this volume recognize in one way or another, and call attention to, the way in which Ratzinger has featured and therefore made visible the element of "introducing" as an element proper to all of theology. We could call this theology under the exigence of "introducing" the invitation of revelation to hearts, including our own, that seem to have closed themselves to it on intellectual grounds. And, although the division of papers into the sections provided in the Table of Contents has an element of arbitrariness because the papers themselves cross the boundaries, it is designed to help the reader see this fundamental connection among all of them, in that each of them have noted, and uplifted, some dimension of Ratzinger's fundamental contribution in this book, which is to have called

2. Ratzinger, *Introduction*, 43.
3. Ratzinger, *Introduction*, 340.
4. *Dei Verbum*, §2.

attention to theology in its "introductory" mode, which is to say all of theology at its best, which is to claim that all of theology, at its best, is properly speaking "introductory," which ultimately is to offer a model for the renewal of theology in the spirit of Vatican II.

Section One: Overview and Context

This is nowhere more evident than in the first group of papers, those in the section of "Overview and Context," all of which treat the *Introduction* as a post-conciliar work that had its genesis in the work of the Council itself. The title of the first and keynote essay, by Bishop Rudolf Voderholzer, announces this idea in so many words, treating the *Introduction* as "integral faith formation in the spirit of the Second Vatican Council." Voderholzer emphasizes the value of "re-reading the *Introduction to Christianity*" after the passage of so many years since its publication, and the value of this retrospect in understanding its significance and impact. He observes, "again and again I notice how many of the topics that I reflected on for the first time while reading it—without my being aware of *this* origin—have belonged since then to the inventory of my deepest theological convictions." Voderholzer's thesis is that the *Introduction* "is an analysis of the Christian faith precisely in the spirit of this [Second Vatican] Council." This spirit is "Christocentric," following the orientations of the two dogmatic constitutions *Lumen Gentium* and *Dei Verbum* and the pastoral constitution *Gaudium et Spes*, thus "gaining clarity about who this Jesus of Nazareth is . . . must be one concern—if not the chief concern—of an introduction to Christian-ity [sic]" in the spirit of the Council. The spirit is also one of *aggiornamento*, and in this connection Voderholzer notes that "the accuracy with which the young professor managed to put into words the questions and needs of his contemporaries in relation to the faith (and to let his own analysis of the faith be challenged by them) may have contributed substantially to the extraordinary success of Ratzinger's *Introduction*." Finally, the spirit of the Council is biblical, and Voderholzer adds that Ratzinger's *Introduction* models "in an exemplary fashion" what *Dei Verbum* meant when it said that the study of Sacred Scripture must be "the soul of sacred theology." Ratzinger accomplishes this "not by lining up proof texts" but rather "through a theology and analysis of the faith that draws from the overall dynamic of Sacred Scripture . . . "

The title of the second keynote contribution, that of Fr. Richard Schenk, OP, also gets at the deeper meaning of what "introducing" Christianity means in the *Introduction*. Schenk proposes that the various types of critical reception of Ratzinger's *Introduction* generally tended to sort themselves out according to the various types of critical reception of the Council itself. Criticized by traditionalists as "modernist" because of its "alleged adoption of subjectivism, historicism, and relativism," it also faced "the precisely opposite criticism" from those liberals who critiqued it as "Platonist," even while the precise content of that charge remained mostly unarticulated. Recalling the distinction between "memory" (*mneme*) and "recollection" (*anamnesis*) made by Plato himself and then by Aristotle and, following him, Ricoeur, Schenk characterizes Ratzinger's *Introduction* as "The Articulation of Faith Between Memory and Recollection." For between memory and recollection lies the relation of both to "forgetting." Both traditionalist and liberal critics have a stronger confidence in their "memory" of the tradition than does the *Introduction*. The former "display little worry that their own memory of the tradition is a faded one, which might require extensive anamnetic efforts at ressourcement," while in the latter there is "an unstated 'Platonic' confidence that Catholic identity is already well enough established and present within us to recognize with ease and facility the pastoral and theological significance of trends read simply as benevolent 'signs of the times.'" Theology under the exigence of "introduction" goes deeper into our own collective forgetfulness: "In comparison to its accommodationalist and traditionalistic critics, the *Introduction* is less sanguine about, because more familiar with, the painful godlessness that continues to haunt the faithful." Its concern for ressourcement, from this perspective, turns out to be "a search in the imagination for places of the earliest experience of what in good part has been forgotten." Ironically, in that sense, the *Introduction* "was arguably less 'Platonic' than many of its sharpest critics." In any event, it is clear that the *Introduction* is an "introduction" more by way of "re-introduction" to what our attachment to an idealized past or present has caused us to forget, namely, the "very basics of faith in the personal divine Other" and the difficulties in understanding what they mean for the contemporary faithful.

Tracey Rowland's contribution is devoted to a more detailed analysis of the critical reception of Ratzinger's *Introduction*. This essay is especially valuable for providing Ratzinger's reactions to the criticisms, especially to that tendered by Walter Kasper, who, it should be noted, also praised the book for its "profound theological depths," especially in the sections on Christology, atonement, the theology of the cross, and the connection between pneumatology and ecclesiology. Kasper noted that in these areas, "Ratzinger succeeds in a valid new interpretation" of these dogmas of the Church, "a courageous effort and a notable achievement." And while these laudatory comments can be easily overlooked because of the criticism

Kasper also tendered, it is interesting to note that these areas are all singled out for their "notable achievement" by contributors to this volume as well. Kasper famously went on to indict Ratzinger's theology as Platonizing—as prescinding from, rather than proceeding from "'the concrete complexity of man and his embedded state within nature, society, culture and history.'" In Rowland's analysis the accusation of Platonism is something of a red herring: "Rather than Plato being the problem, it might be argued that the reception of Hegel is the point of issue between Ratzinger and Kasper, and especially the idea, made fashionable by the Hegelians of the Left, of the priority of *praxis*." Kasper's criticism had echoed an earlier charge of Platonism, leveled by an anonymous reviewer in the journal *Kritischer Katholizismus*, and Ratzinger's response tends to support the thesis of Rowland, since he alleged that, for the group behind *Kritischer Katholizismus*, "'which pays homage to a consequential Neo-Marxism, there is no enduring truth towards which man can stand receptive, but rather reality is constant change.... Truth exists as *pragma* alone; as intervention within the process of changing the world.'" Ratzinger noted further that it is true that "'theology does not revolve upon itself,'" and that "'its goal is praxis,'" but that "'the properly practical task of theology lies in teaching men to believe, to hope and to love and thereby opens up meaning which helps him to live.'" Again, "'its proper praxis consists in giving man something which other "organizations" are not in a position to give,'" and then adds, hoping, he says, not to appear boastful, that theologians who had originally judged his theology as "'impractical,'" later confessed to him "'that they had completely revised their opinion, because they find that neither children in schools, nor the sick, nor the helpless are interested in which changes to ecclesial structures are still possible, but rather wish to know what message the Church still now has to offer.'" Here is the idea surfacing, once again, of what I am calling theology under the exigence of "introducing." It is that which addresses the thirst to find meaning in life and so reaches the profundity that Kasper himself acknowledged. Interestingly, Ratzinger begins to sound like Pope Francis here, who has repeatedly warned us against a Church that is too inwardly focused, too interested in internal matters, and not in evangelization: "'In loudly proclaiming reform we speak only of ourselves; the Gospel hardly seems to rate a mention.'" In fact, the *Introduction*, drawing attention to the "gulf between [the biblical] conception and Platonic, absolute Being," mentions in particular God's naming of Himself in Exodus 3 as an invitation to relationship, once again foreshadowing Pope Francis in that "a fundamental feature of Christianity is that it is personal. It is not I believe in something, but 'I believe in Thee.'"

Section Two: Fundamental Theology

The section on Fundamental Theology opens with an essay by Cyril O'Regan. He reads the *Introduction* in the light of the 1982 *Principles of Catholic Theology*, which has the subtitle, "Building Stones for a Fundamental Theology." O'Regan places Ratzinger in the tradition of Kierkegaard and Dostoyevski, each a "prophetic figure who diagnoses the crisis in modernity concerning the viability of Christianity." Theology under the exigence of introduction is theology that comes from a sense of crisis and "it is precisely this sense of crisis and thus the necessity of . . . intervention that has made the text the classic that it is." There is a "patent sense of emergency which demands that the basics of the Christian faith be boldly as well as clearly expressed." In large part this "explains the energy of [the] text" and its "continuing persuasiveness." Further, the choice of the Apostles' Creed as the substrate for the *Introduction* is explained because the Creed is oriented to "baptism and full entry into the Church," and thus to decision and "confession." It is ordered, in other words, towards persuasive apologetic teaching, catechesis and preaching, in accordance with the crisis that called it forth. This has implications for the practice of ecumenical and inter-religious dialogue, where the goods of proclamation should not be marginalized or officially excised from a dialogue that would then proceed simply "for dialogue's sake." Triumphalism is to be avoided, but our age is more inclined to the "prejudice . . . increasingly in favor of a dialogue thought to fare best if the participants in the dialogue in general, but especially Christianity, make all aspects of their faith matters of negotiation." One can see, in turn, how such a tendency towards effective relativism makes the exigence of introducing all the more of an "emergency," since people can no longer discern what the Church has to offer that is distinctive. In the "now moment" of the "contemporary crisis of the relation between faith and reason . . . what is therefore needed is a bold declaration of Christian faith, and a spirited defense of its possibility as well as actuality." Apparently fifty years' worth of readers agree!

In this crisis of the relation between faith and reason, Ratzinger, according to Fr. Aaron Pidel, "underscores reason's need of faith." Pidel examines Ratzinger's choice of a "sparring partner" in articulating reason's dependence on faith—not Marx, but Lessing, famous for the "broad ugly ditch" he posited between, on the one hand, the historical and contingent posits or facts of Christianity, the *vérités de fait*, and the truths of reason, the *vérités de raison*, on the other, which need no chain of evidentiary proof to back them up. Such proof is in any event ultimately unsatisfying in comparison to the truths of universal reason "immediately and independently verifiable by individual reason." Lessing's ditch defines the crisis of modernity to which Ratzinger responds. It is the "scandal" of such questions as "Why the Jews among the nations? Why the Incarnation in the 'middle' of history rather than in our own lifetime? Why wheat for the Eucharist, when rice is the staple of so much of the world? Can a God who reputedly desires the salvation of all really put much stock in any doctrine or duty he has not made equally plausible and accessible to all?" The answer that "modern rationalism" gives, based on Lessing's ditch, is negative. Instead, "reason's reflection on human nature discloses every important religious duty." This amounts to the "regulative ideal of rational autonomy," where "the highest mode of reason is the most sufficient unto itself." One way to deal with Lessing's ditch is to try to cross it by demonstrating the compatibility or correlation of the seemingly contingent truths of the faith with truths universally available to transcendent reason, but this tactic, both in its "'conservative' (e.g. neo-scholastic) and 'liberal' (e.g., Rahnerian)" forms, if it is even possible, would generate "too costly a victory." It would overcome Lessing's broad, ugly ditch "by marginalizing Christianity's stubbornly positive elements—its history, symbols, sacraments, scriptures, hierarchy," and thus "if we could actually succeed in rendering Christianity rationally transparent, we would at the very moment render it existentially superfluous." In its "chastening of rationalist pretensions," the *Introduction* recovers an Augustinianism that provides it with an "ongoing timelessness," enabling it to remain fresh even fifty years after its publication. The *Introduction* resolutely rejects the terms of Lessing's ditch insofar as it denies the "dependence" of creaturely reason, which is not self-sufficient and cannot manufacture its own meaning without defeating itself. Pidel comments that "if God limited his ways and demands to those strictly deducible from the *vérités de raison*, God would remain ultimately indistinguishable from our reason." In the *Introduction*, Ratzinger comments that "'the contingent, the external is what is necessary to man; only in the arrival of something from the outside does he open up inwardly.'" Thus theology under the exigence of introduction is indeed a theology under the exigence of promoting an encounter not with the impersonal absolute of Platonism or German idealism, but with the positive concrete Person of the Word made flesh.

In place of the "regulative ideal of rational autonomy," the *Introduction* presents the regulative ideal of Tradition, and it is anything but an account of autonomy, as Catherine Cavadini's essay explains. Instead, because faith does not arise from autonomous reason, but "'comes from hearing'" and is thus "'the reception of something that I have *not* thought out,'" as Ratzinger says in the *Introduction,* faith, as a response to what is revealed, always retains its character as intrinsically dialogical. Revelation is necessarily a living reality, living in the one who hears and receives, and thus "'the person who receives it also is a part of the revelation . . . for without him [or her] it does not exist."' The locus of the "handing on" of what is revealed is therefore the communion of hearers and proclaimers that is the Church. As *Dei Verbum* teaches, in Tradition the "'Church, in her teaching, life and worship, perpetuates and hands on to all generations all that she herself is, all that she believes.'" The *Introduction* offers itself as a moment in this handing on. As Cavadini explains, "this kind of handing-on involving the whole person and all that the Church herself is, makes for a persuasive public appeal." It drives back to the roots of faith, to the roots of personal assent to the basic proclamation: "Ratzinger invites his readers to contemplate Christ and ask again and again, 'Are you really he?' The reader may feel this is a rather elementary question to ask—too introductory—but Ratzinger shows it is a question to be asked again and again. It is the point of entry into dialogue." Theology under the exigence of "introducing" is always bringing us back to the moment of encounter as the source of plenipotentiary meaning that is anything but self-referentially and autonomously constituted. Instead it provides the opportunity to open our hearts to it and to each other in sharing it. The success of the *Introduction* is thus precisely its "traditional" character. "It expresses Ratzinger's own participation in the 'we' of the Church in a way that invites others into this 'we.'" Cavadini notes that this way of characterizing tradition is peculiarly Marian: "with Ratzinger . . . we examine the dialogue between Christ, John and Mary [at the foot of the Cross] as a particular historical point in which the life that is 'completely' for others becomes the life of the Church." As Mary was entrusted to John, "the Church is entrusted to each and every individual whose 'Amen' receives the Church into his or her own home," a kind of "sacrificial hospitality," which is intrinsically open to sharing both the question, "Are you really he?" and the "Amen!" which hands on the gift of self that this answer entails. Theology under the exigence of introducing is itself personal and exigent, itself living. It shares that "Amen!" in a way that engenders understanding of it so as to invite the same response from the reader. In this sense, too, it is Augustinian. In the prologue of the *De doctrina*, Augustine insists on a mode of revelation which is constitutively mediated, constitutively "traditional," in his belief "that God is present through 'men and women,' the community of believers, and the Church's sacramental life."

The relational character of revelation continues as a feature of the essay by Anthony Pagliarini on the role of Scripture in the *Introduction*. Pagliarini enters into a detailed consideration of the criticisms, also underscored by Imbelli, of the draft document *De fontibus* which was to be the Second Vatican Council's constitution on revelation. Critiquing its claim that revelation has "two sources, Sacred Scripture and Tradition," Ratzinger alleged that "in this view, God's self-disclosure is restricted to 'a teaching that one acquires from different "sources"—a view typical of the age of historicism and its emphasis on the "positive."'" Instead, "Ratzinger sought to place Christ at the center." He is the "one source" of revelation. It is He who, in revelation, addresses Himself "to men and women in the entirety of their being, and the goal of this personal address is 'fellowship' and a coming to 'share in the divine nature,'" as *Dei Verbum* eventually puts it. The goal of revelation is not simply to secure intellectual assent to a set of propositions but it "'necessarily reaches . . . into the personal center of man, it touches him in the depths of his being, not only in his individual faculties, in his will and his understanding.'" Scripture itself is thus not "revelation" unless and until "'its inner reality has itself become effective after the manner of faith.'" Pagliarini observes that the *Introduction* "aims to elicit from its audience the act of faith which the Church herself makes in its profession of the Creed," drawing its audience "toward the confession, 'I believe in you.'" This confession is prompted by an encounter with the God who addresses himself to human beings in revelation. "Scripture is put forward in the *Introduction* as the site of this encounter." Ratzinger "introduces" us to the way that "God present[s] himself in Scripture," and he does it in such a way that the "encounter" with the God who presents Himself "becomes possible for the audience of the *Introduction*." In a sense, God introduces *Himself* to us in Scripture, and the *Introduction* is thus a kind of introduction to an introduction, in a way that hopes to bring out the intention of the original introduction in a way that makes its inherently efficacious character available for the reader who may have dismissed the texts of Scripture as hopelessly ancient, outdated, and irrelevant. In this way, the *Introduction* becomes itself the site of an encounter, which does not abstract from Scripture, but is essentially and irreducibly Scriptural.

Section Three: Philosophical Theology

The next section contains our two essays in philosophical theology. Each of them discusses the *Introduction* as a sample, within the larger context of Ratzinger's theology, of the relationship between Ratzinger and particular philosophies or theological uses of philosophy. Donald Wallenfang examines the characteristic philosophical tone or tendency of Ratzinger's theology. He notes overall that it "resists any facile identification with one or more trending schools of philosophy, be they ancient, medieval, or modern," and this is true especially because for Ratzinger philosophy and theology "are inseparable by virtue of their common font in the pre-existent *Logos* who is

Jesus Christ, the Incarnate Word of God the Father, spoken simultaneously with the exhaled Breath of God the Holy Spirit." Ratzinger's antecedents in this way of thinking are Augustine and Bonaventure. This in turn sets him apart from neo-Thomism most particularly, but even from Thomas himself, who allows natural reason a relative independence and thus allows philosophy a kind of independent or semi-independent validity. Most importantly, there is a "both . . . and" character to Ratzinger's theological/philosophical synthesis. It respects the "dialectical alterity" proper to truth that prohibits it from collapsing into an "exclusionary monism." It thereby has the ability to resist reductionism, whether in its relativistic form or its fundamentalist form. Ratzinger "teaches us to 'think in Franciscan' (Augustinian, Bonaventurian), while at the same time pointing to the possibilities of thinking in Dominican, Benedictine, Jesuit, Carmelite, and so many more styles and spiritual traditions that are the Catholic heritage." Wallenfang presents Ratzinger's particular brand of inter-penetration of theology and philosophy as offering integrative possibilities for use in the new evangelization, and we can add that the fact that Ratzinger's philosophical approach is conducive to, instead of restrictive of, evangelization is one thing that has helped make the *Introduction* such a success.

Anthony Sciglitano, Jr. juxtaposes Ratzinger's account of the normativity of Christianity with that of the philosopher Charles Taylor, and demonstrates their ultimate divergence. Our modern world is "Post-Durkhemian" as Taylor sees it, meaning that religion is divorced from political discourse and polity. If Christianity retains any normativity, it does so only insofar as its particular claims for Jesus and the Church are "backgrounded" in favor of allowing the "universality" of other of its goods to be "recognized and socially embedded," such goods as "the general egalitarianism of the Gospel, the value of ordinary life . . . , a larger scale of empathy for human suffering, a communal or dialogical mode of authenticity as opposed to atomistic relativism, and perhaps even a sense of depth meaning(s) or immanent transcendence." Without being interested in a "return to some former age" of Constantinian polity, this vision sounds too much like an accomodationalist bridging of Lessing's ditch, privileging the *vérités de raison* (to use the terms of Pidel's essay), for Ratzinger, for whom "Christ does not point to some past, present, or future socio-cultural moment, but instead offers a unique and singular opening onto an Absolute Future for or against which one decides in the present." Decision always in some way creates an "us" and a "them," and this is precisely what Taylor fears in religion socially speaking. But for Ratzinger the "us" is ordered toward the "them," because the "us" is formed by the "Being-for" that is Christ, who configures His Church to Himself in the sacraments. "Being-for" precludes the triumphalism that Taylor fears.

For Ratzinger "what is non-negotiable is the formation of a witnessing, sacramental community that has decided on its obligation to loving service as primary over any power or powers that threaten to enslave us." The Church by its nature is this very community, even though one must equally say it is always in need of conversion towards the Future to which it bears witness—an Augustinian theology of the Church if there ever was one.

Section Four: Dogmatic Theology

Fr. Robert Imbelli's essay, "Joseph Ratzinger's Spiritual Christology," leads off the next section. As others, especially Voderholzer, have emphasized, the focus of Vatican II, and in particular of its four constitutions, was Christocentric. In declaring that the central focus of his *Introduction* is Christ, Ratzinger therefore aligns it in a central way with Vatican II. Imbelli, again echoing Voderholzer, notes that the Christocentric focus of Vatican II defies standard dichotomies such as academic vs. pastoral, or doctrinal vs. spiritual, because "Vatican II's *re-Sourcement* sought to know Christ in a new way: to re-discover the Person of Jesus Christ—not only through propositions *about him*, but by inviting and fostering a personal encounter *with him*," an encounter that leads "not merely to an assent of the mind, but also a consent of the heart, and hence to transformation of life." Ratzinger's Christology is fully in this spirit. As such, it is a "spiritual Christology," not spiritual at the expense of being dogmatic nor dogmatic at the expense of being spiritual. Here we are returned to the secret of the success of the *Introduction*, which "turned out to be an oasis in a parched land" dried up by dichotomies that deadened theology and that sentimentalized the spirituality divorced from it. The "theological-spiritual crisis" to which Ratzinger adverts as one of the reasons for his writing *Introduction* "was—and remains—fundamentally a *Christological crisis*." As Imbelli quotes him, "'Ultimately, all the reflections contained in this book . . . revolve around the basic form of the confession: "I believe in you, Jesus of Nazareth, as the meaning (*logos*) of the world and of my life."' Theology under the exigence of introducing helps the reader understand who Jesus is in the Church's profession, and that, in turn, doctrinal exposition is at once an invitation to encounter the Person of Christ and to make the Church's confession most truly one's own as a result. Ratzinger's spiritual Christology "advocates and guides our entering into the mystery of Christ, a 'Christification' that goes beyond mere moralism." But since the "I" of this Person is "'not at all something exclusive and independent, but rather is Being completely derived from the 'Thou' of the Father and lived for the 'You' of men,'" as Ratzinger says in the *Introduction*, this "Being-for," to use the terms of the previous essay, is realized only in communion. Entering the mystery of Christ is fundamentally Eucharistic, as Ratzinger clarifies more explicitly in later writings, namely, that "'communion with Christ is, of necessity, a communion with all those who are his: it means that I myself become part of this new "bread" which Christ creates by transubstantiating all earthly reality.'"

Perhaps the doctrine of soteriology is the most remote of all from any kind of contemporary intelligibility. Francesca Murphy says that, on the topic of soteriology, "Ratzinger does not seem to write as a 'theologian's theologian' in *Introduction*. Anselm's satisfaction theory seems to take us into 'theological' territory which makes civilian Christians itch and feel uncomfortable," let alone those who are not believers at all. Ratzinger seems to anticipate Pope Francis once again in his requests for theologians to eschew "desk-bound theology"[5] in favor of a theology ordered towards encounter. As Murphy notes, the *Introduction* opts for a "non-juridical conception of atonement" because "some kind of 'objective' satisfaction does not satisfy the need for a *personal* redeemer." Even the doctrine of original sin, while certainly not denied, takes a back seat in Ratzinger's presentation. The fallen state is described in a way that is "phenomenologically accessible" to contemporaries, that is, the "condition of pure loneliness," and the concomitant "horror of plummeting alone into a closed and exitless abyss." Ratzinger's audience can relate to this horror. Jesus's cry of dereliction is "'simply the abyss of loneliness of man in general, of man who is alone in his innermost being, . . . in fundamental contradiction with the nature of man, who cannot exist alone; he needs company.'" Christ overcomes "original death" more than "original sin": "death, says Ratzinger, really is 'what theology calls "hell,"'" where hell "'denotes a loneliness that the word love can no longer penetrate . . . , a night into whose solitude no voice reaches.'" Christ's descent into hell is the destruction of this death. Fallen humanity, "fallen into hell, encounters his face and his outstretched hands," and thus hell ceases to be hell because he is there. Theology under the exigence of "introducing" evokes the hell we all know and fear, not a science fiction fantasy, and allows us to encounter Christ just there, if we are willing.

Arriving at the third article of the Creed, Patrick Gardner's contribution announces itself as wholly congruent with all of the preceding essays in observing that what Ratzinger says about the Holy Spirit and the Church is "not primarily a matter of getting the doctrine right for its own sake"—perhaps another foreshadowing of Pope Francis. Rather "his main concern is with the credibility of the Creed's third section" in the face of obstacles that

---

5. *Evangelii Gaudium*, §133.

are all too familiar, the principal one being "not the lure of atheistic arguments or the prevalence of skepticism, but the Church itself." The Creed's claims that the Church is "one" and "holy" do not appear credible, given the scandals attendant upon the Church's history and present, and the obvious disunity which not even the best ecumenical efforts seem to mitigate. The issue also involves our culture's privileging of *techne,* Ratzinger's term for the domain of the humanly made and makeable, which claims our attention as the only reality which can really be known by human beings. "If *techne* or what is makeable is the highest value informing our vision of reality, it will subtly constrain what we imagine our words can refer to," and this will affect what the Creed has to say about the Church, if the Church is indeed more than human making. It will sound as if the Creed is saying that "'the Church's members and institutions are themselves holy' or 'Christians have joined themselves together.'" But if the Spirit is recovered from the "homelessness" He exhibits when He is treated only in Himself, as an eternal Person of the Trinity relegated to the seemingly useless remoteness of the Godhead; if He is placed back where He also belongs, namely, in the spiritual economy constituting the Church, then we can understand that the "holiness" of the Church refers first and foremost to this divine Person: "The Holy Spirit just is the Church's holiness: he is the *power* to affect forgiveness, conversion, and penance." And thus the holiness of the Church is "something it receives in spite of its sins, not something it achieves." In confessing the third article of the Creed, one is confessing that "the Spirit is the power by which holiness is realized and sin overcome, and that this power is given in or through the Church: 'it is really and truly the holiness of the Lord that becomes present in her.'" Likewise, *communion* is simply a reference to the Spirit, the "mode of being of the Holy Spirit" into which we enter upon becoming a Christian, the communion of saints. "It follows that the Creed is not locating the Church's holiness and catholicity in its institution." This goes for the papacy and the episcopal hierarchy which, though important, are not ends in themselves but "simply a means of mediating the Spirit's *communio.*" When it comes to the Holy Spirit and the Church, "we need to resist the urge to moralize and to scandalize nonbelievers by giving the impression that the Spirit and the Church are only where the most moral human efforts are found," and in the *Introduction*, Ratzinger helps us make sure that our own confession regarding the Church "does not simply mirror the meaningless dogmas of our technocratic age."

Leonard DeLorenzo in the next contribution shows that Ratzinger's *Introduction* displays the same inventiveness in subverting theological clichés about eschatology as we have seen in the other essays on other topics. Provocatively, DeLorenzo begins by saying "It is *not* the point of

Christianity to 'get into Heaven.'" DeLorenzo is echoing the *Introduction* here, where Ratzinger says that God is not a local deity: "'the God of our fathers . . . is not the god of a place but the god of men, . . . seen on the plane of I and You, not on the plane of the *spatial*.'" Commenting on the Ascension, the *Introduction* observes, "'Heaven was not a place that, before Christ's Ascension, was barred off by a positive, punitive decree of God's . . . On the contrary, the reality of heaven only comes into existence through the confluence of God and man. . . . This confluence . . . took place once and for all in Christ when he went beyond *bios* through death to new life.'" The mystery of the Ascension, which, as Imbelli notes in his paper, has in contemporary theology and preaching often languished in neglect, is featured in this eschatology. Christ's Ascension is Christ "blazing the path unto everlasting communion with God"; it "turns our gaze to Heaven, but what is to be seen in this heavenly vision is a place that is no place," the communion in God "into which Christ gathers his disciples, and that can only be seen through participation and not from the safe distance of some *other* place," from the vantage point from which we create Heaven as distant. DeLorenzo shows that, just as everything is Christologically focused in the *Introduction*, so is its eschatology. With regard to the elect, "'in their being together as the one Christ, they *are* heaven.' Heaven is determined Christologically and therefore anthropology is likewise determined Christologically, for the destiny to which man is called is one of sharing in who Christ is: the Song of God in whom many are gathered." This gathering is already a present reality in the Eucharistic "restructuring of the space of worship" as the "'logicizing of man' in the encounter with the Word made flesh."

Timothy O'Malley's essay on the liturgy furthers this insight. His contribution features Ratzinger's liturgical theology as a credible challenge to Louis-Marie Chauvet's rejection of sacramental metaphysics where there is "no beyond in the sacraments, no eternal order of divine love separate from the linguistic and ritual event of mediation," and the Eucharist is a sacrament of the "presence of the absence" of God. It is the sacrament of God "crossing himself out" in the Crucified One. There is nothing "beyond" this absence to mediate. Ratzinger's Christological focus in the *Introduction*, much mentioned in the essays in this volume, comes to the fore here with a theology of the cross, and therefore of the sacraments, which is more positive, more robust, and more consistent with traditional theology, be it Augustinian or Thomist. For Ratzinger, the cross "is the revelation of the totality of divine and human love in a visible, tangible act by the God-man," and therefore, in the words of the *Introduction*, "'Christian worship consists in the absoluteness of love, as it could only be poured out by the one in whom God's own love had become human love; and it consists in the new form of representation included in this love, namely, that he stood for us and that we let ourselves be taken over by him.'" This love is that of the *Logos* who, though outside of all time and space, is the meaning or order of creation in the first place, revealed in the love of the Cross as gift. The original meaning of creation is its status as "a gift to the human person, an invitation to enter into relationship with God," not a particular act of love so much as "the very possibility of love to begin with." In this sense, creation is a "sacrifice," a free self-gift on the part of the Creator, and His Logos, his Reason and rationale in creating, is perfectly revealed in the sacrifice of the God-man. He thereby definitively tenders the invitation to participation in the primordial worship to which creation was the original invitation. The sacraments, which always involve created material that mediates "insertion into the history that originates in Christ," provide a new horizon for materiality itself. And thus, while not a "neo-Platonic account of sacramental grace," it is nevertheless an account "that recognizes that a supererogatory divine love is made present through the sacramental economy, one that transcends the material itself." From one perspective it is a recovery of the original meaning of matter and of all creation; from another, it is an elevation, in a sense, the completion of creation, tending, in its original *Logos*, towards its eschatological fulfillment.

Section Five: Spiritual Theology

The first essay in the next section seems to present an oxymoron—an essay on the spirituality of structures. But Clemens Sedmak provides just that, starting from the question in the *Introduction*, "'Does God dwell in institutions,'" with its reply, "'To this we must first of all simply say "yes."'" But what could this mean? Sedmak intends to "sketch a spirituality of institutions in conversation with Ratzinger's insights into structures." He shows that "spirituality" is the proper word here, since an "ethics" of institutions, or "institutional ethics," runs into the limits of a self-enclosed structure of reason (and here we have an echo of the essays on fundamental theology). These limits "allow space for theology." Sedmak identifies four "dimensions" of a spirituality of institutions, theologically articulated, starting from the oft-mentioned "principle of 'For'" or of "Being-for." Structures must demonstrate an awareness that institutions are "not self-serving; they are not ends in themselves." They must evince an "exodus" spirituality of "departure from self," resisting the "anti-kenotic tendencies" to produce "self-preserving and self-aggrandizing patterns of institutional agency along with actions that are irreducibly 'self-referential.'" Structures which are "prepared to 'die,' to sacrifice, to accept the reality of kenosis" are structures displaying the second dimension of an institutional spirituality, that of foundation on truth. The truth is first and foremost the Person of Jesus Christ, who is all self-gift. This is the principle of gratuitousness, of the refusal to allow a "rationally calculating" utilitarian ethics to define an institutional culture. Third, a spirituality of institutions will emphasize the material reality of human being: "We have all heard about the debates concerning the relationship between Ratzinger's thought and Platonism. It may be worthwhile pointing out that the *Introduction* in the excursus on Christian structures gives us a clear idea that we as humans are embodied beings." This requires the recognition and provision for the vulnerability that embodiment entails. Vulnerability, theologically speaking, "can be understood as dependence, ultimately on God." Recognizing and providing for vulnerability means respecting the bodily integrity of people. Finally there is the "vertical dimension." Institutions should have a "spiritual infrastructure" which refuses the modern tendency to "'resolve the Christian religion completely into brotherly love, "fellowship,"'" and not to admit any direct love of God or adoration of God.'" The "spiritual infrastructure" will necessarily be "intangible," because grounded in the "'invisible as the truly real,'" and yet "intangible" does not mean inoperative. The vertical dimension is implicated in all three of the earlier dimensions, and means that it is God who ultimately provides stability, not the structures. In this spirituality, "there is no room . . . for structural complacency and self-righteousness." "Making space for God implies the readiness to be disrupted by God." We have to inhabit our structures, again, "by way of an exodus, by way of inviting God to abide."

Jennifer Newsome Martin's contribution recapitulates many of the themes already raised in the preceding essays by sounding them in the key of theological aesthetics. Theology under the exigence of "introducing" correlates to an aesthetic sensibility as it evokes experiences and positions that underwrite doubt in our time, "representing" in this way "the utter pathos of the universally experienced 'exposed nature of [human] existence.'" Ratzinger's "out-Nietzsche-ing of Nietzsche" enables him to adopt "without compunction the phrase that 'God is dead' into 'the tradition of Christian Passiontide piety.'" It thereby invokes a particular sensibility to an "aesthetic formlessness," not the formlessness of nihilism or Chauvet's "presence of the absence of God," but instead, and ironically, "the very form of the disclosure of Trinitarian love." The radically relational character of the Trinity participates in invoking a sensibility, a kind of post-figural aesthetic. For Ratzinger, "'Father' is purely a concept of relationship. Only in being for the other is he Father. In his own being in himself he is simply God." Likewise, "what marks divine Sonship for Ratzinger is precisely the Johannine principle of 'being-for,' a radical openness, transparency, and porosity of the borders of the self." In the spirituality of "Being-for" that marks Ratzinger's Trinitarian theology, there is implied post-figural sensibility. Contemplating the blood and water flowing from the side of the "Pierced One," Ratzinger presents the Gospel of John as "offering to us an aesthetic imperative," to *look*, to behold, in the image presented in the text, the "completely open man, in whom the dividing walls of existence are torn down." He is "entirely 'transition,' a person who 'knows no . . . firm boundaries but is essentially openness,'" perfectly revealing His divine Sonship. The Holy Week meditations in Ratzinger's *The Sabbath of History*, originally written at the time of the *Introduction*, were published thirty years later accompanied by paintings of the Crucifixion by the Catholic artist William Congdon. Over time, his paintings became increasingly less figural. In *Crucifix 90* the radical porosity of the Son is evoked as the circumscribed borders of the body of Christ dissolve. The painter describes *Crucifix 90* as "a flat squashed dry lava flow, but trampled as if the traffic of 'sin' had crossed over it for or since all eternity, until the body, what was body, became a stain. . . . The tar of the road becomes Christ who became tar in order to let himself be flattened until he flowed, in the fire of love, beyond any boundary." Out-Nietzche-ing Nietzsche indeed. Martin compares this image to Augustine's, in the *De Doctrina*, of Wisdom Incarnate as the pavement under our feet, the "Way" we can return to the Father. Well, Augustine was always going to be Nietzche's nemesis.

Epilogue

The final brief essay, an epilogue, is my own on the pedagogy of introducing. In the first place it is a pedagogy of continual question-raising, persisting to the end, questions which often very poignantly ask if belief is still truly possible, even in our day, as the seemingly defeating implausibility of each Christian mystery is raised one by one, culminating in what seems the utterly irreducible implausibility of believing in the Church, as Patrick Gardener evoked so well. Ratzinger's questions probe so deeply that both believers and non-believers are invited, compelled if they are honest, to hear themselves asking them, wondering too, if belief is still possible in our time, the believers' way of putting it, or, for non-believers, if unbelief can carry on as untrammeled as before these questions were raised. Theology under the exigence of "introducing" manages to voice the questions which spur the reader, believer or non-believer, to seek, with the author, to "understand" what might make the implausible plausible, what might make belief seem credible, and in the process entertaining the "Amen" of the Creed as a lively possibility, whether for the first time or as a deeper appropriation of one's faith. I suggest that Ratzinger's pedagogy of "introducing" is essentially different from that of another popular "introduction," that of C. S. Lewis's *Mere Christianity*. Lewis offers an apology for "Christianity" as "merely" a set of propositions, abstracted from any particular church or communion, as though these were simply places adventitious to the propositions themselves. Ratzinger, on the other hand, introduces us not to propositions in the first place, but to an encounter with the "Pierced One," asking again and again, "Are you truly he?" and showing that this encounter is irreducibly an encounter with the Church, with the communion in the porosity of His "Being-for," with the living of this One, as Katie Cavadini has shown, in the dialogic handing on of the "Yes, I believe you are truly He." There is no such thing as "mere Christianity," meaning an abstract Christianity, dis-incarnated from the Church, despite the difficulties that the Church herself presents to the would-be believer—difficulties C. S. Lewis is hoping to avoid. But the cost is too high, for it is the very implausibility the Church presents, as a *verité de fait* and not a *verité de raison*, that impels one outside of oneself, like the Marius Victorinus of Augustine's *Confessions*, to the deepest level of encounter in the "being-for" that is ecclesial communion. The pedagogy of "introducing" refuses the seemingly easy answer of the abstraction of the Christian faith into a set of propositions. Rather it is irreducibly relational, irreducibly existential, irreducibly ecclesial. "Christianity" cannot be reduced to a set of propositions, but instead is the result of a concrete encounter with Christ, mediated by and in the Church.

Bibliography

Francis, Pope. *Evangelii gaudium*. 2013. http://www.vatican.va/content/francesco/en/apost_exhortations/documents/papa-francesco_esortazione-ap_20131124_evangelii-gaudium.html.

Ratzinger, Joseph. *Introduction to Christianity*. With a New Preface. Translated by J. R. Foster and Michael J. Miller. San Francisco: Ignatius, 2004.

Vatican II. *Dei verbum*. 1965. https://www.vatican.va/archive/hist_councils/ii_vatican_council/documents/vat-ii_const_19651118_dei-verbum_en.html.

I. Overview and Context

1

Integral Faith Formation in the Spirit of the Second Vatican Council

Joseph Ratzinger's *Introduction to Christianity* (1968)

Most Rev. Rudolf Voderholzer

Ladies and Gentlemen, I thank you very cordially for the invitation to your Symposium on the occasion of the "Fiftieth Anniversary of *Introduction to Christianity*" by Joseph Ratzinger. Your initiative in planning this event and the invitation to it made me almost a little ashamed. For in all of Europe—apart from a few articles in Catholic newspapers and scholarly journals—nobody even thought to make use of this truly noteworthy date for such a large-scale re-reading of this work, and for an evaluation of its place in intellectual and theological history, as your Symposium is doing. The *Introduction to Christianity* was not only a bestseller, but as an epoch-making work helped many readers, both men and women, to understand the faith more deeply, and to experience new joy in being Christian. Allow me in this connection to start with a short autobiographical note.

I. Personal Introductory Note

I myself perhaps would not be standing here, if I had not read—besides many other important books—Joseph Ratzinger's *Introduction to Christianity* too in the final phase of my secondary-school years, which were very influential for me and my vocational decision. I had the good fortune of taking a very demanding religious course that was offered in the final year of *Gymnasium* in Munich. Our religion teacher, a Capuchin priest, who expected a lot of "conceptual effort" from us, assigned us to read selected chapters from Karl Rahner's *Foundations of Christian Faith*, and then for "recreation," so to speak, from Joseph Ratzinger's *Introduction to Christianity*, which for me acquired additional significance from the fact that in 1977 its author, the successor to Julius Cardinal Döpfner (1915–1976), who had died so surprisingly early, had just become Archbishop of Munich and Freising, and therefore my local ordinary. I still remember so many exhilarating reading experiences. Karl Rahner's transcendental-anthropological method confirmed me in the conviction that every human being, in his spiritual self-transcendence, by an intrinsic necessity not only poses the question about a final horizon of being, but existentially *is* that question. On the other hand, in the discourse of Joseph Ratzinger, which was rich in imagery and stylistically beautiful as well, arguing in turn biblically, philosophically, and on the basis of the history of dogma, the answer of faith acquired for me flesh and blood, so to speak, as well as a face. What has stuck with me in particular since this reading has been the conviction that the Mystery of the Holy Trinity is not the "translation of the inconceivable into the incomprehensible" (Jörg Splett), but rather the interpretation of the sure tenet of faith: "God is Love."[1] This fundamental article of faith presupposes differentiation in God and the relatedness of Persons to one another.[2] The fact that "Father" and "Son" are relational concepts and refer to the unity and differentiation in God became clear to me then as a student, and I am profoundly grateful that, since then, the central mystery of the Christian faith never again became a hurdle or a puzzling wall set up in front of the faith, but rather its center, which is comprehensible in principle although still inexplicable. As in my case, countless readers—a whole generation of theologians and lay persons—found that the *Introduction to Christianity* by Joseph Ratzinger, either in the original German edition or in one of the by now twenty-three translations, became for them a genuine aid to understanding the faith. After graduating and serving in the military, I applied in the summer of 1980 for admission to the major seminary in Munich, where I then met Joseph Ratzinger personally too for the first time. Re-reading the *Introduction to Christianity* is for me therefore always an encounter with my own faith history, too. Again and again I notice how many of the topics that I reflected on for the first time while reading

---

1. "To him who believes in God as tri-une, the highest unity is not the unity of inflexible monotony. The model of unity or oneness toward which one should strive is consequently not the indivisibility of the atom, the smallest unity, which cannot be divided up any further; the authentic acme of unity is the unity created by love. The multi-unity that grows in love is a more radical, truer unity than the unity of the 'atom.'" Ratzinger, *Introduction*, 179.

2. See de Lubac, *The Christian Faith*. Inspired by the motto, "*De la Trinité à la Trinité*" ("from the Trinity to the Trinity"—compare Joseph Ratzinger's Preface to the book), I myself as a professor began my introductory seminar with an analysis of the Trinity.

it—without me being aware of *this* origin—have belonged since then to the inventory of my deepest theological convictions.

II. My Thesis: A Question Worth Asking

Against this personal background, I have already dealt for some time with a particular question in relation to the *Introduction*, which brings me to the thesis of my lecture. I will try to demonstrate that the *Introduction to Christianity*, which had already been planned in the 1950s and was then published three years after the conclusion of the Second Vatican Council by a young theology professor who had collaborated influentially at that Council, is an analysis of the Christian faith precisely in the spirit of this Council also.

This thesis is less trivial than it looks at first. After all, one could ask: What else should this *Introduction* have breathed but the spirit of this great ecclesiastical assembly and of its teaching, especially since it was penned by one of those who knew the Council best and helped to shape it? As the *peritus* of Cardinal Frings, Joseph Ratzinger had collaborated influentially in drafting the Dogmatic Constitutions. In highly-acclaimed talks about the Council, he lectured on the Council for countless people who were interested in it. His four small published volumes of Council reports are among the most substantial and most lucid things that were written about it.[3] The first two years after the Council were the time of the composition of the major series of German commentaries on the conciliar documents, and Joseph Ratzinger participated very actively in that. How could all this not flow automatically into the *Introduction*? On the other hand, we should consider that, very soon after the conclusion of the Council, a vehement dispute started precisely about the interpretation of the conciliar statements. At first Joseph Ratzinger could still speak positively about a spirit of the Council,[4] but then after 1972 talk about the "spirit of the Council" becomes for him more connected with the attempt to pursue a particular ecclesiastical-political agenda contrary to the insights set down in print in the conciliar documents. Then too, some may find it downright exasperating that nowhere in his early masterpiece does Joseph Ratzinger explicitly cite the documents of the Second Vatican Council. Not one single verbatim citation can be found. Only in the context of ecclesiology does the author point out that the Council struggled

---

3. The four volumes were translated into English and published as one: Ratzinger, *Theological Highlights of Vatican II*.

4. Cf. Voderholzer, "'Der Geist des Konzils.'"

to arrive at the decision no longer to speak merely about the "holy" Church but also about the "sinful" Church.[5]

So to me it seems theologically exciting to find evidence for the following thesis: The *Introduction*, without saying so explicitly, adopts the decisive insights and messages of the ecclesiastical assembly, and presents an analysis of the Christian faith that is both well explained (philosophically and theologically) and also appealing (existentially and spiritually). Now this is to be demonstrated.

III. On the Systematic Methodology of the Conciliar Statements (or: "The Spirit of the Council")

1. A Council of the Church about the Church?

Looking at the sixteen documents, can we discern at all an inner systematic methodology of the Second Vatican Council? Is there anything like a theological blueprint that brings the different texts into relation again and allows us to speak about the Council's message? Can we identify something like the chief statement of the Council? In the *Kleines Konzilskompendium* edited by Karl Rahner and Herbert Vorgrimler, it says that the Council was a Council of the Church about the Church, therefore a Council of the Church about herself.[6] Accordingly, the documents are divided into two groups, in the first texts that concern "the inner life of the Church," and in the second texts about "the external mission of the Church."[7] I consider this systematization dubious, if not even misleading. It is correct, though, that, with regard to its historical proposal of its tasks, Vatican II had to work through the unfinished ecclesiological themes of Vatican I: the contextualization of its statements about the papal ministry in ecclesiology as a whole, in particular a theology of episcopal ministry, was the major challenge.

---

5. Ratzinger, *Introduction*, 344. Ratzinger plainly refers here to *Lumen gentium*, §8: "Christ, 'holy, innocent and undefiled' (Heb 7:26) knew nothing of sin (2 Cor 5:21), but came only to expiate the sins of the people (cf. Heb 2:17). The Church, however, clasping sinners to her bosom, at once holy and always in need of purification, follows constantly the path of penance and renewal."

6. Rahner and Vorgrimler, *Kleines Konzilskompendium*, 24: "Dieses Konzil war ein Konzil der Kirche über die Kirche."

7. Rahner and Vorgrimler, *Kleines Konzilskompendium*, 25.

2. The Christocentrism of the Dogmatic Constitutions

With its Dogmatic Constitution on the Church *Lumen gentium* (1964), the Second Vatican Council then in fact produced—for the first time in history—a comprehensive presentation of the Church's self-understanding, and integrated into it an understanding of the episcopal ministry. Yet we must not overlook the fact that the Council's document starts with a "self-relativization" of the Church.[8] The programmatic opening words of *Lumen gentium* take up an expression of the prophet Isaiah (Isa 42:6) that the aged Simeon, according to the Gospel of Luke, uses in reference to Jesus (Luke 2:32). They do not refer to the Church—as was apparently intended at first and as the reader might assume at first glance now as before—but rather to Christ: *Lumen gentium, cum sit Christus*: "Christ is the light of the world!" We cannot emphasize enough the importance of this: the first statement in the Church's presentation of herself in Vatican Council II is a profession of faith in Christ. The nature of the Church, accordingly—to use the old symbol of the moon that was already so dear to the Church Fathers—is to let the light of Christ be reflected on her face. It is essential for the Church to point away from herself—not to revolve around herself, but to become transparent to God, who in His Son became man. The statements about the sacramentality of the Church follow the same lines.[9] The Church is not an eighth sacrament alongside the seven classic sacraments, but rather the theandric reality that lives on the celebration of the sacraments, is constituted anew again and again through them, and precisely in this way becomes a "sign and instrument both of communion with God and of unity among all men."

Similarly we have the same result in the second Dogmatic Constitution on Divine Revelation, *Dei Verbum* (1965). The programmatic opening words do not mean Sacred Scripture but rather mean Christ, the Eternal Word of the Father, the Logos, who in the fullness of time became man. God's revelation is not the entrusting of a book or the communication of particular truths about God. According to the Christian understanding of faith, revelation is a Person, indeed Jesus Christ. In the Pastoral Constitution on the Church in the Modern World, *Gaudium et spes*, finally, the orders of creation and salvation are related to each other, and the importance of Christ as the New Adam is defined as follows: "Christ, the new Adam, in the very revelation of the mystery of the Father and of His love, fully reveals man to [man] himself and

---

8. Karl Rahner was the one who campaigned for the replacement of *ecclesia* with *Christus* in the first sentence of the schema. Cf. Wassilowsky, *Universales Heilssakrament Kirche*, 366.

9. See *Lumen gentium*, §1.

brings to light his most high calling."[10] Gaining clarity about who this Jesus of Nazareth is whom the Church professes as the Christ (cf. Matt 16:16) and after whom the disciples were named "Christians" already in the New Testament period (Acts 11:26), must be one concern—if not the chief concern—of an introduction to "Christian-ity."

3. The Responsorial Character of Faith and the Ecclesial Character of Faith

This Word is aimed at a word in response (in German: *Ant-Wort*); this Word is an invitation to dialogue. In his studies on Bonaventure, Joseph Ratzinger had already elaborated in the 1950s the thesis that, generally speaking, revelation fully becomes revelation only in man's faith-response, because without acceptance in faith nothing would be revealed to anyone. "The receiving subject is always also a part of the concept of 'revelation.'"[11] In §5 of the Constitution on Divine Revelation, faith is then presented also as the response owed to God who reveals Himself. This response, just like revelation itself, has a historical character, which means a human and, most importantly, a communal character. Without using the word a single time, Ratzinger analyzes the nature of Tradition in the corresponding chapter.[12] The conciliar document reads as follows: "What was handed on by the Apostles comprises everything that serves to make the People of God live their lives in holiness and increase their faith. In this way the Church, in her doctrine, life, and worship, perpetuates and transmits to every generation all that she herself is, all that she believes."[13]

Thus even the conciliar documents leave no doubt about the essential connection between faith and the Church. With all due recognition for the historical-critical methods, exegetes must refer to the spirit in which Scripture came to be, and that is the Church's faith, which precedes the writing-down of Scripture—as a previous Tradition, etc. I do not need to spell that out further here. Ratzinger's analysis in the *Introduction*, however, is noteworthy: "Faith demands unity and calls for the fellow believer; it is by nature related to a Church. A Church is not a secondary organization of

---

10. *Dei Verbum*, §22.

11. This remark, taken from Ratzinger's autobiographical *Milestones*, 108, serves as the motto to Volume 2 of Joseph Ratzinger Gesammelte Schriften (JRGS), which contains his studies on Bonaventure.

12. Shortly before that (1965), he had composed the article "Tradition" for the *Lexikon für Theologie und Kirche*. It is now reprinted in JRGS 9:432–41.

13. *Dei Verbum*, §8.

ideas, quite out of accordance with them and hence at best a necessary evil; it belongs necessarily to a faith whose significance lies in the interplay of common confession and worship."[14]

When we talk about the "spirit of the Council" which, according to my thesis, the *Introduction to Christianity* breathes from start to finish, then after these thematic aspects we must also discuss two more aspects that are rather formal.

4. Two "Formal" Aspects: *Aggiornamento* and the Biblical Orientation

The first formal aspect is *aggiornamento*, the demand of Pope John XXIII, associated already with the convocation of the Council, to "update" the proclamation of the faith, not in the sense of a superficial adaptation of the faith to the spirit of the age, but rather by taking up and taking seriously contemporary questions, whether philosophical or scientific or of other sorts, which cannot be answered adequately by merely repeating well-known abstract formulas. The accuracy with which the young professor managed to put into words the questions and needs of his contemporaries in relation to the faith (and to let his own analysis of the faith be challenged by them) may have contributed substantially to the extraordinary success of Ratzinger's *Introduction*.[15]

The second formal aspect is the biblical orientation of the whole book. The Constitution on Divine Revelation *Dei Verbum* had cited in §24 the statements of Leo XIII and Benedict XV that the study of Sacred Scripture must be "the soul of sacred theology." What may appear self-evident to us today was modeled in an exemplary fashion not least importantly by Ratzinger's work,

---

14. Ratzinger, *Introduction*, 98.

15. One example from among many others is found in *Introduction*, 52–3: "The basic paradox already present in belief as such is rendered even more profound by the fact that belief appears on the scene in the garb of days gone by and, indeed, seems itself to be something old-fashioned, the mode of life and existence current a long time ago. All attempts at modernization, whether intellectual, academic 'demythologization,' or ecclesiastical, pragmatic aggiornamento, do not alter this fact; on the contrary, they strengthen the suspicion that a convulsive effort is being made to proclaim as contemporary something that is, after all, really a relic of days gone by. It is these attempts at modernization that first make us fully aware just how old-fashioned what we are being offered really is. Belief appears no longer as the bold but challenging leap out of the apparent all of our visible world and into the apparent void of the invisible and intangible; it looks much more like a demand to bind oneself to yesterday and to affirm it as eternally valid. And who wants to do that in an age when the idea of 'tradition' has been replaced by the idea of 'progress'?"

which thus also sets standards. Reference to Sacred Scripture, not by lining up proof texts ("*dicta probantia*") but rather through a theology and analysis of the faith that draws from the overall dynamic of Sacred Scripture, observes the Old and New Testaments in their tension and unity, is in dialogue with the leading representatives of the exegetes, and is one of the outstanding hallmarks of the *Introduction to Christianity*.

5. Lectures about the Apostles' Creed *as* an Introduction to Christianity

Against this background it becomes clear: The plan for a series of lectures on the Apostles' Creed for auditors from all faculties, sponsored by the Faculty of Theology in Tübingen in the summer semester of 1967, which resulted in the book *Introduction to Christianity*, is the royal road of introduction to Christianity, once again precisely in the spirit of the Second Vatican Council.

This characteristic of Ratzinger's *Introduction* once again acquires sharper contours if we compare the work with other books of this "Introduction" genre. In the year 2000, Mariano Delgado, Professor of Church History on the Faculty of Theology of the University of Fribourg, had taken the one hundredth anniversary of the lectures by Adolph von Harnack about the nature of Christianity as the occasion to sift through and describe all comparable publications.[16] Often a glance at the table of contents of the books in question is enough to see how different Ratzinger's work is. Karl Adam's *The Spirit of Catholicism* (1924), for example, lays emphasis on Christ's relation to the Church. Karl Rahner's *Foundations of Christian Faith* (1976) certainly does have the main themes of the Christian creed in view in its nine "courses" (*Gängen*) and is oriented to them. Transcendental-theological reflection dominates, of course, in a language that is far removed from the biblical message. Walter Kasper's *An Introduction to Christian Faith* (1972) makes the concept of faith the red thread running through his remarks. Similar explanations of the Creed were produced by Wolfhart Pannenberg, Hans Küng, and Theodor Schnitzler. Wolfhart Pannenberg tries to make accessible the "reasonable character of the Christian faith"; Hans Küng claims to develop the "Creed for Contemporaries" (1992), but leaves unanswered the question of whether many statements of faith are not stifled after all by the doubt of our contemporaries. In his larger book, *On Being a Christian* (1974), he probably did succeed in formulating the questions of

---

16. See Delgado, *Das Christentum der Theologen*. This collection also includes the essay by Wiedenhofer, "Joseph Ratzinger."

his contemporaries, but not in answering them in a way consonant with the traditional faith. That is the difference. The introduction that comes closest to Ratzinger's is surely the very substantial book by Theodor Schneider, *Was wir glauben* (*What We Believe*, 1985). I can only suggest this here and make you curious about these other books, which are in some ways comparable. They are apt to make us understand better the uniqueness and the quality of Ratzinger's work, which of them all surely had the widest circulation and also the most thoroughgoing reception.

In the Preface to the new edition in the year 2000, the author writes that, in comparison to the years immediately after the Council, further questions and topics have been raised (in particular, in interreligious dialogue), which in a revision of the book would have to take up more room, but that he "was not mistaken as to the fundamental approach," inasmuch as he "put the question of God and the question about Christ in the very center."[17] As a result of this concentration on the question of God and Christology, we must turn to this presentation in the following sections.

IV. The Logos as Dialogue—the Question of God

Faith in the Divine Trinity is not just one aspect of the Christian faith among others, but the *specificum christianum*—the specifically Christian belief—that helps to define all articles of the faith. From their original *Sitz im Leben* (setting in Christian life) in the baptismal liturgy, where candidates were (and are) questioned about their faith in God the Father, the Son, and the Holy Spirit, both the Apostles' Creed and the Niceno-Constantinopolitan Creed have a Trinitarian structure. With regard to the Apostles' Creed, a secondary observation caused this Trinitarian structure to recede into the background for a long time. Namely, the fact that it is composed of exactly twelve articles of faith gave the legend about the apostolic origin of the Apostles' Creed its plausibility. Thus, for good reasons, Part One of the *Introduction* about the question of God has to focus mainly on an analysis of the Trinitarian faith.[18]

---

17. Ratzinger, *Introduction*, 29.

18. Ratzinger, *Introduction*, 331: "To that extent the oldest form of the Creed with its tripartite arrangement is indeed one of the main roots of the trinitarian image of God. It was only the gradual expansion of the baptismal questions into a detailed creed that somewhat obscured the trinitarian structure."

1. Biblical Development from the Name of God (Ex 3:14)

Unlike in the theological manuals dominated by neo-Scholasticism, Joseph Ratzinger does not start Part One on the question of God with the "proofs of God's existence." Rather, after an introduction very sensitively describing the present-day need with regard to the question of God, the Christian belief in God is developed from the definition of the biblical category of the name. The elucidation of the revelation of God's Name handed down in Ex 3:14 takes up a lot of space. According to the biblical understanding, a name is in a certain way the person himself. In the communication of the name "Yahweh," of course, revelation and veiling are combined, for God nevertheless still remains the Incomprehensible and Ever-Greater One. "The idea of the name here," Ratzinger says, "enters a decisive new phase. The name is, no longer merely a word, but a person: Jesus himself."[19] With the revelation of the Name, the inauguration of the dialogue with the recipient of the revelation already exists. "When God names himself after the self-understanding of faith, he is not so much expressing his inner nature as making himself nameable; he is handing himself over to men in such a way that he can be called upon by them. And by doing this he enters into coexistence with them; he puts himself within their reach; he is 'there' for them."[20]

2. A Positive Definition of "Hellenization" in the Sense of the Reasonableness of the Faith (Claim to Rationality)

Whereas in the neo-Scholastic methodology, in the sense of multi-story thinking, one progresses from the level of philosophy to the level of theology illuminated by revelation, Ratzinger in his *Introduction*—schooled in this certainly by Augustine and Bonaventure—reverses the train of thought. Through the translation of the Divine Name Yahweh from Hebrew into the Greek of the Septuagint by *Ego eimi ho ōn*, the biblical faith in God is now communicable also to a philosophy that reflects on being. What Ratzinger spelled out in detail in his inaugural lecture in Bonn in 1959, and what was expressed again in the 2006 Regensburg Lecture on the rationality of faith in God in dialogue, is presented in detail also in the corresponding chapter of the *Introduction*. With this connection to philosophical thought, Christian reflection on faith underscores its claim to rationality as a matter of principle. "Christ called himself truth, not custom." This remark by Tertullian is a commonplace that is quoted again

---

19. Ratzinger, *Introduction*, 133.
20. Ratzinger, *Introduction*, 134.

and again by Ratzinger.[21] At the same time, however, thought too finds itself extended once again by revelation itself and lifted out of constricted perspectives. The biblical experience of God causes us to understand reflexively that God is not simply pure thought alone, but love. "It becomes apparent that truth and love are originally identical; that where they are completely realized they are not two parallel or even opposing realities but one, the one and only absolute."[22] Starting from this, it is evident how philosophical thought was broadened by God's revelation.

3. The Re-Evaluation of Relation through Faith in the Trinity and the Overcoming of "Objectifying Thought"

In this encounter between thought about revelation and Greek philosophy, nothing less than an intellectual revolution took place, inasmuch as the category of relation, which in the Aristotelian table of categories was considered the weakest accident, is raised to the height of substance. Ratzinger writes:

> With the insight that, seen as substance, God is One but that there exists in him the phenomenon of dialogue, of differentiation, and of relationship through speech, the category of *relatio* gained a completely new significance for Christian thought. To Aristotle, it was among the "accidents," the chance circumstances of being, which are separate from substance, the sole sustaining form of the real. The experience of the God who conducts a dialogue, of the God who is not only *logos* but also *dia-logos*, not only idea and meaning but speech and word in the reciprocal exchanges of partners in conversation—this experience exploded the ancient division of reality into substance, the real thing, and accidents, the merely circumstantial. It now became clear that the dialogue, the *relatio*, stands beside the substance as an equally primordial form of being.[23]

Ratzinger, who in these reflections takes up important insights of the dialogical philosophy of Franz Rosenzweig and Martin Buber, but even more the personalist thought of Romano Guardini, shows thereby how precisely in the area of a rediscovery of the category of relation, new worlds and at the same time new tasks open up for purely philosophical thought:

---

21. Ratzinger, *Introduction*, 141.
22. Ratzinger, *Introduction*, 148.
23. Ratzinger, *Introduction*, 182–83.

> Therein lies concealed a revolution in man's view of the world: the sole dominion of thinking in terms of substance is ended; relation is discovered as an equally valid primordial mode of reality. It becomes possible to surmount what we call today "objectifying thought"; a new plane of being comes into view. It is probably true to say that the task imposed on philosophy as a result of these facts is far from being completed—so much does modern thought depend on the possibilities thus disclosed, without which it would be inconceivable.[24]

With this reformulation of the doctrine of the Trinity, which for his time was altogether new and unusual, but ultimately derived from Augustine and his thought about relation, Joseph Ratzinger inspired many subsequent authors. We see in the 1970s the rediscovery of *De Trinitate* by Richard of Saint Victor. Authors like Klaus Hemmerle, Jörg Splett, and others speak about "Trinitarian ontology" or "Trinitarian anthropology." And Gisbert Greshake correctly points out that the doctrine of the Trinity is not merely an isolated treatise of theology, but a dimension of systematic theology as a whole. Along the path from a neo-Scholastically isolated theology of the Trinity toward this insight, which could link up directly with Sacred Scripture and patristic theology, Joseph Ratzinger's *Introduction to Christianity*, in aligning its introduction with the Trinitarian Creed of the Church, is a decisive step.

If with respect to ontology and also in relation to the systematic arrangement of the Credo the doctrine of the Trinity has the primacy, then with regard to epistemology, that is, the way of knowing, Christology takes first place, for only the revelation of the Son brings to completion the revelation of the Father.

V. Part Two: Christology

1. Jesus Christ: Mediator and Fullness of All Revelation
(*Dei Verbum* §2)

In our attempt to identify the chief statements of the Council, we have come across the Christocentrism of the two Dogmatic Constitutions, both the one on the Church and the one about Divine Revelation. It is the nature of the Church to point away from herself to Christ, who is the Light of the nations.

Revelation, moreover, is not in primarily a book, but rather the Word-made-flesh, whose life, work, passion, and above all whose death and

---

24. Ratzinger, *Introduction*, 184.

resurrection for the salvation of mankind is attested in the writings of the New Testament. Jesus Christ is the mediator and fullness of all revelation. Therefore an introduction to Christianity must deal in the first place with the figure of Jesus Christ and, while considering all attempts to call Him into question, demonstrate through historical and systematic theology that, even and precisely when using historical-critical methods, one can in all intellectual honesty place faith in Jesus the Christ.

2. The Decisive Challenge: Overcoming the Division between the Jesus of History and the Christ of Faith

The modern dilemma that confronts Christology was powerfully formulated by Adolph von Harnack in his lectures on the nature of Christianity (1900): "Not the Son but only the Father belongs in the Gospel as Jesus preached it."[25]

The struggle with the ensuing disempowerment of Christology and overcoming the fatal division of the Jesus of history and the Christ of faith is one of the great lifelong themes of Joseph Ratzinger.[26] Through the decades, down to the Jesus trilogy of the later Pope (2007–2012), extends the fundamental hermeneutical assumption that the faith-filled view of the figure of Jesus found in the Gospels and in dogma grasp His true being and nature, and that renouncing the faith perspective merely leads to all sorts of reductionism. This struggle is carried out, of course, not on the basis of a rejection of historical-critical exegesis, but rather in the comprehensive yet critical reception of it. For Ratzinger there is no going back behind the serious insights of exegesis. In his commentary on the Second Vatican Council's Constitution on Revelation *Dei Verbum*, which in §12 finally declares the methods of historical criticism to be necessary instruments for investigating the meaning of Scripture, Ratzinger in 1967 also identifies the theological reasoning for this. For the Second Vatican Council did not admit historical criticism *nolens volens* (like it or not) simply because it could no longer be warded off. The human-historical character of the words of Scripture, which is ultimately rooted in the Incarnation of the Logos, demands also a historical confirmation, and thus historical-critical exegesis corresponds to the claim and the structure of Christianity itself.[27]

---

25. Cited by Ratzinger, *Introduction*, 199.

26. See Voderholzer, "Schriftauslegung im Widerstreit."

27. Cf. Joseph Ratzinger, "Einleitung" (reprinted in JRGS 7:715–91). See also Benedict XVI, *Jesus of Nazareth*, vol. I, 14–15 (reprinted in JRGS 6:132): "The first point is that the historical-critical method—specifically because of the intrinsic nature of

These hermeneutical reflections, which take seriously §12 of the Constitution on Divine Revelation with its joining of historical exegesis and traditional approaches to Sacred Scripture (and see it not as a lazy compromise, but rather as a task that can be carried out), appear just as important as the concrete development of Christology in the *Introduction*. I can single out only a few aspects and, in keeping with my guiding interest, consider then also (above all) the teaching of the Second Vatican Council.

3. Christ, the Eschatological Adam

In the concrete development of the Christological chapter of his *Introduction*, Ratzinger discusses important theories of the history-of-religion and the form-critical school, and criticizes their objective inconsistency, indeed also their historical implausibility. He objects as follows to the theory that the early Church restyled the simple Jewish rabbi into the Son of God under the influence of the Hellenistic intellectual heritage: "To anyone accustomed to think historically, the whole theory is absurd, even if today hordes of people believe it; for my part I must confess that, quite apart from the Christian faith and simply from my acquaintance with history, I find it preferable and easier to believe that God became man than that such a conglomeration of hypotheses represents the truth."[28] It is historically exact, and meanwhile also accepted by scholars, to observe that the Incarnation of God to which the New Testament bears witness is without analogy and means something completely different from the alleged parallels in ancient mythology.[29] The title "Son" is not a foreign interpretation, but rather has its origin in Jesus' prayer, in which his relation to Abba, His Father, is most profoundly realized.[30] According to the Gospel of John, this expresses the total relatedness of His existence to the Father.[31]

---

theology and faith—is and remains an indispensable dimension of exegetical work. For it is of the very essence of biblical faith to be about real historical events.... If we push this history aside, Christian faith as such disappears and is recast as some other religion. So if history, if facticity in this sense, is an essential dimension of Christian faith, then faith must expose itself to the historical method—indeed, faith itself demands this."

28. Ratzinger, *Introduction*, 215.

29. Ratzinger, *Introduction*, 203.

30. Ratzinger, *Introduction*, 210. He continues: "We have a glimpse of Jesus' experience of prayer, of that closeness to God that distinguishes His relation to God from that of all other human beings, yet is not at all intended to be exclusive, but rather is aimed at taking others up into His own relationship with God" (211 *sic*; translated from German).

31. Ratzinger, *Introduction*, 211.

The key to understanding Jesus' being and mission is the Cross.[32] In view of the Cross and the *Titulus Crucis* composed by Pilate, it becomes possible to identify Jesus and Christ.

With regard to the path of Christology, Ratzinger discusses the two emphases of Incarnation-theology and the theology of the cross, which identify lasting polarities that must continue to exist but ultimately are complementary.[33] Ratzinger's insistence on the unity of Christology and soteriology, of the being and ministry of the Redeemer, is of lasting importance, not only for the history of theology, but also for systematic theology.[34]

Under the heading "Paths of Christology," Ratzinger devotes comparatively the most space to the explication and classification of the Pauline idea of Christ as the "last/eschatological Adam" (1 Cor 15:45). The following reflections from the *Introduction* can be read furthermore as a commentary on *Gaudium et spes* §22:

> Man's full "hominization" presupposes God's becoming man; only by this event is the Rubicon dividing the "animal" from the "logical" finally crossed for ever and the highest possible development accorded to the process that began when a creature of dust and earth looked out beyond itself and its environment and was able to address God as "You." It is openness to the whole, to the infinite, that makes man complete. Man is man by reaching out infinitely beyond himself, and he is consequently more of a man the less enclosed he is in himself, the less 'limited' he is. For—let me repeat—that man is most fully man, indeed the true man, who is most unlimited, who not only has contact with the infinite—the Infinite Being!—but is one with him: Jesus Christ. In him "hominization" has truly reached its goal.[35]

It would be worthwhile at this point to look more thoroughly at Ratzinger's analysis both of the creedal article about the descent into hell,[36] which

---

32. "The unfolding of the understanding that we call faith thus happens in such a way that Christians first hit upon the identification of person, word, and work through the Cross. Through it they recognized the really and finally decisive factor, in the presence of which all else becomes of secondary importance. For this reason their profession of faith could be restricted to the simple association of the words Jesus and Christ—this combination said it all. Jesus is seen from the Cross, which speaks louder than any words: he is the Christ—no more need be said." Ratzinger, *Introduction*, 206.

33. Ratzinger, *Introduction*, 205–6.

34. Ratzinger, *Introduction*, 217–18.

35. Ratzinger, *Introduction*, 235. On this topic, see also Meiers, "Jesus Christus—Eschatos Adam."

36. Ratzinger, *Introduction*, 293–301.

is nonetheless matter found only in the Apostles' Creed, and also of the Ascension of Jesus.[37] I must limit myself to the observation that Ratzinger (I find) succeeded masterfully in making both the theological and the existential meaning of these faith statements comprehensible, apart from any demythologizing unraveling of them on the one hand or naively objective attempt to render them harmless on the other.

One more skillfully wrought miniature deserves mention: the overall biblical classification of Mariology in the elucidation of the creedal article about the conception of Jesus by the power of the Spirit. After detailed debate, the Council had situated Mariology as part of ecclesiology and presented it in the eighth chapter of *Lumen gentium*. Mary appears here as the archetype and model of the Church. As a way of deepening this insight, in his *Introduction* Ratzinger places Mary in the series of great Old Testament women:

> The Old Testament contains a whole series of miraculous births, always at decisive turning points in the history of salvation: Isaac's mother, Sarah (Gen 18), Samuel's mother (1 Sam 1–3), and the anonymous mother of Samson (Judg 13:2ff.) are all barren, and all human hope of their being blessed with children has been abandoned. With all three, the birth of the child who eventually contributes to Israel's salvation comes to pass as a manifestation of the gracious mercy of God, who makes the impossible possible (Gen 18:14; Lk 1:37), elevates the lowly (1 Sam 2:7; 1:11; Lk 1:52; 1:48), and puts down the mighty from their thrones (Lk 1:52). With Elizabeth, John the Baptist's mother, this process is continued (Lk 1:25, 36), and it reaches its climax and goal with Mary. The meaning of the occurrence is always the same: the salvation of the world does not come from man and from his own power; man must let it be bestowed upon him, and he can only receive it as a pure gift. The Virgin Birth is not a lesson in asceticism, nor does it belong directly to the doctrine of Jesus' Divine Sonship; it is first and last theology of grace, a proclamation of how salvation comes to us: in the simplicity of acceptance, as the voluntary gift of the love that redeems the world.[38]

In the small but very substantial booklet *Daughter Zion* (1977), Joseph Ratzinger elaborated this sketch into a Mariology, and also cleared up the misunderstandings that had appeared with regard to his interpretation of the Virgin Birth in the *Introduction to Christianity*.

37. Ratzinger, *Introduction*, 310–18.
38. Ratzinger, *Introduction*, 277–78.

We come now to Part Three of the *Introduction*. It is the devoted to the explanation of the third section of the Creed, which professes faith in the Holy Spirit and His activity.

VI. The Holy Spirit and the Church

Even a short glance at the table of contents teaches us that, in comparison to the two previous parts, the third one turned out to be extraordinarily short.

1. Reasons for the Comparatively Meager Extent of Part Three

First of all, there is an altogether trivial reason for this: the 1967 summer semester was drawing to a close, and there simply was no more lecture time left. Yet the restriction of the theme Holy Spirit and Church to a few points can certainly be justified objectively too—and again, quite in harmony with the teaching of Vatican II and its Christocentrism and Theocentrism. The Holy Spirit is not given to the Church primarily to compose treatises on Pneumatology, but rather, inspired by the Holy Spirit, to know Jesus as the Christ and to profess Him as the Savior of the world sent by the Father. The decisive task is not to speak *about* the Holy Spirit, but rather to speak and to act *in Him*. The same is true in a certain way about the Church. The Church is first and foremost the acting subject of faith, and only in a second step also the object of faith. As necessary as self-reflection on ministries and structures may be in certain historical situations, it is also dangerous when ecclesiastical thought and speech is devoted exclusively to navel-gazing and looking into the mirror. Nevertheless, with my attempt to make a theological virtue out of the difficulty of being short of time, I do not want to exaggerate, either.

Nevertheless, Ratzinger follows up at least two important aspects of the Second Vatican Council's teaching about the Church.

2. The Holy Church Made Up of Sinful Human Beings

By way of introduction, I already mentioned that the only explicit reference to the Second Vatican Council is the note that the conciliar debates led it to speak also about the sinful Church. These remarks have a fascinating and disturbing relevance. It is as if Ratzinger were writing for our present situation when he says: "And so for many people today the Church has become the main obstacle to belief."[39] "The Second Vatican Council itself ventured to the point of speaking no longer merely of the holy Church but of the sinful Church, and the only reproach it incurred was that of still being far too timorous; so deeply aware are we all of the sinfulness of the Church."[40]

To clarify this, Ratzinger refers then of course to an important distinction between "holiness" as a moral quality and "holiness" as God's gift of grace so as to represent and to communicate His holiness: "As we have already seen, in all these statements of faith the word 'holy' does not apply in the first place to the holiness of human persons but refers to the divine gift that bestows holiness in the midst of human unholiness."[41] Ratzinger then tries to resolve the tension with a very personal statement, which does not presuppose a Lutheran *simul-justus-et-peccator* (just and sinner at the same time) dialectic, but rather the Catholic theology of grace and the sacraments: "I must admit that to me this unholy holiness of the Church has in itself something infinitely comforting about it. Would one not be bound to despair in face of a holiness that was spotless and could only operate on us by judging us and consuming us by fire?"[42]

The statements about the sacramentality of the Church are taken from the center of the Second Vatican Council's teaching about the Church.

3. The Sacramentality of the Church

Besides the Church's self-denial as witness to Christ, as we have seen, the sacramentality of the Church stands in the foreground among the fundamental statements of *Lumen gentium*. The theme "Eucharistic ecclesiology," which is very closely connected with it and was prepared by Henri de Lubac and other representatives of the so-called *Nouvelle Théologie* in the 1950s, was accepted in its entirely by Joseph Ratzinger, and sketched at least in Part Three of his *Introduction*. The occasion for mentioning it is offered by the creedal article *communio sanctorum* (communion of saints), which along with the profession of the *descensus ad inferos* (descent into hell) is part of the distinctive matter of the Apostles' Creed. "The saying about the communion of saints refers, first of all, to the eucharistic community, which through the Body of the Lord binds the Churches scattered all over the earth into one Church. Thus originally the word *sanctorum* (of the holy ones) does not refer to persons but means the holy gifts, the holy *thing*, granted

---

39. Ratzinger, *Introduction*, 340.
40. Ratzinger, *Introduction*, 339.
41. Ratzinger, *Introduction*, 340.
42. Ratzinger, *Introduction*, 343.

to the Church in her eucharistic feast by God as the real bond of unity."[43] While in the Catholic context today we might associate it with the saints who have been perfected and are now with God, and in the Lutheran context think about the *congregatio fidelium* (congregation of the faithful), the original meaning in fact is the *participatio sacramentorum* (participation in the sacraments) in the sense of "Eucharistic ecclesiology." These insights, which were brought again to the attention of the Catholic Church (not least through her encounter with Orthodoxy), have ecumenical significance in many respects, and have not yet sufficiently entered the general consciousness of the faith. Once again, expressed differently in Joseph Ratzinger's words: "Church and sacrament stand or fall together; a Church without sacraments would be an empty organization, and sacraments without a Church would be rites without meaning or inner cohesion."[44]

In 1953, Henri de Lubac had already written: "*C'est l'église qui fait l'Eucharistie, mais c'est aussi l'Eucharistie qui fait l'Église*" ("it is the Church that makes [effects, brings forth through her liturgy] the Eucharist, but it is also the Eucharist that makes the Church"). It is a mutually constitutive relation.[45] This sentence, it is often reported, was an oft-cited sentence at the Council, and was eventually reflected in the foundational first chapter of *Lumen gentium*. The way in which Joseph Ratzinger communicates the same thought in Part Three of his *Introduction* in the briefest form shows once again how much his commentaries on the Apostles' Creed breathe the spirit of the Council, without citing it verbatim. *Quod erat demonstrandum*.

VII. Outlook—The Primacy of Logos over Ethos (Guardini/Ratzinger)

Ladies and Gentlemen, this year another classic work of theological literature is celebrating a jubilee of its appearance. Whereas fifty years ago Joseph Ratzinger's *Introduction to Christianity* was published, it has been exactly one hundred years since the first edition of Romano Guardini's *The Spirit of the Liturgy*. There is no doubt that Guardini, whose cause for beatification was started one year ago in Munich, was of decisive importance for Joseph Ratzinger's thought. With his own book *The Spirit of the Liturgy*, Cardinal Ratzinger very deliberately took his place in the line of tradition founded by Guardini. And in the *Introduction* too there is a clear reference, which I

---

43. Ratzinger, *Introduction*, 334.
44. Ratzinger, *Introduction*, 338.
45. See Voderholzer, *Meet Henri de Lubac*.

place at the conclusion of my remarks, not least importantly because of its present and future relevance.

When Ratzinger speaks in his *Introduction* about the "primacy of the Logos" at the beginning of Part Two, he is probably indirectly adopting a formula of Guardini. While Ratzinger then distinguishes the primacy of the Logos from matter, Guardini spoke about the "primacy of the Logos over ethos." These words serve as the inscription for the last chapter of his early work. The primacy of ethos over Logos—of orthopraxis over orthodoxy that prevailed in the Protestantism of his day—completely contradicts the Catholic spirit, according to Guardini. If nothing is left of faith but a "personally moving experience of faith," then the fixed content of faith is replaced by "the demonstration of right-mindedness through action." Guardini viewed this as the source of the distress in his time: "Nothing remains, nothing stands firm, everything changes." The Catholic Church decisively opposes this intellectual attitude: the violation of the principle of the priority of Logos over ethos, of dogma and profession over praxis, of being over doing, would in Guardini's view "lift the sacred order off its hinges."[46]

"Doesn't the distress described by Guardini resemble the distress of our day, too?" I ask myself. And where can we find a better orientation than with the author of the *Introduction to Christianity*, who as Professor, Archbishop, Cardinal, and Pope leaves to us a magnificent theological work, which is acquainted as very few others are with the questions of its time, and answers them in the light of the faith?!

Translated by Michael J. Miller

Bibliography

Benedict XVI, *Jesus of Nazareth*, vol. I. Translated by Adrian J. Walker. New York: Doubleday, 2007.

Delgado, Mariano, ed. *Das Christentum der Theologen im 20. Jahrhundert: Vom "Wesen des Christentums" zu den "Kurzformeln des Glaubens."* Stuttgart/Berlin/Cologne: W. Kohlhammer, 2000.

Karger, Michael. "'Das Drama am Altar.' Vor hundert Jahren erschien Romano Guardinis 'Vom Geist der Liturgie.'" *Die Tagespost* (4 November 2018).

Lubac, Henri de. *The Christian Faith: An Essay on the Structure of the Apostles' Creed.* Translated by Richard Arnandez. San Francisco: Ignatius, 1986

Meiers, Anna Elisabeth. "Jesus Christus—Eschatos Adam: Christologie und ihr existentieller Anspruch bei Joseph Ratzinger/Benedikt XVI." *Trierer Theologische Zeitschrift* 127 (2018): 308–24.

---

46. Cf. Karger, "Das Drama am Altar."

Rahner, Karl, and Herbert Vorgrimler. *Kleines Konzilskompendium.* Freiburg: Herder, 1966; 1980.

Ratzinger, Joseph. "Einleitung." In "Einleitung und Kommentar zum Vorwort und zu Kapitel I, II und VI der Offenbarungskonstitution Dei Verbum." In *Lexikon für Theologie und Kirche.* 2nd ed. Ergänzungsband II, 498–528, 571–81, 499. Freiburg, 1967.

———. *Introduction to Christianity.* Translated by J. R. Foster. San Francisco: Ignatius, 2004.

———. *Milestones: Memoirs: 1927–1977.* Translated by Erasmo Leiva-Merikakis. San Francisco: Ignatius, 1998.

———. *Theological Highlights of Vatican II.* New York and Mahwah: Paulist, 1969, 2009. (German edition, 1964).

Voderholzer, Rudolf. "'Der Geist des Konzils': Überlegungen zur Konzilshermeneutik." *Trierer Theologische Zeitschrift* 123 (2014) 169–86.

———. *Meet Henri de Lubac.* Translated by Michael J. Miller. San Francisco: Ignatius, 2008.

———. "Schriftauslegung im Widerstreit." In *Der Glaube ist einfach: Aspekte der Theologie Papst Benedikts XVI,* edited by Gerhard Ludwig Müller, 54–85. Regensburg: Pustet, 2007.

Wassilowsky, Günter. *Universales Heilssakrament Kirche: Karl Rahners Beitrag zur Ekklesiologie des II. Vatikanums.* Innsbrucker theologische Studien 59. Innsbruck: Tyrolia, 2001.

Wiedenhofer, Siegfried. "Joseph Ratzinger—'Einführung in das Christentum: Vorlesungen über das Apostolische Glaubensbekenntnis." In *Das Christentum der Theologen im 20. Jahrhundert: Vom "Wesen des Christentums" zu den "Kurzformeln des Glaubens,"* edited by Mariano Delgado, 174–85. Stuttgart/Berlin/Cologne: W. Kohlhammer, 2000.

2

The Articulation of Faith between Memory and Recollection

Rev. Richard Schenk, OP

I. Books and Their Fates

As Terentianus Maurus told us in the second century, the fates which books have are in good part a matter of how their readers take them. *Pro captu lectoris habent sua fata libelli.* "Books have their destinies according to the grasp of the reader." It belongs to the fate of the book in our discussion here that it found immediately and over the decades uncommonly many readers, and then with quite varied and even contradictory understandings. Printed and reprinted in German some fourteen times in the first five years after its initial publication, and translated eventually into more than twenty languages, Joseph Ratzinger's *Introduction to Christianity* enjoyed immediate and lasting attention from the time of its first edition in 1968, in good part because it shared many of the same readers and much the same fate as the texts of the Second Vatican Council. The lecture that it published had been a "studium generale" offering, designed for students and professors of all faculties at the University of Tübingen in the summer semester of 1967, less than two years after the conclusion of the Council. The broad initial public, the foundational nature of the issues that the book addressed, and the ongoing discussion of the Council, helped to make the book more accessible to a wide range of readers than many more specialized studies. Ratzinger's book also shared with the post-Conciliar readings of the Conciliar texts the fate of very uneven interpretations, often contradictory of one other, and at points seemingly in tension even with themselves—a legacy which we still are struggling to assimilate into the Church and theology of our own times. The contributions gathered in this volume ask the question of how we ourselves might best read and understand this book and its place in former and future decades.

This diversity of understanding was widened by the social, political, and ecclesial unrest that had intensified in the months between the lecture itself in 1967 and the first publication of the work in 1968. In his replies to some of the more critical readings of his work, the young author was keen to point out the often contradictory nature of their demands. Not rarely, however, Ratzinger's critical readers had leveled much the same charge against this best-seller, that it seemed at times less and in other passages then again more in continuity with the past. The open questions and the rival views about the letter and the spirit of the Council's texts found their echo in the divergent readings of this theological work that, even after later re-readings, was anything but an open and shut case. The pre-understanding of "The New Ratzinger," as the book was called at the time of its first editions, knew that it had something controversial to say about pre- and post-Conciliar theology, about pairing the re-reading of the traditional articles of faith with a critique of some other recent attempts to do something along similar lines, and about the confrontation of faith and unbelief.

This anticipation of conflict has contributed to the readership of the work to the present day. Ratzinger was himself not just a contributor to but also a reader of the Council, engaged in the post-Conciliar debates about its conflicts and its authentic reception and development. Perhaps more than any other section of his work, the two page preface to the first printed edition of 1968 did much to shape the pre-understanding that readers brought to this work, which begins by comparing the trend of recent theology to the central figure of a "Schwank" or popular tale, "Hans im Glück," the happy-go-lucky Hans (or better, if you will, a happy-go-unlucky Hans). Denoted in the English translations also as Clever Hans or Poor Jack, the character begins with a heavy gold nugget of significant worth, but makes a series of capricious exchanges for simpler goods of ever lesser worth, the last and least of which, a small whetstone, he simply chucks into the lake.

After 1968, Ratzinger never ceased to be a prominent player in the post-Conciliar "trading negotiations" to develop with greater success than happy-go-lucky Hans the genuine legacy of the Council. Several of the papers gathered in this volume inscribe this early work of the then forty-three-year-old theologian into the larger development of Ratzinger's theological thought and its place in the often heated discourses that were to unfold. Like any author who lives to see the publication of his or her work, Ratzinger was a reader of his own work and its reception, as well as of the post-Conciliar context common to both. Ecumenical Councils tend to provide not just solutions to older controversies but also impulses for newer ones,[1] and this was especially true of the Second Vatican Council. The competition for the most coherent hermeneutic of the Council did not end with the fiftieth anniversary of its conclusion. Its contemporary readers are caught up in a common fate. With apologies to Joseph Ratzinger, who in this remarkable book began with a remarkable effort to look for a Church that was not preoccupied first and foremost with itself, we cannot avoid beginning with a short attempt to situate the questions that the book poses by recalling what were and what are the chief readings of the Second Vatican Council. Given that this essential part of the narrative is dealt with in greater depth by other contributions in this volume, a brief and schematic sketch of the hermeneutical options for reading the Council will suffice here.

II. Readings of the Council and of Ratzinger

In the first decades after the Council, much of the debate about its legacy was set in terms of two questions: whether it had been in discontinuity or continuity with the past, and whether this stance was to be embraced or not. Each of the four logical possibilities for answering these two questions found convinced proponents: (1) The Council as a clear break and long overdue innovation (whether or not sustained after the Council); or (2) it was a sad and sudden loss of identity (perpetuated afterwards); or (3) the Council was a welcome reaffirmation of tradition (whether or not sustained after the Council); or rather (4) it was itself a missed chance for direly needed self-reform (perpetuated afterwards). As a result of historical studies (most notably of the "Bologna school" around Guiseppe Alberigo) for the fortieth anniversary of the Council, the discussions and texts of the Council were documented as a mix of discontinuity and continuity in greater detail than ever before. The hermeneutical directions around the fiftieth anniversary and until today for interpreting this mix have absorbed aspects of the older four models, but now with a clearer sense of the compromises in the agreed texts of the Council itself. Two hermeneutical options, not unknown before, have come to the fore with new force and detail: (1) the polarizing view that only the innovations belong to the genuine spirit of the Council and are in need of something like a Third Vatican Council to distill them from the compromises at or after the Council and to translate them into pastoral practice; and (2) the view that the Council's conscious and accepted ambiguity was a mandate for a future theological synthesis of the heterogeneous moments and for pastoral reforms corresponding to such a synthesis.

1. Cf. Daley, *God Visible*.

Especially the early reviews of Ratzinger's work and his responses to them, notably the responses of 1969/70 and 2000, now collected in volume 4 of the Regensburg edition (Joseph Ratzinger Gesammelte Schriften 4), suggest that all six readings of the Council have provided contexts and continue to do so for reading and re-reading the *Introduction*. These early discussions are also dealt with in greater depth by other contributions gathered in this volume, for, despite the many unforeseeable twists and turns of secular and ecclesiastical history in the last fifty years, they continue to suggest where the questions raised by *Introduction* are situated. The two most extreme criticisms found their proponents at different paces, and I wish to begin with the younger of the two criticisms of the *Introduction*.

As Karl-Heinz Menke (Bonn) recently observed,[2] the Italian traditionalist Enrico Maria Radaelli published a short time ago a manifesto of eighty theses. Where his mentor Romano Amerio's *Iota unum. A Study of Changes in the Catholic Church in the Twentieth Century* had referred exclusively to Ratzinger's work as prefect of the Congregation of Faith,[3] Radaelli's *Al cuore di Ratzinger. Al cuore del mondo* is focused on the *Introduction to Christianity*. The alleged adoption of subjectivism, historicism, and relativism by the 1967 lecture is said to manifest and continue the "modernistic" rupture with the older ecclesial tradition that the Council itself had begun, in good part due to Ratzinger's influence, notably on *Dei Verbum*.

The precisely opposite critique had found its way into the earlier discussion. An anonymous author, who identifies himself only as an academic assistant at a theological faculty, published a scathing attack on Ratzinger's "dangerous" work in the second issue of the short-lived periodical, *Kritischer Katholizismus* (1968), following the imitation of the civil dissent of 1968 at the Katholikentag held in Essen in the same year,[4] and boasting as its motto a mélange of Marx and the New Testament, the latter (and only the latter) read ironically against the grain (Matt 13:12 as a capitalist manifesto). The telling image depicted on the cover is of the pantocrator with his hand raised not in blessing but as a fist. This particular review opened a series of short columns aimed at stating just how unprogressive the so-called "progressive German theologians" at the Council had been and had remained. The second piece in the series, a somewhat less fundamental critique of Karl Rahner's transcendental argumentation,[5] would be signed

2. See *Al cuore di Ratzinger*.
3. So the title of the translation by John P. Parsons.
4. Cf. also Seeber, *Katholikentag im Widerspruch*; and van Onna and Stankowski, *Kritischer Katholizismus*.
5. The author of the more measured reflections on Karl Rahner, Oskar Rubicek (Berlin), would likely have seen his position only strengthened by Rahner's less

by its author. The first, anonymous piece dismisses as "naïve" the use of Scripture by the Council itself and by Ratzinger. In his brief but brusque review, the presumably youngish author accuses Ratzinger several times of a lack of awareness of the contemporary problems surrounding the matters he discusses. The most serious issues for the *anonymus*, however, seem to be the sense that Ratzinger had built a "bastion of orthodoxy" in matters of faith that would prevent the kind of political and ecclesial revolution called for in the practical order. The *Introduction*'s treatment of the final articles of the Creed on the Church, the *communio sanctorum*, the forgiveness of sins, the resurrection of the flesh, and life everlasting all as in a special sense the work of the Holy Spirit, and correspondingly its emphasis on a primacy of the Spirit's inner graces before ecclesiastical structural re-organization or social-political accommodation, is dismissed by the *anonymus* as the language of "the Platonist Ratzinger."

The dismissive or even more decidedly pejorative sense of the heritage of Plato is not the invention of theologians. It began no later than with Aristotle in his attempts to distinguish with stark emphasis his own philosophy from that of his predecessors.[6] In its theological adaptation, the term "Platonic" only rarely acknowledges theology's complicity in the problematic dimensions of Plato's legacy, unlike Augustine's famous self-critique, formulated in his *Retractationes*, that he had allowed the maxim of Porphyry, "corpus est fugiendum," too great an influence over his own earlier thought. More frequent is the discrepancy between the openly pejorative label of "Platonism" for the ideas of other theologians and the unidentified presence of Platonic tendencies in one's own. Even less attention is directed in the main to the breadth and internal differentiation of the Platonic tradition.[7] The limitations of Plato's legacy are better known than its strengths, tempting the theologian towards the easy choices of a lack of gratitude and consistency. The resulting ambivalence was present in the early readings of *Introduction*, where the "accusation" of Platonism was an easy enough charge to level against a young author known chiefly for his works on Augustine and Bonaventure. Ratzinger will defend himself against the "charge" of Platonism, but shows himself at one point willing to accept the title, if by it were meant merely the affirmation of abiding truths (setting aside the question of the historically varied access to abiding truths that the authors of both the *Republic* and the *Introduction* had done much

transcendental, direct contributions to the Council, still unavailable at the time. Cf. Rahner, "Animadversiones de Schemate."

6. Cf. Cherniss, *Aristotle's Criticism of Plato and the Academy*.

7. But cf. von Ivánka, *Plato Christianus*, and Richard Schenk, "From Providence to Grace."

to elucidate). Ratzinger sees his own work and a second review by Walter Kasper as reflecting an interpretation of Platonism more nuanced than that suggested by the earlier reviews. The issues at stake in the context of the Platonist controversy in the early reviews were the alleged alternatives (arguably more contraries than contradictions) between the spiritual and the political and between the unchanging and the historical. Still implicit was a third issue that will occupy us below, on the presence and absence of what is or should be remembered or recollected.[8]

What makes the cited review in the second issue of *Kritischer Katholizismus* memorable are three of its references, one active and two passive. The review begins by citing the call by Johann Baptist Metz for a "second courage," adding to the Conciliar reforms newer and more stringent measures. Metz would repeat this appeal in 1969, when he united a previous talk and an open letter to Karl Rahner into a longer essay, "Reform and Counter-Reformation Today."[9] Metz would use the phrase again in 1989, this time to celebrate the legacy of Karl Rahner.[10] While not explicit, a judgment about the contents of such a legacy had much to do with the ability to describe them as courageous. In his review of 1968, the anonymous assistant makes no note of the differences in content between his own position and the positions expressed in the contemporary thought of Metz, such as the latter's more positive reading of the Council or his worry that those most concerned with reform might be defamed for a kind of "liberal minimalism"[11] arguably quite like the positions espoused by the review. No mention is made by the reviewer of those areas where points of congeniality appeared between Metz and Ratzinger, e.g., in their esteem for the Council, the concern for ecumenism, or their insistence that the Church not be focused first and foremost on herself. Metz and Ratzinger made no direct mention of each other in these publications, but one line of "reading" Ratzinger's text and its critics was forming, and both theologians would be vocal about their divide in future venues.

The passive references that make the anonymous review especially memorable are Ratzinger's discussion of the review and his initial association of its positions with those formulated by Walter Kasper in the first of two more nuanced reviews of Ratzinger's work, the first in 1969 and then, following a first response by Ratzinger, again in 1970. The second review by

---

8. On the topos "Platonism" in the early reception of *Introduction,* cf. now Jall, *Erfahrung von Offenbarung,* 456–58.

9. Metz, "Reform und Gegenreformation heute," esp. 26–27.

10. Metz, "Zeuge für den 'zweiten Mut,'" esp. 349.

11. Metz, "Reform und Gegenreformation heute," esp. 24.

Kasper was likewise followed by a second response from Ratzinger.[12] Kasper's analysis of the *Introduction* anticipates something akin to what will develop as the fifth interpretation of the Council noted above, in that it distinguishes positions in continuity (notably the Christology) from those in discontinuity (notably the eschatology) with earlier interpretations of the faith, seeing the two strands, however, as incompatible with one another. In his reviews of Ratzinger's work, Kasper tended to acknowledge only the transformative readings as tenable for today. At the very least, he had identified with his remarks three of the issues which continue to play a role in current assessments of Ratzinger's early work: the interrelated questions of alleged Platonism, which would be bracketed out only in the second set of exchanges between the two theologians, of historical awareness, and of the relation between theology and praxis. Behind these three was a fourth issue that remained implicit for the most part: inner-Christian ecumenism.

III. Synthetic Intentions

Ratzinger's own sense of what the complexity of the Conciliar documents could contribute positively for future theological synthesis developed only gradually. In his commentary on *Dei Verbum* for the *Lexikon für Theologie und Kirche*, written in the same year as the *Introduction*, it was not meant as praise or hope, when Ratzinger wrote: "With its very brief form and in the logical fissures that it can barely paste over, the Prologue quite clearly reveals the confused prehistory out of which it developed."[13]

In 2003, perhaps with an image before him of the confluence of the Inn and Danube Rivers at Passau, Ratzinger would offer a less pejorative image of conciliar compromise:

> The Constitution on the Sacred Liturgy drew together the manifold streams and rivers of the Liturgical Movement and united them into one deep river which "brings joy to God's city" (Ps 46:5). Of course there remained behind some residual, free-standing waters, so to speak, which couldn't be channeled into this river, and in the river itself the different tributaries that united in it can still be identified. The currents still show where they came from. Internal tensions have remained, and we will need to discuss them: tensions between the desire to renew the

---

12. Cf. Walter Kasper, "Das Wesen des Christlichen (B)." For Ratzinger's responses, cf. "Glaube, Geschichte und Philosophie," and "Schlusswort."

13. "Das Prooemium lässt in seiner kargen Form und in den nur mühsam verdeckten logischen Brüchen, die es enthält, noch recht deutlich die verworrene Vorgeschichte erkennen, aus der es hervorgewachsen ist."

liturgy of the ancient Church once again in its primordiality and the need to situate the liturgy in the present age; tensions between the conservative and the creative element of liturgy; tensions between the worshipping character of the liturgy and its catechetical and pastoral tasks. These of course are tensions that are rooted ultimately in the very essence of the liturgy and do not merely reflect different currents of liturgy. The Council sought in impressive ways to establish the right internal balance between these different aspects. But in carrying out the commission of the Council, it could easily happen that the balance of the Conciliar text got dissolved in a one-sided way into just one particular direction. This is why there is always a need to reflect anew on the actual statement of the Council. The general ease with which anyone could lay claim to "the Council" to support his or her own wishes led to a false reading of the great task which the Conciliar fathers bequeathed to us.[14]

On December 22, 2005, at his first Christmas address to the Curia, Pope Benedict XVI argued for a "hermeneutic of reform." Though interpreted at first by some—friends and critics—as a simple hermeneutic of the Council's continuity with the past, it soon became clear that this alternative to a hermeneutic of rupture was meant as that synthesis of *nova et vetera* expected since Matt 13:52 of the reader of the Scriptures who had become a disciple. It suggested a path for reading not just the Council but the *Introduction* that surfaced in its wake.

These two more recent possibilities for reading the Council that followed the detailed documentation of Conciliar controversy and compromise are mirrored by the two leading developments in the current German discussion of an intentionally "local theology," which, inspired by the so-called "spatial turn" in contemporary social sciences, has expanded on the suggestions made by Melchior Cano's *De locis theologicis*, first published in 1563, three years after Cano's death. Retrieving especially Cicero's *Topica*, Cano distinguished seven topoi or loci that are proper to theology from three topoi or loci that, while not stemming from faith traditions, are nonetheless necessary for theology. The three "loci theologici alieni" identified by Cano are human reason (expressed in the sciences and disciplines of a university), the history of philosophy and philosophers and—Cano's last and most original discovery—human history. The seven "loci proprii" identified by Cano in *De locis* include: (1) Scripture, (2) the oral tradition of Christ and the Apostles, (3) the universal Church, (4) the Council, (5) the

---

14. Ratzinger, "40 Jahre Konstitution über die heilige Liturgie." Translated here from Joseph Ratzinger Gesammelte Schriften (JRGS) 11, 696–97.

Roman Church or Apostolic See, (6) the saints of the early Church, as well as (7) scholastic theology and canonistic thought. Current local theology seeking to develop *De locis* tends to agree that the loci are somewhat more numerous than those mentioned by Cano, but the discussion has focused more on the generic distinction between the two genera of loci. One line of development running from Elmar Klinger to Hans-Joachim Sander sees in *loci alieni* privileged resources for the development of theology, and so this line of interpretation might be described as the alienational model. The alternative direction might well be called an "integrative model" of interpretation, notably articulated after Max Seckler by Bernhard Körner, as it stresses the need to bring both genera of loci into a synthesis of all the relevant sources, an "epistemological Catholicity," as Seckler called it. In what might be described as an experiment in local theology of the alienational model, H.J. Sander recently presented a long and widely received commentary on *Gaudium et spes* arguing that the "signs of the times" originating outside the faith community should in accord with the Pastoral Constitution be accorded a privileged place in shaping the future course of doctrine and pastoral practice. From the critical viewpoint of a more integrative reading, such a demand would rob the category of human history of much of its diachronic alterity, and forget too much of the ecumenical and political nuance which the Council itself and post-Conciliar liberation theology had brought to the understanding of the *signa temporum*. How these current debates may be used to understand Ratzinger's work and its relation to the Council, is one of the questions to which we will return below.

IV. The Believer's Familiarity with Disbelief and Israel's Struggle for a Divine Name

If Ratzinger's anything but innocent inclusion in his preface of 1968 of the story of happy-go-lucky Hans did much to shape the controversial pre-understanding of the *Introduction* as a whole, there were three further, also more literary references in the first of the original lectures that pointed to the heart of Ratzinger's intentions and to the distinctive, argumentative goals of the entire work. For the first hundred pages, more than a fourth of the whole work, the work dwells on the basic character of faith before proceeding to a direct discussion of the "object" of first article on God. Even then, that first main section on the "one God, the Father Almighty, Creator of heaven and earth," will echo and deepen the initial reflections on what it means to believe at all ("Credo in"). Together, these two sections, on "Credo in . . . " and on the words " . . . unum Deum . . . ," constitute more than half the entire work. The light of the problematic developed there, including the surprising emphasis on the familiarity of the believer with the gravitational pull to disbelief, will provide the light under which the larger body of the Apostles' Creed will be considered. Ratzinger chooses and explicates his three references with special intent.

The first one is taken from Harvey Cox and his 1965 bestseller, *The Secular City*, which recalled Søren Kierkegaard's parable of a clown in full array, who, sent from a burning circus to near-by villagers threatened by the approaching conflagration, still unknown to them, cannot convince them of the seriousness of his warning or the peril they face. It is the opening passage of Ratzinger's first lecture in the 1967 series. The *Introduction* includes as all too true the more obvious implications implied here for the difficulty of proclaiming the Gospel in our times, and for the impossibility of attaining credibility simply by divesting ourselves of seemingly outlandish and outmoded trappings. But then Ratzinger extends the application of the story in a direction that, while not explicit in his sources, is even more to his point. "But perhaps our examination of conscience should go still deeper," as he begins to describe the clown's own self-doubt.[15]

> In the strangeness of theology's aims to the men of our time, he who takes his calling seriously will clearly recognize not only the difficulty for the task of interpretation [for others] but also the insecurity of his own faith, the oppressive power of unbelief in the midst of his own will to believe . . . [He will] have to understand that his own situation is by no means so different from that of others as he may have thought at the start. He will become aware that on both sides the same forces are at work, albeit in a different way.[16]

The solidarity of the believer with those who feel most the gravitational pull towards disbelief is not arbitrary. To begin with this emphasis is, however, an uncommon opening for a work seeking to renew and strengthen the faith. A second reference continues the theme, this time with a story borrowed from Martin Buber's collection of stories of the Chassidim. An enlightenment atheist visits Rabbi Levi Yitschak of Berditchev for the purpose of chiding him for his dogmatism, but he catches him unaware as the Rabbi, meditating a sacred text, says first to himself, "Perhaps it is true after all," and then soon to the visitor, "But think my son, perhaps it is true." This "perhaps" reveals to the Enlightenment figure for the first time his own dogmatism and faith commitments, but, as Ratzinger is even more

15. Ratzinger, *Introduction*, 40.
16. Ratzinger, *Introduction*, 41.

intent on showing, it also reveals the non-arbitrary solidarity of the Rabbi with him. "[B]oth the believer and the unbeliever share, each in his own way, doubt *and* belief, if they do not hide from themselves and from the truth of their being. Neither can quite escape either belief or doubt."[17] The kinds of faith in another singular Thou that simply could not be false, could also not be true faith. The faith as mere custom and the faith as politically functional might have their undeniable practical advantages. As such, they are far more self-understood, but as such not yet the medium of the bold claim to the truth of a non-self-explanatory faith in a benevolent and beneficent divine Thou, as belief which is also far from the secure expressions of a loose metaphoric or a tight metaphysics. Ratzinger will cite in this regard several times in his works the remark by Tertullian: "Dominus noster Christus veritatem se, non consuetudinem cognominavit."[18] The admission of something like what Ratzinger will later call the "experience of inexperience" (*die Erfahrung der Nichterfahrung*)[19] is seen throughout his work as a necessary condition for the possibility of the truth claim of that belief in the divine "You" which is sought by Israel and the Church.

The third literary reference also involves contrasting and yet interconnected figures, who in this case are portrayed as siblings, the protagonists in Paul Claudel's *The Satin Slipper* (1931). The Jesuit missionary, brother to the main protagonist Rodrigue, suffers shipwreck and survives only by clinging to a wooden plank. Ratzinger's reading: "Fastened to the cross—with the cross fastened to nothing, drifting over the abyss. The situation of the contemporary believer could hardly be more accurately and impressively described. Only a loose plank bobbing over the void seems to hold him up, and it looks as if he must eventually sink. Only a loose plank connects him to God."[20] As in the other two allusions, Ratzinger has again the dimension of solidarity between the two figures foremost in mind. "This picture contains in addition yet another dimension, which indeed seems to me the really important thing about it. This shipwrecked Jesuit is not alone, he foreshadows, as it were, the fate of his brother, the destiny of his brother is present in him, that brother who considers himself a non-believer, who has turned his back on God because he sees his business, not in waiting but as 'possessing the attainable, as though he could be anywhere else than where Thou art.'"[21] The

17. Ratzinger, *Introduction*, 46–47.

18. Tertullian, *De virginibus velandis* I, 1 (CCSL 2:1209).

19. Ratzinger, *Theologische Prinzipienlehre*, 367. Cf. Mark 9:24: "Credo; adiuva incredulitatem meam."

20. Ratzinger, *Introduction*, 44.

21. Ratzinger, *Introduction*, 44.

conquistador will fall from his position of wealth and control, captive on a slave ship, mirroring the fate of his brother, and sharing his experiences of profound solitude and isolation.

Ratzinger draws on this narrative by Claudel to reflect more broadly on the sense of "loneliness" or solitude that is the abiding condition of belief in the other and in the gift of divine-human conviviality, rather than a self-understood confidence in the self-sufficiency of human arts and religious sentiment. "The same thing could be demonstrated in the theme of loneliness and security [Einsamkeit und Geborgenheit]. Loneliness is indubitably one of the basic roots from which man's encounter with God has risen. Where man experiences his solitariness, he experiences at the same time how much his whole existence is a cry for the 'You' and how ill-adapted he is to be only an I' in himself."[22]

Ratzinger has a human experience in mind that points beyond even the sacramental solace of human community to the question of a God who is Other than "the work of human hands" (Ps 115:4). This opening of humankind to divine alterity is a condition of the possibility of *timor filialis* and its genuinely dialogical veracity. It is what also saves inter-human relationships from the impossible demand that they provide their partners with final beatitude. Recalling "the great concluding dialogue between Dona Prouhèze and Rodrigue" in Claudel's *The Satin Slipper*, Ratzinger continues:

> This loneliness can become apparent to man on many levels. To start with, it can be comforted by the experience of a human "You." But then there is the paradox that, as Claudel says, every "You" found by man finally turns out to be an unfulfilled and unfulfillable promise; that every "You" is at bottom another disappointment and that there comes a point when no encounter can surmount the final loneliness: the very process of finding and having found thus becomes a pointer back to the loneliness, a call to the absolute "You" that really descends into the depths of one's own "I".[23]

As in all things that are "in the genus of a sign," the sacramental gift of a loving human "You" signifies not only by revealing that it is "merely" a sign, but first of all and foremost in its direct, positive mediation:

> But even here it remains true that it is not only the need born of loneliness, the experience that no sense of community fills up all our longing, that leads to the experience of God; it can just as well proceed from the joy of security [der Freude der

22. Ratzinger, *Introduction*, 106.
23. Ratzinger, *Introduction*, 106.

Geborgenheit]. The very fulfillment of love, of finding one another, can cause man to experience the gift of what he could neither call up nor create and can make him recognize that in it he receives more than either of the two could contribute. The brightness and joy of finding one another [des Sichfindens] can point to the proximity of absolute joy and of the simple fact of being found [des schlechthinnigen Gefundenseins] that stands behind every human encounter [Sichfinden].[24]

Introduction to Christianity concretizes this sense of the never self-understood character of belief in its treatment of the first article regarding belief "in God, the Father Almighty, Creator of heaven and earth." Here Ratzinger seeks to retrieve and bring together again two of the historical sources of Christian belief, diachronical to one another and to us. The first was the quest of Israel for the name of God, expressed notably in the story of Jacob/Israel of Genesis 32, where after wrestling in the night with God at Penuel Israel received his own name as a result of seeking God's name. Even more central to Ratzinger's recovery of this pre-history is the revelation to Moses in Exodus 3 of the name of the God of Abraham, Isaac, and Jacob, which sets Israel on its path to faith in the God who is above all and yet Creator of heaven and earth, and as such the author of the salvific hope of Israel's history. Yet far from following B. Pascal's sharp opposition between this God of faith and the God of the philosophers, Ratzinger surprises many of his readers by a second retrieval, the option in the early Church not to see its faith practice as an easy addition to the other religions of the time, although they all had something that recommended them. As Ratzinger had already developed the theme in his inaugural lecture at Bonn in 1959, the early Christians saw the Highest Being that Greek philosophers had identified in the process of their critique of conventional narrative and political religions to be unsurpassable as the God that Christians were called to venerate.[25] In *Introduction*, neither the ecumenical context nor its relation to the legacy of Thomas Aquinas (who is never mentioned in the work, prior to the preface of 2000, which even then merely notes the decline of research in this direction) is as evident as in the 1959 lecture, where Emil Brunner's reflections on the search for the proper name of God, together with his objections to any generalized natural theology of the type commonly proposed in Catholic thought as a development of Thomas Aquinas, are brought into a well argued synthesis that reaffirms the early Church's efforts to embrace

---

24. Ratzinger, *Introduction*, 106.

25. Ratzinger, *Der Gott des Glaubens*. On the development of the key insight of the inaugural lecture at Bonn beyond *Introduction*, cf. Striet, "Benedikt XVI."

both its biblical and its philosophical heritage.[26] The *Introduction* is an attempt to find the grammar that makes an articulated faith possible in its mix of second and third person language. The lecture might seem to echo a line in Paul Celan's poem, "Es war Erde in ihnen," from the same year as the lecture in Bonn, with its sense of the nearly forgotten and never self-understood quest for the name: "O einer, o keiner, o niemand, o Du": "O someone, or not, O no one, O Thou . . . "[27] The *Introduction* is an attempt at the retrieval of a nearly forgotten and never self-understood articulation that distinguished early Christian faith from the many conventional or politically instrumentalized cults of its day. Recalling Varro's distinction of three basic types of religion, Ratzinger saw in the faith of the early Church the universalism of cosmic religion and the philosophical critique of conventional or political religions joined to that second-person naming of the Creator which had been granted to Israel.

V. Looking for Plato

In the terms developed by "local theology," Ratzinger's 1967 lectures can be described as the search for a better understanding of the *loci proprii* associated with the Creed by devoting careful attention to the *loci alieni* identified by local theology as: natural reason, all too aware of its own limits; the work of philosophers, whose religiously critical sense of God was identified by the early Church with the God of the Judeo-Christian faith; and diachronically recollected human history, in particular the history of Israel and the history of its Christian legacy, sensitive to the concerns in the separated churches and in contemporary culture to re-read and re-shape that legacy. While several questions of historical-critical method remained open in the

26. Ratzinger might have recalled here an insight from Thomas Aquinas' first series of regular disputations as a professor of theology: "Inde est etiam quod in credente potest insurgere motus de contrario eius quod firmissime tenet, quamvis non in intelligente vel sciente" (*Quaestiones disputatae De veritate* 14, 1 co.). Despite his largely favorable interpretation of Thomas in the inaugural lecture in Bonn, Ratzinger's reading of Thomas before and after 1959 has been marked more generally by his critique of a semi-Pelagian optimism not unknown among some Thomistic trends prior to the Council. Cf. more recently the remark by Pope Emeritus Benedict XVI, "Gnade und Berufung ohne Reue," 391: "Wenn bei Thomas von Aquin mit einer neuen Sicht der Theologie die Allegorie grundlegend abgewertet wird (nur der Wortsinn ist argumentativ zu gebrauchen) und de facto die Nikomachische Ethik des Aristoteles zur Grundlage christlicher Moral wird, so ist die Gefahr des Bedeutungsverlustes für das ganze Alte Testament offenkundig." For an alternative view of the encounter between biblical and pagan thought in Thomas Aquinas which arguably is closer to the reading of Ratzinger's 1959 lecture cf. Mansini, "Similitudo, Communicatio."

27. Celan, *Die Gedichte*, 125, 673.

Introduction and would be revisited in Ratzinger's later writings, notably in the exegetical works on *Jesus of Nazareth*, another dimension of Ratzinger's sense of history already in evidence here has something to do with the unarticulated issue of "Platonism," raised but rarely articulated in the early, critical reviews of the *Introduction*. The question of historical sensitivity has much to do with the distinction mentioned by Plato,[28] and then taken up and accentuated by Aristotle, as the difference between *mneme* and *anamnesis*, between memory and recollection.[29] It was a distinction received and pondered for example by Thomas Aquinas in his commentary on Aristotle's *De memoria et reminiscentia*,[30] but also by Paul Ricoeur as the starting point of his late monograph, *Memory, History, Forgetting*.[31] Memory in the sense of *mneme* serves to make the past present. Nearer to the passive impression made by events, it can be stronger or weaker in its service of re-presenting. But recollecting or *anamnesis* involves on Aristotle's account the active search for a past known to be no longer fully present in memory. Recollection not only suffers forgetfulness, but it reacts to it intentionally. It searches for the early experiences not accessible by memory. More than a reliance on memory, it is an active answer to forgottenness.[32] Ricoeur makes clear that the need for arts of memory and recollection is due to the possibility that both memory, forgetting, and recollection know both uses and abuses, and thus an art is needed by each to embrace its uses and restrain its abuses. Some past wrongs are too easily and too gladly ignored or forgotten, others are kept too present to allow their forgiveness at the fitting time. While Aristotle examined personal memory and recollection, Ricoeur widened his study programmatically to include collective modes of the same. Political forgiveness with the partial forgetting that it requires and the conditioned freedom that it makes possible is the final interest of the philosopher in

---

28. Cf. Plato, *Philebus* 34a-c.

29. For Aristotle's text *De memoria et reminiscentia*, cf. his *Parva naturalia. A Revised Text with Introduction and Commentary by Sir David Ross*, and the very helpful, annotated English translation of Aquinas' commentaries by Kevin White and Edward M. Macierowski cited in the following note.

30. Thomas Aquinas, *Commentaries on Aristotle's 'On Sense and What is Sensed' and 'On Memory and Recollection.'* As recently shown by Müller (Würzburg), *Albertus Magnus über Gedächtnis*, Albert's commentary is far less concerned than that by his earlier student to accentuate the contrast between the acts of remembering and recollecting, mneme and anamnesis.

31. Ricoeur, *Memory, History, Forgetting*.

32. Cf. the commentary by R. A. H. King in Aristotle, *De memoria et reminiscentia*, 55: "Bei beiden Phänomenen handelt es sich um frühere Erkenntnis, nur dass sie im Falle des Gedächtnisses <memoria> parat ist, und in der Erinnerung <reminiscentia> gesucht (wiederaufgenommen) werden muss."

this study. Ricoeur had already accomplished much in his several mediations in famous philosophical and cultural disputes, early on for example between the understanding of the proximate other that Hans-Georg Gadamer proposed on the basis of that Wirkungsgeschichte of which our self-understanding is a part, and the critique of just that history by Jürgen Habermas. This pattern of well argued mediation might serve theologians well in an age of political polarization as an alternative model to ecclesiastical polemics in an age of social media. Ricoeur remained indebted to Gadamer *inter alia* for his reminder of Nietzsche's sense of not just any, but of certain forms of forgetting as " . . . a necessary condition for the life of our mind. It is only by forgetting that our mind receives the possibility of a thorough-going renewal, the ability to see things anew with a fresh look, so that what was old and familiar now blends with what is newly seen into a multidimensional unity. In ways that are largely overlooked, forgetting belongs to the relation between retaining and remembering . . . ,"[33] or, as may be said, to the relation between memory and recollection.

Aristotle took his distinction several steps further. Human beings share with many higher animals the gift of memory and its keeping present the past, but it is proper to human beings to be aware of their forgetfulness and to search intentionally for what has been forgotten. Recollection seeks to return in the imagination to the place of the first experience of what has been forgotten. And, as Aristotle twice points out in this brief work (at 449B and 453A), those with good memories and those good at recollection are not the same persons. It is something that will distinguish Christian theologians as well: Those with robust memories represent other trends in theology than what is sought by those more inclined to recollection.

That final point is much in evidence in recent theology. The most prominent forms of transcendental theology, for example, had always assumed something like a good memory, that every human being had from the beginning of its mature existence the *mneme* of God and the benefactions that God had long since begun to share. For that reason, the best known theological systematizations of what was deemed transcendental method displayed comparatively little interest in history. Likewise, following the manifold displacement of transcendental arguments by more categorial concerns in the 1980s, and notably following the spatial turn among several

---

33. Gadamer, *Wahrheit und Methode*, 13: "Dem Verhältnis von Behalten und Sich-Erinnern gehört in einer lange nicht genug beachteten Weise das Vergessen zu, das nicht nur ein Ausfall und ein Mangel, sondern, wie vor allem F. Nietzsche betont hat, eine Lebensbedingung des Geistes ist. Nur durch das Vergessen erhält der Geist die Möglichkeit der totalen Erneuerung, die Fähigkeit, alles mit frischen Augen zu sehen, so dass das Altvertraute mit dem Neugesehenen zu vielschichtiger Einheit verschmilzt."

of the more prominent theologians and clerics of the "alienational" bent in recent local theology, privileging the "loci alieni" in the accommodationalist reform of faith and practice, there is an unstated "Platonic" confidence that Catholic identity is already well enough established and present within us as to allow us to recognize with ease and facility the pastoral and theological significance of trends read as benevolent "signs of the times."[34] At the other extreme of the spectrum, traditionalist critics display little worry that their own memory of the tradition is a faded one, which might require extensive anamnetic efforts at ressourcement. In comparison to both of these sources of critique, Ratzinger's *Introduction* evidences the stronger awareness of the forgetfulness required by and calling for recollection by all theologians than either of the alternatives suggested by its early critics. Each of these two alternative readings shows a greater confidence in its own memory of the past than theological movements with a sensed need of ressourcement. In comparison to its accommodationalist and traditionalistic critics, the *Introduction* is less sanguine about (because more familiar with) the painful godlessness that continues to haunt the faithful, making ressourcement by older and younger witnesses to a difficult faith a pressing but still unfinished task of ecclesial *anamnesis*. From this sense that the very basics of faith in the personal divine Other have been largely forgotten, it directs its attention both to the early history of Israel, and to its critical encounter with Hellenism, re-read in the horizon of more recent struggles for faith. From here stems generally its concern with ressourcement and the search in the imagination for places of the earliest experience of what in good part has been forgotten. At least in this sense, the *Introduction* was arguably less "Platonic" than many of its sharpest critics.

What is closer to Ricoeur than even to Aristotle is the observation that, among rememberers and recollectors, no one has a completely developed and encompassing sense of the same events of the past. Taken as a collective, any given body of memory, forgetting, and recollection will be a "corpus mixtum" of the use and misuse of memory, forgetting and recollection, at best a work in progress, the work of the Spirit (the term in John 14:26 is *hupomnései*) needed to correct and heal what begins and remains imperfect in this ecclesial life. A certain memory, a certain forgetting, and a certain recollection are necessary but still insufficient conditions of the passion and action of a flourishing Church, which must be animated by the divine Vivificator.

---

34. For the sometimes forgotten, growing nuance regarding the "signs of the times" that the Vatican II achieved and communicated as a result of its ecumenical listening during the Council, cf. Schenk, *Officium signa temporum perscrutandi*.

For our topic, it should be conceded that the anamnetic capabilities displayed in the *Introduction* did not yet have a robust sense of the place of anamnesis for recalling the political tasks of theology. Arguably this reduced scope of recollection was conditioned by the excesses of political claims on academic discourse not just in the late 1960s and 70s, but all too present in the still fresh memory of the 1930s and 40s. This field of recollection arguably became stronger for Ratzinger with time, as shown, say, by Benedict XVI's address before the German parliament in 2011 (urging a robust sense of natural law),[35] the conversations of Cardinal Ratzinger with the philosopher Marcello Pera (insisting on the acknowledgement of human rights),[36] and Ratzinger's remarks on the profound, if partial, consensus between himself and Johann Baptist Metz at the colloquium for the latter in Ahaus in 1998.[37]

"Books have their fates according to the grasp of the readers," as we heard at the beginning of this talk. But the best sense of fate had always left room for freedom, just as the best sense of freedom had always recognized both its situatedness, or thrownness, and its still open possibilities. Ratzinger's *Introduction* stresses throughout that God intended this freedom for his beloved human creatures. Our hope is that, by recalling key but somehow forgotten themes of the *Introduction*, contemporary theology might make use of its own freedom, in the midst of an already eventful history of reading Ratzinger and his times, and in the midst of recent resurgent polarization, to renegotiate the "Vorgriff" of a future interpretation that, rather than simply dig a bit deeper and shore up the trenches of twentieth century disputes, might succeed in preparing an anamnetic path in the direction of genuine forgiveness.

Bibliography

Amerio, Romano. *Iota unum. A Study of Changes in the Catholic Church in the Twentieth Century*. Translated by John P. Parsons. Kansas City, Sarto House 1996.

Aristoteles. *De memoria et reminiscentia*. In *Werke in deutscher Übersetzung*, ed. Hellmut Flashar. Band 14, Teil II: *Parva naturalia*. Translated and commentary by R.A.H. King. Berlin: Akademie, 2004.

———. *Parva naturalia. A Revised Text with Introduction and Commentary by Sir David Ross*. Oxford: Clarendon, 1955.

---

35. Available on the Vatican website.
36. Cf. Pera and Ratzinger, *Without Roots*.
37. Peters et al., *The End of Time?*

Benedict XVI. "Address of Holiness Benedict XVI" (to the German Parliament in Berlin). September 22, 2011. https://w2.vatican.va/content/benedictxvi/en/speeches/2011/september/documents/hf_ben-xvi_spe_20110922_reichstag-berlin.html.

Celan, Paul. *Die Gedichte. Kommentierte Gesamtausgabe*, edited by Barbara Wiedemann. Frankfurt: Suhrkamp, 2005.

Cherniss, Harold F. *Aristotle's Criticism of Plato and the Academy*, vol. 1. Baltimore: John Hopkins University Press, 1944.

Daley, Brian E. *God Visible: Patristic Christology Reconsidered*. Oxford: Oxford University Press, 2018.

Gadamer, H. G. *Wahrheit und Methode*. Auflage. Tübingen: Mohr, 1975.

Ivánka, Endre von. *Plato Christianus. Übernahme und Umgestaltung des Platonismus durch die Väter*. Einsiedeln: Johannes, 1965.

Jall, Andreas. *Erfahrung von Offenbarung. Grundlagen, Quellen und Anwendungen der Erkenntnislehre Joseph Ratzingers*. Ratzinger-Studien 15. Regensburg: Pustet, 2019.

Kasper, Walter. "Das Wesen des Christlichen: Ein Fundamental-Theologe und ein Dogmatiker zu dem Buch von Joseph Ratzinger: *Einführung in das Christentum* (B)." *Theologische Revue* 3 (1969) 182–88.

———. "Theorie und Praxis innerhalb einer theologia crucis: Antwort auf J. Ratzingers 'Glaube, Geschichte und Philosophie.'" *Hochland* 62 (1970: März/April) 152–57.

Mansini, Guy, OSB, "Similitudo, Communicatio and the Friendship of Charity in Aquinas." In *Thomistica. Recherches de Théologie Ancienne et Médiévale: Supplementa* 1, edited by E. Manning, 1–26. Leuven: Peeters, 1995.

Metz, Johann Baptist. "Reform und Gegenreformation heute. Zwei Thesen zur ökumenischen Situation der Kirchen." In *Lerngemeinschaft Kirche. Gesammelte Schriften* 6/1, 15–41. Freiburg, Herder 2016. (Originally published 1969).

———. "Zeuge für den 'zweiten Mut': 'Wer retten will, muss wagen.'" In *Lerngemeinschaft Kirche. Gesammelte Schriften* 6/1, 347–54. Freiburg, Herder 2016. (Originally published in 1989).

Müller (Würzburg), Jörn. *Albertus Magnus über Gedächtnis, Erinnern und Wiedererinnerung. Eine philosophische Lektüre von* De memoria et reminiscentia *mit Übersetzung*. Lectio Albertina 17. Münster: Aschendorff, 2017.

Onna, Ben van, and Martin Stankowski, *Kritischer Katholizismus*. Frankfurt am Main and Hamburg: Fischer Bücherei, 1969.

Pera, Marcello, and Joseph Ratzinger. *Without Roots. The West, Relativism, Christianity, Islam*. New York: Basic, 2006.

Peters, Tiemo Rainer, et al., eds. *The End of Time? The Provocation of Talking about God*. Mahwah: Paulist, 2004.

Pope Emeritus Benedict XVI, "Gnade und Berufung ohne Reue. Anmerkungen zum Traktat 'De Iudaeis." *Internationale Katholische Zeitschrift (Communio)* 47 (2018) 387–406.

Radaelli, Maria. *Al cuore di Ratzinger, al cuore del monde*. Aurea Domus 2017.

Rahner, Karl. "Animadversiones de Schemate 'De ecclesia in mundo huius temporis.'" In *Sämtliche Werke* 32/1, *Ergänzungen*, edited by Albert Raffelt, XVIII–XIX and 289–325. Freiburg: Herder 2016.

Ratzinger, Joseph. "40 Jahre Konstitution über die heilige Liturgie. Rückblick und Vorblick." In *Theologie der Liturgie*, 695–711. JRGS 11. Freiburg: Herder, 2008. (Originally published in *Liturgisches Jahrbuch* 53 [2003] 209–21).

---. *Der Gott des Glaubens und der Gott der Philosophen. Ein Beitrag zum Problem der theologia naturalis*, edited by Heino Sonnemans. Trier: Paulinus, 2006.

---. *Einführung in das Christentum. Bekenntnis—Taufe—Nachfolge*. JRGS 4. Freiburg: Herder, 2014.

---. "Glaube, Geschichte und Philosophie. Zum Echo auf meine 'Einführung in das Christentum.'" *Hochland* 61 (1969) 533–43.

---. *Introduction to Christianity*. Translated by J. R. Foster and Michael J. Miller. San Francisco: Communio/Ignatius, 2004.

---. "Schlusswort zu der Diskussion mit Walter Kasper.'" In *Einführung in das Christentum: Bekenntnis-Taufe-Nachfolge, Band 4 Gesammelte Schriften*, 323–42. Freiburg: Herder & Herder, 2014. (Originally published in *Hochland* [1970]).

---. *Theologische Prinzipienlehre. Bausteine zur Fundamentaltheologie*. Munich: E. Wewel, 1982.

Ricoeur, Paul. *Memory, History, Forgetting*. Chicago: University of Chicago Press, 2004.

Schenk, Richard. "From Providence to Grace: Thomas Aquinas and the Platonisms of the Mid-Thirteenth Century." *Nova et Vetera* 3 (2005) 307–20.

---. "*Officium signa temporum perscrutandi*. New Encounters of Gospel and Culture in the Context of the New Evangelisation." In *Scrutinizing the Signs of the Times in Light of the Gospel*, edited by Johan Verstraeten, 167–203. Bibliotheca Ephemeridum Theologicarum Lovaniensium CCVIII. Leuven: Leuven University Press, and Leuven/Paris/Dudley: Peeters, 2007.

Seeber, David Andreas. *Katholikentag im Widerspruch. Ein Bericht über den 82. Katholikentag in Essen*. Herder Bücherei 328. Freiburg: Herder, 1968.

Striet, Magnus. "Benedikt XVI., die Moderne und der Glaube. Anmerkungen zur Regensburger Vorlesung des Papstes." *Herder Korrespondenz* 60 (2006) 551–54.

Tertullian, *De virginibus velandis*. In *Tertulliani Opera. Pars II: Opera Montanistica*, edited by A. Gerlo, 1209–26. Corpus Christianorum Series Latina 2. Turnholt: Brepols, 1954.

Thomas Aquinas. *Commentaries on Aristotle's 'On Sense and What is Sensed' and 'On Memory and Recollection.'* Translated with introductions and notes by Kevin White and Edward M. Macierowski, 169–260. Washington, DC: Catholic University of America Press, 2005.

3

The Reception of *Einführung in das Christentum* among the Reviewers

Tracey Rowland

Cardinal Ratzinger's best-selling book sounded a classical tone amidst the dissonance of 1968. While the typical *soixante-huitard* intellectual was interested in Buddhism, Shamanism, Taoism, or varieties of New Age Paganism, in addition to Marx, Freud, Nietzsche, and Gurdjieff, in his *Einführung in das Christentum* Ratzinger defended creedal Christianity. As a consequence, reviews of the book quickly appeared in the theology journals in 1969. A common theme was Ratzinger's attempt to navigate his way through a narrow theological strait, avoiding the rocks of history without ontology on the one side (historicism), and ontology without history on the other (varieties of pre-Christian Greek philosophy, partially sound, but without the grace of the Incarnation) on the other. In the journal *Theological Studies*, Patrick J. Burns, SJ, concluded:

> [Ratzinger] does his best to explain the Creed's classic categories to a contemporary audience beyond the post-Tridentine catechisms of their childhood and yet bewildered by the *Dutch Catechism*. Above all, he emphasizes the *Positivität* of Christian faith, its historical background in particular events in human history, its scandalous dependence on a particular human person named Jesus of Nazareth.[1]

In a 2017 review in the ecumenical journal *Fare Forward*, which markets itself as a quarterly Christian Review of Culture and Ideas for millennials, Joshua Tseng-Tham began by arguing that a proper introduction to Christianity—one that appeals to the entire human psyche (heart, imagination and memory, as well as intellect)—ought to incorporate both intellectual rigor

---

1. Burns, Review (Shorter Notice) of *Einführung*, 748.

and spiritual depth. He then showcases *Introduction to Christianity* as an example of a work that manages to achieve both of these ends. It offers spiritual wisdom alongside intellectual argument.

Perhaps for this reason, the sales of the book quickly took off after its 1968 release, prompting the German journal *Kritische Katholizismus: Zeitung für Theorie und Praxis in Gesellschaft und Kirche* to offer a review under the banner of a series tilted "Just how progressive are our progressive theologians?" The review of Ratzinger's book was the first in the case study. The anonymous reviewer for *Kritische Katholizismus* judged the work to be "extremely dangerous"—the statement was "Ratzingers Buch ist ausgesprochen gefährlich." The bill of indictment included the following: it obscures essential results of contemporary theology, it does not fight openly but secretly taunts the proponents of modern theology such as Bultmann and the contemporary champions of political theology. While Ratzinger's outward tone is one of humility, beneath the surface he is constantly evaluating, confessing, and judging. There is no provocation to critical thinking. Ratzinger exhaustively draws attention to the dangers and bottlenecks of the historical-critical method. There is little talk of the profit we owe to these methods of theology. Ratzinger suffers from a methodological naiveté which is very obvious in his treatment of the virgin birth. He simply assumes that Our Lady was and remained a virgin. This lack of method consciousness corresponds to a language that uses concepts of the New Testament as directly as if they naturally originate from today's experience. Sometimes one acquires the impression that Ratzinger cannot follow the post-Kantian critical way of thinking. Moreover, Ratzinger in his ecclesiological statements rightly points out that the church in its structure is an interweaving of the holy and the unholy, but nonetheless he is critical of those who are critical of church structures for not seeing beyond the organization to the church's presentation of the word and the sacraments. In this context the anonymous author accuses Ratzinger of operating under a Platonic influence according to which the real is not found in the structures (not in the bureaucracy, one might say), but only in the mediation of grace and truth which goes on behind the structures. The reviewer then asserts that, according to the understanding of the prophets (and here it is not clear which particular prophets the reviewer has in mind), tearing down is essential to the existence of a believer and his or her exercise of critical responsibility. He or she laments that there is nothing of this understanding of the importance of demolition work in Ratzinger's *Introduction*.[2]

---

2. Anonymous author, "Wie progressive sind unsere Progressiven?" 9.

Kritischer Katholizismus: Zeitung für Theorie und Praxis in Gesellschaft und Kirche was a German monthly newspaper that operated from 1968–1974. It was founded at the eighty-second German Catholic Congress in 1968. Its writers had been inspired by the social opposition movements in the universities and sought to apply the same principles of political opposition and critique to the hierarchical structures in the Church. They found little in Ratzinger's book to merit him with the appellation of a progressive theologian. On the contrary the work was declared dangerous.

The reviews that received even more attention, however, were those published in the *Theologische Revue*, the journal of the Theology Faculty of the University of Münster, Number 3 of 1969. The first was by Hubertus Mynarek (who was then a Professor of Religionswissenschaft at the University of Vienna), and the second by Walter Kasper (who was then teaching dogmatic theology at the University of Münster).[3]

Mynarek began with the clipped statement: "This work concerns the concrete form of the Christian faith in the guidelines of the so-called Apostolic Creed." He further stated that "Ratzinger sets out with this book a compact and large-scale belief system whose foundation, middle and high point as well as whose continuous explanatory principle seems to me to be love."[4] Quite simply, the logic of love, provides Ratzinger with the clue to the great Christian truths and mysteries. Mynarek explained:

> If love plays a decisive role in the fundamental determination of the act of faith, this applies even more to the content of the faith. In contrast to the essentially self-referential God of philosophy, the God of faith is fundamentally determined by the category of relationship. The highest is not the absolute self-contained self-sufficiency, but . . . relatedness . . . creative power that creates, sustains and loves others. It is connected with the fact that the philosophical God is a self-thinking thought, while the God of faith is love as thought and thought as love. The absolute is the identity of truth and love.[5]

Mynarek went on to argue that love is also the key to understanding the whole of Ratzinger's Christology since the "monstrous union of logos and sarx" or the "philosophical unheard of Incarnation of God" becomes more

---

3. In 1972 Mynarek wrote an open letter to Pope Paul VI, calling for the lifting of celibacy and the democratization of the Catholic Church. In the same year he left the church and married. According to him, he was the first university professor of German-speaking theology in the twentieth century to leave the Catholic Church.

4. Mynarek, "Das Wesen des Christlichen (A)," 177.

5. Mynarek, "Das Wesen des Christlichen (A)," 178.

comprehensible when one considers that, for the lover, the great is not too heavy and the least not too low. With love, Mynarek suggests, "there is thus a revaluation of all values, a revaluation of maximum and minimum, of greatness and life, which is characteristic of the Christian understanding of the real."[6] Mynarek also thought that love is at the centre of Ratzinger's ecclesiology, since Ratzinger views the Church as a community of love and a communion that is sacred because of the gift of divine love.

Mynarek then suggested that the work could be subjected to criticism from three angles: the perspective of philosophical reason, the perspective of comparative religions, and the perspectives of the leading authorities in the various sub-fields of theology. Specifically he suggested that the first may regard Ratzinger's account as too ontological, the second may ask why Ratzinger covered polytheism, monotheism, and atheism, but omitted a consideration of pantheism, and the third (he suggested) may be astonished by what he called the "mythological elements" in the treatment of such subjects as the Ascension, the Descent into Hell, and the Virgin-Birth. In other words, the sub-text here is that those for whom the historical-critical method of biblical exegesis is the only valid foundation for theology might be upset by Ratzinger's approach to biblical exegesis and to fundamental theology which is far less skeptical of the value of tradition.

Overall, Mynarek concluded that, if one wanted to locate Ratzinger in the history of theology, one would have to classify him as a neo-Augustinian along with Max Scheler and Romano Guardini. He also noted that Ratzinger's literary style was similar to Guardini's, which he defined as elegant, fluent, and easily understandable. He suggested that just as Guardini was regarded in his time as the "most subtle apologist of Catholic Christianity," this mantle was now likely to be passed to Ratzinger following the publication of *Einführung in das Christentum*.[7]

One may argue that Mynarek was 'on the money,' to use a popular game-show expression. Love is certainly a recurring theme in Ratzinger's theological counter-point. As Ratzinger wrote in another work: [The] Christian God is not just reason, objective meaning, the geometry of the universe, but he is speech, relation, Word and Love. He is sighted reason, which sees and hears, which can be called upon and has a personal character. The "objective" meaning of the world is a subject, in relation to me.[8]"

The notion that God is love is also the central theme of Hans Urs von Balthasar's *Glaubhaft ist nur Liebe*, first published in 1963, which became

6. Mynarek, "Das Wesen des Christlichen (A)," 178.
7. Mynarek, "Das Wesen des Christlichen (A)," 182.
8. Ratzinger, *Dogma and Preaching*, 94.

Love Alone is Credible in its English manifestation. It is highly probable that Ratzinger had read this work before writing his own introduction to Christianity. In the preface to *Glaubhaft ist nur Liebe*, Balthasar wrote that never in the history of the Church have Christian thinkers thought it adequate to answer the question of what specifically is Christian about Christianity with reference to a series of mysteries one is required to believe. Instead they have always aimed at a point of unity that would serve to provide a justification for the demand for faith. He further argued that it was only an account of revelation based on the notion that God is love which can provide such a point of unity.

Mynarek was also on target in his comparison of Ratzinger with Guardini, not only in terms of their literary style, but also their fundamental theology. Although *Einführung in das Christentum* is often treated as an attempt to do for the generation of '68 what Karl Adam had attempted to do for the post-World War I generation in his *Das Wesen des Katholizismus* published in 1924, there is an even stronger comparison to be made with Romano Guardini's essay *Das Wesen des Christentums* published in the magazine *Die Schildgenossen* in 1929. In that essay, Guardini argued that the core essence of Christianity is not a doctrine of truth nor an interpretation of life, but rather Jesus of Nazareth in his concrete existence. Guardini's imprint on Ratzinger is clearly evident in Ratzinger's *Einführung in das Christentum*, especially in what Patrick J. Burns, SJ, called its emphasis on the positivism of the Catholic faith. Echoes of Guardini and Balthasar are not only evident in this landmark 1968 work, but reach the level of a fugue in Ratzinger's papal triptych on the theological virtues. In *Lumen Fidei*, drafted by Ratzinger/Benedict but published under the name of Francis, truth and love are said to be inseparable.[9]

It is therefore fair to say that all the reviewers so far covered were generally accurate in their judgments. Burns was right about Ratzinger trying to avoid a warmed-up Tridentine theology on the one side and the musings of Dutch theologians, spellbound by the *Zeitgeist* of the 1960s, on the other. The anonymous contributor to *Kritische Katholizismus* was right to judge the book "very dangerous" from the point of view of those who want to abolish the hierarchy and turn the Church into an international network of communities for social activists for whom beliefs like the virgin birth are mere mythology. Tseng-Tham could explain the book's best-seller popularity by the fact that it simultaneously offers spiritual consolation alongside intellectual content, and Mynarek had accurately discerned the importance of the Johannine motif of love for Ratzinger. Mynarek was also right to make the

---

9. See especially §27.

judgment that people who do not accept anything as an element of revelation and/or Christian tradition unless it can withstand the solvency test of the historico-critical method would be dismissive of some of Ratzinger's claims. The only questionable note in these reviews was the suggestion by the anonymous reviewer that Ratzinger's ecclesiology is Platonic. To do justice to the complexity of Ratzinger's ecclesiology one would have to carefully analyse his 1953 dissertation on "The People and the House of God in St. Augustine's Doctrine of the Church," and this was not done.

However, the Platonic criticism reappears in the review by Walter Kasper.[10] Kasper begins his contribution by noting how different Ratzinger's *Einführung in das Christentum* is from Karl Adam's 1924 work *Das Wesen des Katholizismus*. Whereas Adam's was ecclesio-centric and the problem was the alternative Protestant form of Christianity, Ratzinger's work was anthropocentric and the problem is not Protestantism but atheism. Kasper also acknowledged that Ratzinger was correct to see an affinity between his own work and Kierkegaard's "Practice in Christianity." Just as Kierkegaard was concerned with the mediation of existence, Ratzinger was also concerned with communication, not mere information. Kasper then offered a paragraph-long encomium:

> Many of Ratzinger's interpretations have an almost liberating effect; one agrees to them all the more readily because they do not lead to a shallow liberalism, but rather to profound theological depths and are thereby enriching in a Christian as well as theological sense. This applies, above all, to the two Christological chapters and their attempt—principally oriented towards K. Barth—to mediate functional and ontological Christology (163, 182ff.). It is here that Ratzinger succeeds in a valid new interpretation of the Christological dogmas of the ancient Church. The same goes for the interpretation of the notions of atonement and redemption (186ff., 230ff.) and the accentuation of the significance of the dynamic of the theology of the cross, as compared with a one-sided and static theology of the incarnation (184ff.), as well as the connection between Pneumatology and Ecclesiology (277). Thus J. Ratzinger's *Einführung in das Christentum* represents a courageous effort and a notable achievement.[11]

---

10. The author is indebted to Sebastian Condon for the English translations of the reviews of Walter Kasper and responses from Joseph Ratzinger. The translation of the review of Hubertus Mynarek and that of the anonymous reviewer are her own.

11. Kasper, "Das Wesen des Christlichen (B)," 183–84.

Nonetheless while Kasper approves of Ratzinger's treatment of Christology, Pneumatology, and Ecclesiology, and his interest in faith as a practice, he is highly critical of Ratzinger's approach to systematic theology. He writes:

> J. Ratzinger's delineation of the essence of Christianity brings us, in a particularly pressing way, to the question of the approach and method of a systematic theology. If, in this regard, one attempts to proceed from the concrete complexity of man and his embedded state within nature, society, culture, and history—rather than from the platonic dialectic of visible-invisible, which lies at the foundation of Ratzinger's delineation—then both methodological as well, indeed, as several other theological consequences are revealed. With this more concretely historical starting point, the invisible can only be made accessible or inaccessible in and from the concrete, historical engagement with the world, other people, and the witnesses of history. The question of meaning is then only to be posed and answered within a historical mediation, and often by means of an arduous passage through concrete historical problems.
>
> With this starting point, one first arrives at an attitude of far greater earnestness with regard to the concrete problems of man—and thereby also to the modern question as to the *factum* and the *faciendum* (33ff.)—than is the case with Ratzinger. Science and technology and the realm of the political are now no longer able to be simply pushed aside or skipped over, but are rather the locus wherein man today finds himself, where he must be met, and where the question of meaning and of God must be made accessible to him. Within this concrete, historically determined world, where injustice, hunger, and violence prevail, it is no longer so easy to speak of the connection of reality to the Logos, or of the law of superfluity and of the givenness of man (210ff.). Nevertheless, it is possible to disclose and articulate the question of salvation directly from the historical reality of today, for in the philosophies, ideologies, and utopias of modernity, many originally Christian approaches are operative in a more secularized form. Modern thought thus provides us with categories that must be at least as suitable as those of Greek philosophy which grew from a basis in mythology.[12]

Kasper thus begins what becomes a life-long criticism (and indeed, what might be called Kasper's "meme") that Ratzinger is a Platonist, and that this alleged Platonism is the defective corner-stone of Ratzinger's theology.

---

12. Kasper, "Das Wesen des Christlichen (B)," 186.

Kasper also adds that in some ways Ratzinger's account of the Christian faith follows the trajectory of German Idealism, and that this approach occludes any account of what is uniquely Christian about Christianity. Specifically, he accuses Ratzinger of trying to prove that an accidental truth of history (the Incarnation) is a necessity from a philosophical point of view. Without mentioning Mynarek, Kasper concurs with Mynarek's judgement that for Ratzinger the essence of Christianity is the principle of love, but he disparagingly quips that "Hegel and Feuerbach had been able to say that."[13] While he acknowledges that the idea is "very far from being theologically false," he asserts that, with this conclusion alone, that which is specifically Christian has not yet been brought to expression.

Ratzinger first responds to Kasper in the article: "Glaube, Geschichte und Philosophie. Zum Echo auf meine 'Einführung in das Christentum'" in the following words:

> With regard to the brilliantly written review to which Walter Kasper subjected my book, I must register marked objection to a number of points. That goes for both the foundational thesis of Kasper as well as for the majority of the individual claims that he makes. His foundational thesis is that there exists a "marked platonic approach" in my work (184), and he thus speaks of the "latent idealism" and ultimately even of the "latent idealism and secularism" of my position, which he then once again attributes to its "platonizing point of origin" (185). He says that I virtually accept the answer "which Schelling and Hegel gave to the question of Lessing" (184); on my summarizing identification of the essence of Christianity. Kasper opines: "Hegel and Feuerbach could equally have said that" (185). I must admit that, despite detailed reflection, these theses remain largely incomprehensible to me. The "horizon of an historical thought" which Kasper indicates as the correct solution with regard to my undertaking (186) remains completely vague, insofar as commonly known ideas are not recapitulated therein. Perhaps the word 'historical' ought to be absolutely forbidden for use by theologians for some time, as it is truly becoming a label for everything and nothing. Some formulations in the concluding section of Kasper's analyses, however, do mark somewhat more clearly the thrust of his argument: " [. . .] a theological interpretation is thus always false, if it only accounts for that which is extant and is no longer concrete and critically oriented towards action" (186). Now, I did not wish to provide recipes for how one could change the Church, but rather directions as to how one can believe. Herein

---

13. Kasper, "Das Wesen des Christlichen (B)," 185.

> Kasper's diagnosis of Idealism-(Platonism) vividly recalls the verdict of [the journal] *Kritischer Katholizismus*, which rejected my book precisely with the reproach of Platonism. Naturally Kasper's thesis is differentiated from those of that circle, yet one can only understand it if one holds this reference point in view. In any case, I have found no other possibility—even after conversations with readers of my book and attendees at my lectures—of making sense of this peculiar theory. The reproach of Platonism on the part of *Kritischer Katholizismus* has a very explicit and clear meaning: for this group, which pays homage to a consequential Neo-Marxism, there is no enduring truth towards which man can stand receptive, but rather reality is constant change; thus the relationship of man to that reality is the active alteration of the world. Truth exists as *pragma* alone: as intervention within the process of changing the world. Everything else—the "Yes" to a truth that simply *is* and which I, as a human being, simply receive and which transforms me to the extent that I receive it—is "Platonism." In this sense I am indeed a "Platonist" and wish to be one.[14]

Having addressed the Platonism point, Ratzinger then went on to address the 'priority of praxis' point. In this context he stated:

> Before I pass onto questions of detail, I wish to add a short remark on the much-discussed bearing of theology to praxis. It is true that theology does not revolve upon itself. Its goal is "praxis." It is simply a question of what one understands by the term "praxis." For me, the properly practical task of theology lies in teaching men to believe, to hope, and to love, and thereby opens up meaning which helps him to live. It does not lie in inventing new costumes for clerics, new forms of ecclesial organization, and new forms of liturgical celebration. If it is necessary, it can and ought to also do those things, and I myself had sufficient opportunity during the Council to contribute to such changes. However, I emphasize once again that is not the actual "praxis" of theology. Its proper praxis consists in giving man something which other "organizations" are not in a position to give ... I hope I do not appear boastful if I mention that theologians who, during the course of their studies, felt my theology "impractical" later confessed to me that they had completely revised their opinion, because they find that neither children in schools, nor the sick, nor the helpless are interested in which changes to ecclesial structures are still possible, but rather wish to know

---

14. Ratzinger, "Glaube, Geschichte und Philosophie," 328–29.

what message the Church still now has to offer. I fear we are on the best path to blunder into a clericalism that is far worse than that which has gone before—the seven spirits which the exorcised demon brings with it are already in the process of entering into the house. In loudly proclaiming reform we speak only of ourselves; the Gospel hardly seems to rate a mention.[15]

Kasper responded to Ratzinger's reply with an article in the journal *Hochland*, titled "Theorie und Praxis innerhalb einer theologia crucis; Antwort auf J. Ratzinger's Glaube, Geschichte und Philosophie." In this article he reiterates the criticism that Ratzinger's notion of freedom is unwittingly idealist and thus (he asserts) dangerously secularist. He then defends the fashion for political theology as a specific contemporary form of St. Paul's theology of the cross, and he compares Erich Przywara's concept of the *analogia entis* with Hegel's notions of negative mediation and concrete negation. The macro-level thrust of the argument is that Ratzinger should be supportive of a priority of *praxis* approach to theology since it is, according to Kasper at least, authentically Pauline.

Ratzinger then responded again to Kasper in *Hochland* with what he called his final word on the matter—"Schlusswort zu der Diskussion mit Walter Kasper." He stated:

> It appears to me necessary to name at least two points in which I am misunderstood by Kasper. I have not (as he opines in note 14) defined Platonism as the "Yes" to a truth that simply is, but rather delineated in that sentence the conception of Platonism held by *Kritischer Katholizismus*, which suspects every commitment to abiding truth of Platonism and thereby incorrectly classifies everything which contradicts its own pragmatic thought as belonging to the historical phenomenon of Platonism. Furthermore, I feel it important to establish that I self-evidently did not speak of "squaring the circle" in such a way that I imagine I have made the *mysterium* transparent and the interplay between necessity and freedom rationally comprehensible. My comparison had a very narrowly defined meaning: I believed I had illustrated a point by which it can be made somewhat understandable precisely why, through the accidents of a unique history, man is redeemed and how, in this apparently so extrinsic and contingent an event, man finds that which is most inherent and necessary to himself. I have thereby neither pronounced myself in favour nor opposed to the transcendental method of Rahner, nor did I arrive at the position of idealism; I have merely attempted to

15. Ratzinger, "Glaube, Geschichte und Philosophie," 330–31.

approach one step closer to the perennially necessary question of *Cur Deus Homo* under the conditions of our time.

The core of the discussion truly lies, however, in the phrase concerning the necessarily critical orientation of all theology to action. Even after the clarifications which Kasper has now provided, and for which thanks are due, I still find this phrase fatal and difficult to bear . . . Naturally, faith as a whole is act-oriented and as an anticipation of judgment, as the anticipated crisis of this world (cf. Jn 5:24–9; 12:31), it is "critical" vis-à-vis the world. Insofar as theology as a whole is related to faith, it obviously shares in its "critical" and "practical" character. Yet can that be made the one (albeit only one!) measure of every theological interpretation? That must be contested most forcefully even if one adopts Kasper's programme of a theology, "which proceeds from a concrete analysis of human and societal praxis and wishes thereby to arrive at the access to grace." Must the attempt to understand something of the mystery of the Trinitarian God as such be "concrete and critically act-oriented"? Or the matter of the Lord Jesus Christ? Or the search for the connection between creation and evolution? Even the matter of the Church can never be determined principally and entirely from the canon of a critical act-orientation: where, in fact, in the Pauline Letters does it state that it is for Christians to change the Church? I remain of the opinion that that which we are able to change about the Church [and there is much], is—at the same time and in the final analysis—that about her which is insignificant, namely that which we ourselves do to her. For she is indeed significant by virtue of that alone which does not come from us. Incidentally, I ask myself how, according to this canon, the Bible itself would be assessed: is the Letter to the Ephesians concrete and critically act-oriented in the sense that Kasper specifies? Or the Letter to the Colossians? Or the Apocalypse?[16]

The above reviews and exchanges are arguably of much greater significance than knowing the history of theology in the 1960s. They highlight issues in fundamental theology which are playing out today.

Karl Rahner once wrote that, after the Second Vatican Council, Catholic scholarship was characterized by a high degree of gnoseological concupiscence. By this it seems he meant that Catholic theologians were hooking up elements of Christian revelation to all manner of philosophies and social theories hitherto unknown in the world of Catholic letters. Foremost

---

16. Ratzinger, "Schlusswort," 341–42.

among these was the Critical Theory of the Frankfurt School. In his article "Theology and Praxis" published in 1973, Charles Davis, one of the big British Catholic names of the 1960s (and by 1973 a laicised priest) described the attraction of the Frankfurt School's Critical Theory to Belgian and Dutch theologians of the 1960s in the following terms:

> Fundamental for them as a consequence of their acceptance of the Marxist unity of theory and *praxis* is a conviction that the permanent self-identity of the Christian faith cannot be presupposed . . . Truth does not yet exist; it cannot be reached by interpretation, but it has to be produced by change. For these theologians, therefore, faith is in a strong sense mediated in history through *praxis*. *Praxis* is not the application of already known truth or the carrying out of a transhistorical ideal; it is that process in and through which one comes to know present reality and future possibilities.[17]

Davis goes on to note that if faith is mediated in *praxis*, it must renounce any claim to universality.[18] In the final paragraph of his article, Davis posed the following question: "Is theology, as [Edward] Schillebeeckx says, the critical self-consciousness of Christian *praxis*, or is [Leszek] Kołakowski right when he says: 'For theology begins with the belief that truth has already been given to us, and its intellectual effort consists not of attrition against reality but of assimilation of something which is ready in its entirety.'"[19] Kasper (it seems) followed the Schillebeeckxian trajectory, while Ratzinger stood shoulder to shoulder with the agnostic philosopher Kołakowski. In *Einführung*, Ratzinger wrote: "Meaning that is self-made is in the last analysis no meaning. Meaning, that is, the ground on which our existence as a totality can stand and live, cannot be made but only received . . . [To believe as a Christian] means affirming that the meaning which we do not make but can only receive is already granted to us, so that we have only to take it and entrust ourselves to it.[20]"

Ratzinger went on to argue that such a disposition of receptivity is "not a blind surrender to the irrational" but "a movement towards the logos, the ratio, towards meaning and so towards truth itself, for in the final analysis the ground on which man takes his stand cannot possibly be anything else but the truth revealing itself."[21] For Ratzinger, moreover, this revelation

17. Davis, "Theology and Praxis," 167.
18. Davis, "Theology and Praxis," 167.
19. Davis, "Theology and Praxis," 167.
20. Ratzinger, *Introduction*, 43.
21. Ratzinger, *Introduction*, 44.

occurs with the Incarnation, Christ's life on earth, and the Paschal mysteries. It is not found in contemporary social movements which themselves can only be understood if they are judged according to the truths revealed by Christ. The idea that the truth of Christianity might be found in the spirit of contemporary social movements is, for Ratzinger, a case of putting the cart before the horse. According to Ratzinger, Christ's exhortation to his disciples to read the signs of the times was not a recommendation that they study sociology. He was trying to help them to grasp the eschatological point that they were now living in the era of the Incarnation—that He, Christ, was the sign of their time. A transition had taken place between the time before the Incarnation and the ages after the Incarnation.

Precisely because the Word was made flesh, Ratzinger is able to distinguish Christianity from Platonism. Again, as he wrote in *Einführung*:

> Christian belief is not merely concerned, as one might at first suspect from all the talk of belief or faith, with the eternal, which as the "quite other" would remain completely outside the human world and time; on the contrary it is much more concerned with God *in* history, with God as man. By thus seeming to bridge the gulf between eternal and temporal, between visible and invisible, by making us meet God as a man, the eternal as the temporal, as one of us, it knows itself as revelation.[22]

In other words, "a fundamental feature of Christianity is that it is personal. It is not I believe in something, but 'I believe in Thee.'"[23] Moreover, Ratzinger explicitly addressed the Platonism issue at the end of his introduction to the *Einführung*. He spoke of the conversion of the Platonist Marius Victorinus to Christianity and explained this in terms of a realization that the Church is "something more and something other than an external institutionalization and organization of ideas." Victorinus had understood that "Christianity is not a system of knowledge but a way." In the very last paragraph of the introduction to the *Einführung*, Ratzinger fired a missile into the Platonism criticism for those who may have been sleepy when reading the earlier paragraphs. He stated: "Christian belief is not an idea but life; it is not mind existing for itself, but incarnation, mind in the body of history and its 'We.' It is not the mysticism of the self-identification of the mind with God, but obedience and service: the outstripping of oneself, liberation of the self precisely through its being taken into service

---

22. Ratzinger, *Introduction*, 27.
23. Ratzinger, *Introduction*, 47.

by something not made or thought out by myself, the liberation of being taken into service for the whole.[24]"

As if this were not enough to attend to the Platonism issue, in the substantive body of the text Ratzinger again returned to the subject of the relationship between Platonism and Christianity. With reference to the biblical "I Am Who I Am" statement found in the book of Exodus at 3:13–15 he observed: "If one adds that it is an important detail of the text that one can only name God because he has named himself, then one only deepens still further the gulf between this conception and Platonic, absolute Being, the final stage of ontological thinking, which is not named and names itself still less.[25]"

Arguably, given all these statements, the real debate between Ratzinger and Kasper has very little to do with Plato (although it is true that Ratzinger has much more time for Greek philosophy even if it began its life as mythology) than he has for philosophies whose genealogies represent secular mutations of the Judeo-Christian synthesis. While Kasper believes that "it is possible to disclose and articulate the question of salvation directly from the historical reality of today, for in the philosophies, ideologies, and utopias of modernity many originally Christian approaches are operative in a more secularized form," Ratzinger's position is that while, as a matter of intellectual history, it is the case that many of the philosophies, ideologies, and utopias of modernity are indeed secularized versions of Christian teachings, nothing of value has been gained by the pastoral projects of Dutch and Belgian theologians "correlating" or "re-contextualizing" the Catholic faith to these ideologies and utopias of modernity. Leaving aside the intellectual problems associated with the correlational and re-contextualization projects, the sociological fact is that, after half a century of such experiments in Holland and Belgium, the result has been that these countries have witnessed the most dramatic drops in sacramental participation rates of any countries in the world. At the Synod on the Family held in 2015, Dr. Anca-Maria Cernea of the Catholic Doctors' Society of Bucharest suggested that, if Church leaders seriously wanted to understand the crisis within family life, they should be holding a Synod on the influence of Frankfurt School philosophy on Catholic theology.[26]

Rather than Plato being the problem, it might be argued that the reception of Hegel is the point of issue between Ratzinger and Kasper, and especially the idea, made fashionable by the Hegelians of the Left, of

24. Ratzinger, *Introduction*, 6
25. Ratzinger, *Introduction*, 79.
26. Cernea, "The World Needs Real Freedom, Liberation from Sin."

the priority of *praxis*.[27] In a later work, *Principles of Christian Morality*, Ratzinger wrote:

> Christian *praxis* is nourished by the core of Christian faith, that is, the grace that appeared in Christ and that is appropriated in the sacrament of the Church. Faith's *praxis* depends on faith's truth, in which man's truth is made visible and lifted up to a new level by God's truth. Hence, it is fundamentally opposed to a *praxis* that first wants to produce facts and so establish truth. By holding to the Creator, faith's *praxis* protects the creation against such a total manipulation of reality. By looking to the example of Jesus Christ, faith recognizes fundamental human values and rescues them from all manipulation. It protects man by protecting creation; the apostles' successors have an indestructible commission to maintain apostolic teaching and make it present. Since grace refers to both the creation and the Creator, apostolic exhortation (as a continuation of Old Testament admonitions) is involved with human reason. Contrary to appearances, the flight into pure orthopraxy, as well as the attempt to banish substantive morals from the realm of faith (with the teaching authority that is an integral part of the realm of faith), turn reason into heresy.[28]

In his *Principles of Catholic Theology*, in another reflection on the priority of *praxis* subject, Ratzinger added:

> If the word "orthopraxis" is pushed to its most radical meaning, it presumes that no truth exists that is antecedent to *praxis* but rather that truth can be established only on the basis of correct *praxis*, which has the task of creating meaning out of and in the face of meaninglessness. Theology becomes then no more than a guide to action, which, by reflecting on *praxis*, continually develops new modes of praxis. If not only redemption but truth as well is regarded as "*post hoc*", then truth becomes the product of man. At the same time, man, who is no longer measured against truth but produces it, becomes himself a product.[29]

In contrast to Ratzinger, Edward Schillebeeckx argued that "an authentic faith in God only seems to be possible in the context of a *praxis* of liberation and of solidarity with the needy. It is in that *praxis* that the idea

---

27. For an extensive analysis of the Platonic criticism and defense of Ratzinger against the charge, see McGregor, *Heart Speaks to Heart*.
28. Ratzinger, *Principles of Christian Morality*, 70–71.
29. Ratzinger, *Principles of Catholic Theology*, 318.

develops that God reveals himself as the mystery and the very heart of humanity's striving for liberation, wholeness and soundness."[30] Juan Luis Segundo went even further and asserted that "not a single dogma can be studied under any other final criterion than that of its social impact on the *praxis*."[31] The fact that a priority of *praxis* principle turns much of classical Catholic fundamental theology on its head was not lost on Jon Sobrino, who concluded that the priority of *praxis* means, among other things, that Christology must be based on the "historical Jesus" rather than on the Christ of the Chalcedonian doctrines.[32] Arguably, however, the most systematic account of the priority of *praxis* was that offered by Clodovis Boff in his *Theology and Praxis: Epistemological Foundations*, published in English in 1987. In this work Boff offered no less than ninety-eight principles for a correct understanding of the *praxis* process. Louis Dupré has highlighted the irony that the alleged priority of *praxis* over theory is itself an *idea*.[33] In the case of Boff it was ninety-eight ideas.

Within the context of contemporary Catholic systematic theology, Matthew Lamb has identified five common models of the theory-praxis relationship: (I) the primacy of theory, (II) the primacy of *praxis*, (III) the primacy of faith-love, (IV) critical theoretic correlations, and (V) critical *praxis* correlations.[34] Under the primacy of *praxis* heading, Lamb offered a further 3 sub-divisions. He distinguished between (I) *praxis* understood as cultural-historical activity, (II) liberal socio-political reform activity, and (III) radical Marxist revolutionary *praxis*. He traced the cultural-historical primacy of *praxis* to Luther's repudiation of speculative theology, and to the Enlightenment's rejection of metaphysics. He traced the notion of *praxis* as socio-political reform activity to a marriage between "the Kantian relation of religion to morality and the Ritschlian distinction between the speculative judgements of science and the value judgments of religion." And finally, he traced the Marxist theories back to the dialectical materialism of Marx. The choice for the priority of *praxis* theorists, at least as Lamb sees it, is between a *praxis* à la Luther-Kant, a *praxis* à la Kant-Ritschl, or a *praxis* à la Hegel-Marx.

Lamb summarised his analysis of these three types of primacy of *praxis* theories with the statement:

---

30. Schillebeeckx, "The Role of History," 318.
31. Segundo, "Capitalism-Socialism," 16.
32. Sobrino, *Christology at the Crossroads*.
33. Dupré, *Marx's Social Critique of Culture*, 287.
34. Lamb, *Solidarity with Victims*.

These primacy of *praxis* types agree in rejecting classical metaphysics. If Christianity is to be faithful to its task, it must be intrinsically involved in historical, cultural, political, social and/or revolutionary *praxis*. Doctrinal theory is at best extrinsic and secondary. The reflex character of theory-*praxis* tends toward a reduction of theory to reflection on *praxis* as variously understood. The normativity tends toward an identification of Christianity with modern, secular (liberal or Marxist) processes.[35]

It is precisely here that one finds Ratzinger and Kasper to be at the greatest distance from one another. Ratzinger did not abandon metaphysics, and he has never identified Christianity with modern, secular processes. Precisely where Walter Kasper fits within Lamb's taxonomy could form the subject of a doctoral dissertation. Without undertaking such a project, my preliminary assessment is that he would fit within Lamb's category five—the critical *praxis* correlationist theorists—whose flag holders are Schillebeeckx and Johann-Baptist Metz. Kasper's enthusiasm for correlating Christianity to the "philosophies, ideologies, and utopias of modernity" is evocative of the pastoral strategies of Schillebeeckx and of Marie-Dominique Chenu's concept of *pierres d'attente* or "toothing stones." Both Schillebeeckx and Chenu had the idea of hooking up or correlating the faith to 'toothing stones' within the culture of modernity. Such stones were often elements of philosophies, ideologies, and utopian projects that Schillebeeckx and Chenu thought were capable of offering Christianity an entry point into modern culture. In contrast, Ratzinger's stance towards what he treated as mutations of Christian ideas was always one of critique rather than an attempted baptism. His starting point for evangelization is not "toothing-stones" with a dubious heritage, but the Trinitarian God of love. In Lamb's taxonomy this would have him classified as a primacy of the faith-love type. Lamb had classified Balthasar, the author of *Love Alone is Credible*, as his star exhibit in this category, and it could easily be argued that Ratzinger would find himself at home here as well alongside his friend and mentor.[36]

One of the obvious problems with the fundamental theology of those who operate from a priority of *praxis* position is that it is difficult to find two of them who have the same understanding of how the priority of *praxis* works. Furthermore, it seems that whatever beliefs or ideas are extracted

---

35. Lamb, *Solidarity with Victims*, 73.

36. Karl Rahner is offered as an example of the critical theoretic correlations type (in his case the correlating partners are the philosophies underpinning liberal modernity) and Johann-Baptist Metz is offered as an example of a critical *praxis* correlations type (who occupies a position between Rahner on the one side and Liberation theologians on the other).

from the *praxis* will be dependent on changing historical conditions. For some theologians the moral relativism which flows from the second of these issues is not a problem. Hence we have moral theologians promoting "situation ethics" and biblical theologians saying that it is not what Christ said or did that matters, but how he related to his social context. Assuming this is true, it raises another issue: how do we understand the universality of the Church if reflection upon social practices may give rise to different discernments in different social milieu? Could something be ethically unproblematic in South Bend, Indiana, but a mortal sin in Beijing?

If we do not receive the truth, if we create it for ourselves, then we are in the dangerous territory of gnosticism. As the Canadian philosopher Kenneth L. Schmitz suggested, "it seems to be that exile and liberation through a cognitive mode of knowledge constitute the very essence of the gnostic spirit once it is transformed by modernity."[37] Ratzinger has also identified in the gnostic disposition a fear of being dependent on something we cannot make ourselves but only receive from another. Gnosticism, Ratzinger argues, "will not entrust itself to a world already created, but only to a world still to be created."[38] Ratzinger has described the mentality that wants to prioritize *ethos* over *logos*, to use Romano Guardini's terminology, or to start with *praxis* and word backwards to something like truth, as "the Hinduization of the faith."[39]

The division identified by Charles Davis in 1973 between Schillebeeckx and Kołakowski was already present and evident in the exchanges between Kasper and Ratzinger in 1969 prompted by the publication of *Einführung in das Christentum*.[40] In Ratzinger's final response to Kasper there is a tone of exasperation. His question "must the attempt to understand something of the mystery of the Trinitarian God as such be 'concrete

---

37. Schmitz, "The Transfiguration of Gnosis," 704.

38. Ratzinger, *'In the Beginning,'* 97. These thoughts also appear in a condensed form in §34 of Ratzinger/Benedict's encyclical *Caritas in Veritate*: "Gift by its nature goes beyond merit, its rule is that of superabundance. It takes first place in our souls as a sign of God's presence in us, a sign of what he expects from us. Truth — which is itself gift, in the same way as charity — is greater than we are, as Saint Augustine teaches. Likewise the truth of ourselves, of our personal conscience, is first of all *given* to us. In every cognitive process, truth is not something that we produce, it is always found, or better, received. Truth, like love, 'is neither planned nor willed, but somehow imposes itself upon human beings'" (quoting *Deus Caritas Est*, §3).

39. Ratzinger, *The Nature and Mission of Theology*, 91. The expression 'Hinduization of the faith' was adopted by Ratzinger from Albert Görres.

40. Kołakowski was not himself a Catholic but an open-minded philosopher. He was also an authority on Marxism, and somewhat bemused by the openness to Marxism he found among Catholic theologians of the 1960s and 70s generation.

and critically act-oriented?'" underscored the gulf that separates their approaches to theology. Ratzinger remains firmly on the side of the primacy of the faith-love relationship with Balthasar and other theologians in the circles surrounding the journal *Communio* which he, Balthasar, and Henri de Lubac founded in 1972.

When de Lubac was asked to write the introduction to Paul Claudel's *Commentary on the Apostles' Creed*, he selected the following passage from Claudel for special mention:

> When in my village church I hear the Creed being recited, one article after another, by the harsh voice of the soloist, to which the naïve whine of the little girls responds, I tremble with an inner ecstasy; it seems to me that I am present at the creation of the world. I know the cost of each one of those formulae printed in eternal truth—with what rending of heaven and earth, what rivers of blood, by what effort, what mental travail, and with what overflowing grace they came to be born. I see those great masses of dogma emerge and take form before my eyes one after the other; I see man struggling painfully and finally succeeding in tearing out of his own heart the final affirmation. It is like a cathedral, immovable and yet advancing with all its columns from porch to choir.[41]

One might imagine that Ratzinger would strongly identify with Claudel's sentiments. They echo something of the importance of the Ricouerian themes of memory, recollection, and forgetting to which Fr. Schenk refers in his essay in this volume. In his *Principles of Catholic Theology*, Ratzinger wrote that the "seat of all faith is the *memoria Ecclesiae*, the memory of the Church. It exists through all ages, waxing and waning but never ceasing to be a common *situs* of the faith ... there can be a waxing and waning, a forgetting or remembering, but no recasting of the truth in time."[42]

For Ratzinger, contemporary social practices, including social evils, can be the subject of theological reflection, but it is the *memoria* of the Church which serves as the framework for discerning the signs of the times. This is extremely difficult medicine to swallow for those of a more Hegelian disposition.

---

41. Claudel, *I Believe in God*, 38.
42. Ratzinger, *Principles of Catholic Theology*, 23–24.

Bibliography

Anonymous. "Wie progressive sind unsere Progressiven? 1: Joseph Ratzinger—Theologie als Suggestion." *Kritischer Katholizismus: Zeitung für Theorie und Praxis in Gesellschaft und Kirche* 2 (1969) 9.

Benedict XVI. *Caritas in Veritate*. June 29, 2009. http://w2.vatican.va/content/benedict-xvi/en/encyclicals/documents/hf_ben-xvi_enc_20090629_caritas-in-veritate.html.

Burns, Patrick J. Review (Shorter Notice) of *Einführung in das Christentum: Vorlesungen über das apostolische Glaubensbekenntnis* by Joseph Ratzinger. *Theological Studies* 30 (1969) 748–49.

Cernea, Anca-Maria. "'The World Needs Real Freedom, Liberation from Sin,' Says Romanian Doctor at Synod." 17 October 2015. http://wwwvoiceofthefamily.com/the-world-needs-real-freedom-liberation-from-sin-saysromani.

Claudel, Paul. *I Believe in God: A Commentary on the Apostles' Creed with Introduction by Henri de Lubac*. London: Harvill, 1965.

Davis, Charles. "Theology and Praxis." *Cross Currents* 2 (1973) 154–68.

Dupré, Louis. *Marx's Social Critique of Culture*. New Haven: Yale University Press, 1983.

Kasper, Walter. "Das Wesen des Christlichen: Ein Fundamental-Theologe und ein Dogmatiker zu dem Buch von Joseph Ratzinger: *Einführung in das Christentum* (B)." *Theologische Revue* 3 (1969) 182–88.

———. "Theorie und Praxis innerhalb einer theologia crucis: Antwort auf J. Ratzingers 'Glaube, Geschichte und Philosophie.'" *Hochland* 62 (1970: März/April) 152–57.

Lamb, Matthew. *Solidarity with Victims: Towards a Theology of Social Transformation*. New York: Crossroad, 1982.

McGregor, Peter John. *Heart Speaks to Heart: the Spiritual Christology of Joseph Ratzinger*. Eugene: Pickwick, 2016.

Mynarek, Hubert. "Das Wesen des Christlichen: Ein Fundamental-Theologe und ein Dogmatiker zu dem Buch von Joseph Ratzinger: *Einführung in das Christentum* (A)." *Theologische Revue* 3 (1969) 177–82.

Ratzinger, Joseph. *Dogma and Preaching: Applying Christian Doctrine to Daily Life*. San Francisco: Ignatius, 2011.

———. "Glaube, Geschichte und Philosophie. Zum Echo auf meine 'Einführung in das Christentum.'" In *Einführung in das Christentum: Bekenntnis-Taufe-Nachfolge, Band 4 Gesammelte Schriften*, 323–39. Freiburg: Herder & Herder, 2014.

———. *'In the Beginning' . . . A Catholic Understanding of Creation and the Fall*. Grand Rapids: Eerdmans, 1995.

———. *Introduction to Christianity*. Translated by J.R. Foster. London: Burns & Oates, 1969.

———. *The Nature and Mission of Theology: Approaches to Understanding its Role in the Light of the Present*. San Francisco: Ignatius, 1995.

———. *Principles of Catholic Theology: Building Stones for a Fundamental Theology*. San Francisco: Ignatius, 1987.

———. *Principles of Christian Morality*. San Francisco: Ignatius, 1986.

———. "Schlusswort zu der Diskussion mit Walter Kasper.'" In *Einführung in das Christentum: Bekenntnis-Taufe-Nachfolge, Band 4 Gesammelte Schriften*, 323–42. Freiburg: Herder & Herder, 2014.

Schillebeeckx, Edward. "The Role of History in what is called the New Paradigm." In *Paradigm Change in Theology*, edited by Hans Küng and David Tracy, 307–19. T&T Clark, 1989.

Schmitz, Kenneth L. "The Transfiguration of Gnosis in Late Enlightenment German Thought." *Communio: International Catholic Review* (Winter 1997) 691–713.

Segundo, Juan-Luis. "Capitalism-Socialism: A Theological Crux." In *Mystical and Political Dimensions of the Christian Faith*, edited by Claude Geffré and Gustavo Gutiérrez, 105–23. New York: Herder & Herder, 1974.

Sobrino, Jon. *Christology at the Crossroads: A Latin American Approach*. Maryknoll: Orbis, 1978.

Tseng-Tham, Joshua. "Review of Joseph Ratzinger's *Introduction to Christianity*." *Fare Forward* 8 (Dec. 2017). https://farefwd.com/index.php/2020/12/23/introduction-to-christianity/.

II. Fundamental Theology

4

The *Introduction to Christianity* in Light of *Principles of Catholic Theology*

CYRIL O'REGAN

WHEN JOSEPH RATZINGER WROTE *Introduction to Christianity*, he could rely not only on an established twentieth-century theological genre of commenting on the Apostles' Creed both within and without Catholicism,[1] but also in a certain sense on a genre that could trace its ancestry back to the early Church.[2] Incredibly rich as the text is, Ratzinger neither offers a literary analysis of the Creed in terms of its twelve elements and governing triadic structure of belief in Father, Son, and Holy Spirit,[3] nor handles questions

---

1. See Ratzinger, *Einführung in das Christentum*. In this essay, I cite from the English translation. Since Ratzinger's specific interest is looking for specifically Catholic precedents, it is hardly surprising that he would recall the lectures by Karl Adam that issued in *Das Wesen des Katholizmus* (1924). This occurs in the original 1968 Preface. See Ratzinger, *Introduction to Christianity*, 32. It is interesting to see an example of reverse influence. Hans Urs von Balthasar, whose communion theology so influenced Ratzinger, produces an interpretation of the Apostles' Creed in the last year of his life (1988): *Credo*. There is, of course, a venerable Protestant tradition for this kind of Introduction—one that is established by Adolf von Harnack in his *Das Wesen des Christentums* (1900). The major contemporary Protestant theologian who has offered an interpretation of the Apostles' Creed is Wolfhart Pannenberg. Roughly at the same time of Ratzinger's *Einführung*, Pannenberg published his own meditation on the Apostles' Creed, especially as it throws light on the contemporary situation and the contemporary situation throws light on it. It would be an interesting exercise to compare these texts in terms of their relative willingness to entertain modern thought on its own terms.

2. Given Ratzinger's Augustinian proclivities, I am thinking especially of Augustine's *Enchiridion*. I have sketched the Augustinian contours of Ratzinger's thought in "Benedict the Augustinian."

3. For example, although Luther's *Small Catechism* (1529) does more than interpret the Apostles' Creed, to the extent to which it does, it brings out very clearly its triadic structure.

such as the historicity of the Creed, nor analyzes and critically evaluates ancient and modern precedents, which would be the traditional Catholic and at the same time quintessentially German way of proceeding. Somewhat ironically, Ratzinger's very patient text quite impatiently intervenes, and on his account does so necessarily, given the general dilution of literacy regarding both the truths of faith and their principle of integration, the confusion of modern Christians in the post-Conciliar world,[4] and finally because of both general cultural assumptions regarding faith, reason, and their connection that,[5] in his view, are unfounded, and theological and philosophical definitions and conjugations that he deems simply to be wrongheaded. Of course, it is precisely the sense of crisis and thus the necessity of the intervention that has made the text the classic that it is. Ratzinger manages at once to point to an apocalyptic moment of decision without imitating an apocalyptic tone, and it is this patent sense of emergency which demands that the basics of Christian faith be boldly as well as clearly expressed that explains the energy of a text that exhibits an extraordinary appearance of unity, despite the more or less episodic character of its initial production in lectures. This energy in turn perhaps also explains at least in part its continuing persuasiveness. At the same time this incredibly sober text, which aims at once to elucidate Christian faith and offer a defense of it, inserts itself in the prophetic milieu of the nineteenth century,[6] and more specifically within the warnings of Kierkegaard against the demise of genuine Christianity,[7]

---

4. In chapter 1 of *Introduction*, "Belief in the World Today" (39–81), Ratzinger sketches the challenges faced by the Church from secular culture. This chapter represents something of an advisory with regard to an over-confidence on the part of the Church regarding alignment with the modern spirit in the post-Vatican II situation.

5. Throughout the first chapter of *Introduction*, Ratzinger challenges the secular assumption that faith and reason are binaries, and more specifically that faith does not naturally have a cognitive dimension any more than reason has an orientation towards God as a finality. This continues to be a crucially important theme for Ratzinger, and it is arguably what the Regensburg Address (2006) is really about (rather than an attack on Islam as an inherently violent religion).

6. Of course, Kierkegaard is the prophetic figure who is appealed to in *Introduction*. But it is quite clear that, for Ratzinger, Kierkegaard is not the only precursor in prophetic tradition of viewing modernity as the scene of the crisis of Christianity. Throughout Ratzinger's oeuvre, Dostoyevski is routinely appealed to as a kind of prophetic figure who diagnoses the crisis in modernity concerning the viability of Christianity. Dostoyevski's mediation (also Soloviev's) on the Anti-Christ is recalled in *Spe Salvi* (2007). Ratzinger's interest in the prophetic exposure of the ideological foundations of modernity has precedents in *nouvelle théologie*—in the case of de Lubac especially (but not exclusively) his *Drama of Atheistic Humanism*, which appeared in French in 1944; and in the case of Balthasar especially (but not exclusively) his *Apokalypse der deutschen Seele*, 3 vols. (1937–1939).

7. Kierkegaard's fundamental distinction is that between authentic Christianity

famously given by the ultimate outcast to society, the clown.[8] To inscribe your text in a prophetic template is to repeat it—even if non-identically. And while Kierkegaard's clown is not necessarily a Christian insider, and thus the alarm sounded is not prophetic in the strict biblical sense, still it cannot but hark back to biblical prophecy in which, in light of the exercise of God's judgment, there is the need for a fundamental decision for or against faith, or more precisely a fundamental decision for or against this God and this God's plan for humankind and cosmos.

Indeed, the interventive quality of the text is such that it is easy to lose sight of the fact how what is superordinate and what is subordinate in the Apostles' Creed accounts for what might be regarded as surprisingly slim treatments of Church[9] and resurrection,[10] which on the basis of other texts we know that Ratzinger is deeply committed to theologically, and about which he has so much to say. Still, in the white heat of intervention, as indicated above, there are any number of points that could and perhaps should have been made. I want to suggest, without prejudice to the importance given to the Nicene-Constantinopolitan Creed in part one of *The Principles of Catholic Theology*, that a good way to read this part of the text, portions of which date back to the early 1970s, is to understand it as offering a supplement to *Introduction to Christianity* by providing a retroactive historical and systematic justification for the choice of the Creed as a platform from which to elaborate the basics of Christian faith. This reading provides the basis for the other two major moves in this essay. The first of these—and thus part two of the paper—argues that de Lubac's own commentary on the Apostles' Creed, that is, *The Christian Faith* (1970),[11] which was published shortly after *Introduction*, provided major assistance in supplementing Ratzinger's *Introduction to Christianity* along both the historical and systematic fronts. The second of these—and thus the third part of the essay—will touch very briefly on two corollaries concerning a shared theological principle that the confession is definitional for Christianity. The first corollary concerns the nature and limits of ecumenism and what

---

and inauthentic Christianity, the latter nominated as "Christendom." For Kierkegaard, Christendom is Christianity high-jacked by modern rationalism and fatally attenuated. This distinction is operative in *Introduction*, although obviously Ratzinger and Kierkegaard do not agree regarding the details of genuine Christian faith. As a Catholic, Ratzinger has far more confidence than Kierkegaard, the somewhat idiosyncratic Lutheran, in doctrine, tradition, and the Church.

8. Ratzinger, *Introduction*, 39.
9. Ratzinger, *Introduction*, 39.
10. Ratzinger, *Introduction*, 39.
11. Lubac, *La Foi chrétienne*. For a convenient English translation, see *The Christian Faith*. Page references will be taken from this English translation.

would count as realistic and unrealistic expectations concerning dialogue. In the second part of *Principles* Ratzinger offers an analysis of ecumenism which moves freely between the languages of principle and prudence, indicating what is and is not negotiable. For the purpose of this paper, I am emphasizing that underscoring confession as defining of Catholic faith ensures that ordinary Catholic believers as well as those who lead them recognize fully that there are ineluctables. At the very least, formulated doctrines as well as the Creed cannot be regarded as fungible. The second corollary has to be with the theology of religions. Dissatisfaction with Ratzinger's particular elaboration of the theology of religions often takes the form of a psychological typing in which Ratzinger is supposed to find inter-religious dialogue more or less uncongenial. Here I want to argue that the kind of understanding of the confession of the Apostles' Creed exhibited first in *Introduction* and supplemented in *Principles*, while by no means prejudicial regarding interreligious dialogue, attempts to set realistic limits to our expectations of it, given the claim to truth that is enacted in the Christian's proclamation of the Apostles' Creed.

Retrogressive Justification in *Principles of Catholic Theology*

Principles of Catholic Theology (German, 1982) is one of Ratzinger's more important and (by the look of it) one of his least read texts. Despite the fact that it consists for the most part of essays published in the previous decade and thus proximate to the production of *Introduction to Christianity*, very much like Ratzinger's most famous and extraordinarily well-received text, it comes across as at once comprehensive in scope and integrated in terms of argument. If this text contains one of Ratzinger's most sustained reflections on ecumenism (part two),[12] I would like to suggest that a fruitful way of reading the first part of the text is to see it as presenting, *ex post facto*, a justification for the selection of the Apostles' Creed as the ground of catechesis and apology, which are the two fundamental aspects of *Introduction to Christianity*. On my reading of part one of *Principles*, there are two dimensions with regard to this retrogressive justification: the first historical, the second systematic.

With regard to the historical justification, without directly appealing to the age of the Creed as some theologians do, Ratzinger implicitly speaks to the antiquity of the Creed by insisting on its baptismal context and telos.

---

12. Ratzinger, *Principles of Catholic Theology*, 193–331. Ratzinger's other major treatment of ecumenism—again a collection of essays—can be found in *Church, Ecumenism, & Politics*, Part 2, "Ecumenical Problems," 69–138.

Baptism is the original site of the formulation of faith,[13] and catechesis is ordered towards baptism and full entry into the Church. The implied antiquity of the Creed is further reinforced in two different but related ways. One of these ways is through appeal to the interpretation of the Creed in the Patristic period. While Ratzinger provides both Eastern and Western examples, it should not surprise that Augustine's catechetical texts, especially the *Enchiridion*, are prominent.[14] In *Principles of Catholic Theology*, of course, this is simply a specification of the much larger point of the constitutive—and thus enduring—importance of Patristic thought for the Catholic Church in general and Catholic theology in particular.[15] The more specific as well as more general point has less to do with antiquity (although proximity to the fontal sources of Christianity should not be summarily dismissed) than with the high level of integration illustrated in Patristic thought, which contrasts positively with Christian thought's later manifestation not simply with regard to the analytical breakdown into theological topics, but with regard to the level of cohesiveness between theology and liturgy, on the one hand, and theology and Christian life, on the other. The influence of *nouvelle théologie* here is obvious.

The other feature of the Apostles' Creed underscored by Ratzinger is that all of the language of the Creed is biblical. For Ratzinger, this speaks eloquently to the connection between scripture and theology, which he supports throughout his entire theological career. At the same time, it hardly needs to be pointed out that, for Ratzinger, the support of biblical language as primitive does not provide warrant against the use of philosophical language to explicate it. Not only does Ratzinger in *Principles of Catholic Theology* and *Introduction to Christianity* endorse the general compatibility of faith and reason, he also endorses the general compatibility of biblical and philosophical language, thereby refusing both Luther's polemics against the 'whore reason' and any and all versions of the pejorative construction of "Hellenization."[16] Here he speaks to the Bible express-

---

13. Ratzinger, *Principles of Catholic Theology*, 108–12.

14. Ratzinger, *Principles of Catholic Theology*, 47, 147.

15. Ratzinger, *Principles of Catholic Theology*, 133–52 (esp. 142–52). In *Introduction*, Chapter 2, "The Ecclesiastical Form of Faith" (82–100), Ratzinger mentions Patristic figures such as Augustine (95, 98–99). Interestingly, while there is obvious appreciation, Ratzinger is critical of Augustine's distinction between exoteric and esoteric forms of Christian faith. Here, however, it is the Augustine of the *Confessions* rather than the *Enchiridion* who is suspect.

16. Resistance to the Hellenization hypothesis is at the core of Ratzinger's theology. See, for example, his essay, "Variations on the Theme of Faith, Religion, and Culture," which is written in the early 1990s. This essay can be found in *Truth and Tolerance*, 80–114 (see esp. 90–95). Rejection of the Hellenization hypothesis is also a feature of the Regensburg Address (2006).

ing a word to which reason, understood holistically rather than narrowly as instrumental reason,[17] responds. While this particular formulation is not especially illuminating, at this juncture in the text it is patently evident that Ratzinger is convinced that philosophical language is not only permissible but necessary in the actual formulations of faith—perhaps nowhere more needful than in the formulation of the doctrines of the Trinity and the Sonship of Christ. The very technical language of *ousia* and *hypostasis*, on the one hand, and divine person and divine and human nature on the other, not only do not obscure the disclosure of God's salvific economy rendered in scripture, but help to protect it.[18]

Before the writing of *Principles of Catholic Theology*, and even before *Introduction to Christianity*, Ratzinger was convinced that scripture as such is not the Word, but rather that it gives testimony regarding the Word's actions in history that render who God is. In real time this was his interpretation of *Dei Verbum*, which he was convinced enriched what might be referred to as "the Catholic difference" that his two major theological influences, Henri de Lubac and Hans Urs von Balthasar, had gone to considerable trouble to make in distinguishing a Catholic reading of the Bible from Protestant readings that tend to identify the Word and the biblical text as such.[19] Even if fairness might require softening the harsh

---

17. As is well-known, Ratzinger thinks that, as there are pathologies of religion, there are also pathologies of reason. In the Western world, the regnant pathology is the reduction of reason to instrumental reason, with deleterious ethical and political consequences. It comes up on a number of occasions throughout the *Introduction* (in chapter 1, see 58, 64, 66, 70–71). The complaint is made frequently throughout his later essays. See, for example, *Values in a Time of Upheaval*, 24, 109 (*inter alia*). Ratzinger also makes this point in the Regensburg Address. While it is true that, in the main, Ratzinger simply opposes the classical Catholic view of reason to what he regards as its modern deformation, sometimes his view goes under the banner, as it did also to some respect in German predecessors such as Erich Przywara and Hans Urs von Balthasar. See especially Ratzinger's fine essay, "If You Want Peace, Conscience and Truth," in *Values in a Time of Upheaval*, 75–99.

18. This is in line with the position advanced by Newman in *The Development of Doctrine* (1845), as well as *The Arians of the Fourth Century* (1833). It is also in line with strategy exhibited by Augustine in *de Trinitate*.

19. The 'Catholic difference' is advanced more or less self-consciously by Hans Urs von Balthasar and Henri de Lubac. For Balthasar's full rendering of the biblical text, see especially *Herrlichkeit*, Bd. 3, which dates from the late 1960s. For an English translation of these two important volumes which perform a Catholic interpretation of scripture rather than argue for it, see *The Glory of the Lord: A Theological Aesthetics*, vol. 6, *The Old Covenant*; and vol. 7, *The New Covenant*. For a very useful synoptic view of the Catholic reading of scripture, see Balthasar, "Word, Scripture, and Tradition." For de Lubac, see *Exégèse médiévale*. Volume 1 is key. For a convenient English translation, see *Medieval Exegesis*.

judgment of Neo-Scholasticism made by Rahner and Balthasar alike, still for Ratzinger it is necessary to place scripture and not theological proof at the center of Catholic faith. While neither de Lubac nor Balthasar thought that ecumenical dialogue was entirely incidental to their own recommendation of the shift back to scripture—this was especially true in the case of Balthasar who conducted a decades' long dialogue with Barth[20]—both ressourcement thinkers were convinced that the Church Fathers indicated a level of integration between scripture and theology not matched in the medieval period—or at the very least not uniformly matched. Whatever the limitations of Patristic theology and exegesis (and both de Lubac and Balthasar were mindful of them), they serve as both measure and correction of the Protestant principle of *sola scriptura* and the insistence on historical-critical method as the only justifiable method of biblical interpretation. In the wake of Vatican II, Ratzinger doubles down on these *nouvelle théologie* convictions. Ratzinger judges that a significant number of Catholic biblical scholars now follow their Protestant colleagues in setting up a cordon sanitaire around the study of the Bible which happily no longer has to deal with ecclesiastical interference. This was also not an entirely unhappy result for Catholic theologians who accepted the division of labor as convenient and felt encouraged to proceed beyond Scholastic propositionalism, without necessarily having to be responsible to the wild text that is the Bible and the conflict of interpretation that marks its checkered history.

The second dimension to the retrogressive justification of the selection of the Apostles' Creed is more nearly systematic and normative, although, of course, this dimension is merely analytically separable from the historical dimension. Indeed, from Ratzinger's point of view the historical and the systematic are two sides of a single retrogressive argument. Baptism, Ratzinger insists, is the normative and not simply historical context of the expression of Christian faith.[21] This point is once again indicative of the broader point of the intrinsic connection between the Church and faith, and more specifically liturgy and faith. Crucially, for Ratzinger confessing the Creed implies that it has existential valence.[22] The baptismal context of the utterance helps us to see that the Creed is not simply a string of propositions enunciated by the person who has been catechized. At the very least implicitly, presupposed is an act of conversion[23] that concerns not merely the intellect but the

---

20. The trace of this is evident in Balthasar's great book on Barth originally published in German in 1951. For a good English translation, see *The Theology of Karl Barth*. See especially chap. 4, "The Catholic Standpoint," 30–43.

21. Ratzinger, *Principles of Catholic Theology*, 27–43 (esp. 34, 35).

22. Ratzinger, *Principles of Catholic Theology*, 26.

23. Ratzinger, *Principles of Catholic Theology*, 35 (also 17–18).

whole person.[24] One would not be mistaken were one to hear an echo of *A Grammar of Assent*. Overall though, Ratzinger's point is broadly biblical and democratic and does not depend on a particular religious epistemology, even one he rates as highly as Newman's.[25] This by no means suggests that Ratzinger never recurs to religious epistemology to bolster his general case. In fact, by speaking of the language of the Creed as being performative[26] in that it aims to support practices and bring out intentional forms of life,[27] Ratzinger evokes the linguistic theory of J. L. Austin, who drew attention to forms of language which, in addition to referential function, had illocutionary (rhetorical) and perlocutionary (broadly performative force).[28]

As is well established in analytical philosophy, these distinctions made their way into mainline philosophy of religion through Donald Evans' application to statements of Christian belief, that is, *The Logic of Self-Involvement*. One should not overrate Ratzinger's foray into the arcana of linguistic analysis. There is no evidence in *Principles of Catholic Theology*, or for that matter any other text of Ratzinger that I am aware of, that he pursues the linguistic angle comprehensively and deeply. Nor for that matter is there any evidence that he has read Evans' landmark text. Ratzinger is likely registering a German theological adaptation of a linguistic reframing of the language of belief without feeling called on to delve more deeply into the subtleties of this mode of analysis or develop it. In any event, in *Principles of Catholic Theology*, the reference to what might be called the logic of self-involvement in the confession of faith serves a supporting rather than foundational role regarding the commitment that is implied in the baptized person's entrance into the Christian community. This entails a conversion,[29] a turning away

---

24. Ratzinger, *Principles of Catholic Theology*, 69, 73–74.

25. I have already (in note 18) pointed to Ratzinger's support of Newman's view of the prospect of access to truth. But the agreement is simply part of a broader alliance between these two Catholic thinkers with regard to diagnosing secularity as the constitutive modern problem for Christian faith to the extent to which it misinterprets faith, reason, and their relation, wishes to cut ties with the historical tradition, and is impatient regarding doctrine. In *Introduction*, Ratzinger emphasizes the existential and personal dimensions of faith, and doubles down on these dimensions in the talks that make up *Glaube und Zukunft* (1970), published only two years after the German publication of *Introduction*. For a convenient English translation, see *Faith and the Future*.

26. Ratzinger, *Principles of Catholic Theology*, 124.

27. Ratzinger, *Principles of Catholic Theology*, 65–75.

28. Austin, *How to Do Things with Words*, was a compilation of the William James Lectures given by Austin between 1957–1960. It was Originally published in 1962. What is now the standard edition was published by Harvard University Press in 1975.

29. To be fair, this is not entirely a new point. Ratzinger says as much in *Introduction* (see 88).

from a previous form of life, marked by sin, death, and alienation, and a turning towards a new form of life, marked by forgiveness and participation in Christ and, through him, with the living triune God.

It is a truism with regard to Ratzinger that, though his particular texts may be more nearly catechetical or apologetic/polemical, whatever the dominant, the other will be present in some way. Similar to *Introduction to Christianity*, while the later *Principles of Catholic Theology* in general is more nearly referred to *ad intra*, this is not entirely the case. There are major and minor indicators in both texts of the challenges of modernity that need to be met by any articulation of Christian faith that would claim to be adequate. In the case of *Introduction*, the major indicators in the text of the problems for faith in the modern world are provided in the two Prefaces as well as chapter one; in the case of *Principles of Catholic Theology*, arguably, the major indicator of the problematic modern horizon of faith is addressed in the Epilogue.[30] Needless to say, throughout both texts there are numerous critical remarks made about the contemporary situation that encourage the reflection on the possibility of faith and theology, and the difficulties of expressing anything like an Augustinian account of *fides quaerens intellectum*. Ratzinger's response in *Principles of Catholic Theology* is typical. Certainly, Catholic theology dialogues and critically engages modern culture, yet neither this dialogue nor critical engagement exhausts its responsibilities.[31] It falls on Catholic theology also to underscore the necessity of proclamation. There seems to be two reasons for this. The first is that, for Ratzinger, both the situation and the intrinsic logic of Christian faith require it. On the one hand, in these confusing times, proclamation is an empirical necessity.[32] The faithful do not know what to believe. This need is met in part at least by putting them in contact with the synopsis of faith or what has been called a 'symbol' of faith.[33] On the other hand, there is a 'logical' need for proclamation. To proclaim the Creed is to claim as meaningful and true a particular perspective on God and God's relation to the world and to human beings. It is also to claim that one bears an existential relation to the content of faith, that is, that proclamation calls one to be true to it.[34] The second point is not stated explicitly, but is a corollary of the double necessity of proclamation. Since proclamation is not a contingent feature of Christian faith, it follows

30. Ratzinger, *Principles of Catholic Theology*, 367–93.
31. Ratzinger, *Principles of Catholic Theology*, 380–82.
32. Ratzinger, *Principles of Catholic Theology*, 133.
33. In *Introduction*, Ratzinger demonstrates that he fully grasps the meaning of the Creed as "symbol." See 96–100.
34. Ratzinger, *Principles of Catholic Theology*, 74–75.

that it does not automatically yield to secular constructions of the world, other Christian confessions, and other religions. Ratzinger fully embraces the good of dialogue that is enshrined in *Gaudium et Spes*, just as he also recognizes the theological necessity of encounter and dialogue with other Christian confessions. This is so much the case that the second part of *Principles of Catholic Theology* is devoted to ecumenism. And finally, in line with *Nostra Aetate*, Ratzinger consistently affirms the value of major world religions, including Hinduism, Islam, and Buddhism.

Nevertheless, in each case Ratzinger typically adds a rider. He reserves his most frequent rider for the failure in the reception of Vatican II to receive *Lumen Gentium* as well as *Gaudium et Spes*, and effectively to have made a choice in favor of the latter over the former.[35] As is evinced for obvious reasons far more in *Principles of Catholic Theology* than in *Introduction to Christianity*, respect for Protestant and Orthodox forms of Christianity does not rule out the possibility that there might be circumstances under which one might bruit the Catholic case. For example, the understanding of the relation between the Word and words of the scripture might be one, and the linking of the activity of the Holy Spirit to Christ might be another. On a somewhat more formal level, the affirmation of the relation between faith and right reason, that is, non-instrumental reason, moves towards the condition of a Catholic ineluctable. While Ratzinger believes that Catholicism should avoid a noxious triumphalism, nonetheless, he is unshakable in his conviction that Catholics have the responsibility to own their identifying beliefs that differentiate them from their Protestant and Orthodox brethren, whether these beliefs concern the understanding of the Church and magisterial authority, or some other article of Catholic faith. And finally, seeing the good in other religions and taking heed of the imperatives of dialogue and keen listening does not in principle render nugatory the proclamation of the full truth of Catholic faith. In the final part of this essay, as I leave the reception of Vatican II concerning the Church in brackets, I will attend to the ecumenical and world religious consequences of the kind of emphasis on proclamation that characterizes both *Principles of Catholic Theology* and *Introduction to Christianity*.

---

35. Of course, for Ratzinger, to have thus chosen is also in effect not to have received *Gaudium et Spes*. For this text can only be received if it is viewed in connection with or in parallax with regard to *Lumen Gentium*.

Ratzinger's *Principles* and de Lubac's *The Christian Faith*

In *Introduction to Christianity*, Ratzinger does not refer to Henri de Lubac's reflection on the Apostles' Creed. The reason is the fairly obvious one that the first edition of de Lubac's *The Christian Faith* came out in 1969, one year after the German publication of the *Introduction*. In *Principles of Catholic Theology*, however, de Lubac is mentioned a number of times, and here *The Christian Faith* is quite prominent, with Ratzinger citing the second edition of 1970,[36] rather than the first edition which appeared a year earlier. Unsurprisingly, given Ratzinger's agenda of establishing the fundamentals of Christian faith, the other text of de Lubac that receives some measure of attention is *Catholicism*.[37] Since I am reading the relation between *Introduction* and *Principles* as retrogressive justification of the choice of the Apostles' Creed in *Introduction*, this is at the very least interesting. Before I get to the details of my analysis, however, I should say that, while I refuse to make a genetic argument regarding *The Christian Faith* and *Introduction*, it needs to be noted that much of the work for de Lubac's commentary on the Apostles' Creed was completed well before Vatican II.[38] De Lubac's research was updated after Vatican II as a clarification of the classical view on faith and as an act of resistance to emerging understandings of faith after the Council and with which he disagreed. Effectively, then, only the last three chapters are new, the other six chapters having been published in some form before the beginning of the Council.

Conceivably, then, Ratzinger could have been familiar with a considerable portion of *The Christian Faith*. Still, whatever the case in terms of a genetic link, it has to be said that the substance and style of both commentaries are very different: de Lubac's commentary is deeply historical in a way that Ratzinger's *Introduction* is not. De Lubac enacts a retrieval which allows in some measure a merely historical interest, even if ultimately its *raison d'être* is to assist Christians here and now to rediscover and articulate their faith. Still, there is too much existential urgency animating *The Christian Faith* to sustain the thesis that de Lubac's commentary on the Apostles' Creed is reductively historical. Still, by way of contrast, in *Introduction to Christianity* Ratzinger almost never makes a point for purely historical purposes;[39] his commentary seems irreducibly to be ordered to the now moment, and more specifically the contemporary crisis of the relation between faith and

---

36. Ratzinger, *Principles of Catholic Theology*, 21–23.

37. Ratzinger, *Principles of Catholic Theology*, 49, 111.

38. In fact, before 1959.

39. This is true even in regard to the most historical section of *Introduction*, 82–100.

reason in which what is needed is a bold declaration of Christian faith, and a spirited defense of its possibility as well as actuality. A second distinction, that is, a distinction of style, follows from the first. De Lubac's commentary on the Apostles' Creed in *The Christian Faith*, while captivating, is also diffuse. On the one hand, as in *Catholicism*,[40] de Lubac seems satisfied to compile voluminous material across the centuries and in a huge variety of forms that express Christian faith as a rich tapestry that necessarily shows up modern attenuation, and at the same time shows us the way forward which will involve a step back, although clearly not an identical repetition. While de Lubac is very obviously more interventive in those sections of *The Christian Faith* written after Vatican II, there is still the sense that it is not so much him prophetically speaking out against the current state of the understanding of faith, as allowing the premodern theology to speak against what effectively is its intended and thoroughly vacuous replacement.

Introduction to Christianity reveals a theologian who, if every bit as self-consciously ecclesial as de Lubac (moreover, one who shares many of his historical interests, especially in Augustine and Bonaventure), is far more comfortable with being an author, that is, taking personal responsibility for voicing the tradition on behalf of the Church. There is no blending of author and a rich and pluriform tradition of reflection as often happens in de Lubac. In this effacement of the authorial "I" in de Lubac's texts, there is a sense in which the tradition rather than Henri de Lubac is the real author of the text. The contrast with Ratzinger in *Introduction to Christian Faith* is conspicuous. If the writing is characterized by a genial objectivity, it is quite clear that in *Introduction to Christianity* Ratzinger comfortably inhabits and exhibits the authorial "I." This is not to suggest in the slightest, however, that Ratzinger accepts the post-Schleiermachian mantle of the theological author as an individual creative talent.[41] Not only does he find this Romantic or Romanticist model of theological authorship uncongenial; more and more in the years after the Council, he finds the injection of such a model into Catholic theology problematic. He judges that there is a need for a basic understanding of Christian faith, such that his own *Introduction* necessarily shows his keen awareness of the fragmentation of theology into personal points of view. One might even think that this is far more the issue for him

---

40. Lubac, *Catholicisme* (Paris, 1938). The first English translation was made by L. Shepard and E. Englund in 1950. Their translation is reissued in *Catholicism: Christ and the Common Destiny of Man* (1988). Needless to say, there is a major discrepancy between the French subtitle and the English. Crucially, the English subtitle fails to capture the 'social' element of de Lubac's thesis.

41. See Thiel, *Imagination and Authority*.

than the issue of "dissent" raised by the likes of Hans Küng.[42] For in the end it is this scattering into individual points of view and thus actual and potential authorship that encourages dissent, indeed, makes it possible. Ratzinger's voice is the voice of an "I" rather than a "We." Crucially, however, the "I" is an ecclesial "I," that is, an "I" pledged to support the "We." It is through this pledge to the "We" that Ratzinger both affirms and subverts the purely idiosyncratic "I" point of view. Moreover, it is this non-identical union of voice and community that allows Ratzinger to have the kind of consistency in forensic tone that he has in *Introduction to Christianity*, which even by this time is becoming an indelible marker of his thought.

It is my contention then that in *Principles* de Lubac's *The Christian Faith* provides enormous assistance in Ratzinger's retrogressive justification on historical and systematic grounds of the Apostles' Creed as the basis of Christian faith. In chapter one of *The Christian Faith*, entitled "History of a Legend," de Lubac non-anxiously admits that the Apostles' Creed is not formulated until long after the Apostolic period. Despite the late date for fully explicit evidence of its canonic status, however, from de Lubac's perspective there is no reason to doubt that this eighth century formulation represents but a slight modification of an ancient Roman Creed. In any event, its use is reliably affirmed by major Patristic thinkers such as Ambrose,[43] Augustine,[44] and Rufinus.[45] It should not come as a surprise that the author of *Catholicism* adds a host of others to his pivotal three. Other testimonials regarding its antiquity cited include those of Origen, Cyril of Jerusalem, and Theodore of Mopsuesta. The value of the testimony depends in equal parts on the quantity and the quality of the testimonial, where the quality refers more nearly to the caliber of the theological mind. On this score Augustine does well, even if de Lubac agrees with the main line of scholarship that it is Ambrose who provides the clearest evidence for the early functioning of the Creed. Of course, it should be noted that, while admitting that it is basically a Western Creed, de Lubac adduces the testimony of Greek as well as Latin authors for its use and general relevance. The confidence that Ratzinger displays regarding the antiquity of the Apostles' Creed is buoyed up in no small way in *Principles* by de Lubac's comprehensive rehearsal of the evidence, with special attention given to the Patristic sources. Of importance also for Ratzinger in *Principles* with regard to retrogressive justification of the Creed as the basis

---

42. While dissent is an intrinsic feature of Küng's entire work, the idea finds exemplary expression in *The Church*, and the small book co-edited with Moltmann, *Right to Dissent*.

43. Lubac, *The Christian Faith*, 21–23, 27, 28, 34.

44. Lubac, *The Christian Faith*, 22–23, 29–31.

45. Lubac, *The Christian Faith*, 24–25, 28, 34.

of Christian faith is that in significant part he relies on de Lubac's rehearsal in *The Christian Faith* for the baptismal context of the Creed.[46] This is a hugely important point for Ratzinger, who is anxious to underscore the connection between liturgy and confession.

Similarly, regarding the systematic dimension of Ratzinger's movement beyond *Introduction*, de Lubac marks a number of features of the Creed highlighted in *Principles*. There are four features worth brief mentioning. The first feature is that the Apostles' Creed is unreflective,[47] that is, the Creed is an expression of faith on the first-order level without those traces of explanation that one finds in the Nicene-Constantinopolitan Creed, which moves fluidly between first and second-order discourse. With regard to the latter, I am referring specifically to the language of "essence" (*ousia*) and "consubstantial" (*homoousios*) when speaking to the triune God, and to a lesser extent the contrast between "begotten" and "made" in speaking of Christ. When de Lubac makes this point about the first-order nature of the discourse of the Apostles' Creed, he is being purely descriptive. Certainly, in elevating this point Ratzinger does not understand de Lubac to say (or for that matter any of the Patristic writers adduced by de Lubac to say) that the Apostles' Creed is more important than the Nicene-Constantinopolitan Creed because the former is purely unreflective and the other only relatively so. Ratzinger will not sanction any leveraging of the Apostles' Creed over the Nicene Creed. When it comes to interpreting Father, Son, and Spirit, on the one hand, and Christ on the other, although it is not his main business, he has no compunction about using the kind of philosophical terms used in the Nicene-Constantinopolitan Creed to interpret the Apostles' Creed, which does not use philosophical terms. Relatedly, throughout his long and distinguished theological career, Ratzinger has consistently resisted any and all forms of the Hellenization hypothesis that would judge against the use of philosophical terms in more reflective forms of Christian theology. For an Augustinian such as Ratzinger, convinced that Augustine had spoken the definitive word regarding the dynamic of faith seeking understanding, unreflective faith, while fully integral, naturally proceeds to reflective clarification. A second emphasis in *The Christian Faith* that allows Ratzinger in *Principles* to retrogressively justify and/or supplement what he said in *Introduction* is the insistence not only that the expression of faith is existential all the way down, but that this is written on the surface of the expression of faith. This is brought out clearly, de Lubac argues, when we consider faith with respect to Father, Son, and Spirit where it is not sufficient for the believer merely

---

46. Lubac, *The Christian Faith*, 60–61, 66–67 (see also 63, 77).
47. Lubac, *The Christian Faith*, 96.

to use the locution "I believe that." The believer feels called on to use the preposition "in": I believe in the Father, Son, and Holy Spirit.[48] Now, while Ratzinger does not repeat exactly de Lubac's distinction between "believe in" and "believe that," nonetheless, he does seem to read de Lubac as drawing attention to the fact that the very language of faith provide clues of existential commitment to the Trinitarian persons, and through that commitment also to the truth of the salvific acts associated with them.

Third, between *Introduction* and *Principles*, de Lubac can be viewed as assisting Ratzinger to come to a clearer understanding of the subject of the profession of faith, which seems to unstably hover between "I" and "We." It is probably the case that de Lubac provides an assist at least when he underscores that that the "I" in the "I believe" of the profession of faith is the ecclesial "I" rather than monadic "I": the ecclesial "I" always involves a reference to others that constitutes a "We."[49] It would be going too far to say that this is a new thought in Ratzinger, who shows himself to be something of a presiding genius in *Introduction* regarding prepositions ("with," as well as "to" and "for"). Yet in *Principles*, it is a sharpened thought, and de Lubac has helped Ratzinger to become at once more clear and more traditional in underscoring the "I," without fear of falling into modern subjectivism on the one hand, or collectivism on the other.[50] For Ratzinger, both of these tendencies must be studiously avoided when it comes to identifying the subject of Christian faith. Fourth, and finally, de Lubac helps bring out more explicitly a conviction that underlies *Introduction*, that is, that confession is a defining feature of Christian faith. At an important point in *The Christian Faith*, de Lubac seems to make a shift from description to normative proposal.[51] This is a point that Ratzinger seems perfectly comfortable with in *Principles*, even if he does not press one of the implications of de Lubac's account, that is, that confession or proclamation is not simply a definitive feature, but a unique feature of Christianity.[52]

---

48. Lubac, *The Christian Faith*, 136–42; 174–75; see also 140–43.

49. Lubac, *The Christian Faith*, 185.

50. The avoidance of both is constitutive of the thought of Ratzinger. Throughout his oeuvre, he inveighs against modern individualism. But he is equally harsh regarding collectivist experiments, whether fascist or communist. With regard to the latter, see *Eschatology*, xviii–xix, 3–4, 12. See also *Spe Salvi*, especially the section called "The Transformation of Christian Faith-Hope in the Modern Age," §§16–23.

51. Lubac, *The Christian Faith*, 279–81.

52. Lubac presses this point of contrast (as well as others) in his still useful comparison between Christianity and Buddhism, *Aspects du Bouddhisme* (1955). It is evident that Ratzinger continues to take seriously de Lubac's contribution to the theology of religions, which was the fruit of his enforced silence.

Two Corollaries Regarding Ecumenism and Theology of Religions

As is well-known, Ratzinger has written widely on ecumenism and the theology of religions, much of which has been controversial. The level of production on both topics is such that it is impractical to engage these aspects of Ratzinger's thought outside of the context of their relation to the profession of faith. Still, we should be aware that this epoche freezes to the falsehood if we think that ecumenism or the theology of religions has nothing to do with the confession of faith. On the basis of what we have disclosed thus far about Ratzinger's understanding of the dynamics of Christian faith, it is antecedently unlikely that he would agree that a general confession of faith or even the avowal of specific Catholic doctrines has no place in dialogue. At the very least, what is asserted in the Creed to be true cannot tolerate the contrary assertion in another Christian confession or in another religion with which Christianity is in dialogue.

Addressing Ecumenism first, it should be remarked that in *Principles*, after considering in part one the formal principles of Catholicism in which Creeds as well as scripture play an important role, Ratzinger turns to ecumenism both to lay out its general principles, and to discern what are the difficulties between Catholicism and Orthodoxy on the one hand, and Catholicism and Protestantism on the other. *Principles* is fairly typical of Ratzinger's contribution to ecumenism, in that by and large the focus is on different interpretations of the Church and Church governance,[53] although it needs to be said that, even outside the explicit intent of ecumenism, Ratzinger tends to be involved with both Eastern Orthodoxy and the other churches when it comes to a whole host of issues (for example, the Eucharist, proper biblical interpretation, and the nature of Christ). In any event, in *Principles* Ratzinger is anxious to deflate expectations in ecumenical dialogue since, unlike individuals, the representatives of the Churches have responsibilities to their Church's specific articulation of faith that is presupposed in all dialogue, and necessarily has to be preserved in and through it. In ecumenical dialogue charity is the horizon. Among other things this means that "the claim to truth ought not be raised where there

---

53. Ratzinger, *Principles of Theology*, Part 1, chapter 1 offers a general overview of the hopes and obstacles regarding dialogue between the Catholic Church and the other major Christian confessions (193–237). Chapter 2 is on the dispute between Catholicism and Protestantism on the fundamental issue of apostolic succession (239–84). The other major collection of essays (largely from the 1980s) on ecumenism is gathered in *Church, Ecumenism, & Politics*, Part 2, 69–137.

is not a compelling and indisputable reason for doing so."[54] Just as much as indifferentism, in dialogue chauvinism should be avoided.[55] Still, in certain situations such confession may be unavoidable, and unavoidable for all parties in ecumenical conversation.[56]

Now, if we think that the structure of *Principles* is not arbitrary, and that the reflections on ecumenism not only follow on but from the formal principles of Catholicism which have as one of their pivots the Creed or creeds, then ecumenism cannot conform to the secular model of unrestricted conversation in which everything is negotiable. There are truth claims embedded in creeds, theology, and practices of the churches that are not obviously compatible, and which may or may not admit of resolution. Ecumenism, says Ratzinger, is not a form of politics,[57] and most certainly not the liberal politics of vacuous agreement, where the parties to the conversation have sidelined their creeds and evacuated the claim to truth of their pivotal theological formulations.[58] This structural difficulty in ecumenical dialogue should be recognized by all parties and expectations adjusted accordingly. Specifically, representatives of Roman Catholicism should expect that the other Churches not only are unlikely to shift on fundamentals in discussion, but that they can't. Indeed, in some sense they should not.

Ratzinger does not produce in *Principles* a theology of religions that follows on his discussion of ecumenism and which devolves from his reflections on the formal principles of faith. Undoubtedly, this disappoints some Catholic theologians who think that interreligious dialogue is just as

---

54. Ratzinger, *Principles of Catholic Theology*, 198.
55. Ratzinger, *Principles of Catholic Theology*, 203.
56. Ratzinger, *Principles of Catholic Theology*, 198.
57. Ratzinger, *Principles of Catholic Theology*, 198.
58. Arguably, while what he writes is totally congruent with what he writes in *Principles of Catholic Theology*, Ratzinger's reflections in *Church, Ecumenism, & Politics* are more trenchant. In his essay on Catholicism's dialogue with Anglicanism (69–99), Ratzinger insists that, notwithstanding the goods of dialogue (84–89), dialogue itself is a relative rather than absolute good (85, 93). Ratzinger is perhaps at his declarative best in his essay "Luther and the Unity of the Churches" (100–31). There he insists that ecumenism is not a "political manoeuver" (113; see also 134). Unity without content is not a genuine unity (107), and such unity cannot be brought into being by dialogical procedures or "interpretive tricks" (105). In this volume, however, one can find a take on ecumenism that is strikingly different in tone. "On the Progress of Ecumenism" (132–38) proposes a view of ecumenism as involving patience, suffering, acceptance of diversity, and openness to the future. While it would be easy to judge that this essay contradicts those in which Ratzinger is very reserved about ecumenical dialogue, it is perhaps best to think of the essay as complementing his more deflationary account. Ecumenical discussion is valuable in itself, and the goods that it bears may be more nearly eschatological than historical.

important as ecumenism, and especially those theologians who think that, in the wake of Vatican II, a theology of religions ought to be one of the "building stones for a fundamental theology," to invoke the subtitle of *Principles of Catholic Theology*.[59] Now, while it is logically possible that the focus on ecumenism to the exclusion of a theology of religions might be indicative of a fundamental theological preference in Ratzinger, it could equally be the case that Ratzinger's treatment of ecumenism serves as a synecdoche for dialogue in general, and that more specifically ecumenical dialogue could be considered to provide examples of a number of critical judgments that can help guide or at least inform interreligious dialogue. Three judgments particularly come to mind: (a) our relative lack of progress in ecumenical dialogue where the discussants have texts, traditions, and practices in common should helpfully deflate expectations regarding Christianity's dialogue with other religions where such commonalities are lacking; (b) at the same time, these more narrowly focused discussions should also aid us regarding hearing and seeing what other religions regard as non-negotiable and negotiable; (c) in addition to bringing to light the above, the experience of the Catholic church in ecumenical dialogue can serve to highlight the additional complication that, when it comes to dialogue with Asian religions, their tendency to relativize doctrine makes for more rather than less difficulty in conversation. Ratzinger does not feel sufficiently informed to adjudicate the claim of the conceptual elasticity of major East Asian religions, although he suspects that the so-called apophaticism of these religions uplifted by Western theologians feeds a relativist agenda of the prohibition of truth claims. Ratzinger, however, does not think that, as a religion, Christianity is unique in making truth claims, and that a religion which does not is likely the exception rather than the rule. In any event, as *Introduction* had intimated and *Principles* confirmed and developed, it is a logical rather than contingent property of Christianity to make truth claims and to be existentially invested in the making of them.

That the concerns intimated in ecumenical dialogue are pertinent also to interreligious dialogue is amply illustrated in the essays on Christianity's relation to other religions gathered together in *Truth and Tolerance* and in *Many Religions—One Covenant*. The claim to truth cannot be dispensed

---

59. A sophisticated supporter of Christian-Buddhist dialogue is Joseph Steven O'Leary. See *Religious Pluralism and Christian Truth*. O'Leary avails of Buddhist agnosticism as well as postmodern philosophy, especially in its mode of deconstruction, as a solvent of Christian truth claims. See also his more recent elaboration in which interreligious dialogue is a key component of a Catholic fundamental theology, *Conventional and Ultimate Truth*. See my review article, "Stephen Joseph O'Leary and the Return of Correlationist Theology."

with in interreligious dialogue,[60] nor can mission.[61] Ratzinger realizes that the modern rationalist culture, based on the European Enlightenment, does not sustain the claim to truth in general and especially in the specific case of Christianity.[62] Indeed, he thinks that the relativization of truth claims is expressive of the so-called 'tyranny of relativism' that is an indelible feature of the modern secular, social unconscious. Although the secular embargo is on confession and proclamation in general, Ratzinger has no doubt that Christianity rather than the other major world religions is the target of choice.[63] He is adamant that the prohibition can safely be ignored, and that Christianity may experience the obligation from time to time to criticize another culture. Again, however, as is the case in ecumenism, listening is crucial,[64] responsible proclamation is discreet rather than loud, and criticism of another religion or culture can only be prosecuted if Christianity is prepared to go through the crucible of self-criticism. Ratzinger makes it perfectly clear that he regards the pluralist position advocated by the likes of John Hick[65] and Paul Knitter[66] to have succumbed to modern relativistic culture. Against this vacuous form of pluralism, Ratzinger proposes a "radical pluralism"[67] that accepts the variety of religions in the world that are at once irreducible to each other,[68] and whose claims cannot be harmonized. One particular tactic in a pluralist theology of religions that Ratzinger seems especially interested in cutting off is the appeal in dialogue to those elements of the relativization of symbols in non-Christian religions[69] which, subsequently and consequentially, become the measure not only of one of the dialogue partners, but of all. While Ratzinger remains agnostic about whether relativization defines Hinduism and Buddhism as a whole, he has no doubt that the appeal by Western theologians to such discursive strategies serves the relativism of Western post-Christian culture.

Given that always and everywhere Ratzinger is an ecclesial theologian, his defense of the intrinsic connection between proclamation and dialogue

---

60. Ratzinger, *Truth and Tolerance*, 57. See also *Many Religions—One Covenant*, 100, 109, 112.

61. Ratzinger, *Truth and Tolerance*, 105.

62. Ratzinger, *Truth and Tolerance*, 70–71, 117–19, 162–63.

63. Ratzinger, *Truth and Tolerance*, 88.

64. Ratzinger, *Many Religions—One Covenant*, 113.

65. Ratzinger, *Truth and Tolerance*, 52, 119–21, 126, 131.

66. Ratzinger, *Truth and Tolerance*, 52, 113, 126, 131.

67. Ratzinger, *Truth and Tolerance*, 81.

68. Ratzinger, *Truth and Tolerance*, 109.

69. Ratzinger, *Truth and Tolerance*, 125–26, 176–79.

in *Truth and Tolerance* and elsewhere is warranted in and through an appeal to the broad tradition of the church. Ratzinger makes a number of appeals to the Patristic 'seeds of the Word' tradition,[70] in which the religions are valued as partial realizations of the full truth, which is given in the revelation of God in Jesus Christ. Of course, Ratzinger is fully aware that this idea provides one of the basic platforms of *Lumen Gentium* (§16–17) as well as *Nostra Aetate*. Ratzinger also appeals to the *logos spermatikos* view in *Dominus Iesus* (§10) in the context of a spirited defense of Christ, confessed in the Catholic tradition and consistently affirmed by the magisterium as the definitive disclosure of the divine (§4, 8). There can be no doubt that among the pluralist targets in *Dominus Iesus* is the theology of religions of Jacques Dupuis. Although Dupuis denies the assignation of pluralism in the strict sense (and his position on dialogue is not as radical as either that of Knitter or Hick), he is reluctant to affirm either the need of proclamation or its value vis-à-vis dialogue.[71] More important than adjudicating this particular point is the deliberate and concerted warranting procedure enacted by *Dominus Iesus*, which involves not only the Vatican II documents, but also a particular line of reception of Vatican II deliberations on other religions. Especially important in *Dominus Iesus* are *Evangelii Nuntiandi* (1975) by Paul VI, *Redemptor Hominis* (1979), and *Redemptoris Missio* (1990) by John Paul II.[72]

Conclusion

The question being asked in this essay is as important as its execution is modest. The question is the reflective or reflexive one of asking, on the basis of the performance of confessing faith elaborated in *Introduction to Christianity*, what are its theological warrants, and how the relation between proclamation and ecumenism and between proclamation and the theology is to be understood within the parameters of a fundamental Catholic theology. I judged that a good way to get purchase on this question is to envision *Principles of Catholic Theology* as providing retrogressive justification of Ratzinger's decision in *Introduction to Christianity* of the Apostles' Creed as the basis of Christian faith. I also made the argument that, with regard to the supply of warrants, *Ratzinger* is assisted in significant ways by de Lubac's *The Christian Faith*, which was published a year after the *Introduction*

---

70. Ratzinger, *Truth and Tolerance*, 81, 97, 171.

71. For Jacques Dupuis, see *Towards a Christian Theology of Religious Pluralism*. See also my article, "The Theology of Religions of Benedict XVI," which goes into some detail on the relationship between Benedict and Dupuis. For a fine introductory essay on Benedict and dialogue with Asian religions, see Robert M. Gimelo, "A Depth of Otherness."

72. In addition to the ones named, a case could also be made for the inclusion of *Dominum et Vivicantem* (1986).

to *Christianity*. In addition, however, I paid attention to the fact that, in *Principles*, Ratzinger raises explicitly the question of the relation between proclamation and ecumenism (again, an issue that is not addressed in *Introduction to Christianity*). Ratzinger clearly sees the tension between the goods of proclamation and dialogue, but insists that neither can be sacrificed. While Catholic chauvinism, Ratzinger believes, remains a perennial possibility, in the current climate in which there is a massive introjection in Christianity of secular norms, there is, he believes, far more danger that dialogue for dialogue sake becomes absolute, and proclamation marginalized in fact or in principle. What is a dangerous unbalance in the practice of ecumenism is an ever present danger also in ecumenical dialogue. Although in *Principles of Catholic Theology* Ratzinger only speaks to ecumenical and never to interreligious dialogue, I have argued that this by no means suggests that Ratzinger is denying it a role in the elaboration of a fundamental Catholic theology. Here too, however, there is the necessary tension between the goods of proclamation and dialogue, and also the ever present danger of a procrustean reduction either to willful Catholic self-assertion, or affirmation of dialogue for dialogue sake, which either marginalizes or officially excises proclamation from religious encounter. Once again, however, in our increasingly secular age, the prejudice is increasingly in favor of a dialogue thought to fare best if the participants in dialogue in general, but especially Christianity, make all aspects of their faith matters of negotiation.

Bibliography

Austin, J. L. *How to Do Things with Words*. Cambridge: Harvard University Press, 1975.
Balthasar, Hans Urs von. *Credo: Meditation on the Apostles' Creed*. Translated by David Kipp. San Francisco: Ignatius, 2005.
———. *The Glory of the Lord: A Theological Aesthetics*, vol. 6, *The Old Covenant*. Translated by Brian McNeil C. R. V and Eraamo Leiva-Merikakis. San Francisco: Ignatius, 1991.
———. *The Glory of the Lord: A Theological Aesthetics*, vol. 7, *The New Covenant*. Translated by Brian McNeil C. R. V. San Francisco: Ignatius, 1989.
———. *The Theology of Karl Barth: Exposition and Interpretation*. Translated by Edward Oakes. San Francisco: Ignatius, 1992.
———. "Word, Scripture, and Tradition." In *Explorations in Theology*, vol. 1 *The Word Made Flesh*. Translated by A. V. Littledale with Alexander Dru, 11–26. San Francisco: Ignatius, 1989.
Dupuis, Jacques. *Towards a Christian Theology of Religious Pluralism*. Translated by Philip Berryman. New York: Orbis, 1997.
Evans, Donald. *The Logic of Self-Involvement: A Philosophical Study of Everyday Language with Special Reference to Christian Use of Language about God as Creator*. New York: Herder & Herder, 1963.

Gimelo, Robert M. "A Depth of Otherness: Buddhism and Benedict's Theology of Religions." In *Explorations in the Theology of Benedict XVI*, edited by John Cavadini, 114-41. Notre Dame: University of Notre Dame Press, 2012.

Küng, Hans. *The Church*. London: Burns and Oates, 1967.

——— and Jürgen Moltmann, eds. *Right to Dissent*. Edinburgh: T&T Clark, 1982.

Lubac, Henri de. *Catholicism: Christ and the Common Destiny of Man*. Translated by L. Shepard and E. Englund. San Francisco: Ignatius, 1988. (Originally published in 1950).

———. *Catholicisme: les aspect sociaux du dogme*. Paris, Éditions du Cerf: 1938.

———. *The Christian Faith*. Translated by Brother Richard Arnandez, FSC. San Francisco: Ignatius, 1970.

———. *Exégèse médiévale:Les quatre sens de l'écriture*. 4 vols. Paris: Aubier, 1959, 1961, 1964.

———. *La Foi chrétienne: Essai sur la structure du symbole des Apôtres*. Paris: Aubier-Montaigne, 1969.

———. *Medieval Exegesis: The Four Senses of Scripture*. Translated by Marc Sebanc. Grand Rapids: Eerdmans, 1998.

O'Leary, Joseph Steven. *Conventional and Ultimate Truth: A Key to Fundamental Theology*. Notre Dame: University of Notre Dame Press, 2015.

———. *Religious Pluralism and Christian Truth*. Edinburgh: Edinburgh University Press, 1996.

O'Regan, Cyril. "Benedict the Augustinian." In *Explorations in the Theology of Benedict XVI*, edited by John Cavadini, 21-60. Notre Dame: University of Notre Dame Press, 2012.

———. "Stephen Joseph O'Leary and the Return of Correlationist Theology," *Modern Theology* (forthcoming).

———. "The Theology of Religions of Benedict XVI." In *Evangelization as Interreligious Dialogue*, edited by Donald Wallenfang and John C. Cavadini, 45-79. Eugene: Pickwick, 2019.

Ratzinger, Joseph Cardinal. *Church, Ecumenism, & Politics: New Endeavors in Ecclesiology*. Translated by Michael J. Miller et al. San Francisco: Ignatius, 2008.

———. *Einführung in das Christentum*. Munich: Verlag GmbH, 1968.

———. *Eschatology: Death and Eternal Life*. 2nd ed. New Foreword by Joseph Ratzinger. Translated by Michael Waldstein and Aidan Nichols, OP. Washington, DC: Catholic University of America Press, 1988.

———. *Faith and the Future*. San Francisco: Ignatius, 2004. (Originally published by Franciscan Herald, 1971).

———. *Introduction to Christianity*. With a new Preface. Translated by J. R. Foster and Michael J. Miller. San Francisco: Ignatius, 2004.

———. *Many Religions—One Covenant: Israel, the Church, and the World*. Translated by Graham Harrison. San Francisco: Ignatius, 1999.

———. *Principles of Catholic Theology: Building Stones for a Fundamental Theology*. Translated by Sister Mary Frances McCarthy, SND. San Francisco: Ignatius, 1987.

———. *Truth and Tolerance: Christian Belief and World Religions*. Translated by Henry Taylor. San Francisco: Ignatius, 2004.

———. *Values in a Time of Upheaval*. New York: Crossroad, 2006.

Thiel, John. *Imagination and Authority: Theological Authorship in the Modern Tradition*. Minneapolis: Fortress, 1992.

5

Ratzinger on Lessing's "Ugly Broad Ditch"

Augustinian *Ressourcement* and Modern Rationalism

Rev. Aaron Pidel, SJ

Anyone acquainted with Joseph Ratzinger's writings will know how vigorously he defends both faith's need of reason and reason's need of faith, emphasizing one direction of dependence or the other, according to the occasion. In his papal address to the University of Regensburg (2006), for instance, Ratzinger, in the face of rising religious terrorism, recalls that faith needs reason to avoid sinking into a kind of dark, violent fanaticism.[1] In his earlier and much-admired *Introduction to Christianity* (1968), by contrast, Ratzinger, addressing a Tübingen university community then thrall to the Marxist "science of history," underscores reason's need of faith.[2] In articulating his central and characteristic argument for reason's dependence, however, Ratzinger chooses for his sparring partner not Marx—though he is implicitly included—but the Enlightenment philosopher Gottfried Ephraim Lessing (1729–1781). Against Lessing's claim that everything essential to religion can be deduced from the necessary truths of reason, Ratzinger counters that God's choice to make the ordinary path of salvation historically contingent also has a certain necessity. The necessity of the Incarnation and an elected people, however, follows not from rules of logical inference, but from the human person's status as fallen creature, who requires liberation from the self-imprisonment of exaggerated rational autonomy. In presenting sacramental positivity as a help to creaturely humility, this essay will argue, *Introduction to Christianity* both consciously

---

1. See "Faith, Reason, and the University."

2. For Ratzinger's impression that Marxist social criticism left many university students disaffected from Christianity in the late 1960s, see *Salt of the Earth*, 76–78; *Milestones*, 136–38.

revives an Augustinian apologetic strategy and reveals one of the distinctive features of Ratzinger's theological style.

Showing both the Augustinian roots and representative quality of Ratzinger's response to Lessing requires an exposition in several stages. The first step is simply to unpack *Introduction to Christianity*'s treatment of Lessing's "ugly broad ditch," noting how it presents the positive and contingent origins of Christianity as a dependence that creaturely reason can never "outgrow." The second step involves profiling Ratzinger's anti-rationalist apologetic against its nineteenth-century precursors, noting the shift from a juridical to a sacramental positivity. With the distinctive features of Ratzinger's anti-rationalist apologetic established, we can then proceed to the third step, to show its origins in Ratzinger's first published work: his dissertation on Augustine's ecclesiology. The fourth will be to show how Ratzinger invokes the Augustinian logic of humility both before and after *Introduction to Christianity*, using it to explain both the Church's mission in the modern world and his growing disenchantment with the theology of Karl Rahner. In the final analysis, Ratzinger's high regard for Christian positivity not only marks his distinctive theological "style," but also forms a strong basis for *Introduction to Christianity*'s ongoing relevance.

I. Ratzinger's Response to Lessing and Modern Rationalism

Few deny that "social location" leaves an impress on the mind, stimulating ways of thinking and shaping questions of enduring interest. Ratzinger's own location within the German academy, with its pervasive debt to Enlightenment and Idealist thinking, doubtlessly left him with an acute sensitivity to a certain intellectual "scandal": the ineluctable contingency of Christian path to salvation. Why the Jews among all the nations? Why the Incarnation in the "middle" of history rather than in our own lifetime? Why wheat for the Eucharist, when rice is the staple of so much of the world? Can a God who reputedly desires the salvation of all really put much stock in any doctrine or duty he has not made equally plausible and accessible to all? Modern rationalism answers this question negatively, proposing that reason's reflection on human nature discloses every important religious duty. But *Introduction to Christianity* argues that God can and does care deeply about such contingent "posits," and has good reasons for doing so.

Appreciating just how Ratzinger tries to "make sense" of Christian positivity requires reviewing the grounds for modernity's rejection of historically revealed religion. Since Ratzinger expressly engages Lessing's "ugly broad ditch," it behooves us to begin with Lessing's arguments, attending to the presuppositions they share more broadly with Enlightenment Rationalism and German Idealism. The famous image of the "ugly broad ditch" comes from Lessing's essay "On the Proof of the Spirit and of Power." There the German philosopher argues that contingent truths of history, such as the miracles and the prophecies of Scripture, can never furnish probable grounds for assent to Christianity. For such *vérités de fait*, by their very nature, make us dependent upon secondhand knowledge. Referring to the ensemble of biblical evidence, Lessing notes that "this proof of the spirit and of power no longer has either spirit or power, but has sunk to the level of human testimonies of spirit and power."[3] Lessing admits that these testimonies give us roughly the same probable grounds for believing that Christ worked miracles and claimed divinity as for believing that Alexander conquered Asia. He nevertheless deems such probability insufficient, asking rhetorically, "But who, on the strength of this belief, would risk anything of great and lasting importance whose loss would be irreplaceable? Who, as a result of this belief, would permanently disavow all knowledge that conflicted with this belief?"[4] In other words, the *vérités de fait*, received through a chain of dependence, can never accumulate so much evidential force as to unseat the *vérités de raison*, immediately and independently verifiable by individual reason. This is the "ugly broad ditch" that cannot be crossed. Implicit in Lessing's depreciation of contingent historical truths, therefore, is the regulative ideal of rational autonomy. That is, the highest mode of reason is the most sufficient unto itself, least dependent on tradition or authority.

Lessing does not hold this regulative ideal alone, of course, but shares it with such figures as Immanuel Kant (1724–1804) and G. W. F. Hegel (1770–1831). Kant's seminal essay "What is Enlightenment?" sums up the rational ethos of the Enlightenment with the rallying cry: *Sapere aude*— "Dare to think!"[5] We should refuse, in other words, to outsource the formation of our worldview to authorities. In religious matters, this means refusing to credit fully religious beliefs that do not fall "within the boundaries of mere reason."[6] Hegel's German idealism, for all its differences with Kantianism, nevertheless concurs in the ideal of full rational autonomy. In his *Lectures on the Philosophy of Religion* of 1827, Hegel concedes that the Christian Scriptures are "given in a positive fashion." He adds, however, that

---

3. Lessing, "Proof of Spirit and of Power," 84.
4. Lessing, "Proof of Spirit and of Power," 86.
5. Kant, "What is Enlightenment?" 8:35–42, here 8:35; in *Practical Philosophy*, 17.
6. For the normative priority of practical reason over religious belief, see Kant, *Religion within the Boundaries of Mere Reason*.

the religious meaning of Scripture emerges only through the "inner witness of the spirit," whose loftiest register remains autarkic reason: "The witness of spirit in its highest form is that of philosophy, according to which the concept develops the truth purely as such from itself without presuppositions. As it develops, it cognizes . . . the necessity of truth."[7] Though Christianity has the outer form of positivity, in other words, the philosophical spirit can distil this outer form into a universal logic. For Kant, Hegel, and Lessing alike, then, intelligibility has come to mean rational necessity, and thinking for oneself has come to mean thinking *by* oneself.

Ratzinger elaborates his logic of creaturely humility in *Introduction to Christianity* against this presumed aseity of "mature" reasoning. He first elaborates this logic as a general human law: "Activity that makes itself into an absolute, that aims at achieving humanity by its own efforts alone, is in contradiction with man's being."[8] Applying this prohibition of self-absolutizing activity to human reason, Ratzinger concludes,

> [O]ur relation to God cannot rest in the last analysis on our own planning, on a speculative knowledge, but demands the positivity of what confronts us, what comes to us as something positive, something to be received. It seems to me that from here the squaring of the theological circle, so to speak, can be accomplished . . . The antithesis, so heavily emphasized by Lessing, between *vérité de fait* (contingent factual truth) and *vérité de raison* (necessary intellectual truth) here becomes surmountable. The contingent, the external is what is necessary to man; only in the arrival of something from the outside does he open up inwardly. God's disguise as man in history 'must' be—with the necessity of freedom.[9]

Here as elsewhere, *Introduction to Christianity* identifies not the Incarnation's alleged metaphysical impossibility but its flagrant historical positivity as the chief scandal to the modern mind.[10] At the same time, the book insists that God "must" scandalize in this way. For if God limited his ways and demands to those strictly deducible from the *vérités de raison*, God would ultimately remain indistinguishable from our reason. We would inevitably experience salvation not as a gracious intervention from outside, but as the

---

7. Hegel, *Lectures on the Philosophy of Religion*, 398–99.
8. Ratzinger, *Introduction*, 202.
9. Ratzinger, *Introduction*, 203.
10. Ratzinger calls the "staggering positivism" of the Incarnation the true "stumbling block for human thinking." *Introduction*, 141–42.

achievement of human ingenuity and industry. We would remain our own lords rather than his creatures.

Though *Introduction to Christianity* mentions only the Incarnation among the indispensable *vérités de fait*, it has already prepared its readers to understand the needfulness of the sacramental Church analogously. This seems to be the point of Ratzinger's lengthy reflection on the conversion of the neo-Platonist Marius Victorinus, related by Augustine in Book VIII of the *Confessions*. Ratzinger interprets Victorinus as a rationalist *avant la lettre*, who for too long kept his distance from the Church because he viewed Christianity as a mere "Platonism for the people, something of which he as a full-blown Platonist had no need." His later decision to accept baptism coincided with his realization that Christianity offers not just a "mere idea . . . bereft of force" but a "way which makes a claim on him."[11] In other words, Victorinus had already in the fourth century accomplished the "squaring of the theological circle," acknowledging his "need" of a "force" or "claim" originating from outside his own reason. Perhaps Ratzinger expects the reader to recall that, in the fuller narrative of the *Confessions*, Victorinus ascribes his initial hesitation to shame at the lowliness of the sacraments.[12] In any event, the episode adumbrates the observations on the "necessary" experience of dependence that Ratzinger would direct against Lessing and post-Enlightenment rationalism more generally.

To sum up, Ratzinger responds to modern rationalism's reduction of intelligibility to logical necessity by drawing attention to a different kind of necessity. Though Christianity's doctrines and practices are not strictly deducible from universal and self-evident rational principles, they nevertheless remain necessary for the "realization" (in Newman's sense of rendering more than "notional") of our own creaturely dependence. Ratzinger understands by the "positivity of what confronts us" both the incarnate Christ and the acting (or sacramental) Church. Ratzinger's use of Augustine to make the latter point, as we shall see below, is far from accidental.

II. Ratzinger's Nineteenth-Century Apologetic Precedents

Before proceeding to Ratzinger's indebtedness to Augustine, we do well to profile *Introduction to Christianity* against its precursors. Catholic apologists of the post-Napoleonic Restoration, such as the Jesuits of the Roman School

---

11. Ratzinger, *Introduction*, 64.
12. See *Confessions* VIII, ii, 4.

and the French traditionalists,[13] also present reverence for "positive" revelation as an index of creaturely rationality. Unlike Ratzinger, these thinkers increasingly oppose rationalism not to the positivity of historical contingency or sacramental agency, but to the positivity of juridical authority.[14] A few examples, drawn from both theology and political theory, will suffice to give a sense of both the structural similarity and tonal difference.

The structural similarity becomes evident in the tendency of nineteenth-century Catholic thought to accentuate humanity's insurmountable dependence on contingent factual truth, transmitted through tradition, over against the individualism of Enlightenment rationalism.[15] This emphasis, common to both politics and theology, emerges in part as a reaction to the violence unleashed by French Revolution in the name of "enlightened" reason. Typical of the political reaction against enlightened rationalism would be the French Catholic layman Louis de Bonald (1754–1840), who argues that the *vérité de fait* enjoys a natural priority over the *vérité de raison*. As a kind of epitome of this ordering, de Bonald adduces the priority of speech to reason. Immersion in the communal medium of language, he observes, constitutes a prior condition for the development of independent reason. Since language makes reason possible, reason cannot invent language.[16] If the emergence of individual intelligence presupposes a linguistic community, and if an infinite regress is impossible, then only a divinely instituted language can account for the fact of human rationality: "[E]verything is explained and can be explained by the hypothesis of a first tongue granted to a first man, spoken in a first family, and transmitted through the generations to all its descendants."[17] Not just faith, therefore, but reason too derives from a primordial "posit" and propagates itself through tradition. In discrediting the *vérité de fait*, reason saws off the limb on which it stands.[18]

13. On this "courant traditionaliste," see Congar, "L'Ecclésiologie de la Révolution Française."

14. Kasper's study on the Roman School suggests that the Restoration (1815–1830) comprises loosely confederated movements—political, theological, papal—all intent on restoring order and authority. See *Die Lehre von der Tradition*, 123.

15. According to Menczer, what unites the nineteenth-century traditionalist thinkers are their "sharp criticisms ... of individual judgment as the basis of modern political institutions." *Tensions of Order and Freedom*, 46.

16. For a helpful summary of Bonald on thought and language, see Koyré and Cohen-Rosenfield, "Louis de Bonald," esp. 66–69.

17. *Recherches philosophiques*, I, ch. ii; *Oeuvres*, VIII, 170–79; cited in Koyré "Louis de Bonald," 68.

18. For Ratzinger's rather more balanced claim that the intellect both shapes and is shaped by its particular linguistic community, see *Principles of Catholic Theology*, 86–89.

The French traditionalist revalorization of historical positivity finds analogous expression in the theology of the Roman School, centered at the Gregorian University, and broadly characterized by its attempt to balance scholastic and positive theology. Giovanni Perrone (1794–1876), an influential representative of the Roman School, identifies German Idealism's fundamentally ahistorical nature as one of its chief defects. Referring to the philosophies of Kant, Schelling, and Hegel, he laments, "Those imbued with the principles of these philosophers have destroyed all *historical* or *real* and *positive* Christianity, considering sufficient a merely philosophical religion, clearly drawn from the human person's moral and intellectual nature alone."[19] Indeed, Perrone goes so far as to imply that any system reducing history to an "inflexible geometry" ends not just in "rationalism" but in "pantheism."[20] Reverence for the initiatives of God's positing will, according to Perrone, goes hand in hand with a sense for the difference between Creator and creature.

Though Ratzinger would surely find himself sympathetic to this nineteenth-century rehabilitation of Christian positivity, *Introduction to Christianity* does not follow its accompanying exaltation of authority. Here the tonal difference becomes become striking. Bonald, for instance, reasons from the sociality of reason to monarchy as the ideal form of human government. If God institutes the human community "from above" with the gift of language, then only governance "from above," i.e., hereditary monarchy, can form a perfect society.[21] Joseph de Maistre (1753–1821) will extend de Bonald's line of thought, arguing that the social order needs not only an apex but an infallible apex. "There can be no human society without government, nor any government with sovereignty, nor any sovereignty without infallibility."[22] Here de Bonald and de Maistre find the "positivity of what

---

19. "Ne quid tamen operi perficiundo [sic] deesset rationalismo *vulgari* in subsidium venit rationalismus *gnosticus* seu *sapiens*. Hic Kantii, Schellingii, ac Hegelii principiis philosophicis transcendentalibus adscitis, omnem christianismum *historicum* seu *realem* ac *positivum* destruxit, ei sufficiendo religionem mere philosophicam, ex sola nempe morali atque intelligenti hominis natura depromptam." *Tractatus de locis theologicis*, pars III, sec. 1, cap. iii [242] (in Perrone, *Praelectiones theologicae*, 288; translations mine, here and below).

20. "Pantheismus ac rationalismus aeque ac in philosophicis systematibus Germaniae *neo-eclectismi* hujus cardines sunt. Deus est ἓν καὶ πᾶν seu universum: creatio est necessaria mundi emanatio a Deo: historia est inflexibilis geometria: christiana vero mysteria omnia pervertuntur." *Historiae theologicae cum philosophia comparatae synopsis* [74] (in Perrone, *Praelectiones theologicae*, li).

21. *Théorie du pouvoir*, tome II, book VI, ch. ii; *Oeuvres*, XIV, 438; cited in Koyré, "Louis de Bonald," 62.

22. *Du Pape*, liv. I, ch. 19, p. 147; cited in Congar, "L'Ecclésiologie," 82.

confronts us" in the angular sovereignty of monarchy and papacy, which stand as keystones in the arch of the human social order.

Theologians naturally showed an intensifying interest in the "authority principle" as well. Perrone often presents the rejection of Church authority as the sympathetic bond uniting rationalists across the ages.[23] Johann-Baptist Franzelin (1816–1886), Perrone's colleague at the Roman College, defines rationalism in opposition to authority, identifying its "fundamental principle" as the "full autonomy and independence of reason from any external authority whatsoever."[24] Hence, whereas Ratzinger tends to assign the lead role in chastening idolatrous reason to historical givenness, the Roman School tends to assign it to ecclesial authority.

These political and theological currents shape the language and conceptuality of the First Vatican Council (1870). *Dei Filius* echoes the language of Perrone and Franzelin, both *periti* at Vatican I,[25] when it defines the essential motive for faith's assent as the "authority of the God who reveals" (*auctoritas ipsius Dei revelantis*).[26] Thomas Aquinas, by contrast, describes the equivalent motive as "First Truth" (*Veritas Prima*).[27] *Pastor aeternus* partially fulfills the aspirations of the French Traditionalists when it identifies the ongoing locus of this divine authority as the papacy, whose *ex cathedra* definitions are "irreformable of themselves, not from the consent of the Church" (*ex sese, non ex consensu ecclesiae irreformabiles*).[28] Nineteenth-century theology thus shows an increasing tendency, notably absent in *Introduction to Christianity*, to oppose rationalism to representative ecclesiastical authority, itself articulated in the categories of political sovereignty.

Synthesizing the previous two sections, we can say that Joseph Ratzinger inherits a nineteenth-century theological tradition that presents both historical positivity and—to an even greater extent—ecclesial authority as external checks on rationalist self-sufficiency. *Introduction to*

---

23. According to Perrone, modern rationalists praise Descartes "because he freed philosophy from theological authority," and they esteem the ninth-century pantheist John Scotus Eriugena as a "champion of reason against the yoke of authority." *Historiae theologicae cum philosophia comparatae synopsis* [61], [40] (in *Praelectiones theologicae*, xli, xxvi).

24. Referring to all those who attribute too much to reason in comparison with faith, Franzelin observes, "ii omnes vel diserte vel saltem practice statuunt principium fundamentale plenae autonomiae rationis et independentiae a quavis auctoritate extrinseca." See "Votum Franzelin," 4–5; in Hermann Pottmeyer, *Der Glaube vor dem Anspruch der Wissenschaft*, 29*–30*.

25. Congar, "L'Ecclésiologie," 99, 113.

26. *Dei Filius*, cap. 3; in *Decrees of the Ecumenical Councils*, 807.

27. I owe the observation to Yves Congar, "L'Ecclésiologie," 112.

28. *Pastor aeternus*, cap. 4; in *Decrees of the Ecumenical Councils*, 816.

Christianity extends the emphasis on historical positivity, while muting the accent on juridical authority. Ratzinger substitutes for the positivity of juridical authority the positivity of sacramentality, presenting Marius Victorinus as a paradigm of conversion to the acting Church. In doing so, Ratzinger not only adopts an Augustinian text but, as we shall see below, a broader Augustinian sensibility.

III. The Augustinian Roots of Ratzinger's Apologetic

Ratzinger's inspiration to refocus the Catholic anti-rationalist apologetic on reason's need of sacramental encounter comes ultimately from his *Promotion* on Augustine, *Volk und Haus Gottes in Augustins Lehre von der Kirche* (1950–51).[29] There the twenty-four-year-old Ratzinger finds in Augustine's critique of neo-Platonist rationalism the model for his own account of modern rationalism's incapacity to liberate the human person.

Volk und Haus Gottes shows many signs of Ratzinger's early interest in the challenge of modern rationalism. In the course of warning his readers against anachronistic readings of Augustine's distinction between divine and human law,[30] for example, Ratzinger digresses to consider how our contemporary way of dividing God's will into "natural law" and "positive divine law" may instill an unconscious bias against positive divine law. In human affairs natural law, rooted in the unchanging ends of human nature, clearly trumps the mutable conventions of human positive law. Since such human affairs provide the basis for our analogical thinking about God, however, we tend unreflectively to subordinate to natural law not only *human* positive law but also *divine* positive law. The consequence is a forgetfulness that divine positive law actually enjoys parity with natural law.[31]

Regardless of its psychological genesis, Ratzinger concludes that any depreciation of the contingent and positive elements of God's saving plan

---

29. Ratzinger, *Volk und Haus Gottes*. Ratzinger wrote the dissertation for entry in an academic competition whose stipulated theme was: "The People and the House of God in Augustine's Doctrine of the Church." Ratzinger, *Milestones*, 97.

30. As Ratzinger reads Augustine, these terms do not distinguish laws enjoying divine authority from laws enjoying merely human authority, but laws governing the Church from laws governing the State. *Volk und Haus Gottes*, 399.

31. "The impression is given that natural law is grounded in the essence of the being [*Seienden*], whereas the positive-divine law, though divine, nevertheless, in that it shares in the property of all positive law, is 'contingent' and mutable, even if grounded in a decree of the *divine* will, since it owes its origin only to a decree of the *will*, in contrast to natural law, which seems to be grounded in the very essence of God. The priority [*Rangstufung*] between the two thus becomes evident." Ratzinger, *Volk und Haus Gottes*, 401. This translation and those that follow are mine.

only strengthens the grip of modern rationalism on the Christian mind. Though rational reflection on nature certainly reveals God's will in part, Ratzinger explains in footnote,

> We must nevertheless consider here that the whole supernatural economy of salvation lies on the side of the "merely" positive decree of the divine will. It is certainly an unmistakable aspiration of theology to base the givens of Revelation in the essential order itself (cf. the theme of the *"praedestinatio absoluta Christi"*). But we may need to raise yet again the question of just how justified this Western devaluation of the *vérité de fait* relative to the *vérité de raison* is, since this strategy [*Verfahren*] is obviously grounded in it.[32]

Ratzinger's choice of the technical terms here is revelatory. In contrasting the *vérité de fait* and *vérité de raison*, he shows that he was wrestling with Lessing's objections as a twenty-four-year-old *Doktorand*. The critical reference to the *"praedestinatio absoluta Christi"* suggests that Ratzinger finds a certain kind of scholastic theology complicit in this marginalization of the *vérité de fait*. Ratzinger suspects, in short, that Augustine offers a better way across the "ugly broad ditch."

In the next footnote, Ratzinger explains that rehabilitating the *vérité de fait* represents a matter not just of intellectual honesty but of pastoral urgency. The unquestioned hegemony of the *vérité de raison*, coupled with a diminishing circle of true believers, has led pastors and theologians alike to believe that the Church can appeal to humanity "only inasmuch as she can show that her demands are founded in nature [*naturgemäß*] and thus universally binding."[33] In less technical language, the Church should aim to produce what everyone would recognize as a "a good person." One can easily guess the reasons for Ratzinger's misgivings about the long-term success of this apologetic strategy. A Church justified in terms of universal human morality quickly becomes redundant.

Ratzinger's concern for the contemporary problem of redundancy attunes him to Augustine's way of evoking the "Church's salvific absoluteness" (*Heilsausschließlichkeit*) vis-à-vis neo-Platonism. Like modern rationalists, ancient philosophers claimed basic agreement with Christians regarding the immaterial and transcendent nature of God. Like modern Christians, ancient Christians described the Incarnation and the whole visible saving economy as a means to this immaterial end. "Could we object," Ratzinger imagines Augustine and his contemporaries asking, "to one who arrived at the end

---

32. Ratzinger, *Volk und Haus Gottes*, 401n6.
33. Ratzinger, *Volk und Haus Gottes*, 401n7.

without the means? Who also lifted his heart on high without the outer signs of the Church?" Neo-Platonism, no less than post-Enlightenment rationalism, would seem to contain all the Christian essentials.³⁴

Yet Ratzinger argues that Augustine refuses to accept the equivalence of Christianity and neo-Platonism on the grounds that the philosophers, in bypassing the outer sign of the Church, leave their autonomy intact. By way of illustration, Ratzinger directs the reader to *City of God* Book X, where Augustine diagnoses the spiritual and intellectual infirmity of neo-Platonism without Christ. Augustine recalls there that even for Plotinus the rational soul "cannot be its own light, but needs to receive its illumination from another, the true Light."³⁵ Had Plotinus' disciples not become "vain in their own thoughts," Augustine continues, they would have realized that the dependent cannot attain blessedness without worshipping the true God: "To Him we owe the service which is called in Greek λατρεία . . . for we are all His temple . . . because He condescends to inhabit each individually and the whole harmonious body, being not greater in all than in each, since He is neither expanded nor divided. Our heart, when it rises [*sursum est*] to Him, is His altar.³⁶"

Augustine, Ratzinger remarks, here replaces the language of neo-Platonic ascent with the sacramental language of the Eucharistic ritual: "*sursum cor(da)*"—"heart(s) upward."³⁷ For Ratzinger, Augustine makes the same point that he made when narrating the conversion of Victorinus:³⁸ that created spirits mount upwards not by intellectual exertion alone, but by attaching themselves to the "positive" sacramentality into which God "condescended."³⁹ Adumbrations of *Introduction to Christianity* abound.

Not content merely to situate Augustine's ecclesiology within the intellectual currents of its own day, Ratzinger offers an excursus on its relevance for the ecclesiological debates of the European *Zwischenkriegzeit*. According to Ratzinger, the generation prior to his own chiefly contested two different

---

34. For all citations in this paragraph, see Ratzinger, *Volk und Haus Gottes*, 313.

35. Augustine, *City of God* X, 2 (p. 306).

36. Augustine, *City of God* X, 3 (p. 306).

37. Ratzinger, *Volk und Haus Gottes*, 292.

38. Ratzinger, *Volk und Haus Gottes*, 303 n9. Ratzinger cites both *Confessions* VIII, 2, 4 and *City of God* X, 29. The latter does not mention Victorinus by name, but only "a certain Platonist" known to Simplicianus.

39. "The purification of the Christian is no intellectual process; it occurs rather through the sacrament and the *res* offered therein; it occurs as grace from above that draws humanity on. The highest ascent of humanity happens in no other way than through the descent of God. The fault of the philosophers is not to have submitted themselves to this order" (Ratzinger, *Volk und Haus Gottes*, 306).

senses of the word *corpus*: "the old concept of the juridical corporation," and the "Pauline, 'pneumatically' inflected concept of the body."[40] Neo-scholastics and *nouveaux théologiens* mooted whether the Catholic Church should present herself primarily as a "church of law," the domain of Christ's sovereign order, or a "church of love," the sphere of his vital presence.

Ratzinger ultimately finds in Augustine's sacramental ecclesiology a refusal of this sharp dichotomy. Inasmuch as the Eucharist presupposes an apostolic succession and a hierarchy of orders, the "sacrament implies the juridical union [*rechtliche Einung*] of the church as a sacramental corporate Christ [*Christus-Körperschaft*]."[41] Yet the Church's supernatural origin simultaneously precludes patterning the Church's authority too directly after human political sovereignty:

> The concrete Church remains a juridical community by virtue of the sacrament, but this sacramental-juridical community is no longer the immediately present posit [*Setzung*] of the divinely-juridical community, but its "sign," while the latter remains, as incomprehensible reality, hidden behind this sign; and this sign in turn begins ever anew to extend itself into the domain of concretely human order.[42]

Ratzinger thus finds in *City of God* Book X not only a vindication of Christianity in all its "positivity," but also a model of positivity different from the juridical model favored by post-Restoration scholasticism. The Church confronts us not primarily as an inappellable sovereignty but as efficacious "sign"—a great sacrament.

Summing up, we can note three ways in which *Volk und Haus Gottes* anticipates Ratzinger's arguments against modern rationalism in *Introduction to Christianity*. First, it finds in Augustine's greater emphasis on the divine positive law a refreshing counterpoint to the devaluation of the *vérité de fait* more common in the Christian apologetics of his own day. Second, he discovers that Augustine prescribes as the remedy for Neo-Platonist rationalism a kind of humble submission to the positivity that confronts us, i.e., to the Word made flesh. Third, Ratzinger finds in Augustine an

---

40. Ratzinger, *Volk und Haus Gottes*, 409. Ratzinger also reflects on this context in the introduction to the new edition of his dissertation (*Volk und Haus Gottes*, 6–7). Pius XII's encyclical *Mystici corporis Christi* (1943) attempted to mediate this dispute, teaching that the Church has indeed received "juridical principles" from Christ, but has nevertheless, in view of the life of Christ permeating her, a kind of social constitution transcending the natural order. See *Mystici corporis Christi* §63.

41. Ratzinger, *Volk und Haus Gottes*, 409.

42. Ratzinger, *Volk und Haus Gottes*, 411.

instance of Christian positivity modeled more after sacramental action than political sovereignty.

IV. Ratzinger's Ongoing Reception of Augustine

Up to this point, this essay has argued that the seminal insights evident in *Introduction to Christianity*'s response to modern rationalism were present nearly twenty years earlier in *Volk und Haus Gottes*. Ratzinger responds to Lessing and company much as Augustine responded to Porphyry and company. Both uphold Christian positivity as a lance to the boil of absolutized reason, while giving this Christian positivity a sacramental (rather than juridical) tonality. However, as we shall soon see, this neo-Augustinian logic represents more than an occasional strategy or ad hoc solution for Ratzinger. It represents a constitutive and recurring element of his theological style.[43] We can appreciate the persistence of this Augustinian sensibility by revisiting two of Ratzinger's other works, heretofore unmentioned: *The Meaning of Christian Brotherhood* and Ratzinger's critique of Karl Rahner in *Principles of Catholic Theology*.

The Meaning of Christian Brotherhood (1958)[44] deploys the same Augustinian logic of creaturely humility, but now applies it to the problem of human community and the attendant intellectual scandal of election. Why does God work through the election of definite historical peoples, whether Israel or the Church, rather than through the ubiquitous medium of universal human nature? Ratzinger lays the groundwork for his reply by observing that a basic tension pervades human social relations: a tension between closed tribalism and empty universalism. Tribalism, on the one hand, divides the world into two different "ethical zones," with diverse ethical obligations toward insiders and outsiders. We can think here of the sharp division between Greeks and barbarians and, to a lesser extent, of Israel and the Gentiles.[45] Universalism, on the other hand, aims at bringing about a single ethical zone by rejecting all considerations of historical descent and basing ethics on common human nature alone. According to Ratzinger, this aspiration to universal fraternity dominates post-Enlightenment thinking. The French Revolution rallied its supporters with the cry of *fraternité—liberté—egalité*. Schiller's *Ode to Joy*

---

43. Ratzinger notes in the introduction to his republished dissertation on Augustine, "I found to my surprise in the tenth book of the *City of God* what were for me the most beautiful and fundamental [insights] about the Eucharist and its human significance." *Volk und Haus Gottes*, 6.

44. The work was originally published as a lengthy article: "Die christliche Brüderlickeit." I cite according to *The Meaning of Christian Brotherhood*.

45. Ratzinger, *The Meaning of Christian Brotherhood*, 5.

rhapsodized about the limitless extension of brotherhood—"Be embraced ye millions." Kant hoped to eliminate all merely "statutary" [sic] human differences, i.e., those historically contingent determinations superadded to humanity's common moral and religious make-up. "The question whether history could be subordinated to nature this way," Ratzinger wryly observes, "was never asked."[46]

Indeed, a moment's reflection indicates why such a subordination is impossible. A community can only stand for something, Ratzinger contends, by becoming visible. To become visible, a community must particularize its ethos against the universal human horizon. Even when the French Revolution adopted the Enlightenment program of universal *fraternité*, it had to differentiate "drastically and bloodily between the inner fraternal circle of the revolutionaries and the outer circle of the nonrevolutionaries."[47] The same holds true of the Christian community: "[T]here must, first of all, be a limitation, the formation of a definite brotherly community which raises the whole from empty romanticism to the level of concrete realizability."[48] A community without a particular ethos loses visibility and, along with it, the ability to act as a leaven in world history.

These preliminary reflections on visibility and historical agency allow Ratzinger to connect the question of election back to the sacramental ecclesiology he discovered in Augustine. Why does God make an ostensibly arbitrary option to communicate through one people rather than another, to attach grace to some cultural forms rather than others? The answer: this allows us to encounter his presence and grace as an active sign, as a gracious intervention from without rather than the fruit of human achievement. Ratzinger makes this point using the eucharistic language of representation:

> We come here to the basic ecclesiological category . . . of *repraesentatio*. Just as it is the essential nature of the sacraments to show forth by signs the hidden mystery of God in the drama of history . . . so it is with the great total sacrament that is the Church herself: she is the sign of God in the world, and her task

---

46. For the previous references see, *Meaning of Christian Brotherhood*, 14–16. Though Ratzinger does not cite a text from Kant, Ratzinger probably has in mind Kant's expectation that "in the end religion will gradually be freed of all empirical grounds of determination, of all *statutes* that rest on history and unite human beings provisionally for the promotion of the good through the intermediary of an ecclesiastical faith." *Religion within the Boundaries of Mere Reason*, 6:121 (p. 127).

47. Ratzinger, *Meaning of Christian Brotherhood*, 16.

48. Ratzinger, *Meaning of Christian Brotherhood*, 70.

is the visible and public witness to the divine saving will before the face of human history.[49]

Here the Church's witness to God's will "before the face of human history" adumbrates what *Introduction to Christianity* calls the "positivity that confronts us." It also suggests the degree to which Ratzinger's neo-Augustinian eucharistic ecclesiology forms the unexpressed backdrop to his attempt to bridge Lessing's "ugly broad ditch." Only by embracing her identity as a *vérité de fait* through which God wants to work universal salvation does the Church exercise a real causality and reveal our creaturely *dependence*. Such was Ratzinger's objection in the late 1950s to the empty cosmopolitanism of Enlightenment rationalism.

By the 1980s, Ratzinger begins to engage the same battle on a different front. In *Principles of Catholic Theology* (German: 1982), he vindicates Christian positivity not only against religion's "cultured despisers" but also against his fellow Catholic theologians. Especially instructive in this regard, precisely for the subtlety of the contrast, is Ratzinger's intensifying criticism of Karl Rahner, his erstwhile collaborator at Vatican II.[50] Ratzinger's differences with Rahner, hinted at earlier in his career,[51] come to a head in the 1980s, after the German Jesuit publishes his *Foundations of the Christian Faith* (German: 1976). Ratzinger finds in Rahner's later theological formulations the same post-Enlightenment tendency to devalue the *vérité de fait* in favor of the *vérité de raison*.

Making Ratzinger's concerns more readily understandable requires us first to recall the basic structure of Rahner's anthropology in *Foundations of the Christian Faith*. Rahner distinguishes within human subjectivity two inseparable poles, a foreground and a background.[52] The foreground (or categorical) pole includes every finite item of our experience, whether conceptual judgments or historical events. The background (or transcendent) pole represents the mysterious horizon against which we apprehend the discrete items of our experience *as* finite. We would never experience finitude unless our spirit somehow transcended finitude, profiling particular

---

49. Ratzinger, *Meaning of Christian Brotherhood*, 89.

50. For Ratzinger's own recollection of their collaboration, see *Milestones*, 128–29.

51. The earliest signs of this disagreement appear in Ralph Wiltgen's *The Rhine Flows into the Tiber*, which reports, "Father Ratzinger, the personal theologian of Cardinal Frings and former student of Father Rahner, had seemed to give an almost unquestioning support to the views of his former teacher during the council. But as it was drawing to a close, he admitted that he disagreed on various points, and said that he would begin to assert himself more after the council was over" (285).

52. For the language of polarity within the subject, see Rahner, *Foundations of Christian Faith*, 19.

objects against an infinite background—a background indirectly co-known in every act of knowing.[53] Since nothing can come from nothing, Rahner concludes, the intellect's self-transcendent dynamism must have a positive and sustaining cause, a mysterious ground that, when made an object for thematic reflection, humanity calls God.[54]

Ratzinger does not object to this religious anthropology in principle, and even praises the attention to historical particularity in Rahner's earlier works. As Ratzinger interprets Rahner's *Hörer des Wortes* (1941), for instance, the "paradox of the being *man* is that he can find the 'universal' in himself only in tension with the 'particular,' with a history that comes from without . . . so that man can be described as a 'hearer of the Word.'" The problem for Ratzinger occurs when *Foundations of Christianity* later relaxes the creative tension between the particular and universal in favor of the universal. *Foundations* does this by assigning the active mediation of grace almost exclusively to the transcendental pole, making any contingent historical location—whether inside the People of God or outside—equally opportune for salvation. Ratzinger finds particularly worrisome Rahner's oft repeated principle, "'Revelation history' is 'coextensive with the totality of world and salvation history.'"[55] If so, then full human liberation depends no longer upon "a *particular* history," the history of Israel and Church. Though Ratzinger is aware that Rahner elsewhere affirms a certain superiority of Christian history within world history, he nevertheless notes that Rahner locates this superiority "not on the level of event, but of consciousness." That is, salvation history does not represent God's sacramental action from the outside but only the "most successful interpretation" of a ubiquitous inner experience. To Ratzinger's sensibilities, this leveling of salvation history savors more of Enlightenment *fraternité* than the biblical doctrine of election.[56]

Ratzinger fears this rather one-sided privileging of the *vérité de raison* for various reasons. Rahner's privileging of the transcendental and universal pole, while it more easily accounts for the possibility of "anonymous Christians," subtly removes the *raison d'être* for both the sacramental

---

53. "In the fact that he affirms the possibility of a merely *finite* horizon of questioning, this possibility is already surpassed, and man shows himself to be a being with an *infinite* horizon. In the fact that he experiences his finiteness radically, he reaches beyond this finiteness and experiences himself as a transcendent being, as spirit." Rahner, *Foundations of Christian Faith*, 32.

54. Rahner, *Foundations of Christian Faith*, 33, 51–55.

55. Ratzinger cites the German equivalent of *Foundations of Christian Faith*, 144.

56. For all citations from this paragraph, see Ratzinger, *Principles of Catholic Theology*, 163–64.

Church and radical conversion. Ratzinger asks rhetorically, "[I]s it enough to declare that all Christian positivity is a realization of the human per se? But will not this explanation . . . soon become just a palliative that does not dispense me from fulfilling my Christian duties but makes it more difficult for me to do so by telling me there are other ways of doing it?" Besides making ecclesial life more burdensome, this distillation of Christianity to the realization of the "human per se" may subtly replace the call to conversion with an ethos of self-affirmation. Rahner sometimes reformulates the Christian imperative in this way: "He who . . . accepts his own existence . . . says . . . Yes to Christ."[57] To Ratzinger's sensibility, the Rahnerian transcendental subject becomes so freed from the particular historical conditions for its self-realization that it assumes "an almost godlike ability for self-action."[58] Rahner has subtly departed from the logic of creaturely humility because, in attempting to span Lessing's ditch, he concedes Lessing's key premise: the devaluation of the *vérité de fait*.

Though one could multiply instances of Ratzinger's refusal to resolve Christianity into the "human per se," the arguments in *The Meaning of Christian Brotherhood* and *Principles of Catholic Theology* suffice to show how a dogged valorization of Christian positivity marks Ratzinger's thought from beginning to end. They also further illuminate Ratzinger's motivations for doing so. *The Meaning of Christian Brotherhood* indicates that Ratzinger calls for a renewed emphasis on Christian positivity not to establish a cultural ghetto, but to mount a more effective missionary witness. Reading *Principles of Christianity* against the backdrop of Ratzinger's larger *oeuvre* likewise helps nuance the narrative of Ratzinger as an "erstwhile liberal" spooked back into conservatism by post-conciliar student riots and liturgical hijinks.[59] The same charge of devaluing the *vérités de fait* that Ratzinger leveled at Rahner in the 1980s, he had already laid at the feet of neo-scholasticism in the early 1950s. And inasmuch as Ratzinger maintains a consistent line of criticism against both "conservative" (e.g., neo-scholastic) and "liberal" (e.g., Rahnerian) theologies, it becomes clear that both his early and late thought defy facile political classification. Ratzinger is ultimately neither a "conservative" nor a "liberal" but, perhaps like his predecessors in

---

57. For the above citations, see *Principles of Catholic Theology*, 167. Ratzinger here cites the German equivalent of *Foundations of Christian Faith*, 228.

58. Ratzinger, *Principles of Catholic Theology*, 170.

59. For Ratzinger as "an erstwhile liberal" converted to conservatism after the trauma of 1968, see especially the eponymous chapter in John Allen, *Cardinal Ratzinger*, 45–88. Though Allen later nuanced his narrative, the first version retains a tenacious hold on the imagination of the theological academy.

the Roman School and the *nouvelle théologie*,[60] a predominantly "positive" theologian—one who takes as his preferred point of departure not human aspiration but what God has "posited" in history.

Conclusion

In the final analysis, Ratzinger would consider too costly a victory any overcoming of Lessing's "ugly broad ditch" by marginalizing Christianity's stubbornly positive elements—its history, symbols, sacraments, scriptures, hierarchy. For if we could actually succeed in rendering Christianity rationally transparent, we would at that very moment render it existentially superfluous. The only logic that can bridge this chasm is the logic of creaturely humility. Only when God approaches us through the rationally ineducible, that is, in an incarnational and sacramental mode, can we perceive him as Other and ourselves as his dependents.

To the extent that our own age remains heir to modern rationalism, moreover, *Introduction to Christianity*'s way of chastening rationalist pretensions remains fresh, even fifty years after its publication. The book perhaps owes its ongoing timeliness to the timelessness of its sources, especially Augustine's sacramentally grounded response to neo-Platonism. It might be objected that we live no longer in the modern but in the post-modern era, in the landscape no longer of monochrome cosmopolitanism but of identitarian tribalism. But however much the influence of "identity politics" waxes, it does not seem to have much affected religious sensibilities. Most Americans would find themselves quite sympathetic to the religious program promoted by Lessing's *Nathan der Weise*, namely, the reconciliation of the world's great religions through their reduction to an underlying ethical core. Even confessional universities do little to challenge this least-common-denominator approach, inasmuch as they routinely translate particular ecclesial commitments into the trans-confessional coin of "values"—inclusion, justice, service, etc. Even as a twenty-four-year-old student, Ratzinger foresaw that the Church's efforts to justify herself in terms of the "human per se" would result in the Church's increasing irrelevance. Perhaps we would do better to try instead Ratzinger's way of bridging Lessing's "ugly broad ditch"—the humbling embrace of Christian positivity.

---

60. Jon Kirwan rightly identifies commitments to historical methodology and positive theology as distinctive notes of the *la nouvelle théologie*. See *An Avant-garde Theological Generation*, 5.

Bibliography

Allen, John. *Cardinal Ratzinger: The Vatican's Enforcer of Faith*. New York: Continuum, 2000.
Augustine. *The City of God*. Translated by Marcus Dodds, introduction by Thomas Merton. New York: Modern Library, 2000.
Benedict XVI. "Faith, Reason, and the University—Memories and Reflections." September 12, 2006. http://w2.vatican.va/content/benedict-xvi/en/speeches/2006/september/documents/hf_ben-xvi_spe_20060912_university-regensburg.html.
Congar, Yves. "L'Ecclésiologie de la Révolution Française au Concile de Vatican, sous le signe de l'affirmation de l'autorité." In *L'ecclésiologie au xixe siècle*, edited by M. Nédoncelle, 77–114. Unam Sanctam 34. Paris: Cerf, 1960.
Dei Filius. In *Decrees of the Ecumenical Councils*, edited by Giuseppe Alberigo, translated by Norman Tanner, SJ, 804–11. London: Sheed & Ward; Washington, DC: Georgetown University Press, 1990.
Hegel, G. F. W. *Lectures on the Philosophy of Religion: The Lectures of 1827*. Edited by Peter C. Hodgson, translated by R. F. Brown et al. Oxford: Clarendon, 2006.
Kant, Immanuel. *Religion within the Boundaries of Mere Reason*. Cambridge Edition of the Works of Immanuel Kant, edited and translated by Allen Wood and George di Giovanni, introduction by Robert Merrihew Adams. Cambridge: Cambridge University Press, 1998.
———. "What is Enlightenment?" In *Practical Philosophy*. Cambridge Edition of the Works of Immanuel Kant, translated and edited Mary J. Gregor, general introduction by Allen Wood, 17–22. Cambridge: Cambridge University Press, 1996.
Kasper, Walter. *Die Lehre von der Tradition in der Römischen Schule*. Gesammelte Schriften 1. Edited by George Augustin and Klaus Krämer. Freiburg: Herder, 2011. (Originally published 1962).
Kirwan, Jon. *An Avant-garde Theological Generation: The Nouvelle Théologie and the French Crisis of Modernity*. Oxford: Oxford University Press, 2018.
Koyré, Alexandre and Leonora Cohen-Rosenfield, trans. "Louis de Bonald." *Journal of the History of Ideas* 7 no. 1 (1946) 56–73.
Lessing, Gottfried Ephraim. "On the Proof of Spirit and of Power." In *Philosophical and Theological Writings*, edited and translated by H. B. Nisbet, 83–8. Cambridge: Cambridge University Press, 2005.
Menczer, Béla. *Tensions of Order and Freedom: Catholic Political Thought, 1789-1848*. Introduction by Russel Kirk. New Brunswick: Transaction, 1994. (Originally published 1952).
Perrone, Giovanni. *Praelectiones theologicae*, vol. 1. Barcelona: Pons et Soc., 1847.
Pius XII. *Mystici corporis*. June 29, 1943. http://w2.vatican.va/content/pius-xii/en/encyclicals/documents/hf_p-xii_enc_29061943_mystici-corporis-christi.html.
Pottmeyer, Hermann. *Der Glaube vor dem Anspruch der Wissenschaft: Die Konstitution über den katholischen Glauben 'Dei Filius' des Ersten Vatikanischen Konzils und die unveröffentlichten theologischen Voten der vorbereitenden Kommission*. Freiburg: Herder, 1968.
Rahner, Karl. *Foundations of Christian Faith: An Introduction to the Idea of Christianity*. Translated by William V. Dych. New York: Crossroads, 1978.
Ratzinger, Joseph. "Die christliche Brüderlickeit." *Der Seelsorger* 26 (1958) 387–429.
———. *Introduction to Christianity*. San Francisco: Ignatius, 1990.

———. *The Meaning of Christian Brotherhood*, 2nd English ed. San Francisco: Ignatius, 1993.

———. *Milestones: Memoirs, 1927–1977*. San Francisco: Ignatius, 1998.

———. *Principles of Catholic Theology: Building Stones for a Fundamental Theology*. Translated by Sr. Mary Frances McCarthy, SND. San Francisco: Ignatius, 1987.

———. *Salt of the Earth: The Church at the End of the Millennium, An Interview with Peter Seewald*. San Francisco: Ignatius, 1997.

———. *Volk und Haus Gottes in Augustins Lehre von der Kirche: Die Dissertation und weitere Studien zu Augustinus und zur Theologie der Kirchenväter*. Gesammelte Schriften 1, edited by Gerhard Ludwig Müller. Freiburg: Herder, 2011.

Wiltgen, Ralph. *The Rhine Flows into the Tiber: A History of Vatican II*. Rockford: TAN, 1985.

6

An Introduction to Tradition in Ratzinger's *Introduction to Christianity*

Catherine R. Cavadini

Introduction

To become a Christian is to enter into the dialogue that has constituted salvation history since its beginning. God speaks us into existence and waits for the "obedient" response of our faith. This dialogue, then, has been spoken between God and humankind and then Christ and the Church, and still unfolds today in the words and deeds of the faithful. We could describe tradition as this dialogue, occurring simultaneously between Christ and his Church and the souls unified by this dialogue. Here obedience and seeking each do their part to better understand God's revelation and further the conversation of words and deeds.

Ratzinger's *Introduction to Christianity* invites readers into tradition's dialogue. He invites their hearts and minds to seek and respond within the intellectual and doxological contours of Christian faith, as questions and answers are handed down across the centuries. These questions and answers are both those of the Apostles' Creed, as spoken by the Church, and those of each believer who seeks to understand his or her response of faith. Indeed, Ratzinger's *Introduction* invites readers into this dialogue precisely by opening his own ecclesial process of seeking and believing to the consideration of others also seeking to understand. In his encyclical *Deus Caritas Est*, Ratzinger (then Pope Benedict XVI) instructs the Church to do her seeking at the foot of the Cross, in the company of Mary.[1] Here the very heart of God can be contemplated, pierced open for us to gaze upon. In many ways, Ratzinger's *Introduction* brings us to the foot of the Cross, but only because, as tradition

---

1. Benedict XVI, *Deus Caritas Est*, §12.

has taught him, we arrive there through the seeking of his own heart and mind, opened before us on the pages of this book.

The task of this essay, in celebrating the fiftieth anniversary of the *Introduction*'s first publication, is to treat the role of tradition within the *Introduction to Christianity*. Such a treatment will be most properly done by approaching the *Introduction* as Ratzinger's invitation to dialogue about Christianity. The *Introduction*, in laying bare the ecclesial heart and mind of its author, offers to hand the Christian faith on to a new generation of believers. Tradition, then, is not only a resource for Ratzinger, but is that in which Ratzinger participates when writing and offering this *Introduction* to his readers.

This way of considering tradition in Ratzinger's *Introduction* naturally invites us to also enter into the dialogue. In his preface to the 2000 edition of the *Introduction*, Ratzinger reminds us that the Second Vatican Council intended to "endow Christianity once more with the power to shape history."[2] Ratzinger's reminder serves as inspiration to his own readers: our efforts at introducing Christianity illuminate our history as salvation history. Our own methods of teaching and instructing should imitate Ratzinger's dialogue with Christ and the Church, and so with tradition. He will teach us to participate in this dialogue, too, by handing over our hearts and minds in conversation with God and new generations of seekers.

We will proceed with such arguments by first treating the place of tradition within the *Introduction to Christianity* more fully. As articulated above, we will find that its "place" is in the heart and mind of its author, and then in their acts of handing-over. The second part of the essay then examines the ways in which Ratzinger seeks to better understand the Creed as the Church's dialogue with God. We will see his own seeking taking place within the contours of tradition—at the intersection of giving and receiving. Thus, we will also see all the more clearly that Ratzinger has entrusted himself and his questions to the Church, and so to Christ.

Together, the sections of this essay will support Ratzinger's understanding of the Church as tradition, and this essay's own understanding of tradition as essentially sacrificial, beginning with the self-gift of God in Christ, and continuing in the response of the Christian. The Church, as exemplified in Ratzinger's method of introducing her, is a gift meant not only to be received, but also to be given. Along the way of this two-fold argument, we will use Mary as our guide. With Christ from the beginning and an image of the Church, Mary gives (her) life and limb to tradition. Understanding the Marian character of Ratzinger's *Introduction*, then, only

---

2. Ratzinger, *Introduction*, 13.

serves to further illuminate the ecclesial reality embraced in its authorship and so encountered by its readership. Ratzinger calls his readers to a Marian "Amen" in their own lived introductions to Christianity.

I. The Place of Tradition in the *Introduction*

The Dogmatic Constitution on Divine Revelation, *Dei Verbum*, begins with these words: "Hearing the word of God with reverence and proclaiming it with faith, the sacred synod takes its direction from these words of St. John: 'We announce to you the eternal life which was with the Father, and has appeared to us.'"[3] With such an introduction, the Council takes up the "we" of St. John's letter and vivifies it, announcing the Word Incarnate, the source and summit of Revelation. In other words, the magisterial authors of *Dei Verbum*—including Joseph Ratzinger—take their place in the Tradition, enfleshing the "we" of the Church. I argue, then, that the *Introduction to Christianity* corresponds to this ecclesial enfleshment: it expresses Ratzinger's own participation in the "we" of the Church in a way that invites others into this "we." The *Introduction* introduces a new generation to the Eternal Life, allowing Him to "appear" among us. We will see that for Ratzinger hearing and proclaiming the word of God with faith are crucial to such "appearances."

In order to treat this approach to tradition within the *Introduction* most fully, let us hear first about tradition from *Dei Verbum*. As Ratzinger's own commentary on *Dei Verbum* tell us, the goal at Vatican II was to give a "positive and clear account of tradition."[4] I divide *Dei Verbum*'s account of sacred tradition (*De sacra traditione*) into two parts, which I will call the apostolic and the Marian character of tradition.

First, consider these words:

> Christ the Lord in whom the full revelation of the supreme God is brought to completion (see 2 Cor. 1:20; 3:13; 4:6), commissioned the Apostles to preach to all men that Gospel which is the source of all saving truth and moral teaching, and to impart to them heavenly gifts . . . This commission was faithfully fulfilled by the Apostles who, by their oral preaching, by example, and by observances handed on what they had received from the lips of Christ, from living with Him, and from what He did, or what they had learned through the prompting of the Holy Spirit. The commission was fulfilled, too, by those Apostles and

---

3. *Dei Verbum*, §preface.1.
4. Ratzinger, "Commentary on *Dei Verbum*," 184.

apostolic men who under the inspiration of the same Holy Spirit committed the message of salvation to writing.[5]

In sum, this is the apostolic tradition with which we are likely most familiar. Thinking of the opening words of *Dei Verbum*, the "we" are the apostolic men, some of whom received the word of Christ from the very lips of Christ. This is the lineage of our faith, handed down and taught by apostolic men across the generations. Put differently, it corresponds to handing on "all that she [the Church] believes."[6]

We also read the following words: "Now what was handed on by the Apostles includes everything which contributes toward the holiness of life and increase in faith of the peoples of God; and so the Church, in her teaching, life and worship, perpetuates and hands on to all generations all that she herself is, all that she believes."[7] Here our understanding of tradition explicitly coincides with our understanding of the Church, her life, and her worship.[8] Clearly this handing-on requires a lived response of faith from each member of the Church, by hearing and receiving her teaching, living her life, and participating in her worship. Each member of the Church hands "who she is" on to the next generation. While Ratzinger clearly teaches the faith with all the authority of the magisterium, structuring the *Introduction* as a commentary on the articles of the Apostles' Creed, he also participates in the more personally intimate handing-on of the "we" who is the Church in the *Introduction to Christianity*. This will be our focus in the first part of this essay. This kind of handing-on, involving the whole person and all that the Church herself is, makes for a persuasive public appeal.

Let me be clear, however, that I don't wish to dichotomize the tradition by focusing our treatment of the *Introduction* in this way. Tradition, as a single stream of revelation, is absolutely and essentially ecclesial: it expresses who the Church is *and* what she believes. What I do wish to do is to draw our attention to what I have called the "Marian" character of the tradition. The Church, born not just from the preaching of Christ's lips, but from his deeds, too—from, let us remember, his open heart and side—is also rooted in the very heart of Mary, whose faith and life enfleshed the Word incarnate in a unique way. As Theotokos, Mary also became an image of the Church where Christ is still made present. *Dei Verbum*'s emphasis on the Church as tradition is radically Marian—a *resourcement*, indeed!

---

5. *Dei Verbum*, §II.8.
6. *Dei Verbum*, §II.8.
7. *Dei Verbum*, §II.8.
8. Rowland, *Ratzinger's Faith*, 55.

And thus, I structure my examination of the "place" of tradition within Ratzinger's *Introduction to Christianity* by quoting one short sentence from his third volume of *Jesus of Nazareth*, on the infancy narratives. There he writes, "Only Mary could report the event of the annunciation, for which there were no other human witnesses."[9] This striking observation about the Annunciation, somehow only obvious to me once pointed out, summarizes Ratzinger's understanding of tradition and points to the idea that the "Church *is* tradition."[10] Mary is a living dialogue between God and the Church.

Ratzinger's observation about the Annunciation summarizes the place of tradition within the *Introduction* in three ways. First, Mary's response of faith as developing not only a conversation about God, but with God. As a stream of Revelation, tradition requires a free response of faith. Second, Mary's proclamation handed on the word of God as revealed to her. The Church has enfleshed this response and this call to faith through the ages. Third, we will see that Ratzinger's own proclamation of the apostolic faith in the *Introduction* has a Marian quality. In listening to Mary through the Body of her Son, and by imitating her response to God's word, Ratzinger vivifies our faith, inviting his readers into a living dialogue with God. Let us take these three in turn.

First: Tradition and the Response of Faith

In the discussion of the infancy narratives found in the third volume of *Jesus of Nazareth*, Ratzinger depicts Mary as a living agent of revelation, first hearing God's word through the angel Gabriel, then responding to God's word, and reporting it to Luke. To put this in the idiom of the *Introduction to Christianity*, Ratzinger might say that Mary entered into a living dialogue with God, a conversation that includes her hearing God's word, responding to it, and proclaiming it.

In the *Introduction*, Ratzinger comments on St. Paul's assertion that "faith comes from what is heard." "[The nature of faith]," Ratzinger writes, "lies in the fact that it is not the thinking out of something that can be thought out and that at the end of the process is then at my disposal as the result of my thought. On the contrary, it is characteristic of faith that it comes from hearing, that it is the reception of something that I have *not* thought out . . . "[11] Here Ratzinger delineates the obedience of faith, a re-

---

9. Benedict XVI, *Jesus of Nazareth: The Infancy Narratives*, 16.
10. See Rowland, *Ratzinger's Faith*, 55.
11. Ratzinger, *Introduction*, 91. Emphasis mine.

sponse that can only be given by listening. Mary was obedient, conceiving the Christian faith in her hearing.[12]

Luke's Gospel re-sounds Mary's response to God's Word. At first she is perplexed at Gabriel's greeting, pondering what it might mean as she never imagined a *Theotokos*. Yet she responds with her *fiat*. With these words Mary becomes a living vehicle for Revelation. "Revelation," writes Ratzinger, "only arrive[s] where . . . its inner reality has itself become effective after the manner of faith. Consequently, the *person* who receives it [the revelation] *also is a part of the revelation* to a certain degree, for without him [or her] it does not exist. You cannot put revelation in your pocket like a book you carry around with you. It is a living reality that requires a living person as the locus of its presence."[13] In the language of the *Introduction*, Mary's unique "yes" was a decision "made in answer to a question, in the interplay of Do you . . . and . . . I do!"[14] Mary became God's "living tent"[15] through her response of faith in which she embraced the "inner reality" of love. She is the locus of God's presence, in dialogue with the reality living within her. Thus Mary is at the root of tradition, and a part of its revelation.

Mary's response to God's revelation also includes her proclamation of faith. We have noted with Ratzinger how Mary must have confided her experience of the Annunciation in Luke. As Tracey Rowland rightly points out, this proclamation is part of God's "giving activity" for Ratzinger. Luke further reported Mary's visit with Elizabeth. In this conversation between cousins, Mary communicated what she received, visible now in her very person, the Word enfleshed in her own flesh. Elizabeth, in turn, joins the conversation, the first to call Mary the "Mother of my Lord." We might add that Ratzinger also points out that Elizabeth tells us how John had also "leapt" into the conversation, having perceived Christ's presence. We, in our turn, hear this growing conversation about God and with God through the written Gospel, but only because Mary relayed her experience of hearing and receiving God's word.

Second: Tradition and the Church

In *Spe Salvi*, Ratzinger comments on Mary's trip to Elizabeth's home: "When you [Mary] hastened with holy joy across the mountains of Judea to see your cousin Elizabeth, you became the image of the Church to come, which carries

---

12. Cf. Ratzinger, *Jesus of Nazareth: Infancy Narratives*, 36–37.
13. Ratzinger, *God's Word*, 52.
14. Ratzinger, *Introduction*, 98.
15. See Benedict XVI, *Jesus of Nazareth: The Infancy Narratives*, 28.

the hope of the world in her womb across the mountains of history."[16] We continue to contemplate the Annunciation and the Visitation today, because the Church has received the revelatory experiences of Mary and Elizabeth and John and Luke. The Church carries on Mary's living conversation with God, voiced across generations, across time and space. And so we hope, with Ratzinger, that the Church and the faith she embodies has the power to shape history, rather than simply withstanding it.

Let us return now to Ratzinger's *Introduction* in consideration of the dialogue carried out across time and space. Here Ratzinger discusses the larger conversation between ourselves and God: "Man's conversation with God and men's conversation with one another are mutually necessary and interdependent. Indeed, perhaps the mystery of God is from the start the most compelling challenge . . . ever issued to man to take up the dialogue that, however much it may be constructed and disturbed, causes the *logos* to resound, the real word from which all words proceed and which all words constantly and inchoately attempt to express."[17] The reality of Revelation resounds and lives within the Church's conversation, as she receives and proclaims the Mystery of God. The Church, then, is a communion of so many living loci of reception and proclamation: the dialogue of the faithful that occurs in the "real word" who became incarnate and spoke to us as a man. Language, Ratzinger continues, "unites us with others. It is the way in which intellectual communication takes place, the form in which the mind is, as it were, human, that is corporeal and social. This primacy of the word means that faith . . . is first of all a call to community, to unity of mind through the unity of word."[18]

This call to community and unity is uttered through the Creed. "The creed," writes Ratzinger, "is a formula that forms the residue of the original dialogue"; it is the residue of the Church's conversation about God, even those earliest conversations between cousins surrounding Jesus' conception in Mary by the Holy Spirit. Our faith "is not the result of lonely meditation . . . it is the result of a dialogue, the expression of a hearing, receiving, and answering that guides man through the exchanges of 'I' and 'you' to the 'we' of those who all believe in the same way."[19]

Thus, the Church *is* tradition not only because of her apostolic lineage, but because each of her members receives and hands on all that the Church herself is, done in part by enfleshing "all that she believes." The Church is

---

16. Benedict XVI, *Spe Salvi*, §50.
17. Ratzinger, *Introduction*, 95.
18. Ratzinger, *Introduction*, 93.
19. Ratzinger, *Introduction*, 90.

at once the subject of tradition, handed-on across the hills of history, and the "I and you" who do the receiving and proclaiming. If, as *Dei Verbum* teaches, the Church hands on all that she is, *traditio* depends upon each "I" and each "you" becoming a living locus of the inner reality of revelation *and* of its outward effect in history.

Third: Tradition, the "I" of Ratzinger, and the "You" of His Readers

Much of Ratzinger's *Introduction to Christianity* focuses on re-introducing us to ourselves. We are uniquely situated between the visible and invisible recipients now of all the pondering and seeking of "then." The human situation requires faith and reflection; now and then are bridged by proclamation. Just as tradition depends upon us, we are dependent upon tradition to hand us ourselves. Most fundamentally, believers come to understand themselves as recipients of God's ultimate revelation of love for us, made for and by this love. Reflecting on love as the substance of Christian dialogue with God, believers become the very hands that carry tradition forward, attempting to hand on "all that Church is" to the next generation. This is a great responsibility and a God-given task, endowing us with great dignity, and history with great power.

Ratzinger does not simply write about this God-given task, but embraces it. In writing his volumes on Jesus of Nazareth, works which put *Dei Verbum* into practice,[20] Ratzinger says:

> I have attempted to develop a way of observing and listening to the Jesus of the Gospels that can indeed lead to personal encounter and that, through collective listening with Jesus' disciples across the ages, can indeed attain sure knowledge of the real historical figure of Jesus. . . . Even if there will always be details that remain open for discussion, I still hope that I have been granted an insight into the figure of our Lord that can be helpful to all readers who seek to encounter Jesus and to believe in him."[21]

Articulating such a hope, Ratzinger opens his heart to his readers, where we hear his dialogue with Christ's disciples across the ages, and so with Christ.

In the *Introduction to Christianity*, we are introduced to the "I" who has listened so carefully, both personally and collectively, to the Jesus of the

---

20. Benedict XVI, *Jesus of Nazareth: Holy Week*, xv.
21. Ratzinger, *Jesus of Nazareth: Holy Week*, xvii.

Gospels. We are introduced to an "I" who recognizes himself as a member of Mary's Son. He is, above all, an ecclesial being. As the "you" of his readership, we receive Ratzinger's response, become here a proclamation of faith in a new place and time. We, then, receive our very selves by entering into the conversation opened by Ratzinger for our consideration. With Ratzinger we reflect upon and hopefully come to enflesh the "I believe" and the "Amen" of the Creed, and so the "we" of the Church. The "place," then, of tradition within the *Introduction to Christianity*, is in the heart and mind of its author, communicated through the hands that wrote its pages.

II. An Introduction to Seeking, Questioning, and Responding

What is so persuasive about Ratzinger's *Introduction*, then, is the window it opens into Ratzinger's own seeking, into the heart and mind that asks "Are you really he?" This heart and mind listens to him, ponders his words and deeds, and utters an "Amen." Ratzinger's readers participate in his seeking to understand and enflesh the Christian faith, investigating its origins and expressions over time, and its "inner reality." Thus, we contemplate these things *with him*, moving *with* his thoughts as they understand more fully all that the Church has handed to him.

We should not be surprised to find that the movement of Ratzinger's own thoughts in the *Introduction* mimic the movement of Mary's thoughts at the Annunciation. Today, the Church's Creed annunciates the Gospel, and Ratzinger shows that the faithful rightly respond with a searching faith, and that this is no different even from Mary's response. Questions are not a roadblock, but an entry point into tradition's dialogue. In volume three of *Jesus of Nazareth*, Ratzinger presents the response of Mary's heart and mind as she enters into the dialogue of "Do you . . . and I do!" with the angel Gabriel. The movements of her "obedient" faith unfold in three "steps": (1) an "interior reflection" that seeks to understand the angel's message, (2) questioning, and (3) answering. Ratzinger says that Mary becomes an image of the Church particularly in her seeking.

Thus, these three steps hardly unfold in a clean-cut sequence. Rather, "interior reflection" and seeking go hand in hand with questioning. Such contemplative, intellectual seeking is animated in the *Introduction*, as the words put to the page by Ratzinger's hand invite us further into the contours of his pondering and responding. In this way, the *Introduction* is both a personal appeal and an ecclesial testimony: tradition is streaming forth! The reader already finds himself or herself participating in the Church's creedal dialogue. Put differently, because the *Introduction* invites us into Ratzinger's own creedal dialogue with God, we, as his readers, actively participate in that ecclesial, Mary-like seeking.

Above all the other questions, we hear Ratzinger asking Christ, "Are you really he?"[22] Part of his seeking, though, is to also ask the very Marian question: "How could this be?"[23] We seek with Ratzinger into the Creed's dialogue, spoken by the Mary-Church over time, and join in the response of Ratzinger's "Amen!" This then is to experience the "handing-on" that is tradition.

Accordingly, this second part of this essay takes a closer look at the Marian quality of Ratzinger's own seeking. Doing so will allow us to imitate his method of introduction and invitation, of handing-over. Yet, this is also a window into the inner-workings of tradition, as "God seeks to enter the world" here and now.[24] We will divide this second part of this essay, then, into three sections, which will attend respectively to Ratzinger's way of pondering and seeking, asking, and responding. In each section we will see that the Marian character of tradition is at work, handing the Church to her members, proclaiming the Good News, and offering an authentic encounter with Christ.

First: Seeking & Questioning: "Are You Really He?"

In the *Introduction to Christianity*, Ratzinger invites his readers to contemplate Christ and ask again and again "Are you really he?" The reader may feel this is a rather elementary question to ask—too introductory—but Ratzinger shows it is a question to be asked again and again. It is the point of entry into dialogue. The reader may also feel worried about asking such a question. Could it be the articulation of a doubt that could break our faith? No; rather, such a question should drive us to seek *more* understanding. Moreover, as Ratzinger also points out, such a question is simply part of the human situation—of being positioned between the visible and the invisible, between the "then" of the historical Jesus and now.

Today especially, writes Ratzinger, "[w]e have to pose the question, 'Are you really he?', not only out of intellectual honesty or because of reason's responsibility, but also in accordance with the interior law of love, which wants to know more and more him to whom it has given its Yes,

---

22. Ratzinger, *Introduction*, 80.
23. Cf. Luke 1:34.
24. Ratzinger, *Introduction*, 36.

so as to be able to love him more. Are you really he?"[25] All other questions, says Ratzinger, are "subordinate" to this one.[26] Indeed, in writing the preface to the 2000 edition of the *Introduction*, Ratzinger commented, "I believe that I was not mistaken as to the fundamental approach, in that I put the question of God and the question about Christ in the very center, which then . . . demonstrates that the place of faith is in the Church. This basic orientation, I think, was correct. That is why I venture to place this book once more in the hands of the reader today."[27] In other words, the question of who Christ is, and therefore who the Church is, remains absolutely central for Ratzinger, however many years later. Answering this question is to seek an understanding not only of God, but of our ecclesial selves and so "all that we are."

Ratzinger roots himself in the Church's own seeking when he insists that such a question be posed at the foot of the Cross. The Cross, however, seems to pose a "stumbling block" to our human efforts at seeking, for the God who bridged the visible and invisible in the Incarnation "has come so near to us that we can kill him . . . "[28] "[T]he very thing," explains Ratzinger, "that at first seems to bring God quite close to us, so that we can touch him as a fellow man, follow his footsteps and measure them precisely, also becomes in a very profound sense the precondition for the 'death of God.'"[29] The Incarnation tempts the human heart and mind to merely calculate the tangible and focus on the visible. But such calculations—the "measuring" of Christ's footsteps "precisely"—won't lead to an encounter with God, but to a hasty and false understanding of Christ. Instead of calculating and measuring, Ratzinger says we must contemplate and receive. It will amount not only to the reception of God, but also to the reception of our very selves as ecclesial handmaids at the foot of the Cross.

Thus, it is also at the foot of the Cross that Christ begins to answer Ratzinger's question with the silence of his death. Here we encounter Christ vulnerable in a most literal way, wounded with his heart opened to our gaze. As Pope Benedict XVI, Ratzinger wrote the encyclical *Deus Caritas Est*. This encyclical invites the Church to remain in this silent but revelatory moment, to gaze upon and to contemplate Christ's pierced heart: "By contemplating the pierced side of Christ (cf. 19:37), we can understand [that] "God is love" (1 Jn 4:8). It is there [at the Cross] that this truth can

---

25. Ratzinger, *Introduction*, 80.
26. Ratzinger, *Introduction*, 81.
27. Ratzinger, *Introduction*, 29.
28. Ratzinger, *Introduction*, 55.
29. Ratzinger, *Introduction*, 55.

be contemplated. It is from there that our definition of love must begin. In this contemplation the Christian discovers the path along which his life and love must move."[30] Christ's death reveals God's love for us, which informs our understanding of the human person: reality breaks open. The Cross, therefore, "reveals the unconditional devotion of [God] to men . . . it vouchsafes itself to us as a love that loves me and makes life worth living by this incomprehensible gift of . . . love."[31]

In sum, to ask "Are you really he?" at the foot of the Cross is to seek a better understanding of Christ, and so to encounter him. To ask this question in the very moment of Christ's death, in the very moment in which the whole idea of God seems dubious (more like an idea than an historical reality) is to persevere in asking, seeking, and discovering God's love. It is precisely in this great act of God's self-effacement, by appearing as an immeasurable nothing (the very human things of blood and water running from his side) that the invisible God, now visible, "vouchsafes" love and hands himself over to our gaze and our touch.

"Ask," Ratzinger's questions remind us, "and you shall receive."[32]

Second: Seeking & Receiving

Theologically speaking, to seek is to cultivate receptivity. As Ratzinger has argued, seeking into that which we have not made, is to discover that which must be given. This includes nothing other than the gift of God's self and of ourselves. Thus, receptivity is at the heart of handing-over, and it is sacrificial. This sacrificial quality of tradition has been seen in the handing-over of the Annunciation and upon the Cross. God has handed Himself over to the Church, and, as noted in the first part of this paper, tradition is the Church's way of handing over "*all* that she is." Head and Body are entrusted to the receptivity of the next generation. The generations hand themselves over to the "divine logic," "more deeply reflected" in the Body. Reception and seeking go hand in hand: enfleshing the faith meets its necessary ecclesial environment.

The method of seeking and receiving most prominent in the *Introduction* is Ratzinger's own faith. To read the *Introduction*, is to come to Ratzinger so that *he* might introduce us to Christ and to the Church (and so to ourselves!). As he seeks to understand the Creed in his commentary upon it, he also seeks to hand this understanding over to us.

30. Benedict XVI, *Deus Caritas Est*, §12.
31. Ratzinger, *Introduction*, 79.
32. See Matthew 7:7 (NRSV).

For Ratzinger, seeking and receiving within the Church lead to an encounter with Christ. Because the Church is tradition, this encounter can unfold in many ways. Let us turn again to *Deus Caritas Est*, a text that draws together Ratzinger's Marian receptivity expressed in the *Introduction* and his apostolic proclamation as Bishop of Rome. Indeed, much of *Deus Caritas Est* echoes the central questions of seeking and receptivity that are the heart of his *Introduction to Christianity*. For example, we hear within this the following passage about the resources within the Church for seeking and receiving an encounter with Christ, and how She continues to make the invisible God appear and dwell "amongst us":

> [N]o one has ever seen God as he is. And yet God is not totally invisible to us; he does not remain completely inaccessible. God loved us first, says the *Letter of John* . . . (cf. 4:10), and this love of God has appeared in our midst. He has become visible in as much as he "has sent his only Son into the world, so that we might live through him" (*1 Jn* 4:9). God has made himself visible: in Jesus we are able to see the Father (cf. *Jn* 14:9). *Indeed, God is visible in a number of ways*. In the love-story recounted by the Bible, he comes towards us, he seeks to win our hearts, all the way to the Last Supper, to the piercing of his heart on the Cross, to his appearances after the Resurrection and to the great deeds by which, through the activity of the Apostles, he guided the nascent Church along its path. Nor has the Lord been absent from subsequent Church history: he encounters us ever anew, in the men and women who reflect his presence, in his word, in the sacraments, and especially in the Eucharist. In the Church's Liturgy, in her prayer, in the living community of believers, we experience the love of God, we perceive his presence and we thus learn to recognize that presence in our daily lives. He has loved us first and he continues to do so; we too, then, can respond with love. God does not demand of us a feeling which we ourselves are incapable of producing. He loves us, he makes us see and experience his love, and since he has "loved us first," love can also blossom as a response within us.[33]

As this passage shows, we encounter Christ wherever he reveals his presence: in Scripture's love-story, the liturgy, prayer, and in Church history. This last place of encounter is one that should be emphasized when considering tradition. To see that God is present in history is to see the importance of the human person in handing on the faith and introducing it to new generations. Understanding this is to understand *how* the Church is

---

33. Benedict XVI, *Deus Caritas Est*, §17. Emphasis mine.

tradition. She has been handed her very self, and then turns to hand this "self" on, under the guidance of the Holy Spirit, handed to the Church at Pentecost. This passage from *Deus Caritas Est* mentions not only the way God has come "towards us" in the history recounted by Scripture, not only how God comes towards us in the activity of the Apostles, but also how God can also come "towards us" through the "men and women" who are the "community of believers," and in our "daily lives." "Then" and "now" the Church is a place of encounter and revelation because God has willed to come "towards" us in word and deed.

Let us linger longer on this historical reality, especially as it emphasizes human participation within tradition. Many scholars have recognized how deeply rooted Ratzinger is in the theology of St. Augustine. St. Augustine, too, had the gift of inviting his audience into his own seeking (even an audience removed by 1600 years!). In the prologue to his work *On Christian Doctrine*, Augustine seems to describe just the kind of experience Ratzinger provides in his *Introduction* and describes in *Deus Caritas Est*. Augustine reminds his readers that they should be willing "to go to church to hear and learn the Gospels, or to read a book, or to hear a man reading or teaching" rather than "expect[ing] to be 'caught up to the third heaven,' as the Apostle says, 'whether in the body or out of the body,' and there hear 'secret words that man may not repeat,' or there see Our Lord Jesus Christ and hear the gospel from Him rather than from men."[34] Even Paul, he continues, "although prostrated and taught by the divine and heavenly voice, was nevertheless sent to a man that he might receive the sacraments and be joined to the church . . . "[35] Further, writes Augustine, Cornelius went to Peter for instruction and "he not only received the sacraments from him, but was also taught what should be believed, what should be hoped, and what should be loved."[36] Clearly, Augustine believes that God is present through "men and women," the community of believers, and the Church's sacramental life.

Thinking of the *Introduction*, we are Cornelius and Ratzinger is Peter, teaching us what is to be believed, hoped, and loved. In other words, with Ratzinger, we follow Augustine's instruction to seek understanding where it can be given: in the Church. The Church is the Body of Christ, given to us in his death, and composed of the many members who have died with Christ through Baptism, saying, "Amen! I do. I believe in you, Jesus of Nazareth, as the meaning of the world and of my life."[37] The love,

---

34. Augustine, *On Christian Doctrine*, Prologue, 5.
35. Augustine, *On Christian Doctrine*, Prologue, 5–6.
36. Augustine, *On Christian Doctrine*, Prologue, 6.
37. See Ratzinger, *Introduction*, 81.

then, that is received, even as we are seeking, is the same love that "holds [the Church] together in a knot of unity" and dignifies the faithful as "human temples" from which God speaks, as Augustine says.[38] Through these "temples," then, "the living voice of the Gospel resounds in the Church, and through her, in the world, leads unto all truth those who believe and makes the word of Christ dwell abundantly in them (see Col 3:16)."[39] God "seeks out man in no other way but in his fellow humanity."[40] Truly, history is affected by the power of tradition.

We can say now that the love of God is manifested in the Church's activities of handing-on, and of being handed-over. To hand-on and to hand one's self over are to participate in the tradition that arose from Christ's "historical touch" in handing himself over first to the disciples at the Last Supper, then to Pilate, and ultimately to the Church. Having become the "historical touch" of Jesus, the Church is vulnerable to the human desire to seek and receive, just as Christ first trusted her to receive the gift of his blood and revelation of love. To ask and seek within the Church is to receive the Church's constant attempt to understand better the God who handed himself to her, and so who is still there to be asked, "Are you really he?"

As *Dei Verbum* teaches us, there is still today "growth in understanding of the realities and the words which have been handed down."[41] "This," the document continues, "happens *through the contemplation and study made by believers*, who treasure these things in their hearts (see Luke, 2:19, 51) [and] a penetrating understanding of the spiritual realities which they experience . . . "[42] Ratzinger, whose *Introduction* is the product of Marian reception and proclamation, has "treasured" the articles of faith in his heart by pondering the revelation of God's love in Christ and his Church, and has actively aligned his own deeds of seeking, receiving and proclaiming with God's sacrificial tradition. Ratzinger carries out his study of the Creed at the foot of the Cross, contemplating not only the birth of God, but the death of God, and how this life and death handed God over to history.

---

38. See Augustine, *On Christian Doctrine*, Prologue, 6.
39. *Dei Verbum*, §II.9
40. Ratzinger, *Introduction*, 94.
41. *Dei Verbum*, §II.9
42. *Dei Verbum*, §II.9. Emphasis mine.

Third: Amen

"Amen," writes Ratzinger, is "the little word" in which trust and entrust come together.[43] This means that "Amen" is akin to saying "I believe."[44] It is the response of faith to a love received, and it "expresses the abandonment of oneself" that is "a movement toward" God.[45] God has come "towards us" in revelation and we respond, moving toward God in our "Amen."

Our "Amen," however, is not meant to simply be a word, but a deed. If our "Amen" is truly an acceptance of God's love, then it will be expressed in deeds that have an "inner unity"[46] with our words. This was true of the Incarnation: "For the words of God, expressed in human language, have been made like human discourse, just as the word of the eternal Father, when He took to Himself the flesh of human weakness, was in every way made like men."[47] Our "Amen" becomes the "deed" of our life, lived in the presence of Christ within the Church, and through the Church "to the world."

And so we return to something mentioned only in a sideways manner thus far: the Creed as an ecclesial dialogue. "On the one side," writes Ratzinger, "we have a highly personal process, whose inalienable individuality finds clear expression both in the triple 'I believe' and in the triple 'I renounce' that precedes it. It is *my* existence that must turn here, that is to trans-form itself. But together with this extremely personal element we also find here that the decision of the I is made in answer to a question, in the interplay of 'Do you . . . ' and . . . 'I do . . . '!"[48] Though Ratzinger is here talking about the transformative dialogue of the Creed, he is also describing just what happens in the act of reading the *Introduction*. Therein the question of faith is posed by Ratzinger, but also, through Ratzinger, by the Church. The "interplay" of questions and answers is guided by Ratzinger's theological exploration of the Creed. And he shows us what it means to respond, "Amen." "To believe as a Christian," he writes, "means understanding *our existence as a response*."[49]

The response is love. As *Deus Caritas Est* explains, "'God is love, and he who abides in love abides in God, and God abides in him' (1 Jn 4:16). These words . . . express with remarkable clarity the heart of the Christian faith."[50]

---

43. Ratzinger, *Introduction*, 76.
44. Cf. Ratzinger, *Introduction*, 74–75.
45. Ratzinger, *Introduction*, 75.
46. *Dei Verbum*, §I.2.
47. *Dei Verbum*, §IV.13.
48. Ratzinger, *Introduction*, 88–89.
49. Ratzinger, *Introduction*, 73. Emphasis mine.
50. Benedict XVI, *Deus Caritas Est*, §1.

With this reflection on St. John's introduction of God as love, *Deus Caritas Est* echoes the centrality of the existential questions in the *Introduction* and their ecclesial answers. Ratzinger reads John as offering a summary of the Christian life: "*We have come to believe in God's love*: in these words the Christian can express the fundamental decision of his life. Being Christian is not the result of an ethical choice or a lofty idea, but the encounter with an event, a person, which gives life a new horizon and a decisive direction."[51]

For Ratzinger, it is precisely the encounter with Christ that proves Christianity is more than a lofty idea or ethical choice. Belief, as we have seen, is an entry into the Church's dialogue of love. This dialogue is carried out between God and man, but also within the fellowship of the Church, even across time and space. Belief is "being taken into service by something not made or thought out by oneself . . . being taken into service for the whole."[52]

Let us look at an example of this that draws St. John and Mary together, as studied and explained by Ratzinger at the foot of the Cross. Here, through a dialogue of words and deeds, the life of the Church is described as the Christian response to God's love. "[I]n the bible," writes Ratzinger, "the Cross . . . is the expression of the radical nature of the love that gives itself completely, of the process in which one is what one does and does what one is; it is the expression of a life that is completely being for others."[53] With Ratzinger, then, we examine the dialogue between Christ, John, and Mary as a particular historical point in which the life that is "completely" for others becomes the life of the Church. In John and Mary, then, we meet the horizon of ecclesial fellowship and mutual self-gift toward which we should orient ourselves in receiving and responding to God's love.

In John 19:26–27, Christ hands John to his mother ("Woman, here is your son"), and his mother to John ("Here is your mother"). Considering this biblical scene in the second volume of *Jesus of Nazareth*, Ratzinger comments:

> It is to the disciple [John], a true disciple in loving communion with the Lord, that the Woman is entrusted: Mary—the Church. These words spoken by Jesus as he hung upon the Cross continue to be fulfilled in many concrete ways. They are constantly repeated to both mother and disciple, and each person is called to relive them in his own life, as the Lord has allotted. Again and again the disciple is asked to take Mary as an individual and as

---

51. Benedict XVI, *Deus Caritas Est*, §1.
52. Ratzinger, *Introduction*, 99.
53. Ratzinger, *Introduction*, 282.

the Church into his own home and, thus, to carry out Jesus' final instruction.[54]

Here, as the tradition of biblical interpretation warrants, Ratzinger approximates Mary and the Church. Thus, he entrusts the Church to his disciple, asking him to take the Church into his own home. This scene, then, might remind us of the Annunciation, but with a different corporate dimension than simply Mary's "Let it be done." For Ratzinger, John stands in for every "disciple in loving communion with the Lord." The Church is entrusted to each and every individual whose "Amen" receives the Church into his or her own home. Such sacrificial hospitality—offered by offering oneself!—is Christ's final instruction to his disciples, and it is striking that this hospitality has to do with the one—the Church—who is given *as mother*. The entire scene radiates with tradition's dialogic and sacrificial character. We are asked to make a home out of our minds and hearts for the one we can only receive, and, *through* her, to live in loving communion with Christ. Ratzinger explains the approximation of Mary and the Church in the *Introduction*, writing, "Mary is the image of the Church, the image of believing man, who can come to salvation and to himself only through the gift of love."[55]

If we apply this understanding of Mary as "believing man" to John 19:26–27, we have a single image of the believer in Mary and John. The believer receives the gift of love as a disciple, and learns to give the gift of love as a mother. The Christian is one who gives because he or she has received. Put differently, we have an image of the Church as tradition, both receiving and giving the gift of God's love. Under Ratzinger's guiding hand, all the articles of the Creed point to this reality, if we take the time to contemplate them, "treasuring them in our hearts." When we do, we become living "Amen's."

Conclusion

We have examined Ratzinger's *Introduction* with Mary by our side. She was present at the beginning of this essay, imaging tradition in her response to Gabriel and her visit with Elizabeth. She was present as Ratzinger contemplated the pierced side of Christ, seeking to understand the love that reveals and constitutes the Church. And she was given to John as a mother so as to be taken into all of our homes when considering the transmission of tradition. Thus, Mary has exemplified for us the personal

---

54. Benedict XVI, *Jesus of Nazareth: Holy Week*, 222.
55. Ratzinger, *Introduction*, 280.

and the ecclesial nature of tradition as it was embraced by Ratzinger in penning the *Introduction to Christianity*.

In turn, we have seen how the *Introduction to Christianity* exemplifies the Marian character of tradition in the exchange of faith that occurs between the hands that wrote its pages and the hands that turn its pages. The author, like Mary, receives, treasures, and proclaims the Gospel. The reader, also like Mary, can then contemplate and encounter the reality of God's love in Christ. Thus, author and reader, like Mary (and John!), carry out the sacrificial receiving and giving that constitutes tradition in its historical qualities. The individual and the ecclesial move together toward the horizon of love.

For Ratzinger, a Marian introduction to the faith employs the whole person in handing-on the faith. Embracing the whole reality of the Christian life, a Marian introduction is rooted in the words and deeds of God throughout salvation history—even today, even here and now. This reality cannot be expressed in words alone. It comes to life again in the history of each Christian. Like Ratzinger, and perhaps thanks to moving along the contours of his introduction to Christianity, the Christian is a living, fiat-like "Amen."

Finally, Ratzinger's *Introduction* introduces his readers to a life-long encounter with Christ. In such an encounter, asking, seeking, and receiving only lead to more asking, seeking, and receiving. "Are you really he?" We are always being introduced to Christ, always at the beginning of encounter and understanding. "I believe, Lord, help my unbelief" (Mark 9:24).

Any successful introduction to Christianity will not shy away from the intellectual work of asking, seeking, and receiving. Indeed, part of its persuasive power will lie in inviting its audience into the logic of faith. But, even more than this, an introduction to Christianity will be persuasive because it goes beyond the logic of faith to its personal enfleshment. A successful introduction, therefore, participates, Mary-like, in tradition. But most of all, it will unveil the presence of Christ within the heart of its author, offered as a decisive encounter.

Bibliography

Augustine. *On Christian Doctrine*. Translated by D.W. Robertson, Jr. Upper Saddle River: Prentice Hall, 1958.
Benedict XVI. *Deus Caritas Est*. San Francisco: Ignatius, 2006.
———. *Jesus of Nazareth: Holy Week: From the Entrance into Jerusalem to the Resurrection*. Translated by the Vatican Secretariat of State. San Francisco: Ignatius, 2011.

———. *Jesus of Nazareth: The Infancy Narratives*. Translated by Philip J. Whitmore. New York: Image, 2012.

———. *Spe Salvi*. United States Conference of Catholic Bishops, 2007.

Dei Verbum: Dogmatic Constitution on Divine Revelation. In *Vatican Council II: The Basic Sixteen Documents*, edited by Austin Flannery, OP, 97–115. Northport: Costello, 1996.

Ratzinger, Joseph. "[Commentary on *Dei Verbum*] Chapter II: The Transmission on Divine Revelation." In *Commentary on the Documents of Vatican II*, vol. 3, edited by Herbert Vorgrimler, 181–98. Translated by William Glen-Doepel et al. Herder: Freiburg, Palm: Montreal, 1968.

———. *God's Word: Scripture—Tradition—Office*. Translated by Henry Taylor. San Francisco: Ignatius, 2008.

———. *Introduction to Christianity*. With a new Preface. Translated by J. R. Foster and Michael J. Miller. San Francisco: Ignatius, 2004.

Rowland, Tracey. *Ratzinger's Faith: The Theology of Pope Benedict XVI*. Oxford University Press, 2008.

7

The Role of Scripture in *Introduction to Christianity*

Anthony J. Pagliarini

INTRODUCTION TO CHRISTIANITY AIMS to elicit from its audience the act of faith that the Church herself makes in its profession of the Creed. In short form it draws its audience toward the confession "I believe in you."[1] This confession is, as Benedict later wrote in *Deus Caritas Est*, "not the result of an ethical choice or lofty idea, but the encounter with an event, a person, which gives life a new horizon and a decisive direction."[2] Scripture is put forward in the *Introduction* as the site of this encounter. While it appears throughout, its central role comes with Ratzinger's exegesis of the theophany of the Burning Bush in Exodus. There, Scripture renders actual God's self-presentation as one who is "Being for," as one who comes to draw creation into relationship, and thus it invites the audience to make the confession "I believe in you."

This use to which Ratzinger puts Scripture follows from his theology of revelation. The role of Scripture in the *Introduction* is shaped according to the needs of the book, but it is more correct to say that the opposite is true. The *Introduction* is shaped so as to carry forward God's initiative in revelation. True to the task of theology, Ratzinger's work hands on and clarifies God's self-disclosure and self-gift in revelation.

Introduction to Christianity shares much in common with the Second Vatican Council's dogmatic constitution on divine revelation, *Dei Verbum*. Following the contours of the latter's development will help us grasp the theology at work in the *Introduction*, published a few years after *Dei Verbum* in 1968. Ratzinger served at the Council as an assistant for Cardinal Frings of Cologne and then as *peritus*. In that capacity he played

---

1. Ratzinger, *Introduction*, 79.
2. Benedict XVI, *Deus Caritas Est*, §1.

a significant role in opposing the original schema on revelation, *De fontibus revelationis*. And when John XXIII eventually handed over that text for revision, Ratzinger would contribute to the drafting of what became *Dei Verbum*. That text's emphasis on the personal character of revelation owes much to his intervention.

As soon as the original schema became available, it met with criticism on several points. Contrary to Pope John XXIII's intention that the council be pastoral, *De fontibus* was judged to be narrowly dogmatic. It remained mired in important but ultimately parochial neo-scholastic debates, and at times seemed to address, as Cardinal Bea remarked, "one lone theologian!"[3] So too did it lack any ecumenical sensibility. The point of greatest weakness, however, was the document's failure to treat revelation itself. "It speaks to us," Cardinal Liénhart remarked, "about two sources, Sacred Scripture and Tradition. . . . But the decree fails to treat the other source that is deeper and itself unique, from which these two flow, that is, the word of God."[4] With this, Cardinal Frings conferred. "Neither is this talk of two sources of revelation deeply insightful. True, it can be granted [*verificari*] in the order of knowing appropriate to us human beings, but in the order of existence, the source is one and unique, that is, revelation itself, the word of God. And it is extremely lamentable that nothing, absolutely nothing is said about this matter in the schema."[5]

Much of the above critique, offered in the fall of 1962, found its inspiration in a lecture Ratzinger gave in April of that same year. At the invitation of Cardinal Frings, he spoke at the German seminary in Rome critiquing the draft of *De fontibus*. He took up on this occasion the *leitmotiv* that ten years earlier, at the age of twenty five, he made the center of his inaugural lecture for the seminary of the archdiocese Munich-Freising, namely, the understanding of "truth as person."[6] In Rome, he drew on this to press the understanding of revelation implicit in the title "*De fontibus*." By moving immediately to Scripture and Tradition (the *fontes* of *De fontibus*), the text adopts without comment a particular understanding of revelation centered on theological propositions. In this view, God's self-disclosure is restricted to "a teaching that one acquires from different 'sources'—a view typical of the age of historicism and its emphasis on the 'positive.'"[7] As Ratzinger notes, *De fontibus* thus

---

3. Evans, working translation.
4. Evans, working translation.
5. Evans, working translation.
6. Gaál, *The Theology of Pope Benedict XVI*, 49.
7. Ratzinger, "Dogmatic Constitution on Divine Revelation," 170.

robes "in the garment of ecclesiastical traditionalism"[8] a view that originated in Thomism of the post-Tridentine era.[9]

Contrary to Cardinal Ottaviani and others drafters of the text, Ratzinger sought to place Christ at the center. "Instead of a list of abstract truths," de Gaál says of Ratzinger's position, "there is a concrete truth: Jesus Chris is 'truth in person.'" It follows from this that "Scripture and Tradition are not actually the source of revelation," much as Liénhart and Frings made clear in their interventions. "Rather, . . . God's revelation itself, the unveiling and speaking of God in Jesus Christ, is the *unus fons* (one source) of revelation, while . . . scripture and traditions [are] revelation's *rivuli* (brooks). Jesus Christ is not the mere courier of a corpus of teaching . . . , but rather *he is the message*."[10]

The council adopted this theology in the text of *Dei Verbum*. It is voiced throughout when, for instance, it speaks of "Christ, who is both the mediator and the fullness of all revelation."[11] Far from having a "propositional character," revelation is understood by the Council in much the same way that Benedict would speak of it in *Deus Caritas Est*, namely, as the "encounter with an event, a person."[12] In the judgment of the *Dei Verbum*, God's self-disclosure was addressed to men and women in the entirely of their being, and the goal of this personal address is "fellowship" and a coming to "share in the divine nature."[13] Commenting on the text of *Dei Verbum* shortly after the council, Ratzinger writes that "the mystery of God is ultimately nothing other than Christ himself—it is the person (Col 1:27). From this there follows an understanding of revelation that is seen basically as dialogue." Jesus' words "No longer do I call you servants . . . but . . . friends" (John 15:15) are spoken "with the intention of forcing us to reply."[14] And since this reply in faith introduces one into fellowship with God, Ratzinger can summarize the matter by saying that "it is God himself, the person of God, from whom revelation proceeds and to whom it returns." As such, "this revelation necessarily reaches—also with the person who receives it—into the personal center

---

8. Ratzinger, "Dogmatic Constitution on Divine Revelation," 170.

9. Cf. Rowland, *Ratzinger's Faith*, 48–49, who views this as a Suarezian distortion of the classical Thomist position.

10. Gaál, *Theology of Pope Benedict*, 92.

11. *Dei Verbum* §2.

12. Benedict XVI, *Deus Caritas Est*, §1.

13. *Dei Verbum* §2.

14. Ratzinger, "Dogmatic Constitution on Divine Revelation," 171.

of man, it touches him in the depth of his being, not only in his individual faculties, in his will and his understanding."[15]

The language of personal encounter is not a means for rendering intelligible and attractive more rarefied dogmatic convictions. We should not mistake it as a function of the Council's desire to speak more pastorally. In truth, this turn in the Council's theology recovers a portion of "that treasure of incalculable worth" which John XXIII wished for the Church to "transmit... in all its purity, undiluted, and undistorted."[16] Ratzinger, and the Council with him, understood that the personal character of revelation—an event that culminates in God's entrance into history as a speaking subject—is what differentiates the Christian faith. It is, in the words of Guardini, the essential *Unterscheidung des Christentums*, the essential Christian difference that forms the heart of the Church's and of Ratzinger's theology. As such, it was necessary in the context of the Council to move away from a "legalistic view that sees revelation largely as the issuing of divine decrees,"[17] and to reappropriate a view of revelation directed to man's incorporation into Christ and the Life of the Trinity.

Three components of this theology of revelation inform Ratzinger's use of Scripture in the *Introduction*. First, it captures what it means to speak of God as the object of revelation—as that which is revealed. It is true that we know God through propositional language. We assent in faith to the articles of the creed and to all the Church teaches. Even so, "the believer's act (of faith) does not terminate in the propositions, but in the realities (which they express)."[18] And since the reality that is ultimate object of faith is itself not an abstract concept but the living God, faith opens onto a personal encounter. It is "the substance of things hoped for" (Heb 11:1) and not merely its conceptualization. What God reveals and that to which one ultimately assents in faith is God himself.

Second, Ratzinger's theology plumbs what it means to speak of God as the subject of revelation—as the one who reveals. In these last days God has spoken to us through his Son, but the speaking of this Word into history is, of course, not commensurate with the words of Jesus alone, nor of the confessions of faith to which they give rise. As with God's appearance to Job in the whirlwind, it is not the words alone but the fact of God speaking them to Job that constitutes the heart of the revelation. "I had heard of thee by the hearing of the ear," says Job, "but now my eye sees thee" (Job 42:5). So also is

---

15. Ratzinger, "Dogmatic Constitution on Divine Revelation," 170.
16. Cf. John XXIII, "Opening Address to the Council."
17. Ratzinger, "Dogmatic Constitution on Divine Revelation," 171.
18. Aquinas, *Summa Theologica*, II–II.1.2, ad 2.

this true in the Incarnation. In all that Jesus does, it is the Son who acts. And thus, the whole of his life is mystery in the theological sense of the word. "Christ's whole earthly life—his words and deeds, his silences and sufferings, indeed his manner of being and speaking—is *Revelation* of the Father. . . . Because our Lord became man in order to do his Father's will, even the least characteristics of his mysteries manifest 'God's love . . . among us.'"[19] God is subject of revelation in the whole of his incarnate life and remains so in the Church, which is the sacrament of his presence.

Further still, we should emphasize that the "words and deeds"[20] by which God reveals do not themselves constitute a static body of revelation. "While researching Bonaventure, Ratzinger discovered that in the thirteenth century no term existed that corresponds to the modern understanding of 'revelation.'" There existed," writes de Gaál, "no word for the totality of divinely revealed content. For the High Middle Ages, Revelation refers to an act in which God shows himself to a particular receiving subject."[21] Jesus is not the mere courier of revealed truths. He is himself the Eternal Word through whom God, ever anew, "speaks to men as friends . . . and lives among them . . . so that He may invite and take them into fellowship with Himself."[22] That is to say, he is the abiding subject of revelation as well as its object.

This brings us to a third component of Ratzinger's theology of revelation, the role of the recipient. As an act of communication—a free initiative in which God comes to meet man—revelation requires receptivity. This is not something which is subsequent to the act of revelation but is itself constitutive of God's communication with us. And since that act of communication is not the handing over of a body of truths but a making-known of God's self, only a receptivity that draws upon the whole person is sufficient. It follows, therefore, that

> You can have Scripture without having revelation. For revelation always and only becomes a reality where there is faith. . . . [One] can read Scripture and know what is in it, can even understand at a purely intellectual level, what is meant and how what is said hangs together—and yet [such a person] has not shared in the revelation. Rather, revelation has only arrived where, in addition to the material assertions witnessing to it, its inner reality has itself become effective after the manner of faith. Consequently, the

19. *Catechism of the Catholic Church*, §170.
20. *Dei Verbum*, §§4, 14.
21. Gaál, *Theology of Pope Benedict*, 88.
22. *Dei Verbum*, §2.

person who receives it is also a part of the revelation to a certain degree, for without him it does not exist. You cannot put revelation in your pocket like a book you carry around with you."[23]

The act of faith to which Ratzinger refers is not a matter of ratifying in the intellect truths proposed for belief. Rather, the virtue of faith conforms us to the life of God and therein allows us to begin to know God as God knows himself. In the understanding of St. Thomas, "Faith is a habit of the mind by which eternal life begins in us and which makes the intellect assent to things that are not evident."[24] Were it otherwise, faith would be surer in proportion to the strength of one's mind. This is not true. Faith is rather "an act of the intellect that is determined to its object by the command of the will."[25] It is, we might say, the decision to adhere to God that arises in part from the apprehension of his goodness. "[I]n the last analysis," as Ratzinger says, "believing, trust, and loving are one."[26] God approaches man "in the depth of his being," and, when received in faith, effects in man the very reality which he reveals—divine life. One becomes, as it were, "a part of the revelation to a certain degree."

There is an irreducibly existential character to the act of Faith. Dan Berrigan's crass but pithy remark captures it well. "Your faith is rarely where your head is at and rarely where your heart is at. Your faith is where your ass is at! Inside what commitments are you sitting? Within what reality do you anchor yourself?"[27] Said differently, revelation is God's self-offering, and it requires in faith a response that similarly complete—not merely intellectual, not merely affective. With this understanding in view, the structure of the *Introduction* becomes clear. The precarity and foundationlessness which characterizes the shipwrecked Jesuit in Claudel's *The Satin Slipper* is true not just of the religious believer but of everyone. The rabbi and the atheist in Buber's parable can, as it were, say with him "I am fastened to the cross, but the cross on which I hang is not fastened to anything else. It drifts on the sea."[28] As a kind of prior apologetic, Ratzinger anticipates a discussion of God's personal entry into history by showing the unavoidable existential predicament in which we are all placed. Buber's

---

23. Ratzinger, *God's Word*, 52.
24. Aquinas, *Summa Theologica*, II-II.4.1, c.
25. Aquinas, *Treatise on Faith*, 4.1.
26. Ratzinger, *Introduction*, 80.
27. Rolheiser, "Where Faith Resides."
28. Ratzinger, *Introduction*, 43–44, citing Paul Claudel's *Le Souleir de Satin*, act I, scene I.

"perhaps" lingers over all, and the question with which we are faced is not whether to trust but only whom.

This truth receives its strongest formulation in the "Prolegomena to the Subject of God."[29] There are many to whom we can entrust ourselves, and so the pressing question of our existence would seem to be answerable in many ways. Ratzinger tells us otherwise.

> Where man experiences his solitariness, he experiences at the same time how much his whole existence is a cry for the "You" and how ill-adapted he is to be only an "I" in himself. This loneliness can become apparent to man on various levels. To start with, it can be comforted by a human "You." But then there is the paradox that, as Claudel says, every "You" found by man finally turns out to be an unfulfilled and unfulfillable promise; that every "You" is at bottom another disappointment and there comes a point where no encounter can surmount the final loneliness: the very process of finding and of having found thus becomes a pointed back to the loneliness, a call to the absolute "You" that really descends into the depths of one's own "I."[30]

Indeed, the loved-other disappoints in the end precisely in the measure that they love well. Natural love gives rise to a love which it itself cannot satisfy. *Solo Dios basta*, Theresa of Avila said—"God alone suffices." And so only the only the act of faith to which revelation gives rise can open onto a relation that does not disappoint but that instead grants the rest for which every heart longs. But which components of the Biblical witness make this personal encounter possible and effective? In what principal way does God present himself in Scripture, and how does Ratzinger "introduce" that presentation so that the encounter becomes possible for the audience of the *Introduction*?

Ratzinger turns first to the *Shema* of Deut 6:4. "Hear, O Israel, Yahweh, thy God, is an only God."[31] In the context of Deuteronomy, this command follows closely the recitation of Israel's history in chapters one to four. It bears a close resemblance to the words of Moses as he recalls the covenant and its commands: "Hear, O Israel, the statutes and the ordinances which I speak in your hearing this day, and you shall learn them and be careful to do them" (Deut 5:1). The events at Horeb enter the life of Israel as both revelation and law, as the manifestation of the divine presence and the giving of a burden that is not really a burden but the gift of a life. The *Shema*, spoken at

---

29. Ratzinger, *Introduction*, 103–15.
30. Ratzinger, *Introduction*, 106.
31. Ratzinger, *Introduction*, 110.

the end of the Exodus in Beth Peor, recalls this original revelation and functions, in the mouth of Israel, as a commitment to the burden that that presence imposes. "In its original sense," Ratzinger explains, this profession is "a renunciation of the surrounding gods. It is a profession in the fullest sense of the word, that is, it is not the registration of one view alongside others but an existential decision."[32] In the recitation of this prayer, Israel refuses not only the cults of surrounding people, but so also anything that would govern man's existence and so take to itself a divinity it does not possess. The prayer acknowledges as a "disappointment" the "worship of bread, the worship of love, and the idolization of power."[33]

Within the *Shema* this rejection lies hidden. "The No can only exist by virtue of the Yes,"[34] and it is not the refusal of other gods but the acceptance of Yahweh that constitutes the heart of these verses—"The Lord is our God, the Lord alone." But to whom is it that Israel entrusts themselves with these words? Deuteronomy offers a narrative reply, and the whole of what Moses narrates in the opening chapters is gathered together in the title *Elohenu*, our God. The Lord is, as Ratzinger explains, a *numen personale*. "He is not the god of a place but the god of men. . . . God is seen on the plane of I and You."[35] God reveals himself in his being for a certain people, and in providing them the means by which they might "be holy for the LORD your God is holy" (Lev 19:2).

Rather than develop this idea from the texts of Deuteronomy which surround the *Shema*, Ratzinger points us to the theophany of the Burning Bush at Horeb. It is here, on the cusp on the events that lead the Exodus from Egypt, that God reveals his name. By first addressing himself to Moses with the words "I am the God of your father, the God of Abraham, the God of Isaac, and the God of Jacob" (Exod 3:6), God anchors his name is Israel's past. He is *Elohenu* here as well—our God. The declaration that "this is my name for ever, and thus I am to be remembered throughout all generations" (Exod 3:15) likewise extends the meaning of this name to encompass all that God will yet do for Israel. The name is thus inseparable from the whole history to which it gives rise. It is not a concept—not something that "tries to perceive the nature of a thing as it is in itself."[36] It is rather, a name. It announces and makes possible God's relatedness with Israel. Spoken with the ongoing history of Israel and given so as to carry that history forward, the name "'I Am'

---

32. Ratzinger, *Introduction*, 111.
33. Ratzinger, *Introduction*, 111.
34. Ratzinger, *Introduction*, 114.
35. Ratzinger, *Introduction*, 123.
36. Ratzinger, *Introduction*, 134.

is thus rightly understood as "'I am here'; 'I am here for you.'" As Ratzinger goes on to explain, "God's presence for Israel is emphasized; his Being is expounded, not as Being itself, but as Being-for."[37] Parsed into the categories used above, we can say that God comes to Israel as the subject who authors revelation. What he reveals is himself. And in so doing, he draws Israel—the recipient of this revelation—into a relation by which they might come to resemble the One in whose image they were created.

This emphasis on the personal character of revelation that Ratzinger draws from Scripture is refined in his discussion the Septuagint. In that translation, the first mention of God's name—"I am who I am" (אהיה רש אהיה א, Ex 3:14)—is rendered as "I am he who is" (Ἐγώ εἰμι ὁ ὤν). This seems to render the truth of revelation in terms drawn from philosophy, and Ratzinger raises the possibility that this equivalence eviscerates the very essence of revelation. Paraphrasing Emil Brunner's critique, he writes that the "insertion of an 'equals' sign between the God of faith and the God of the philosophers means turning the biblical idea of God into it's opposite. The name, Brunner says, is here replaced by the concept, and the not-to-be-defined is replaced by a definition."[38]

At first, it would seem that Ratzinger's rejection of *De fontibus* and of the conviction that revelation is propositional places him squarely on the side of Brunner. It does not. For the latter, there is an incommensurability between metaphysics and revelation. For Ratzinger, in contrast, the descent of God into the flesh shows that the whole of what is proper to man can be taken up and perfected in grace. This includes the intellect. While there is a distinction to be drawn between revelation and its explication in theology-*cum*-philosophy, this differentiation is only notional. Like the Incarnation, the whole of revelation appears always in and through what is properly human. One can no more reject philosophy in the reception of revelation than they can reject language. There is every reason, then, to begin with an "insertion of an 'equals' sign between the God of faith and the God of the philosophers." Ratzinger's intervention at the Council in favor of a more personal understanding of revelation rejects nothing of the intellectual character of the position found in *De fontibus*; it rejects the undue restriction it places on the object and receiving subject of revelation. "The purpose of this dialogue between God and the human person is," Rowland observes, "not so much the transmission of information but rather the transformation of the person in the life of the Trinity. For Ratzinger, this is not a matter of removing the intellectual component of faith but understanding it as a component in a

---

37. Ratzinger, *Introduction*, 129.
38. Ratzinger, *Introduction*, 120.

wider whole."³⁹ From the witness of Scripture, Ratzinger insists rather it is to the whole person that God directs himself and that it is the whole person which must receive God's revelation. This, precisely, is what it means to speak of revelation as personal. And it is such an encounter as this that Ratzinger works to facilitate for the readers of the *Introduction*.

The discussion of the Septuagint has a second benefit as well. The rendering of God's name as "I am he who is" augments the mystery of the One who here reveals himself. The translation does not alter the narrative's portrayal of this revelation as in fact the revelation of a name: τοῦτό μού ἐστιν ὄνομα αἰώνιον, "This is my name forever" (Exod 3:15 LXX). The translation with which Brunner took issue does not destroy the person, relational character of the divine name. It shows all the more completely the "I" who says of himself "'I am here'; 'I am here for you.'" It serves to draw the whole of existence into this personal relationship between God and Israel. Belief in God acknowledges "the *logos*—that is, the idea, freedom, love—stands not merely at the end but also at the beginning, that it is the originating and encompassing power of all being."⁴⁰ And it prepares the reader for the full import of the Incarnation—of the *Logos* made flesh—wherein "Gods presence for Israel" extends to the whole of humanity and so speaks to that "disappointment" and longing which is proper to all. In him, writes Ratzinger, "The name is no longer a word, but a person: Jesus himself." He is himself "the real proximity of God coming to meet us, God's mediation to us."⁴¹ His treatment of the *Shema* and the Burning Bush are, in the course of the *Introduction* what they are in the course of the history, preparations for an encounter with "Emmanuel," God with us. Under Ratzinger's guidance, the texts of Scripture become the site of a personal encounter and move the audience towards the confession of faith around which the whole of the *Introduction* takes shape: "I believe in you."

Bibliography

Aquinas, Thomas. *St. Thomas Aquinas: Summa Theologica, Vol. I–V*. Translated by the Fathers of the English Dominican Province. Notre Dame: Ave Maria Press, 1948.
Benedict XVI, *Deus Caritas Est*. Washington, DC: United States Conference of Catholic Bishops, 2006.
Catechism of the Catholic Church. London: Bloomsbury Continuum, 2019.
Dei Verbum §2. In *The Documents of Vatican II*. Grand Rapids: Eerdmans, 1988.

39. Rowland, *Ratzinger's Faith*, 51.
40. Ratzinger, *Introduction*, 152.
41. Ratzinger, *Introduction*, 163.

Evans, Shaun. Working translation of the speeches given in response to *De fontibus* during General Congregation XIX on November 14, 1962.
Gaál, Emery de. *The Theology of Pope Benedict XVI: The Christocentric Shift*. New York: Palgrave MacMillan, 2010.
John XXIII, "Opening Address to the Council." In *The Encyclicals and Other Messages of John XXIII*, 423–35. Washington, DC: TPS, 1964.
Ratzinger, Joseph. "Dogmatic Constitution on Divine Revelation." In *Commentary on the Documents of Vatican II*, Vol. III. Edited by Herbert Vorgimler. New York: Herder & Herder, 1968
Ratzinger, Joseph. *God's Word: Scripture—Tradition—Office*. San Francisco: Ignatius, 2008.
———. *Introduction to Christianity*. San Francisco: Ignatius, 2004.
Rolheiser, Ron. "Where Faith Resides." https://ronrolheiser.com/where-faith-resides/#.XhDrX9ZKgWo. May 5, 2002.
Rowland, Tracey. *Ratzinger's Faith: The Theology of Pope Benedict XVI*. Oxford: Oxford University Press, 2009.

III. Philosophical Theology

8

Nein und doch

Ratzinger's Philosophy of Renunciation in an Augustinian Key

DONALD WALLENFANG, OCDS

TWENTIETH-CENTURY AMERICAN DISCALCED CARMELITE, Jessica Powers, begins her mystical poem entitled "The Vision" with these revelatory words:

> He said: write down the vision that you had,
> and I wrote what I saw.
>
> I saw the world kissing its own darkness.
>
> It happened thus: I rose to meet the sunrise
> and suddenly over the hill a horde appeared
> dragging a huge tarpaulin.
> They covered unwary land and hapless city
> and all sweet water and fields.
> And there was no sunrise.
>
> I strained my eyes for a path and there was no path.
> I bumped into trees and the bushes hissed at me,
> and the long-armed brambles cried in a strident voice:
> never through here!
> But I struggled on, fumbling my beads of no.[1]

Joseph Ratzinger, likewise, is to be found "fumbling (his) beads of no" among his theological works and, in an emblematic way, within his *Introduction to Christianity*. For this short essay, I was tasked with giving a summary of Ratzinger's use of philosophy throughout his *Introduction to Christianity*, and so I hazard to describe his philosophy as one of renunciation. In fact,

---

1. Powers, *Selected Poetry of Jessica Powers*, 2.

we observe a deflection of the very question of Ratzinger's use of philosophy per se inasmuch as his work resists any facile identification with one or more trending schools of philosophy, be they ancient, medieval, or modern. He is unconcerned with aligning himself according to contrived categories of philosophical allegiance, whether they begin with the prefix neo– or end with the suffix –ism. Nevertheless, I would like to investigate the covert yet clear lineage of Ratzinger's thought at the risk of imposing on him a category not of his own making. I hope to avoid the temptation toward postliberal narrative theology that Francesca Aran Murphy rightly critiques when she writes that "positive and negative descriptions of Joseph Ratzinger's thought explore his 'Augustinian' methodology, rather than what he has to say about God and human beings."[2] Instead, in order to pierce into the heart of Ratzinger's theological anthropology, this brief investigation will include three related steps: (1) I will relate Ratzinger's philosophy of renunciation to the rite of Christian baptism, (2) I will apply my concept of the logic of the double negative to Ratzinger's personalist Christology, and (3) I will suggest a new rapprochement in contemporary theology between *nouvelle théologie*, phenomenology, and Thomistic metaphysics.

I. The Renunciation of Renunciation

Christian initiation, inaugurated through the sacrament of baptism, begins not with an affirmation, but with a renunciation. As expressed through a triad of questions put to the initiate and ecclesial community, the liturgical rite of baptism crescendos with sober decisiveness beside the sacred waters: "Widersagt ihr dem Satan? Und all seiner Bosheit? Und all seinen Verlockungen?" "Do you renounce Satan? And all his wickedness? And all his temptations?" Or in the alternative form of the rite: "Do you reject sin so as to live in the freedom of God's children? Do you reject the glamor of evil, and refuse to be mastered by sin? Do you reject Satan, father of sin and prince of darkness?" Christian conversion begins with a renunciation: "Ich widersage," "I refuse," "I renounce." Prior to the *credo* comes the *abrenuntio*. Because human conception is accompanied by the contraction of original sin, to overcome the aboriginal inertia of postlapsarian bondage requires renouncing it. Redemption is ignited by a voluntary renunciation of renunciation. This baptismal renunciation of original sin—and sin *generaliter*—occurs as a leitmotif throughout Ratzinger's *Introduction to Christianity*. The Apostles' Creed, upon which the entire text is based, originates as a baptismal *symbolum* of faith. Ratzinger underscores the threefold renunciation

2. Murphy, *God Is Not a Story*, 5.

that clears a confessional space for the threefold assent to belief in the NAME of the triune God. According to Leonard DeLorenzo, "Ratzinger claims that Baptism itself means being opened up to the communication of love that is God's *communio*, as elsewhere he envisions Christ's creating this space when he stretches out on the cross."³ The movement from renunciation (*Absage*) to assent (*Sage*) is defined precisely as a turn (*Wende/Kehre*) of one's being in the act of conversion (*Bekehrung*).⁴

Further, Ratzinger describes belief as "an adventurous break [*Bruch*] or leap [*Sprung*] . . . because in every age it represents the risky enterprise of accepting what plainly cannot be seen as the truly real and fundamental."⁵ In Platonic, Augustinian, and Bonaventurian fashion, Ratzinger illuminates Christian faith as a "transcendent vector," in the words of Cyril O'Regan.⁶ Overcoming the temptation of what Balthasar and de Lubac have called "the immanentization of transcendence," as well as what Patrick Gardner observes as modern Joachimism with its "monastic utopia and chiliastic eschatology," Ratzinger insists on the other-worldliness of the kingdom of God that is ushered in to the creaturely domain not without the transfiguring waters of baptism and all the renunciations these entail.⁷

So what do these preliminary remarks have to do with the peculiar brand of philosophy in force for Ratzinger? Everything, inasmuch as "the figure of Christ himself (is) the perfect philosopher" and "Christianity itself is true philosophy."⁸ In other words, for Ratzinger, there is no philosophy worthy of the name apart from the waters of baptism and initiation into the mystical Body of Christ. Again, as O'Regan observes of Ratzinger: "separate from each other, faith and reason become pathologies."⁹ Or, as Tracey

3. DeLorenzo, *Work of Love*, 286–87, endnote 97.

4. See Ratzinger, *Introduction*, 87–88.

5. Ratzinger, *Introduction*, 52.

6. See O'Regan, "Benedict the Augustinian," 30.

7. O'Regan, "Benedict the Augustinian," 53, endnote 19, and Gardner, *Modern Pentecost*, 236, footnote 677.

8. Ratzinger, *Pope John Paul II Lecture Series, 1985*, 10; Ratzinger, *The Nature and Mission of Theology*, 28. Cf. Ratzinger, *Principles of Catholic Theology*, 327, where he describes theology as "a rationality that remains within faith itself and that develops the appropriate context of faith"; and Ratzinger, *Church, Ecumenism, and Politics*, 149.

9. O'Regan, "Benedict the Augustinian," 39, and further: "Faith not inflected by reason degenerates into fanaticism, and reason, reduced to being instrumental, loses all contact with the depth of reality and mystery which might cull its promethean pretensions. On their own, faith and reason become sicknesses." Cf. Ratzinger, *Faith, Truth, and Culture*, 29: "Wherever philosophy eliminates totally this dialogue with the thought of faith, it ends up—as formulated once by Jaspers—in a 'seriousness that goes on emptying itself'"; Ratzinger, *The Dialectics of Secularization*, 77–80; and Allen, *Cardinal Ratzinger*, 86.

Rowland puts it in a historical tenor, "Ratzinger thus rejects all philosophies of history which would find in the historical process some dynamic outside the theo-drama of God's offer of grace and the human response to this offer."[10] Altogether, for Ratzinger, theology and philosophy are inseparable by virtue of their common font in the pre-existent *Logos* who is Jesus Christ, the Incarnate Word of God the Father, spoken simultaneously with the exhaled Breath of God the Holy Spirit. He avoids both integralism and extrinsicism by rejecting the false dichotomy between nature and grace, all the while acknowledging the prevenience, advenience and supervenience of grace.[11] Similar to his contemporary, Henri de Lubac, who, as Rudolf Voderholzer observantly notes, rejected the notion of *natura pura*, "that is, a man who could find his perfection in something other than God," Ratzinger, too, resists any neo-Pelagian tendencies toward moral self-sufficiency and self-perfection.[12] Thomas Rausch goes as far as describing Ratzinger "to be much more like Jean Calvin and the Reformers than like Thomas Aquinas and his modern commentators . . . like Luther, he emphasizes a *theologia crucis*, a theology of the cross that stresses the priority of grace over human achievement, philosophical reasoning, or ecclesial power."[13] Since reason has been compromised and tainted through original sin and its just deserts, an *Aufklärung* of the Kantian *Aufklärung* must be accomplished by a sacramental illuminationist epistemology. This is the very inversion of Gnosticism in which the word philosophy does not occur.[14] Yet, as Richard Schenk notes with reference to Erich Przywara's *Analogia Entis*, "the theological stands to the philosophical in the relationship of the '*excedere*,' breaking it open, by being beyond it and leaving it behind emptied. For the same reason, theology perfects philosophy, thoroughly brings it to an end and

---

10. Rowland, *Ratzinger's Faith*, 108.
11. See Rowland, *Culture and the Thomist Tradition*, 28–29.
12. Voderholzer, *Meet Henri de Lubac*, 129.
13. Rausch, *Pope Benedict XVI*, 49–50; cf. 62–63: "[Ratzinger's] own thought, often described as neo-Augustinian, has more in common with Augustine and the Reformers, especially with Luther and his *theologia crucis*, than with Aquinas or modern interpreters such as Karl Rahner and Bernard Lonergan."
14. See Ratzinger, *Pope John Paul II Lecture Series, 1985*, 13: "The Gnostics avoided the use of the word, philosophy . . . faith defends both the greatness and the humility of philosophy . . . faith does not threaten philosophy, but defends it against the pervasive threat of gnosticism"; and Ratzinger, *The Nature and Mission of Theology*, 28–29: "Gnosis turns out to be the negation of philosophy, whereas faith defends both the grandeur and misery of philosophy . . . faith does not menace philosophy but rather defends it against the total claim of gnosis . . . Faith does not destroy philosophy, it champions it. Only when it takes up the cause of philosophy does it remain true to itself."

completion."[15] Theology empties philosophy in order that philosophy not be empty; philosophy fills theology in order that theology not be engorged within a self-insular dogmatic slumber.

It is well known that Ratzinger is not a card-carrying member of the neo-Thomist school. As Tracey Rowland has noted, "the young Bavarian seminarian Joseph Ratzinger found scholasticism to be too impersonal. According to Alfred Läpple, his seminary prefect, scholasticism 'wasn't his beer.'"[16] Likewise it is well known that the genealogy of Ratzinger's distinct form of *nouvelle théologie* runs from Plato through Augustine and Bonaventure, and he certainly does not subscribe to "neo-scholasticism of the strict observance."[17] He is entirely reluctant to capitulate according to the modern and postmodern philosophical trends of methodological atheism or theological indifference that would delineate between philosophy on one hand and theology on the other. Cyril O'Regan reminds us that

> without any animus toward academic theology, and adamant about the positive relation between reason and faith, [Ratzinger] is persuaded that theology goes astray if it becomes reductively apologetic and reduces itself to being the handmaid of other disciplines, whether sociology, political theory, or philosophy . . . his intent is to question the modern penchant in theology for originality, which often issues in an apologetic style theology that tries too hard to please secular disciplines that have come to enjoy authority.[18]

In a similar vein, Aidan Nichols recognizes that, for Ratzinger, "though Scholastic theology, and its various subsequent offshoots, whether speculative, systematic or academic in the modern fashion, has its own value and merits our respect, the attention of the one who theologises is ultimately directed not here but to the eschatological divine peace which passes all understanding."[19] Reminiscent of the baptismal renunciation of all that is not within the reign of Christ and the logic of the cross, Ratzinger

---

15. Schenk, "Analogy as the *discrimen naturae et gratiae*," 177–78. Cf. Nichols, *The Thought of Pope Benedict XVI*, 198–99: "Ratzinger believes that the sharp distinction between philosophy and theology, as respectively the tasks of natural reason and supernaturalised understanding, presses the classic Thomist texts beyond what they can, or should, bear . . . Theology too, it seems, must defend itself against the *a priori* of philosophical knowledge, something which menaces the integrity, and novelty, of faith."

16. Rowland, *Benedict XVI*, 4. Cf. 95: "Those [Ratzinger] regarded as mentors or intellectual heroes were all non-scholastics."

17. See Rowland "Neo-Scholasticism of the Strict Observance."

18. O'Regan, "Benedict the Augustinian," 26, 29.

19. Nichols, *The Thought of Pope Benedict XVI*, 43.

renounces any attempt to sever philosophy from theology insofar as the God of faith is the God of the philosophers.[20] Above all, Christian theology is oriented according to its soteriological impulse that is to be consummated not in the here and now, but in an eschatological rendezvous of *communio* redeemed. Anthony Pagliarini, reflecting on the meaning of the novelty of carnivorous diet introduced in the context of the Noahic covenant following the flood, expresses this sign pointing to consummate redemption as "a refiguring (of) violence in the service of communion."[21] Eating the flesh of animals intimates at once the paschal mystery of death–resurrection and the fortification of personal communion in and through sacrifice shared. For the logic of love: if nothing is lost, then nothing is gained.[22] As sacrament, baptism, along with Eucharist and the other sacramental rites, signifies the in-breaking of this eschatological *communio*, but does not actualize its complete reality.[23] The Christian lives in the dialectical meantime between the always-already and the not-yet. Now that the liturgical and sacramental ethos of Ratzinger's philosophical theology has been established, let us consider the meaning of our title, *Nein und doch*.

II. *Nein und doch*: The Logic of the Double Negative

Nein. No. *Und doch* . . . And yet . . . And yes. John Allen recalls that "in his doctoral essay, Ratzinger wrote that Augustine's ideas were worked out in 'polemic against error'" and goes on to suggest that Ratzinger was influenced by Augustine's *City of God* toward "the idea of Christian estrangement from the world . . . The church must not let its members sleep, Ratzinger says. The church must 'raise her index finger and become irksome.'"[24] In his *Introduction to Christianity*, starting with a fierce confrontation with Marxist ideology, this is precisely the gesture of Ratzinger from the word go: *Nein!* Yet again, with reference to the rite of baptism, a renunciation of renunciation results in affirmation of divine goodness and the universal Christian vocation to love and responsibility, one-for-the-other.

20. See Ratzinger, *Introduction*, 137–50.
21. Pagliarini, "Ordering All Things Well," 569.
22. See Marion, *Erotic Phenomenon*, 67–97.
23. See Ratzinger's discussion of the relationship between shadow, image, and reality in his *Spirit of the Liturgy*, 53–61.
24. Allen, *Cardinal Ratzinger*, 36. Further Allen muses on Ratzinger's eventual assignment as Prefect for the Congregation for the Doctrine of the Faith: "As the saying goes, if all you have is a hammer, sooner or later everything looks like a nail" (86). Cf. Aidan Nichols's assessment of the role of Augustine in Ratzinger's theology in Nichols, *The Thought of Pope Benedict XVI*, 17–33.

Altogether, Étienne Gilson calls the Augustinian existential-intellectual approach to faith taken up by Ratzinger a "philosophy of conversion," a "metaphysics of inner experience," or a "metaphysics of conversion."[25] Moreover, Aaron Pidel writes of Ratzinger's "neo-Bonaventurian model of inspiration (that) reveals on every page the watermark of his theological vision—creative fidelity," while Joseph Lam asserts that "this correlation of philosophical inquiry and theological answer is the very core of [Ratzinger's] concept of *personalism*, which places emphasis on the *performative* dimension of the truth. Thus, philosophy as a form of critical inquiry does not exhaust itself in theoretical knowledge. For [Ratzinger], a philosophy is true only if it provides insights into the authenticity of life."[26] Centered on divine revelation, Ratzinger's creative fidelity to the fullness of this revelation in Christ is expressed as a performative personalism of truth. Become Pope Benedict XVI, he later would write in his first encyclical, *Deus caritas est*, that "being a Christian is not the result of an ethical choice or a lofty idea, but the encounter with an event, a person, which gives life a new horizon and a decisive direction."[27] Truth is performed to the measure that it is personalized, that is, truth taking on flesh through a living human nature, or, to be more precise, through the Word made flesh. God's yes to humanity is at once God's no to anything and everything dehumanizing. In his *Introduction to Christianity* we read a litany of *Nein*:

- No to "the Marxist doctrine of salvation."[28]
- No to secular apocalyptic and immanent political eschatology.[29]
- No to liberation theologies in which "God (has) nothing to do."[30]
- No to an apodictic certainty for faith.[31]

---

25. See Lam, "'We Proclaim the Crucified Christ,'" 422.

26. Pidel, "*Christi Opera Proficiunt*," 711; and Lamb, "'We Proclaim the Crucified Christ,'" 420–21.

27. Benedict XVI, *Deus caritas est*, §1.

28. Ratzinger, *Introduction*, 11.

29. See Ratzinger, *Introduction*, 14–15, 108. Ratzinger says no especially to a Marxist philosophy that "adopts a practical program" as "a 'praxis,' which does not presuppose a 'truth' but rather creates one," and to the coronation of "the primacy of politics and economics, which now become the real powers that can bring about salvation." Cf. Ratzinger, *Values in a Time of Upheaval*, 16–18.

30. Ratzinger, *Introduction*, 16.

31. See Ratzinger, *Introduction*, 46–47, 64.

III. PHILOSOPHICAL THEOLOGY

- No to the notion of "progress" (*Fortschrittes*) confined to a materialist concept alone.[32]
- No to scientism and phenomenalism.[33]
- No to the Cartesian reduction of truth to fact.[34]
- No to technocracy.[35]
- No to historicism.[36]
- No to the Hegelian reduction of Christian doctrines to their pure philosophical senses.[37]
- No to hyper-Aristotelianism and "mere metaphysics."[38]
- No to the primacy of *bios*.[39]
- No to the Kantian "religion within the bounds of pure reason."[40]
- No to the rift between ontological and functional Christology.[41]

And finally, as Anthony Sciglitano recollects, Ratzinger issues a no to "Prometheanism," which "most often indicates rebellion against a personal, transcendent divinity for the good of humankind such that humanity replaces the divine as the center and meaning of value."[42] Once again, through the renunciation of renunciation, the plentitude shines forth in the *doch*, in the yet, in the nevertheless, in the yes. We find a litany of *doch* that runs alongside the litany of *Nein*:

- Yes to the "uniqueness of persons."[43]
- Yes to the primacy of the *Logos*.[44]

---

32. See Ratzinger, *Introduction*, 17, 53.
33. See Ratzinger, *Introduction*, 58, 74, 195, 228.
34. See Ratzinger, *Introduction*, 59, 61, 74, 246. Cf. Ratzinger, *Biblical Interpretation in Crisis*, 6, 15.
35. See Ratzinger, *Introduction*, 60, 64–67, including the takeover of cybernetics.
36. See Ratzinger, *Introduction*, 62.
37. See Ratzinger, *Introduction*, 169.
38. See Ratzinger, *Introduction*, 174, 242.
39. See Ratzinger, *Introduction*, 304–7, 313, 314, 358.
40. Ratzinger, *Introduction*, 310.
41. See Ratzinger, *Introduction*, 332.
42. Sciglitano, "Prometheus and Kant," 387.
43. Ratzinger, *Introduction*, 24.
44. See Ratzinger, *Introduction*, 26, 151, 158, 194.

- Yes to belief that pushes against doubt.[45]
- Yes to the meaning of the universal human vocation as being-for the other.[46]
- Yes to the Christian refusal of the no.[47]
- Yes to the fundamental meaning of the world as "the 'you' . . . an indestructible love . . . 'Jesus of Nazareth.'"[48]
- Yes to "the Christian attitude, in which philosophical and religious orientation become identical."[49]
- Yes to the "struggle for God" (*Kampf um Gott*)—the "dramatic wrestling" (*dramatische Ringen*) of the Church that "lives from the gift of God, without which it could not exist."[50]
- Yes to ontology.[51]
- Yes to the law of excess or superfluity.[52]
- Yes to the primacy of spirit (*Geist*), mind, and meaning (*Sinn*).[53]
- "Yes to God" (*Ya zu Gott*).[54]

---

45. See Ratzinger, *Introduction*, 46–47.

46. See Ratzinger, *Introduction*, 27, 127–29, 183, 186, 251–54.

47. See Ratzinger, *Introduction*, 51, 87–88, 96, 98, on the concept of "turning back" (*Umkehr*) and "con-version" (*Be-kehrung*); 111–14, 127–29, 138, 151, on "the Christian refusal" (*Nein*), renouncing the gods of polytheism, and how Christian belief is "always a process of separation, of acceptance, of purification, and of transformation" (151); 168, 171–72, on the renunciation (*Verzicht*) of knowing the doctrine of the triune God with perfect epistemological certainty; 195, on the a renunciation of the "renunciation of truth" as exerted by positivism; 293: "The truth of man is his complete lack of truth"; 335, on Christianity as "the about-turn" (*Wende*) into real humanity"; 341: "So the paradoxical figure of the Church, in which the divine so often presents itself in such unworthy hands, in which the divine is only ever present in the form of a 'nevertheless' (*Dennoch*), is to the faithful the sign of the 'nevertheless' (*Dennoch*) of the ever greater love shown by God." Cf. Ratzinger, *Principles of Catholic Theology*, 37–38, 55–67, on the concept of sacramental *metanoia*; Boeve and Mannion, *The Ratzinger Reader*, 53.

48. Ratzinger, *Introduction*, 81. Cf. Ratzinger's concept of "Christological physiognomy" in *Introduction*, 85.

49. Ratzinger, *Introduction*, 109; cf. 91–93, 107, 268–69.

50. Ratzinger, *Introduction*, 110, 165, 167, 211, 344.

51. See Ratzinger, *Introduction*, 119.

52. See Ratzinger, *Introduction*, 257–62. Cf. Jean-Luc Marion's concept of the saturated phenomenon in *Being Given*, 199–247; Wallenfang, *Dialectical Anatomy of the Eucharist*, 51–61.

53. See Ratzinger, *Introduction*, 321–22.

54. Ratzinger, *Introduction*, 285–86.

Within this "Yes to God" is revealed that "the disinterested character of simple adoration is man's highest possibility; it alone forms his true and final liberation."[55] And this simple adoration delivers the full force of objectivity, as John Cavadini makes clear: "we are free to be formed in the love which alone makes us truly objective observers in the world."[56] An increase in disinterested love is at once an increase in epistemological and spiritual objectivity, while at the same time an opening to the highest capacities of divine worship. *Nein und doch.* No and yet. No and yes. This is what I call the logic of the double negative. We move now to our final point for consideration: how *nouvelle théologie*, phenomenology, and Thomistic metaphysics could complement one another for the sake of effective evangelization in a postmodern world.

III. Toward a Trilectic Methodology of Evangelization

One of the most striking historical insights gleaned from studying the theology of Joseph Ratzinger is the pivotal Bonaventure–Aquinas divergence that occurred during the high meridian of scholasticism in the thirteenth century. This historical moment is crucial to follow in order to understand the undulation of various Catholic theological currents that swelled throughout the twentieth century—in particular, the sharp rivalry between neo-Thomism and *nouvelle théologie*. The contentiousness between the two theological movements (even if instigated especially by the neo-Thomists) would ferment up until the time of the Second Vatican Council, with several of the *nouvelle théologiens* vindicated through their appointment by Pope John XXIII as *periti* for the council, and in turn witnessing their welcome influence on the conciliar doctrines and reforms.[57] In the most general terms, the primary difference between neo-Thomism and *nouvelle théologie* stems from a distinction of genealogy. The former runs from Aristotle to Thomas Aquinas, while the latter runs from Plato to Augustine to Bonaventure.

---

55. Ratzinger, *Introduction*, 288.

56. Cavadini, "The Anatomy of Wonder," 166.

57. Among the notable *periti* of Vatican II, some invited directly by Pope John XXIII include Karl Rahner, Yves Congar, Jean Daniélou, Marie-Dominique Chenu, Louis Bouyer, Hans Küng, Joseph Ratzinger, Gregory Baum, John Courtney Murray, Bernard Häring, and Henri de Lubac. Another notable *peritus*, perhaps the leading proponent of neo-Thomism and staunchest opponent against *nouvelle théologie*, is Reginald Garrigou-Lagrange, who served as a *peritus* for Cardinal Ottaviani. For further studies on the confrontation between Thomism and *nouvelle théologie*, see the *Josephinum Journal of Theology* 18:1 (2011) volume entitled "Thomism and the *Nouvelle Théologie*."

In his essay entitled, "The Notion of Christian Philosophy," Étienne Gilson writes that "both St. Thomas's philosophy and St. Augustine's philosophy are philosophies of the concrete, but their attitude toward the concrete is not the same. St. Augustine always seeks notions comprehensive enough to embrace the concrete in its complexity. Thomas always seeks notions precise enough to define the elements that constitute the concrete. In a word, the former *expresses* the concrete, the latter *analyses* it."[58] Gilson's telling observation is corroborated by Ratzinger's habilitation, *The Theology of History in St. Bonaventure*. In this illuminating work, Ratzinger juxtaposes Bonaventurian historical theology on the one hand with Thomistic ahistorical philosophical theology on the other. He speaks of the modern controversy of Bonaventure's anti-Aristotelianism that would crystallize as a Bonaventurian Augustinianism that sets itself "against the attempt to make philosophy independent [from theology]" and "reject[s] the Thomistic separation of philosophy and theology which had been worked out from an Aristotelian background."[59] Ratzinger contends that Bonaventure's "rejection of Aristotle is not primarily metaphysical or epistemological; rather, it involves first and foremost the question of the theology of history."[60] Revealed in works such as the *Itinerarium*, the *Breviloquium*, and *De reductione artium ad theologiam*, Bonaventure understands history and knowledge immediately in terms of their theological content according to the Augustinian concept of illuminationist epistemology. Any so-called "natural" meanings—whether physics, mathematics or metaphysics—mean nothing apart from divine revelation. Therefore it is practically impossible to distinguish between philosophy as such apart from theology. Likewise it is un-Christian to think in ahistorical terms that would empty the thought process of the force of divine revelation that is bound up necessarily with history and its gradual unfolding led by divine providence. Ahistorical and autonomous reason is irrational. Gilson observes that "Bonaventure rejected the autonomy of reason including the relative autonomy of Thomistic Aristotelianism. He demanded a philosophy that would be radically Christian, that is, a philosophy centered on Christ and worked out from Christian Revelation . . . the undivided unity of Christian wisdom . . . not simply a Platonic idea."[61] For Bonaventure, unlike Thomas, there is no distinction to be made between preambles of faith (philosophy) and articles of faith (theology). The Angelic Doctor versus the Seraphic Doctor!

58. Gilson, "The Notion of Christian Philosophy," 135.
59. Ratzinger, *Theology of History in St. Bonaventure*, 132–33.
60. Ratzinger, *Theology of History in St. Bonaventure*, 119.
61. Ratzinger, *Theology of History in St. Bonaventure*, 130, 132.

Further, Bonaventure's contrast with Thomistic *sacra scientia* would radicalize even more toward the end of his life, under the influence of his fellow Franciscan, Joachim de Fiore and his historical apocalyptic imagination. Bonaventure became increasingly suspicious of the (Thomistic) movement *en vogue* to extract philosophy from theology, as well as the emerging concept of natural theology that begins with hylomorphic sensible knowledge (Aristotle) instead of eidetic abstraction from matter (Plato) that would begin and end with divine revelation rather than meet up with it midstream. Bonaventure's eschatological consciousness was heightened, asserting that redeemed history was now at hand and that one must resist "the Church's capitulation to the spirit of the anti-Christ."[62] One of the false doctrines affiliated with the (Thomistic) philosophers—"the sign of the Beast!"—was the doctrine of the eternal circle of secondary causes.[63]

62. Ratzinger, *Theology of History in St. Bonaventure*, 115. This sentiment aligns well with Karl Barth's *Nein* to natural theology as the alleged product of the anti-Christ. In addition, a twentieth-century carry-over of Bonaventure's sentiments that runs through the *nouvelle théologie* movement is Henri de Lubac's counterpoint to the classic Thomistic nature–grace distinction. For de Lubac, nature is always a graced nature inasmuch as it is imbued with divine power, creativity, meaning, and love. See de Lubac, *Augustinianism and Modern Theology*. Several dialectical undercurrents keep such theological discussions ever in motion—for example, unity–plurality, same–other, identity–difference, *esse–entia*, individual–communion, and substance–relationality.

63. Ratzinger, *Theology of History in St. Bonaventure*, 147. See Thomas Aquinas, *Summa contra gentiles*, II.32–37; *De aeternitate mundi*. Bonaventure is uncomfortable, to say the least, with Thomas's lingering ambiguity on the question of the eternity of the world and its aggregate series of secondary causes. What is most decisive for Thomas, especially concerning dogmas of faith, is that God is pure act and primary cause of everything that has created being, and that God is not to be confused with any part or even the whole of creation. In other words, the eternity of the universe—as a concept—does not in and of itself annul the concept of divinity that, by definition, transcends even the concept of eternity, temporal or otherwise. Likewise, it is important to note the local synodal and episcopal condemnations of 1210, 1270, and 1277: (1) the Condemnation of 1210 by the Synod of Sens that banned the works of Aristotle and commentaries on them from being read in public or private under pain of excommunication; (2) the Condemnation of 1270 by the archbishop of Paris, Étienne Tempier, that forbade teaching some of the Aristotelian and Averroist doctrines at the University of Paris under pain of excommunication, including thirteen banned propositions; and (3) the Condemnation of 1277, again by Archbishop Tempier, against teaching Peripatetic (Aristotelian) doctrines, 219 propositions in all, including fifteen associated with the work of Thomas Aquinas. See propositions 42, 43, 50, 52–55, 110, 115, 116, 146, 147, 162, 163, and 169 in relation to the works of Thomas. Eleven days following the Condemnation of 1277, the Dominican archbishop of Canterbury called for a condemnation of these and other Thomistic doctrines as dangerous. Such condemnations were fueled by "the adherents to the older Plato-Augustinian Scholasticism," for example John Peckham as leader of the Franciscan movement against Thomism in favor of the Franciscans, Bonaventure, and Alexander of Hales. However, the Dominican Albert of Cologne came to the defense of Thomas and prevented a landslide of anti-Thomism. See Raphael Comeau's essay, "The Condemnation of St. Thomas," 94.

Bonaventure arduously resisted the perceived hubris in becoming so beholden to metaphysical categories—such as act and potency, cause and effect, being itself and beings—that theology is rationalized to the point of leaving little room for the uncanniness of God's personal acting in history, and the intellectually offensive claims of Christianity that cannot be reduced to pure theoretical logic and its necessary consequences. In his *Hexaemeron*, Bonaventure makes a decidedly anti-philosophical and anti-intellectualist turn.[64] His critique "is directed against a philosophy which fails to recognize its true function; which makes itself self-sufficient and thereby becomes an eschatological sign of perdition."[65] Bonaventure indicates a time in history in which "rational arguments will no longer be of value . . . there will be no more possibility of a pact between reason and faith," and he exhibits "a limited anti-philosophical attitude which ultimately develops into an anti-dialectical and anti-scholastic mentality . . . As the *simplex* and *idiota*, Francis knew more about God than all the learned men of his time—because he loved Him more."[66] Bonaventure goes as far as prophesying the end of rational theology and, with his *Hexaemeron*, "we find the final development of his anti-philosophical attitude which here becomes a prophetic anti-Scholasticism in which Franciscan, Joachimite, and Dionysian themes emerge . . . For the final stage which is to come he predicts a theology based only on authority."[67] Perhaps Bonaventure's strong reaction against the flirtation with rationalism toward which Thomistic natural theology could be inclined becomes, in the end, the opposite extreme of fideism pregnant with the concomitant un-Christian possibility of irrational apocalyptic theology. The perennial temptation for human thought is to trade one fundamentalism for another. Ideology manipulates truth to the point of reducing its incomprehensible totality in the name of comprehensible totality and abandoning it.

In her essay entitled "Augustinian and Thomistic Engagements with the World," Tracey Rowland writes that "both Augustine and Aquinas saw the whole of human history from the perspective of salvation history, in which the achievement of the Hebrews, the Greeks, the Egyptians, and all peoples only find their fulfillment, their completion, in the arrival of Christian Revelation."[68] I wonder if, in a similar way, we can think about

---

64. See Ratzinger, *Theology of History in St. Bonaventure*, 151.

65. Ratzinger, *Theology of History in St. Bonaventure*, 153.

66. Ratzinger, *Theology of History in St. Bonaventure*, 156–57.

67. Ratzinger, *Theology of History in St. Bonaventure*, 158, 160. Cf. O'Regan's notion of "pneumatic eschatology" in "Benedict the Theologian," 33.

68. Rowland, "Augustinian and Thomistic Engagements with the World," 443–44.

the achievement of Ratzinger's theological *oeuvre* in relation to two different theological achievements, namely, that of phenomenology as applied within theology, such as in the work of Jean-Luc Marion, and Thomistic metaphysics as distinct from the Plato-Augustinian school of Bonaventure. What Timothy O'Malley calls "a truthful rhetoric of love" is required to express the Christian gospel in a multitude of tongues.[69] If authentic evangelization is rooted in its "Christic Center" and the need "to recover and expand 'a sense of what the Incarnation can mean,'" as Robert Imbelli proposes, then is it not necessary to communicate this Christic Center through a diverse harmonization of methods?

Even though Walter Kasper refers to Ratzinger's Christology as founded upon "a phenomenology of love, which is stronger than death," Ratzinger seems to shy away from explicit use of phenomenology in his theology, oftentimes distancing himself from what he calls "phenomenalism." He admits not to have read Heidegger much and disowns the label of being an existentialist.[70] Moreover, in his review of Edward Schillebeeckx's 1967 book, *Die eucharistische Gegenwart*, Ratzinger signals that "a mere phenomenological understanding does not suffice, since the ontological level is involved," and shows disdain for Schillebeeckx's "flight from ontology into phenomenology." Further he relates that "the reduction of knowledge to perception seems to me very problematic . . . [in the wake of the telescoping of phenomenology and ontology]," and instead Ratzinger elevates "the special character of ontology as opposed to mere phenomenology."[71] Yet what about the effectiveness of Karl Rahner's, John Paul II's, and Edith Stein's blending of phenomenology and Thomistic metaphysics for commanding an intelligible and meaningful apologetic for Christian faith within a scientifically minded world?

If Clemens Sedmak is right about his claim that "Ratzinger has used remembering as a key to identifying the coordinates of his personal identity," should not contemporary Christian theology and evangelization do the same, remembering that its Catholic identity is a united diversity of theological voices, methods, and questions that, as a symphonic whole, cannot be limited to a few of its attractive parts? Is it possible and even necessary for the *nouvelle théologie* of Ratzinger to join forces with the metaphysical bulwark of Thomism and the erotic perception of Catholic phenomenology so as to serve best the pluralist target audience of

---

69. O'Malley, *Liturgy and the New Evangelization*, 38.

70. See Ratzinger and Seewald, *Last Testament*, 78; Ratzinger, *Milestones*, 136–37.

71. Ratzinger's book review of Edward Schillebeeckx's *Die eucharistische Gegenwart: Zur Diskussion über die Realpräesenz* in Ratzinger, *Collected Works*, Vol. 11, 243–46.

evangelization, "becom[ing] all things to all, to save at least some?"[72] If, along with Saint Peter, we would "always be ready to give an explanation to anyone who asks [us] for a reason for [our] hope," is not Jay Martin correct when he says that this admonition "demands not an answer (ἀπολογίαν) as such but rather a readiness (ἕτοιμοι), a readiness to answer of a heart that sanctifies Christ as God?"[73] In order for this readiness to prevail, need we not be equipped with the dialectical and irenic arms of truth that achieve the victory wherein solicitous listening and empathy speak louder than words? If the ardent embrace of Christ—the *amplexus Christi*, as conveyed so poetically by Catherine Cavadini—is to be met by the would-be initiate into the Catholic faith, must not the faithful evangelist join with Christ in extending this ardent embrace to the other—all the way to the religious other!—even if letting him or herself be embraced by the hospitality of the other? "But perhaps it is true after all?"[74]

IV. Catholicism: Between Relativism and Fundamentalism

Nein und doch. No . . . and yet. This is the Catholic way: a renunciation of renunciation that leads to participation (liturgy); a reductionism of reductionism that leads to fullness (phenomenology); a contradiction of contradiction that leads to paradox (metaphysics). As part of a greater whole concerning the Catholic theological tradition(s), Ratzinger's work showcases the complementarity and harmony that exists between the plurality of traditions within the tradition. As Balthasar puts it, truth is symphonic, and Ratzinger's contribution to an itinerant Catholic theology that dialogues with a wounded modernity serves as a paradigmatic model for the next generations of faithful Catholic theologians. Instead of attempting to accomplish every theological task within his work, Ratzinger stakes out a territory according to a specific and manageable trajectory set behind him. On the opening page of his 1971 book, *Method in Theology*, Bernard Lonergan suggests that method is "a framework for collaborative creativity."[75] In

---

72. 1 Corinthians 9:22b. Cf. Wallenfang, "Pope Francis and His Phenomenology of *Encuentro*."

73. Martin, "'As love, the giver is perfect,'" 184.

74. Ratzinger, *Introduction*, 46.

75. Lonergan, *Method in Theology*, xi. Cf. Tracy, *Blessed Rage for Order*, 249: "That no single theologian can any longer hope to systematize fundamental, historical, systematic, and practical theology is now a truism. The full meaning and force of this truism was recently expressed in Bernard Lonergan's critical and eloquent call for a theological method expressive of the real possibilities for critical collaboration."

Ratzinger's case, he has both immediate and remote collaborators. Immediate: Plato, Augustine, Bonaventure (the Franciscan), and Ratzinger's fellow *nouvelle théologiens*. Remote: Aristotle, Thomas (the Dominican), and neo-Thomism. Perhaps even more remote: Parmenides, Gregory of Nyssa, Dionysius the Areopagite, John of Ruusbroec, John of the Cross (the Discalced Carmelite), and apophatic mysticism. Nevertheless, Ratzinger shows a deep appreciation for his remote collaborators, leaving certain theological tasks not his own to their handiwork. For the tasks within Catholic theology are many and varied, with more specialized expertise required of the theologian after each passing day. Ratzinger teaches us that we must depend on one another, given the diversity of tasks assigned to theology at present and into the future. Correspondingly, Ratzinger imparts a theological wisdom that knows how to steer clear of the two menacing ideological strongholds of our era of religious pluralism: relativism and fundamentalism.

On April 19, 2005, the day before being elected pope, in his "Homily at the Mass for the Election of the Roman Pontiff," Ratzinger spoke of global cultures "moving toward a dictatorship of relativism, which does not recognize anything as certain and which has as its highest goal one's own ego and one's own desires."[76] Relativism is virtually an inevitable worldview within a culture of radical skepticism, pluralism, agnosticism, materialism, secularism and individualism. What else is one to think? Can a believer enmeshed in the postmodern vortex claim a stable creed with meanings that are not subject to the nihilistic threshing floor of *différance* (Derrida)? Can a person make a cogent decision in favor of a particular account of divine revelation when there are so many contenders saying contradictory things in relation to one another? Can someone decide for or against God in good conscience when the very concept of divinity has been drained into so many sparkling idols? Ratzinger realizes that relativism rules the day in a post-totalitarianism world, even if relativism itself maintains a hidden totalitarian grip on the secular masses of people hypnotized by its apathetic head of Medusa. For this reason, Ratzinger takes aim at relativism much more vehemently than fundamentalism. However, here again, other theologians are tasked with addressing the errors of fundamentalism from a centripetal vantage point to prevent extremes from meeting.

In his 1975 book *Blessed Rage for Order: The New Pluralism in Theology*, David Tracy unmasks the opposite extreme of relativism that is just as sinister, namely, fundamentalism. Also referred to by him as supernaturalism, literalism, and religionism, Tracy contends that fundamentalism speaks

---

76. Benedict XVI, *Essential Pope Benedict*, 22. Cf. Oakes "Resolving the Relativity Paradox."

of its domestic religion "with a supernaturalist precision that exposes an unacceptable demand for a *sacrificium intellectus*."[77] This type of fundamentalism also can be called traditionalism, archaism, propositionalism, dogmatism, fideism, moralism (with a built-in Pelagian Stoicism), rigorism, and institutionalism. Of course it has its counterpart of the progressive sort that can be called progressivism, permissivism, liberalism (of the general kind), laxism, charismaticism, and even reformism. In either case, but especially concerning the former (which is more often found in things religious), fundamentalism implies a reductionism of the whole to one or some of its parts. It is a prioritization of the part in relation to the neglected (if not almost entirely eclipsed) whole. Therefore it is a highly un-Catholic phenomenon, since the term Catholic is derived from the Greek word *kata-* ("according to") *holos* ("the whole"), and the Catholic epistemological commitment is to the fullness of both faith and reason, divine revelation and nature.[78] Fundamentalism implies an entrenched ideology—"this knowledge that sacrifices everything to power"—that manipulates the diverse unity of truth according to absolutizing grammars and rhetoric, masking a vindictive and painful will to power.[79] Hurt people hurt people. Marxism, for instance, is

---

77. Tracy, *Blessed Rage for Order*, 135. He continues later: "To state the matter with the bluntness needed, for many of us fundamentalism and supernaturalism of whatever religious tradition are dead and cannot return . . . Fundamentalism of whatever tradition and by whatever criteria of truth one employs seems to me irretrievably false and illusory. Christian fundamentalism cannot and will not withstand the force of truth and the transformative power of self-sacrificing love which its own originating limit-language and its own past and present religious dynamism has set loose in our history."

78. See Vatican I, *Dei Filius*, §4. Cf. *Catechism of the Catholic Church*, §170: "We do not believe in formulas, but in those realities they express, which faith allows us to touch. 'The believer's act [of faith] does not terminate in the propositions, but in the realities [which they express].' All the same, we do approach these realities with the help of formulations of the faith which permit us to express the faith and to hand it on, to celebrate it in community, to assimilate and live on it more and more."

79. Marion, *Erotic Phenomenon*, 2. Cf. Pope Francis, *Evangelii gaudium*, §39: "Just as the organic unity existing among the virtues means that no one of them can be excluded from the Christian ideal, so no truth may be denied. The integrity of the Gospel message must not be deformed. What is more, each truth is better understood when related to the harmonious totality of the Christian message; in this context all of the truths are important and illumine one another. When preaching is faithful to the Gospel, the centrality of certain truths is evident and it becomes clear that Christian morality is not a form of stoicism, or self-denial, or merely a practical philosophy or a catalogue of sins and faults. Before all else, the Gospel invites us to respond to the God of love who saves us, to see God in others and to go forth from ourselves to seek the good of others. Under no circumstance can this invitation be obscured! All of the virtues are at the service of this response of love. If this invitation does not radiate forcefully and attractively, the edifice of the Church's moral teaching risks becoming a house of cards, and this is our greatest risk. It would mean that it is not the Gospel which

not a function of relativism but a totalizing fundamentalism. Tracy goes on to say that "the dilemma of the fundamentalist seems to be that he must domesticate his own religious language and experience (for example, through obscurantism) in order to disallow the demands for truth in that language and experience from erupting into his own secure and tamed world."[80] This secure and tamed world is what Tracy means by a person's blessed rage for order. The more blessed the rage—usually precipitated by acute trauma, tragic experience, mental illness, or some manifestation of the *libido dominandi*—the more fundamentalist the order: As if the Tridentine liturgy is the only way to celebrate the liturgy. As if Thomas Aquinas is the only Doctor of the Church. As if Vatican II never happened or never should have happened. As if John Henry Newman was misguided on his notion of the positive development of doctrine. Yet this blessed rage for order can take other forms as well: As if the Tridentine liturgy has no place in the life of the Church today (even in spite of Benedict XVI's 2007 *Motu proprio, Summorum pontificum*). As if Thomas Aquinas has nothing to say to us today, or only what we want him to say. As if Vatican II superseded all previous ecumenical councils, and we have nothing to learn from them now. As if the development of doctrine implies a hermeneutic of rupture rather than one of continuity with the past. Out of fear or hatred, one's blessed rage for order becomes an ideological fundamentalism that can neither detect its own blind spots nor smell the scent of its own rotten stench.

But Catholicism is different than fundamentalism and relativism, and all because of one little word: and. *Nein und doch*. Catholicism is the –ism that deflects every other –ism precisely by relating them all to the whole that Catholicism is. Catholicism is the –ism that thinks further than itself because it is always growing, expanding, reaching, and reforming according to the old and the new. It is a synthesis of truth inasmuch as it is the antithesis of falsehood. It is a synthesis of truth insofar as it prevents the dialectical alterity of truth from collapsing into an exclusionary monism. This dialectical alterity is demonstrated in metaphysics beginning with the ontological difference between being (*ipsum esse*) and beings (*entia*). It is expressed in phenomenology as the essential difference between the self and all that is not the self, namely, all phenomena that give themselves by themselves to the self who experiences something. And finally, this dialectical alterity of truth is attested in theology through the doctrine of *creatio ex nihilo*: the radical otherness of divinity in relation to creation. *A fortiori*,

---

is being preached, but certain doctrinal or moral points based on specific ideological options. The message will run the risk of losing its freshness and will cease to have 'the fragrance of the Gospel.'"

80. Tracy, *Blessed Rage for Order*, 145, endnote 95.

the dialectical alterity of truth is disclosed as the distinction between the three divine Persons—Father, Son, and Holy Spirit—of whom the singular and unlimited divine Substance is comprised. Both personhood and truth are revealed to the degree that unified dialectical alterity is protected from being reduced. It is the appointed mission of Catholicism to protect against any ideological attempt to reduce the whole to only one or some of its parts, no matter how stellar these individual parts may be. Heresy is exactly the name used to describe any hasty reductionism of whole to part, for a heresy—*hairein*, "to take"—takes from the whole only to forget the whole from which its treasured and idolatrous part was taken. Catholicism worships neither the part (fundamentalism) nor nothing at all (relativism). Catholicism worships the one, true, and living God—Father, Son, and Holy Spirit—revealed in God the Son become flesh, Jesus Christ our Lord—a revelation entrusted to his Church to be encountered in its saturating fullness, without lack or remainder.

The theological corpus of Joseph Ratzinger teaches us much. It shows the fruitful interplay of traditions within the tradition. It displays one of the primary exigencies of the theologian: to expose, unmask, and deconstruct any nearby reductionism, whether in the name of unity (in the case of fundamentalism) or plurality (in the case of relativism). It recalls the importance of history for theology, and summons us to admit that we have forgotten that we have forgotten. It illuminates the logic of the double negative and paradox that is peculiar to Christianity, and how this logic overcomes the legion aporia contained within objections to belief.[81] It reminds us of the indispensable role of philosophy within theology and, at the same time, the temptation to let philosophy and theology drift too far away from each other. It cautions us not to do theology at a distance from liturgy, for liturgy is the lifeblood of sound Catholic theology. It calls us to be mindful of the multilayered contexts in which every theological text is encircled and enmeshed, and that there is no view from nowhere— no purely neutral and non-polemical perch from which to expound the perfect and airtight philosophical and theological system. It draws our attention to the necessity of the old to be read in light of the new, and the new to be read in light of the old. It teaches us to "think in Franciscan" (Augustinian, Bonaventurian), while at the same time pointing to the possibilities of thinking in Dominican, Benedictine, Jesuit, Carmelite, and so many more styles and spiritual traditions that are the Catholic heritage.[82]

---

81. For example, see Ratzinger, *Introduction*, 190: "The most paradoxical approach is at the same time the most illuminating and helpful one."

82. See Falque and Solignac, "Thinking in Franciscan: Part I," 32.

In sum, the theology of Joseph Ratzinger teaches us many things, but, above all, it inspires us to believe against all alleged odds and to become "the man who seeks a view of the whole."[83]

Bibliography

Allen, Jr., John L. *Cardinal Ratzinger: The Vatican's Enforcer of the Faith*. New York: Continuum, 2000.

Ashley, Benedict M. *The Way toward Wisdom: An Interdisciplinary and Intercultural Introduction to Metaphysics*. Notre Dame: University of Notre Dame Press, 2006.

Barrio-Maestre, José María. "Circularidad fe–razón en Joseph Ratzinger/Benedicto XVI." *Pensamiento y Cultura* 16 no. 1 (2013) 167–201.

Benedict XVI. *Called to Holiness: On Love, Vocation and Formation*. Edited by Pietro Rossotti. Washington, DC: Catholic University of America Press, 2017.

———. *Deus caritas est*. December 25, 2005. http://w2.vatican.va/content/benedict-xvi/en/encyclicals/documents/hf_ben-xvi_enc_20051225_deus-caritas-est.html.

———. *The Essential Pope Benedict: His Central Writings and Speeches*. Edited by John F. Thornton and Susan B. Varenne. New York: HarperOne, 2008.

———. *The Garden of God: Toward a Human Ecology*. Edited by Maria Milvia Morciano. Washington, DC: Catholic University of America Press, 2014.

———. *Great Christian Thinkers: From the Early Church through the Middle Ages*. Minneapolis: Fortress, 2011.

———. *Heart of the Christian Life: Thoughts on the Holy Mass*. San Francisco: Ignatius, 2010.

———. *Joseph Ratzinger in Communio, Vol. I: The Unity of the Church*. Translated by David L. Schindler. Grand Rapids: Eerdmans, 2010.

———. *Liberating Logos: Pope Benedict XVI's September Speeches*. Edited by Marc D. Guerra. South Bend: St. Augustine's, 2014.

———. *Light of the World: The Pope, the Church, and the Signs of the Times. A Conversation with Peter Seewald*. Translated by Michael J. Miller and Adrian J. Walker. San Francisco: Ignatius, 2010.

———. *Pope Benedict in America: The Full Texts of Papal Talks Given during His Apostolic Visit to the United States*. San Francisco: Ignatius, 2008.

———. *A Reason Open to God: On Universities, Education and Culture*. Edited by J. Steven Brown. Washington, DC: Catholic University of America Press, 2013.

———. *The Yes of Jesus Christ: Exercises in Faith, Hope, and Love*. Translated by Robert Nowell. New York: Crossroad, 1991.

——— and Christoph Schönborn. *Introduction to the Catechism of the Catholic Church*. San Francisco: Ignatius, 1994.

——— and Peter Seewald. *Last Testament: In His Own Words*. Translated by Jacob Phillips. New York: Bloomsbury, 2016.

Blanco Sarto, Pablo. "La razón en el cristianismo. Una reivindicación de Joseph Ratzinger." *Scripta Theologica* 37 no. 2 (2005) 643–59.

———. "Logos and Dia-Logos: Faith, Reason, (and Love) according to Joseph Ratzinger." *Anglican Theological Review* 92 no. 3 (2010) 499–509.

---

83. Ratzinger, *Introduction*, 155.

Boeve, Lieven, and Gerard Mannion, eds. *The Ratzinger Reader: Mapping a Theological Journey*. New York: T&T Clark, 2010.
Bursa, Brad. "According to the Logos: Joseph Ratzinger's Vision for Evangelization." PhD diss., The University of Notre Dame, Australia, 2018.
Carbonell, Claudia. "Filosofía y cristianismo. Algunas aportaciones desde J. Ratzinger." *Pensamiento y Cultura* 16 no. 1 (2013) 139–40.
Cavadini, Catherine. "An Ardent Embrace: Thomas the Cistercian's *In Cantica Conticorum*." *Cistercian Studies Quarterly* 47 no. 3 (2012) 297–311.
Cavadini, John C. "The Anatomy of Wonder: An Augustinian Taxonomy." *Augustinian Studies* 42 no. 2 (2011) 153–72.
———, ed. *Explorations in the Theology of Benedict XVI*. South Bend: University of Notre Dame Press, 2012.
Cavadini, John C., and Donald Wallenfang, eds. *Pope Francis and the Event of Encounter*. Eugene: Cascade, 2018.
Comeau, Raphael. "The Condemnation of St. Thomas." *Dominicana* 27 no. 2 (1942) 93–97.
DeLorenzo, Leonard J. *Work of Love: A Theological Reconstruction of the Communion of Saints*. Notre Dame: University of Notre Dame Press, 2017.
Eslava, Euclides. "La razón mutilada. Ciencia, razón y fe en el pensamiento de Joseph Ratzinger." *Scripta Theologica* 39 no. 3 (2007) 829–51.
Falque, Emmanuel, and Laure Solignac. "Thinking in Franciscan: Part I." Translated by Stephen E. Lewis. *Logos: A Journal of Catholic Thought and Culture* 21 no. 4 (2018) 31–59.
———. "Thinking in Franciscan: Part II." Translated by Stephen E. Lewis. *Logos: A Journal of Catholic Thought and Culture* 22 no. 1 (2019) 147–57.
Fletcher, Patrick James. "Resurrection and Platonic Dualism: Joseph Ratzinger's Augustinianism." PhD diss, The Catholic University of America, 2011. https://cuislandora.wrlc.org/islandora/object/etd%3A95/datastream/PDF/view.
Francis. *Evangelii gaudium*. November 24, 2013. http://w2.vatican.va/content/francesco/en/apost_exhortations/documents/papa-francesco_esortazione-ap_20131124_evangelii-gaudium.html.
Gardner, Patrick X. "Modern Pentecost: Henri de Lubac on Atheism and the Spiritual Posterity of Joachim of Fiore." PhD diss, University of Notre Dame, 2015. https://www.academia.edu/6769556/Modern_Pentecost_Henri_de_Lubac_on_Atheism_and_the_Spiritual_Posterity_of_Joachim_of_Fiore.
Girard, René. "Ratzinger Is Right." *New Perspectives Quarterly* 22 no. 3 (2005) 43–48.
Gourlay, Thomas V. "The Nuptial Character of the Relationship between Faith and Reason in the Thought of Joseph Ratzinger/Benedict XVI." *Heythrop Journal* 59 no. 2 (2018) 265–72.
Imbelli, Robert P. *Rekindling the Christic Imagination: Theological Meditations for the New Evangelization*. Collegeville: Liturgical, 2014.
Kasper, Walter. *Jesus the Christ*. Translated by V. Green. New York: Paulist, 1976.
Krieg, R. "Cardinal Ratzinger, Max Scheler and Christology." *The Irish Theological Quarterly* 47 no. 3 (1980) 205–19.
Lam, Joseph Cong Q. "Athens and Jerusalem: Christian Philosophy according to Ratzinger." *Heythrop Journal* 56 no. 6 (2015) 948–57.

———. "'We Proclaim the Crucified Christ' (1 Cor 2:2): Being, Truth, Beauty and the Cross according to Joseph Ratzinger." *Australasian Catholic Record* 92 no. 4 (2015) 419–32.

Lonergan, Bernard J. F. *Method in Theology*. Toronto: University of Toronto Press, 1971.

Lubac, Henri de. *Augustinianism and Modern Theology*. Translated by Lancelot Sheppard. New York: Herder & Herder, 2000.

Marion, Jean-Luc. *Being Given: Toward a Phenomenology of Givenness*. Translated by Jeffrey L. Kosky. Stanford: Stanford University Press, 2002.

———. *The Erotic Phenomenon*. Translated by Stephen E. Lewis. Chicago: University of Chicago Press, 2007.

Martin, Jay. "'As love, the giver is perfect,': Love at the Limit in the Thought of Cyril O'Regan." In *An Apocalypse of Love: Essays in Honor of Cyril O'Regan*, edited by Jennifer Newsome Martin and Anthony C. Sciglitano. New York: Herder & Herder, 2018.

McGregor, Peter John. *Heart to Heart: The Spiritual Christology of Joseph Ratzinger*. Eugene: Pickwick, 2016.

Moynihan, Robert, ed. *Let God's Light Shine Forth: The Spiritual Vision of Pope Benedict XVI*. New York: Doubleday, 2005.

Murphy, Francesca Aran. *God Is Not a Story: Realism Revisited*. Oxford: Oxford University Press, 2007.

Murphy, Jr., William F. "Thomism and the *Nouvelle Théologie*: A Dialogue Renewed?" *Josephinum Journal of Theology* 18 no. 1 (2011) 4–36.

Neuhaus, Richard John, ed. *Biblical Interpretation in Crisis: The Ratzinger Conference on Bible and Church*. Grand Rapids: Eerdmans, 1989.

Nichols, Aidan. *The Thought of Pope Benedict XVI: An Introduction to the Theology of Joseph Ratzinger*. London: Burns & Oates, 2007.

O'Malley, Timothy P. *Liturgy and the New Evangelization: Practicing the Art of Self-Giving Love*. Collegeville: Liturgical, 2014.

O'Regan, Cyril. "Benedict the Augustinian." In *Explorations in the Theology of Benedict XVI*, edited by John C. Cavadini, 21–60. Notre Dame: University of Notre Dame Press, 2012.

Oakes, Edward T., SJ. "Resolving the Relativity Paradox: Pope Benedict XVI and the Challenge of Christological Relativism." In *Explorations in the Theology of Benedict XVI*, edited by John C. Cavadini, 87–113. Notre Dame: University of Notre Dame Press, 2012.

Pagliarini, Anthony. "Ordering All Things Well: The Role of Eating in the Old Testament." *Communio* 44 (2017) 559–73.

Pidel, Aaron. "*Christi Opera Proficiunt*: Ratzinger's Neo-Bonaventurian Model of Social Inspiration." *Nova et Vetera* 13 no. 3 (2015) 693–711.

Powers, Jessica. *The Selected Poetry of Jessica Powers*. Washington, DC: ICS, 1999.

Ratzinger, Joseph. *Behold the Pierced One: An Approach to a Spiritual Christology*. Translated by Graham Harrison. San Francisco: Ignatius, 1986.

———. *Called to Communion: Understanding the Church Today*. Translated by Adrian Walker. San Francisco: Ignatius, 1996.

———. *Christianity and the Crisis of Cultures*. Translated by Brian McNeil. San Francisco: Ignatius, 2006.

———. *Church, Ecumenism, and Politics: New Endeavors in Ecclesiology*. Translated by Michael J. Miller, et al. San Francisco: Ignatius, 2008.

———. *Collected Works, Vol. 11: Theology of the Liturgy*. Edited by Michael J. Miller. Translated by John Saward, et al. San Francisco: Ignatius, 2014.

———. *Credo for Today: What Christians Believe*. Translated by Michael J. Miller, et al. San Francisco: Ignatius, 2009.

———. *Dialectics of Secularization: On Reason and Religion*, edited by Florian Schuller. Translated by Brian McNeil. San Francisco: Ignatius, 2006.

———. *Dogma and Preaching: Applying Christian Doctrine to Daily Life*. Edited by Michael J. Miller. Translated by Michael J. Miller and Matthew J. O'Connell. San Francisco: Ignatius, 2011.

———. *Einführung in das Christentum: Bekenntnis—Taufe—Nachfolge*. Freiburg: Herder, 2014.

———. *Eschatology: Death and Eternal Life*. Translated by Michael Waldstein. Washington, DC: Catholic University of America Press, 1988.

———. *Europe Today and Tomorrow: Addressing the Fundamental Issues*. Translated by Michael J. Miller. San Francisco: Ignatius, 2007.

———. *Faith, Truth, and Culture: Reflections on the Encyclical Fides et Ratio*. Translated by Patrick Stevenson. Milan: Traces, 2000.

———. *The Feast of Faith: Approaches to a Theology of the Liturgy*. Translated by Graham Harrison. San Francisco: Ignatius, 1986.

———. *Fundamental Speeches from Five Decades*. Edited by Florian Schuller. Translated by Michael J. Miller, J. R. Foster, and Adrian Walker. San Francisco: Ignatius, 2012.

———. *God and the World: Believing and Living in Our Time. A Conversation with Peter Seewald*. Translated by Henry Taylor. San Francisco: Ignatius, 2002.

———. *God Is Near Us: The Eucharist, the Heart of Life*. Edited by Henry Taylor. San Francisco: Ignatius, 2003.

———. *The God of Jesus Christ: Meditations on the Triune God*. Translated by Brian McNeil. San Francisco: Ignatius, 2008.

———. *God's Word: Scripture–Tradition–Office*. Translated by Henry Taylor. San Francisco: Ignatius, 2008.

———. *"In the Beginning . . . ": A Catholic Study of the Story of Creation and the Fall*. Translated by Boniface Ramsey. Grand Rapids: Eerdmans, 1995.

———. *Introduction to Christianity*. Translated by J. R. Foster. San Francisco: Ignatius, 2004.

———. *Jesus of Nazareth: From the Baptism in the Jordan to the Transfiguration*. Translated by Adrian J. Walker. San Francisco: Ignatius, 2007.

———. *Jesus of Nazareth: Holy Week: From the Entrance into Jerusalem to the Resurrection*. San Francisco: Ignatius, 2011.

———. *Many Religions–One Covenant: Israel, the Church, and the World*. Translated by Graham Harrison. San Francisco: Ignatius, 1999.

———. *Milestones: Memoirs 1927–1977*. Translated by Erasmo Leiva-Merikakis. San Francisco: Ignatius, 1998.

———. *The Nature and Mission of Theology: Essays to Orient Theology in Today's Debates*. Translated by Adrian Walker. San Francisco: Ignatius, 1995.

———. *New Outpourings of the Spirit: Movements in the Church*. Translated by Michael J. Miller and Henry Taylor. San Francisco: Ignatius, 2007.

———. *A New Song for the Lord: Faith in Christ and Liturgy Today*. Translated by Martha M. Matesich. New York: Crossroad, 1997.

———. *On Conscience: Two Essays*. San Francisco: Ignatius, 2007.

———. *The Open Circle: The Meaning of Christian Brotherhood*. Translated by W. A. Glen-Doeple. New York: Sheed & Ward, 1966.

———. *Pilgrim Fellowship of Faith: The Church as Communion*. Translated by Henry Taylor. San Francisco: Ignatius, 2005.

———. *Principles of Catholic Theology: Building Stones for a Fundamental Theology*. Translated by Mary Frances McCarthy. San Francisco: Ignatius, 1987.

———. *Salt of the Earth: The Church at the End of the Millenium. An Interview with Peter Seewald*. Translated by Adrian Walker. San Francisco: Ignatius, 1997.

———. *The Spirit of the Liturgy*. Translated by John Saward. San Francisco: Ignatius, 2000.

———. *Teaching and Learning the Love of God: Being a Priest Today*. Translated by Michael J. Miller. San Francisco: Ignatius, 2017.

———. *Theological Highlights of Vatican II*. Translated by Henry Traub, Gerard C. Thormann, and Werner Barzel. New York: Paulist, 1966.

———. *The Theology of History in St. Bonaventure*. Translated by Zachary Hayes. Chicago: Franciscan Herald, 1971.

———. *Theology of the Liturgy: The Sacramental Foundation of Christian Existence*. Edited by Michael J. Miller. Translated by John Saward, Kenneth Baker, and Henry Taylor. San Francisco: Ignatius, 2014.

———. *A Turning Point for Europe? The Church in the Modern World—Assessment and Forecast*. Translated by Brian McNeil. San Francisco: Ignatius, 1994.

———. *The Unity of the Nations: A Vision of the Church Fathers*. Translated by Boniface Ramsey. Washington, DC: Catholic University of America Press, 2015.

———. *Values in a Time of Upheaval*. Translated by Brian McNeil. San Francisco: Ignatius, 2006.

———. *Volk und Haus Gottes in Augustins Lehre von der Kirche*. Freiburg: Herder, 2011.

———. *What It Means to Be a Christian: Three Sermons*. Translated by Henry Taylor. San Francisco: Ignatius, 2006.

——— and Karl Lehmann. *Living with the Church*. Translated by Zachary Hayes. Chicago: Franciscan Herald, 1978.

——— and Vittorio Messori. *The Ratzinger Report: An Exclusive Interview on the State of the Church*. Translated by Salvator Attanasio and Graham Harrison. San Francisco: Ignatius, 1985.

——— and Marcello Pera. *Without Roots: The West, Relativism, Christianity, Islam*. Translated by Michael F. Moore. New York: Basic Books, 2006.

——— and Hans Urs von Balthasar. *Mary: The Church at the Source*. Translated by Adrian Walker. San Francisco: Ignatius, 2005.

——— and Karl Rahner. *The Episcopate and the Primacy*. Translated by Kenneth Barker, Patrick Kerans, Robert Ochs and Richard Strachan. London: Burns and Oates, 1966.

——— and Karl Rahner. *Revelation and Tradition*. Translated by W. J. O'Hara. New York: Herder & Herder, 1966.

———, et al. *Handing on the Faith in an Age of Disbelief*. Translated by Michael J. Miller. San Francisco: Ignatius, 2006.

———, et al. *Pope John Paul II Lecture Series, 1985*. St. Paul: College of St. Thomas, St. John Vianney Seminary, 1985.

———, et al. *Problems of the Church Today*. Washington, DC: United States Catholic Conference, 1976.
Rausch, Thomas P. *Pope Benedict XVI: An Introduction to His Theological Vision*. New York: Paulist, 2009.
Rowland, Tracey. "Augustinian and Thomist Engagements with the World." *American Catholic Philosophical Quarterly* 83 no. 3 (2009) 441–59.
———. *Benedict XVI: A Guide for the Perplexed*. London: T&T Clark, 2010.
———. *Culture and the Thomist Tradition: After Vatican II*. London: Routledge, 2003.
———. "Neo-Scholasticism of the Strict Observance." In *T&T Clark Companion to Henri de Lubac*, edited by Jordan Hillebert, 29–55. London: Bloomsbury T&T Clark, 2017.
———. *Ratzinger's Faith: The Theology of Pope Benedict XVI*. New York: Oxford University Press, 2008.
Sadler, Gregory, ed. *Reason Fulfilled by Revelation: The 1930s Christian Philosophy Debates in France*. Washington, DC: Catholic University of America Press, 2011.
Schall, James V. *The Regensburg Lecture*. South Bend: St. Augustine's, 2007.
Schenk, Richard, OP. "Analogy as the *discrimen naturae et gratiae*: Thomism and Ecumenical Learning." In *The Analogy of Being: Invention of the Antichrist or the Wisdom of God?*, edited by Thomas Joseph White, 172–91. Grand Rapids: Eerdmans, 2011.
Sciglitano, Anthony C. "Leaving Neo-Scholasticism Behind: Aspirations and Anxieties." *Josephinum Journal of Theology* 18 no. 1 (2011) 216–39.
———. "Prometheus and Kant: Neutralizing Theological Discourse and Doxology." *Modern Theology* 25 no. 3 (2009) 387–414.
Sedmak, Clemens. "Spiritual Infrastructure: Memory and Moral Resources." *Israel Affairs* 16 no. 4 (2010) 510–34.
Tracy, David. *Blessed Rage for Order: The New Pluralism in Theology*. Chicago: University of Chicago Press, 1996.
Voderholzer, Rudolf. *Meet Henri de Lubac*. Translated by Michael J. Miller. San Francisco: Ignatius, 2008.
Wallenfang, Donald. *Dialectical Anatomy of the Eucharist: An Étude in Phenomenology*. Eugene: Cascade, 2017.
———. *Human and Divine Being: A Study on the Theological Anthropology of Edith Stein*. Eugene: Cascade, 2017.
Zucal, Silvano. "The Intellectual Relationship between Joseph Ratzinger and Romano Guardini." EWTN Library. http://www.ewtn.com/library/Theology/ratzinguardini.HTM.

9

"Being for" and Normativity in a Post-Durkheimian Age

Anthony C. Sciglitano, Jr.

> "One is not a Christian because only Christians are saved; one is a Christian because for history Christian loving service has meaning and is a necessity."[1]

Introduction

READERS OF CHARLES TAYLOR will recognize "post-Durkheimian" in my title as his label for the relation between religion and culture in our time which he advances in a number of places, including towards the end of his *A Secular Age*.[2] Refounding modern goods such as egalitarianism and the goods of ordinary life on articulate phenomenological and ontological grounds seems near the essence of Taylor's project. Taylor thinks religion takes a post-Durkheimian vector wherever it divorces itself from concerns with political discourse/policy. This contrasts with "Durkheimian" or "paleo-Durkheimian," which indicates an integral relationship between religion and

---

1. Ratzinger, *Introduction*, 249.
2. Durkheimian or "paleo-Durkheimian" indicates "the sense that the church and social sacred are one—although the relation of primary and secondary focus is reversed, since for Durkheim the social is the principal focus, reflected in the divine, while the opposite is true for ultramontane Catholicism" (Taylor, *Secular Age*, 442). He is speaking to the society of post-Napoleonic Catholic restoration in France as an attempt to re-establish Christendom. "Neo-Durkheimian" contrasts to "baroque" Catholicism on the one hand and to "more recent forms in which the spiritual dimension of existence is quite unhooked from the political" (455). The latter will be called "post-Durkheimian" (487). In the neo-Durkheimian dispensation "religious belonging is central to political identity" (455). Neo-Durkheimian will remove the sacred from places and things to an overall design that advocates freedom and supports denominationalism as part and parcel of this larger design.

politics such that discourse about one can serve as discourse about the other, and "neo-Durkheimian," which indicates a separation of Church and State, but with something like a consensus civil religion that informs policy and ethos. American denominationalism, Taylor thinks, exemplifies this type of relation. That we Westerners are broadly "post-Durkheimian" in sensibility is interesting as a descriptive sociological claim, but, I would suggest, serves for Taylor as a normative one as well.[3]

That "post-Durkheimian" has normative weight for Taylor is suggested in three related ways. First, Taylor's philosophical method, aptly labeled "soft-Hegelianism" by Edmund Waldstein, O. Cist.,[4] operates under the idea that the "social imaginary" contains strong goods that beg for full articulation. Articulation of this background is not ancillary but constitutive to moral reasoning and practice as being human is fundamentally to be a "self-interpreting animal."[5] Grasping our setting as post-Durkheimian, then, is to articulate the background of our age, to bring it to light along with its varied goods. Each historical period will possess moral ideals that require articulation given self-interpretation as fundamental to what it means to be human. Secondly, Taylor makes clear that he believes leaving Christendom (an iteration of paleo-Durkheimianism) behind allows gospel goods to become universally available in a way that the division between us and them constitutive of Christendom (even allowing that it was a valiant attempt to incarnate the gospel) would never permit.[6] Third, he seems to reject any possible return to paleo- or neo-Durkheimian culture,[7] even if he thinks some people will find spiritual nourishment within religious communities rather than apart from them. The weakness of the latter option can be a certain superficiality, although I do not experience him that way.[8] But Taylor concludes that the debits of the former option, that is, a version of paleo-Durkheimianism, are significantly more serious.[9] There is, then, in Taylor a large scale historical

---

3. It is also interesting that he chooses "Durkheimian" rather than "Constantinian" for this discussion.

4. Waldstein, "What is Integralism Today?"

5. See especially Taylor, "Self-Interpreting Animals," and Taylor, *Sources of the Self*, 53–90.

6. It should be mentioned here that the distinction between "us" and "them" is central to any notion of mission. It need not designate that the "us" is a finished product without need for conversion, only that as a Christian one thinks being Christian is good for everyone. See Taylor, "A Catholic Modernity?" 16–18, 26, 29.

7. Taylor, *Varieties*, 113–14.

8. Waldstein, "What is Integralism Today?" raises the specter of superficial spirituality.

9. Taylor, *Varieties*, 114.

narrative wherein social imaginaries produce normativity when interpretation explicates goods people experience as undeniable, and that any demurral gets experienced as special pleading or takes an awkward linguistic form.[10] Such "transitions" in the landscape of perceived moral goods serve for Taylor as genuine insight into the good. Language, and with it an adequate ontology or phenomenology, often limps to catch up with perception and even social action. One of these transitions is to a post-Durkheimian ambit where conversion has little to do with participation in a communal mission divinely sanctioned and inspired or, relatedly, the vision of *Gaudium et Spes* wherein the Church tries to act as a leaven in the world for social, cultural, economic, and political transformation.[11] Finally, it is the case that articulation of a background, for Taylor, is never an innocuous procedure. Thus, I am indicating here that for Taylor the "post-Durkheimian" sociological designation provides guidelines for institutional self-understanding, and requirements for appropriate ethical behavior as a Church. It is, then, a normative claim every bit as much as a descriptive one.

In this atmosphere, two questions animate my discussion of Ratzinger. First, precisely how does Ratzinger articulate the normativity and finality of Christian revelation in *Introduction to Christianity*? This question will take us to the heart of Christianity itself, indeed, to the heart of Christ. Second, how might this normativity relate to the "post-Durkheimian" claims of Taylor, especially with respect to the Church?

While I cannot investigate Taylor's claims here at any length, what I can do is explore the extent to which Ratzinger's mission theology contests any normative gravity one might give to the sociological descriptor, "post-Durkheimian." This will be the destination intended. The road to this destination will be populated by prepositions, namely, the relational words, "for," "from," and "with," all of which Ratzinger prefixes with Being and connects with mission. More than anything, then, this paper is a meditation on prepositions, mostly focused on Ratzinger's *Introduction*, but in light of a small range of other texts as well, with episodic commentary on relation to Taylor's project.

The first section begins with a discussion of the purposes of their genealogies, and then Ratzinger's discussion of the three prepositions—for, from and with—within and to some extent outside Ratzinger's *Introduction*

---

10. On the nature of philosophical and ethical argument, Taylor's essays in his *Philosophical Arguments* are indispensable. See especially the first three essays, "Overcoming Epistemology," "The Validity of Transcendental Arguments," and "Explanation and Practical Reason."

11. Taylor lays out the importance of transitions to moral reasoning in his essay, "Explanation and Practical Reasoning," in *Philosophical Arguments*, 34–60.

to Christianity. Section two examines Ratzinger's somewhat episodic genealogical reflections, and relates them to the challenges of sacramental theology with reference to our three prepositions. The third section examines the normativity or unsurpassibility claims he makes for Christ as God's Being-for, what these claims indicate, and how they may relate to sociological claims regarding a post-Durkheimian setting for contemporary theology. This brings us to a confrontation with aspects of Taylor's method and a discussion of the role of the Church in part four. We finish with a brief discussion of the contemporary importance of Ratzinger's ec-static vision of Christian and ecclesial existence.

I. Genealogy and Prepositions

If Taylor enacts massive genealogical narratives, Ratzinger's genealogical forays might be described as *ad hoc* and strategic. This is not to say that they lack significant overlap in both figures discussed and even the issues they instigate (Taylor's range, of course, being far more expansive). Taylor and Ratzinger seek a way beyond the epistemological regime of the seventeenth and eighteenth centuries: they both locate in Vico and Descartes key figures in the development of naturalist assumption and anti-realism, and they both look to significant doses of hermeneutical phenomenology to help "overcome epistemology," to avail of Taylor's phrase.[12] It would not be preposterous to suggest that genealogy in both instances seeks to articulate how or why the immanent frame appears closed to transcendence for so many of our contemporaries, even those, to an extent, who call themselves believers. Certainly Ratzinger's discussion of the exorcised clown[13] and the believer choking on the saltwater of doubt[14] recalls and sharpens any sense of "fragilization"[15] Taylor discusses.

The differences, of course, are equally significant—probably more so. Taylor subsumes confessional self-understanding into a historical narrative of goods that need and achieve greater or lesser articulation. The human

12. Much of Taylor's work addresses this issue, but for the essay by this title see Taylor, *Philosophical Arguments*, 1–19.
13. Ratzinger, *Introduction*, 39–43.
14. Ratzinger, *Introduction*, 45.
15. Taylor, *A Secular Age*, 303–4. He writes, "This mutual fragilization of all the different views in presence, the undermining sense that others think differently, is certainly one of the main features of the world of 2000, in contrast to that of 1500." Cf. 437, 53–32, 556, 595, 833n19. The last is important as he clarifies that "fragilization" does not mean weaker conviction in the end, but more movement among positions prior to arriving at one's own.

being as self-interpreting animal requires articulation for goods to come into the light of speech and be available. This method means, to take one example, that what is central to Luther, namely, Christ crucified, will be neglected in Taylor's discussion of the Reformation for alternative goods such as the value of ordinary life and the priesthood of all believers. These latter can far more easily be translated into a post-Christian idiom. Nor does the finality of Christ's revelation play any role in *A Secular Age*, thus vindicating Ratzinger's observations in a number of places that claims for finality and/or irrevocability play against modern sensibility.[16] In a sense, we might say that for Taylor, philosophical hermeneutics assigns to itself rights of interpretation and/or validation with respect to the religious communities of the West. This does not mean that he seeks no opening for religious truths. Indeed, his arguments are designed to argue for the reasonableness of an immanent frame open to religious goods and even to the importance of goods beyond this life.[17] Nevertheless, in the broad sweep of his narrative, there is a price to pay for this opening and, to the extent to which this price deflates Christian mission or the importance and relevance of ecclesial setting for the vitality of these goods, it may be judged too high. Indeed, the designation of our age as post-Durkheimian would seem to suggest both deflations insofar as I am right to read the label as carrying both descriptive and normative weight. Finally, this is not to argue that Taylor's judgements are wrong, only that neither they nor his method are innocuous with respect to confessional claims and ecclesial commitments within the larger social milieu. Indeed, I would argue that when Ratzinger remarks, in *Principles of Catholic Theology*, that Hegel's historicism is a key turning point, Taylor's work fits his description well:

> The decisive turning point lies with Hegel, since which being and time have been more and more intertwined in philosophical thinking. Being itself is now regarded as time: the logos becomes itself in history. It cannot be assigned, therefore, to any particular point in history or be viewed as something existing in itself outside of history; all its historical objectifications are but movements in the whole of which they are parts . . . In such a view, both Catholic and Protestant interpretation of Christianity have meaning, each in its own way; they are true in their historical moment, but they can remain true only by being abandoned

---

16. See, for examples, Ratzinger, *Principles of Catholic Theology*, 15–16, and *Theology of the Liturgy*, 154.

17. As he nicely puts it at one point, parenthetically, "For Christians, God wills human flourishing, but 'thy will be done' doesn't reduce to 'let human beings flourish.'" See Taylor, "A Catholic Modernity?" 20.

when their hour has come and assimilated into the newly developing whole.[18]

While a full argument in this direction would require more space than is possible here, I hope to return to the issue in the last section of the paper.[19]

Ratzinger's strategic genealogical work serves two functions, closely related. In *Introduction*, he wants to show that the movement from Vico, Descartes, and, to a lesser extent, Kant, leads away from reflective thought to the dominance of *techné*, where the world gets reduced to matter and human beings gain license or power over nature. Otherwise put, his is a genealogy of the loss of Logos or meaning as knowable and inherent to the created world.[20] This same genealogical frame serves to illuminate obstacles to a sacramental sensibility such that things can be no more than things, or, perhaps more accurately, only the surfaces of things. Ratzinger clearly does not think this attenuation of Being a positive development for human behavior towards one another, for human meaning, for purpose and value. This he makes clear.[21] Nevertheless, he does not so much argue the point as show it by contrast. In other words, his rhetorical strategy seems to be to indicate the intellectual conditions for loss and subsequently remind the reader, through a rich existentially urgent treatment of the Apostles' Creed, precisely what one stands to lose. In enacting such a description, Ratzinger exhibits the richness and drama of Christian existence coupled to the beauty of its content. One might say that Ratzinger inscribes what the poet Richard Wilbur recommends to the would-be prophet of apocalyptic doom:

> We could believe,
>
> If you told us so, that the white-tailed deer will slip
> Into perfect shade, grown perfectly shy,
> The lark avoid the reaches of our eye,
> The jack-pine lose its knuckled grip
>
> On the cold ledge, and every torrent burn
> As Xanthus once, its gliding trout
> Stunned in a twinkling. What should we be without
> The dolphin's arc, the dove's return,
>
> These things in which we have seen ourselves and spoken?[22]

---

18. Ratzinger, *Principles of Catholic Theology*, 16.

19. Happily, Carolyn Chau, *Solidarity with the World*, has taken on the burden of this argument previously.

20. Ratzinger, *Introduction*, 58. See also *Theology of the Liturgy*, 153–54.

21. See, for example, Habermas and Ratzinger, *The Dialectics of Secularization*, 65.

22. Wilbur, "Advice to a Prophet."

What are we, Ratzinger asks, when we lose the language of symbol and sacrament?

Central to Ratzinger's remembrance are the three prepositions, "for," "from" and "with." From a methodological point of view, it is perhaps important to note that "being for," from and with are Christian specific designations that emerge primarily through Christ himself and not undeniable givens of an eidetic reduction or transcendental deduction. Ratzinger does not think such a neutral reason affords much knowledge of anything, let alone God.[23] Nor does the conversion from Being for self to Being for others[24] indicate merely a Kantian exchange of hedonistic maxims for duty bound ones for at least two reasons. First, for Kant, a change from hedonistic to moral maxims has no interpersonal or relational setting save for the relation of oneself to the inner call of autonomously verified moral duty.[25] Prepositions become unnecessary in a world populated by autonomous subjects. Secondly, Ratzinger's rendition of "being for" has profound ontological and theological reference points that Kant would have us exclude.[26] The possibility of being for others, for instance, finds its ground for Ratzinger in the "Being for" of God himself, revealed most profoundly in Jesus Christ, entered into in Baptism, and shared through Eucharist. In short, Ratzinger's "being for" goes beyond both Kantian moral considerations and the givens of a putatively neutral phenomenology.[27]

In Ratzinger's text, "being for" indicates both that one ought to be for others,[28] and that, in doing so, one manifests or discloses the "forness" of Being as gift of God who is, in his inner-life, constituted by non-accidental relations of eternal "forness" and "fromness."[29] A decision to be for others,

23. Ratzinger, *Introduction*, 177.

24. Ratzinger, *Introduction*, 252.

25. Dialogue is essential to Ratzinger's entire text as it undergirds the "structure of faith" itself (*Introduction*, 93). The contrast here is between faith (dialogical) and philosophy (monological) and his favored form of the Creed as dialogical (see 92–93). Ratzinger's notion that the dialogue in faith "causes the *logos* to resound" recalls Emmanuel Levinas' *Totality and Infinity*, where justice is defined or constituted through and in dialogue or discourse. They are, nevertheless, quite different in that Ratzinger holds to a more Logos-centric notion of creation itself as inherently meaningful, purposeful, and good.

26. I have addressed both some of Ratzinger's concerns with Kant and my own reading of Kant's work on religion in two essays: "Pope Benedict XVI's *Jesus of Nazareth*," and "Prometheus and Kant."

27. Ratzinger, *Introduction*, 175.

28. Of course the entire book says this, but see Ratzinger, *Introduction*, 249 for an example.

29. See Ratzinger's discussion of the Triune God, *Introduction*, 162–90, esp. 186–90.

then, is simultaneously a decision to manifest the truth of Being as good in its self-giving. Here, Erich Przywara's famous phrase, "become what you are"[30] helps supplement Ratzinger's discussion: Insofar as Being is gift or Being for, and human being as an element of Being is Being for, then one's essential being lies out in front, in the being for that Christians hope to become in the totality of their existence. Essence and existence thus lie apart from one another and require dynamic movement outward, *ec-stasis* or, in Ratzinger's favored symbolic, biblical métier, it requires exodus.[31] He builds on this view in his *Principles of Catholic Theology* when commenting on Henri de Lubac's reflections on the Apostles' Creed: "De Lubac clarifies this thought by adding that, for such a view of faith, God does not exemplify loneliness but ec-stasy, a complete going-out-from himself. This means that the mystery of the Trinity has opened to us a totally new perspective: the ground of being is *communio*."[32]

This same "being for" informs his discussion of metaphysical options and obstacles. Here the centrality of "being for" serves as a measure for materialism and idealism. For Ratzinger the presuppositions of neither materialism nor idealism can coherently promote or sustain the "being for" that is central to Christianly encountered reality.

Materialism must reject both Logos and Love or a metaphysics of Gift: the world is inherently neither gift of another, which would require its "being from," nor supplied with inherent rationality, meaning, or purpose.[33] Any rationality discovered in Being must be accidental to matter itself. Materialism appears to offer Being as manipulable, infinitely consumable gift, but that appearance soon shows itself a projection of human desire as this desire reduces other human beings to mere matter for exchange, or the earth itself shows the dire consequences of such views. Ratzinger is eloquent when he notes the modern irony appearing most obviously in the nineteenth century: "At the very moment when radical anthropocentrism set in and man

---

30. Pzywara, *Analogia Entis*, 124.

31. Ratzinger makes this "exodus being" clear when speaking of the different titles of Jesus, and also the relation between a theology of the incarnation and a theology of the cross: . . . dass das *Sein* Christi (Inkarnationstheologie!) actualitas ist, Uberschritt von sich weg, der Exodus des Herausgehens aus sich . . . Dies Sein ist Exodus, Verwandlung." (German edition, p. 216; for the English, see *Introduction*, 230); the italics are Ratzinger's. He wants to emphasize that the theology of the Cross is not opposed to the Incarnation, for both show God in his going out for others, and thus reveal Christ as the one who *is* Exodus: sent from the Father for the world.

32. Ratzinger, *Principles of Catholic Theology*, 22.

33. Ratzinger, *Introduction*, 156–57.

could know only his own work, he had to learn to accept himself as merely a chance occurrence, just another 'fact.'"[34]

Idealism better represents the Logos aspect of creation that he endorses as part and parcel of the Creator's work,[35] and, as for Augustine perhaps, can serve as an important way station between materialism and Christianity. Like Christianity, Idealism endorses mind, meaning, and value as ineluctable aspects of Being. In addition, idealism presupposes the existence and importance of the invisible, a presupposition of faith and one of three major obstacles to belief in the modern world, according to Ratzinger.[36] Nevertheless, Idealism lacks the personal freedom-in-relation[37]—both divine and human—essential to Being. Idealism slides into an impersonal monism where body, history, diversity, and pluriformity struggle to find any positive ground for their existence or independent reality. By contrast, "... Christian belief in God means that things are the being-thought of a creative consciousness, of a creative freedom, and that the creative consciousness that bears up all things has released what has been thought into the freedom of its own, independent existence."[38]

Unlike Idealism, Ratzinger claims, the very structures of Christian faith and being are rooted in freedom and personal being, the Being of a God who gifts our own "true being,"[39] and, what's more, grants his name, takes on flesh, and thus becomes invocable,[40] the possibility of which itself rests upon the "releasing" of the world into freedom. On this latter point especially, Idealism limps. We might note, too, that if the Giver of gifts is not free, that is, if the "for" is not simultaneously a "from," then gratitude, prayer, and Eucharist suffer severe demotion, perhaps even demolition.

34. Ratzinger, *Introduction*, 63.

35. Ratzinger, *Introduction*, 157.

36. Ratzinger, *Introduction*, 74. Ratzinger notes three obstacles to belief in the modern world, including belief in the invisible (50–52), the importance of tradition or the "antithesis between tradition and progress" (54), and the challenge of such a particular or singular revelation in Jesus Christ (54–55).

37. One of the key differences between faith and philosophy, for Ratzinger, is that faith calls one to relationship, to community, and response, whereas philosophy calls one to individual thought. See *Introduction*, 91–100.

38. Ratzinger, *Introduction*, 157.

39. Ratzinger, *Introduction*, 157.

40. Ratzinger, *Introduction*, 133–35. For Ratzinger, the God of the philosophers is ultimately a selfish God: "The philosophical God is essentially self-centered, thought simply contemplating itself. The God of faith is basically defined by the category of relationship. He is creative fullness encompassing the whole" (*Introduction*, 147).

II. Prepositional Vision and Sacramental Ontology

As noted above, Ratzinger sees the need for at least an ad hoc genealogical account of certain modern presuppositions that hinder Christian commitments and/or vision. He is particularly concerned with modern aversion to a sacramental view of creation. Some of this aversion, he thinks, has to do with the relation of sacraments to Church or Church as institution, which moderns typically fear.[41] But more fundamental is the loss of a sense that the being of things can mean more than they do on the literal or material plane.[42]

Briefly, then, on Ratzinger's account, the Cartesian dualism of mind and matter joins to Vico's view that the only things we can truly know are those things we humans make, for to know something is to have a fully transparent grasp of its causes.[43] Outside of such *techne* or human production knowledge, one can only know appearances, while the inner truth of Being remains concealed. Thus the Cartesian "I think therefore I am" (*Cogito ergo sum*) hides what he thinks is much more fundamental: "I am thought therefore I am."[44]

The movement stemming from Vico and Descartes, and the definitive closing off of Being to knowledge from Kant, finds Logos only in what is made by human hands, or, as he puts it himself:[45] "In a time when we have grown accustomed to seeing in the substance of things nothing but the material for human labor—when, in short, the world is regarded as matter and matter as material for human labor—initially there is no room left for that symbolic transparency of reality toward the eternal on which the sacramental principle is based."[46]

Add this endemic set of theoretical assumptions to his observation that, for contemporaries, while God may be of profound interest, the

---

41. This discussion is mostly from Ratzinger, "The Sacramental Foundation of Christian Existence," in Ratzinger, *Collected Works, vol. XI: Theology of the Liturgy: The Sacramental Foundation of Christian Existence*. It is perhaps worth noting that, given the colon and subtitle, liturgy, for Ratzinger, is hardly confined to what occurs in Church, but rather involves the entirety of Christian existence.

42. Ratzinger, *Introduction*, 154.

43. Ratzinger, *Introduction*, 61: "This means that the equation of truth and being is replaced by the new one of truth and factuality; all that can be known is the *factum*, that which we have made ourselves."

44. Ratzinger, *Introduction*, 247; cf. 246.

45. For the discussion of Descartes, Kant and Vico, see Ratzinger, *Introduction*, 58–63.

46. Ratzinger, "Sacramental Foundation," 153–54.

sacraments are all too "religious" and anachronistic, and the possibility of a sacramental foundation appears near hopeless.

Ratzinger is undeterred. It is really not difficult, he thinks, to see how a sacrament connects meaningfully with the rest of existence. His primary example is the relation of Eucharist to eating and to a meal. Whereas eating indicates a mere animal act (to acquire material sustenance), a meal, in Ratzinger's terms, takes up this basic aim into a higher relation of subjects who share the fruits of their labor, their creativity, and themselves. Here we have being from, for and with: the meal is *from* another, but also *from* the earth and the elements; it is *for* those gathered, *with* whom one enjoys both bodily and spiritual sustenance. Indeed, through a meal, he thinks, we can see the interpenetration of biological or bodily life on the one hand and the life of spirit on the other. A meal integrates human beings into the human community, but also into the "cosmic flow" of life. This suggests to Ratzinger that our very existence is grounded in our being-with of relations to others and the earth itself to such an extent that he can say, "man can only exist in the plural, so to speak."[47] Of course with respect to Eucharist, we enter the space of Christ and his self-offering, his being with us in the Eucharistic meal, and his being sent from the Father for precisely this being with, revealing the inner constitution of Divine Being itself as a communion to which we are invited. If human being is not merely cosmic being, but also historical, bodily, and spiritual being, then it is only fitting that God chooses to be with us where we are.[48]

III. Christologically Specified Prepositions and Normativity

If normativity comes for Taylor from the historical and philosophical assessment of strong goods yielded by each social imaginary, for Ratzinger, normativity or finality arises from Jesus Christ, who is uniquely and singularly *Being from*, *Being for*, and *Being with*. It is Christ who is pure relation to the Father: the one who is sent *from* the Father to be *for* and *with* the world.[49] God's entrance into history makes the sacraments unique, even if they have fittingly deep roots in anthropological and cosmic structures. This entrance into history means that not only is God the God of Abraham, Isaac, and Jacob, but he is the God of Jesus Christ: "the God who is here for men and is defined

---

47. Ratzinger, "Sacramental Foundation," 157.

48. On the importance of historical being and God entering into that being, see *Theology of the Liturgy*, 158 and 163.

49. Ratzinger, *Introduction*, 186–87.

precisely by his being with people. In a word, he appears as the personal God who is knowledge and love, and who is therefore word and love, with respect to us. Word that calls us and the Love that unites us."[50]

Unlike us, Christ is purely from and for: his relations are non-accidental in that they define his person by his very mission. This is why, Ratzinger says, the collapse of the functional title "Christ" into a name is no mere error, but speaks an important truth, namely, the utter identity between Christ's person and work.[51]

Christ's "being for" or self-giving generosity and availability is precisely what for Ratzinger is marked with finality. Ratzinger distinguishes here between revelation that is informational and, we might say, revelation that is personal.[52] Finality comes not from new information, but from the promise embedded in the dialogue with man through Israel in the Old Testament. "Revelation ends here," Ratzinger says, not because God deliberately puts an end to it, but because it has reached its goal."[53] Jesus's titles acquire their meaning in relation to this personal movement from, for and with, the totality of which falls under the ambit of mission: " . . . through the concept of mission, being is interpreted as being 'from' and as being 'for'; once again, being is conceived as absolute openness without reservation."[54] In John, then, the name "Son" "always points away from him and beyond him."[55] All is relatedness here, as "Son" refers to the Father, and the extreme openness of Father and Son to one another suggests a unity beyond the contrast between the one and the many. More to our point: "To John, 'Son' means being from another; thus, with this word, he defines the being of this man as being from another and for others, as being that is completely open on both sides, knows no reserved area of the mere 'I.'"[56]

This anti-atomistic reading of the title "Son" joins to the term "Logos" for Ratzinger, who is everywhere concerned to resist dichotomies between

50. Ratzinger, *Theology of the Liturgy*, 161.

51. Ratzinger, *Introduction*, 203–5.

52. See Ratzinger, *Introduction*, 95, for this discussion. The I–You structure of faith is essential to Ratzinger in the Old Testament's shattering of divine localization/spatialization and, relatedly, to the absolutization of bread, love/eros, and power. Leonard DiLorenzo's paper in this volume addresses the issue of divine spatialization in a most interesting manner as directly related to original sin. In this sense, Old Testament revelation serves a crucial negative theological purpose rooted in the encounter with God.

53. Ratzinger, *Introduction*, 263.

54. Ratzinger, *Introduction*, 188–89.

55. Ratzinger, *Introduction*, 185.

56. Ratzinger, *Introduction*, 186. Much of Ratzinger's section on The Triune God reads as a meditation on the fifth book of Saint Augustine's *De Trinitate*.

Hebrew and Greek thought. Nevertheless, he shows here how Christ's person forces a re-interpretation of a static, impersonal idea found in Greek metaphysics. Logos as instransigent intelligibility becomes Word (*verbum*), dynamically spoken from (the Father) and for (the world): "Thus logos Christology, as 'word' theology, is once again the opening up of being to the idea of relationship. For again it is true that 'word' comes essentially 'from someone else' and 'to someone else'; word is an existence that is entirely way and openness."[57] More concretely still, the normative Logos is Christ crucified, the man who is for others: "the man in the sacrifice, sacrificed man. The future of man hangs on the Cross—the redemption of man is the Cross. And he can only come to himself by letting the walls of his existence be broken down, by looking on him who has been pierced and following him who as the pierced and opened one has opened the path into the future."[58]

If it is true for Ratzinger that Christianity is constituted, in part, through its memory,[59] it is no less true that Christianity looks forward. The finality of Christ marks out a future path or new beginning, a way of being for and with and on the side of others in and from the Church. Ratzinger makes this path clearer still: "But in Christ the countenance of him who is to come is already revealed: it will be the man who can embrace all men because he has lost himself and them to God. For this reason the emblem of him who is to come must be the Cross, and his face in this era of the world must be a bleeding, wounded countenance: the 'last man', that is, the real, the future man, reveals himself in this age in the last men; whoever wishes to stand on *his* side must therefore stand on *their* side (cf. Mt 25:31–46)."[60]

Christian normativity, then, lies not in "superficial codes" that speak to a kind of nomolatry and thus make us all morally dumber.[61] Rather, normativity lies in the Being for, from, and with that moves from Creation, to Israel, to the descent into the flesh, to siding with the poor, and even to the loneliness of our personal hells. Normativity or finality, then, opens up a path to the Being for that God is and calls us to be first, through the sharing together in

57. Ratzinger, *Introduction*, 189.

58. Ratzinger, *Introduction*, 241.

59. For the importance of memory, see *Principles of Catholic Theology*, 24, in the context, partially, of anti-Hegelianism or anti-historicism. Ratzinger thinks that Hegel signals a key turning point towards historicism whereby Being is purely time and change.

60. Ratzinger, *Introduction*, 242–43. He echoes this powerful concern for the poor at the beginning of *Principles of Catholic Theology* (22).

61. See Taylor's criticisms of nomolatry in *A Secular Age*, 707. These criticisms are aimed not only at Christian fetishization of moral codes (especially sexual), but also modern liberal rule based ethical theories, the latter a major target of his earlier *Sources of the Self*.

the Eucharist, the communion of God with and for us, and second, through an exodus for the world, especially for and with the most vulnerable. Such a view of normativity does not suggest a kind of separation from the social, cultural, political, and economic realities of this world, but rather an attempt to more deeply penetrate them with the goods of the Gospel—those that loving service requires and the world so desperately needs.

IV. A Return to Christendom? Church and World in Ratzinger's *Introduction*

The juxtaposition of Taylor's Durkheimian schema with Ratzinger's location of normativity in the Being-for of Christ might give rise to an important misconception that Ratzinger yearns for a return to Christendom, a kind of paleo-Durkheimianism, but unhappily settles for neo-Durkheimianism where the Church at least persists, albeit with profoundly attenuated secular authority. This would suggest a nostalgic orientation to the past. I want to suggest here not only that Ratzinger's position bursts the bounds of this schema, but also pushes Taylor—or Taylorean Catholics—toward some difficult decisions. Moreover, it could be argued that Taylor's position, and not Ratzinger's, implies a merging of Catholic identity and that of modernity in a pseudo-triumphalist fashion.

We can start with two different ways to read Taylor. One might read Taylor to suggest that, while Catholicism offers history genuine moral goods that have been and ought to be taken up into our social imaginary, history requires the backgrounding of more particular claims for Jesus and the Church such that the universality of these goods can be recognized and socially embedded. These goods might be the general egalitarianism of the Gospel, the value of ordinary life that emerges out of late medieval Church reform and especially the Reformation itself (coupled with virulent anticlericalism), a larger scale of empathy for human suffering, a communal or dialogical mode of authenticity as opposed to atomistic relativism, and perhaps even a sense of depth meaning(s) or immanent transcendence. This is a kind of Catholic ethical Hegelianism where the particularity of the community must dissolve for its goods to find universalization and genuine reconciliation. Thus his title: "A Catholic Modernity." The idea here is not that the Church ought to update itself, as in a "Modern Catholicism," which Taylor suggests would be triumphalistic,[62] but that modernity itself ought to come to embrace self-consciously a more nearly communal or dialogical ethos open to spiritual experience and expression found in the Catholic

---

62. Taylor, "A Catholic Modernity?" 15.

heritage (among others). "Self-consciously" is an important phrase here, as we have shown that articulacy about moral goods is nearly as important to Taylor as their very presence. In addition, Taylor believes many of these goods to have already found a place in modern culture. In this sense, ecclesial mission becomes unnecessary and, to the extent that mission calls for a decision for or against, may prove counter-productive to the universalization of goods and their appropriation.

Ratzinger has a less sanguine view of modernity, certainly, but this is not because he longs for a previous age. Indeed, near the beginning of *Introduction* he shuts down romantic return narratives when he questions the perhaps rote subscription to Christian belief and practice due merely to general cultural norms and expectations in past ages. What is important here is that, for Ratzinger, Christ does not point to some past, present, or future socio-cultural moment, but instead offers a unique and singular opening onto an Absolute Future for or against which one decides in the present. Indeed, "decision" has a prevalence and existential urgency in Ratzinger's text that is not to be found in Taylor's texts. Decision, of course, etymologically requires a cutting or splitting that no logical or merely historical flow can satisfy or yield. This, then, re-inscribes a kind of "us" and "them" separation inimical to Taylor's critique of Christendom but fundamental to mission. We might ask, then, two questions. First, what might constitute "us" and "them" for Ratzinger? And secondly, can Taylor be read a second way, that is, can he be read to avoid the critique I offer here by adverting to his intellectual location in philosophy rather than theology?

Ratzinger, as I have noted, is not interested in a return to some former age. Nor does he believe the Gospel hands down a ready made blue-print for social, legal, and moral implementation. He makes this clear in *Jesus of Nazareth*: "Discipleship of Jesus offers no politically concrete program for structuring society. The Sermon on the Mount cannot serve as a foundation for a state and a social order, as is frequently and correctly observed."[63] Nevertheless, the decision not only for Jesus but also for an ecclesial existence offers a concrete witness to goods fundamental to the Christian community that seek to influence modern political culture. This too becomes clearer for Ratzinger in his dialogue with Jürgen Habermas, where he insists on human dignity as the underlying foundation of democracy and even pluralism rather than mere interest, identity, or power politics—each of which threatens those who lack the ability to express their interests and/or identity through power.[64]

---

63. Benedict XVI, *Jesus of Nazareth: From the Baptism*, 114. Cf. Ratzinger, *Introduction*, 113.

64. See Habermas and Ratzinger, *The Dialectics of Secularization*, 71–72.

In this sense, then, Ratzinger rejects any idea of a sociological-historical schema for a more ad hoc approach. What is non-negotiable is the formation of a witnessing, sacramental community that has decided on its obligation to loving service as primary over any power or powers that threaten to enslave us. Ratzinger has no illusions that modern assimilation of Christian goods, apart from a dedicated community, will choose these goods over others when tensions or threats to self- or national interest arise.

Perhaps it is equally important to note here Ratzinger's view of the Church as incomplete and the Church as a place of genuine fellowship and communion in worship. If faith requires reception and reaching out, being from and being for our fellow human beings, the Church is equally ecstatic: the Church is a "broken half" that reaches up and into the future to that which is beyond it.[65] Participation in the mission of Christ presumes the opposite of triumphalism: there is much to be done to bring both the Church itself and the world to the Being-for and being-with of Christ that resists and rejects all totalitarian projects (whether rooted in bread, *eros*, or power) through its very worship. The Christian person and the church have their being beyond them as they strive to travel along the path of history opened up by Christ.

The suggestion, then, is that Taylor enacts a kind of Catholic Triumphalism different from the one he mentions in "A Catholic Modernity." It is a "triumph" in that Gospel goods have assimilated into much of Western culture and evidently no longer require the witness of a liturgically centered community for their furtherance. Indeed, such a community may hinder this advance should they insist on their particular mission. What I do not want to suggest is that Taylor believes everything in contemporary culture to incarnate such goods. Certainly he is attractive to many Catholics for his rejection of atomistic individualism, his ethical realism (i.e., commitment to strong goods), his emphasis on dialogue, and his critique of exclusive humanistic takes on modern Western history. Some point to his discussion of conversion or to his populating of his grand narrative with saints. I would observe, however, that saints mainly provide a counter to exclusive humanism along modern lines of "interiority," and conversion stories, while important, are more nearly conversions to some kind of immanent sense of fullness than to the ongoing and unfinished mission of the Church. The question remains whether his discourse, then, can elide my critique by way of adverting to its ostensibly philosophical rather than theological nature. I do not think it can and do not think he would want it to. I will need to be brief.

65. Ratzinger, *Introduction*, 98.

Taylor is committed to the long story of which the Church is a part. The Church brings forward such goods as *agapic* or other-regarding love, self-sacrifice, a variety of spiritual practices, and even the notions of sin and grace. Underlying these, and requiring both institutional incarnation and later institutional attenuation, is the fundamental equality of all human beings made in the image and likeness of God. Taylor does not, to my recollection, wish to distinguish between faith and reason or revelation and reason; nor does he wish to denigrate faith. Goods may come into human consciousness through a variety of avenues. What matters is that they are recognized as goods and articulated as such, subsequent articulations revealing either depths or further aspects of said goods. Thus the theology/philosophy distinction would not be important to Taylor's work; indeed, revelation gets swallowed up into the grand narrative itself as a particularly informative (if superseded) element of it. It is for this reason that Christian mission qua Christian mission gets severely relativized: not because Christianity has nothing to teach us, but because its lessons have already been learned.

Conclusion

Ratzinger's *Introduction to Christianity* offers a stirring phenomenological description of Christian existence rooted in the mission of Christ, a mission that locates genuine humanity, freedom, and joy in the Being from, for, and with that grounds the inner meaning of creation and history. Ratzinger, however, does not think there is any default participation in such a mission. To participate in Christ's mission for the world is to turn towards God and others such that genuine communion in worship and the liturgy of Christian existence becomes possible. This path of ecstatic existence may look differently in different ages and, examined with care, elements of past formations may appear relevant in the present when they join with newer ideas. But much of this will depend upon prudential considerations as much as anything else. What must remain is the fundamental mission of the Church that moves to reconcile the world to God. This is the fundamental mission of the Church that needs to be renewed each generation, for the message of Christian loving service will never be simply agreed upon and enacted by default. Rather, it is a decision each day on the part of persons, and must mark all institutional decisions as well, lest they lose all authority.

Of course, if Being for, from, and with shape all forms of Christian existence, these same prepositions serve as the eschatological measure in which the Church lives and toward which it strives. Ratzinger's depiction of the ideal form of the Church offers a two-fold reminder: (1) for the Church to collapse in upon itself is to cease being Church; only as an exodus community can the Church be the Church of Christ; (2) the Church (and all its members) must never give in to a triumphalist ethos, as if one's conversion or institutional conversion to the Being-for and with of Christ is ever accomplished. For Ratzinger, the decision to live towards others is also a decision to take stock not only of the larger culture in its many ways of absolutizing bread, power, and sex, but also as to whether one is living up to the promises and indeed the promise of one's baptism that introduces us into the dynamic divine life of self-giving, receiving, and accompanying love.

Bibliography

Benedict XVI. *Jesus of Nazareth: From the Baptism in the Jordan to the Transfiguration.* San Francisco: Ignatius, 2007.

Chau, Carolyn. *Solidarity with the World: Charles Taylor and Hans Urs von Balthasar on Faith, Modernity and Catholic Mission.* Eugene: Wipf and Stock, 2016.

Habermas, Jürgen, and Joseph Ratzinger. *The Dialectics of Secularization: On Reason and Religion.* San Francisco: Ignatius, 2006.

Pzywara, Erich. *Analogia Entis: Metaphysics: Original Structure and Universal Rhythm.* Translated by John R. Betz and David Bentley Hart. Grand Rapids: Eerdmans, 2014.

Ratzinger, Joseph. *Introduction to Christianity.* San Francisco: Ignatius, 2000.

———. *Principles of Catholic Theology: Building Stones for a Fundamental Theology.* San Francisco: Ignatius, 1987.

———. "The Sacramental Foundation of Christian Existence." In *Collected Works, vol. XI: Theology of the Liturgy: The Sacramental Foundation of Christian Existence,* 153–87. San Francisco: Ignatius, 2014.

———. "The Theology of the Liturgy." In *Collected Works, vol. II: Theology of the Liturgy: The Sacramental Foundation of Christian Existence.* San Francisco: Ignatius, 2014.

Sciglitano, Anthony C., Jr. "Pope Benedict XVI's *Jesus of Nazareth*: Agape and Logos." *Pro Ecclesia* 17 no. 2 (Spring 2008) 159–85.

———. "Prometheus and Kant: Neutralizing Theological Discourse and Doxology." *Modern Theology* 25 no. 3 (July 2009) 387–414.

Taylor, Charles. "A Catholic Modernity?" In *A Catholic Modernity: Charles Taylor's Marianist Award Lecture,* edited by James. L. Heft, 13–37. New York and Oxford: Oxford University Press, 1999.

———. "Self-Interpreting Animals." In *Human Agency and Language: Philosophical Papers 1,* 45–76. Cambridge: Cambridge University Press, 1985.

———. *Philosophical Arguments.* Cambridge: Harvard University Press, 1995.

———. *A Secular Age.* Cambridge: Harvard University Press, 2007.

———. *Sources of the Self: The Making of Modern Identity.* Cambridge: Harvard University Press, 1989.

———. *Varieties of Religion Today: William James Revisited.* Cambridge: Harvard University Press, 2002.

Waldstein, Edmund, "What is Integralism Today?" *Church Life Journal* October 31, 2018. http://churchlife.nd.edu/2018/10/31/what-is-integralism-today/

Wilbur, Richard. "Advice to a Prophet." https://www.poetryfoundation.org/poems/43044/advice-to-a-prophet.

IV. Dogmatic Theology

10

Joseph Ratzinger's "Spiritual Christology"

Rev. Robert P. Imbelli

Introduction

This article offers some considerations on the topic: "Joseph Ratzinger's Spiritual Christology." It does so mindful of the frequently alleged disconnect between doctrine and experience, manifest in such slogans as "I'm spiritual, but not religious." This slogan has its ecclesiastical counterpart in the increasingly prevalent disjunction between what is "doctrinal" and what is "pastoral." But I also address the topic in light of an ever-growing tendency towards academic specialization that often deems "spirituality" not ingredient to the theological curriculum, but "extra-curricular," reserved to the chapel and not the classroom.

I will attempt to show, therefore, how theology and spirituality are intimately and exemplarily related in Ratzinger's thought—just as they were for his theological ancestors and mentors: Augustine and Bonaventure, Guardini and de Lubac. For him, as for them, "Mystery" and "mysticism" (faith's objective content and its subjective appropriation) are inseparable, and both have a distinctive "*Christic form*."[1] Ratzinger will come to call this persuasion and approach a "spiritual Christology."

The article will proceed in five parts: (I) Looking Back ... and Forward to Vatican II; (II) Ratzinger on Revelation: the Inextricable Nexus of Theology and Spirituality; (III) *Introduction to Christianity*: Laying the Foundations of a "Spiritual Christology"; (IV) Further Delineating "Spiritual Christology"; and (V) Towards a Eucharistic Mysticism and Spirituality.

But let me first dwell briefly upon the two images that accompany this reflection: the risen/ascended Christ bestowing the Holy Spirit upon the apostles (from the great entrance door of the twelfth century Basilica of Saint

---

1. See de Lubac's important article, "Mysticism and Mystery."

Mary Magdalene in Vézelay, France) and the painting of the Transfiguration (by the late thirteenth century Sienese painter, Duccio di Buoninsegna).

Panel Image from the 12th-century Basilica of Saint
Mary Magdalene in Vézelay, France.

"Transfiguration" by the late 13th-century Sienese
painter Duccio of Buoninsegna.

We know the crucial importance of images and of the aesthetic dimension of existence for Joseph Ratzinger/Pope Benedict. In his well-known 2002 address in Rimini, Ratzinger said: "Looking at icons, and in general at the great masterpieces of Christian art, leads us on an interior way, a way of transcendence, and thus brings us, in this purification of sight that is a purification of the heart, face to face with beauty, or at least with a ray of it."[2] A few years later, explaining why he insisted that images of Christian art be included in the *Compendium to the Catechism of the Catholic Church*, then Cardinal Ratzinger wrote: "In a culture of images, a sacred image can express much more than what can be said in words, and be an extremely effective and dynamic way of communicating the Gospel message."[3]

In this spirit and with this same conviction, I offer these two images to recapitulate aesthetically and affectively all that I write here. They depict imaginatively and strikingly *the absolute* novum *of the risen, ascending Jesus Christ and the transformative way of life to which he calls his disciples.*

2. Ratzinger, "Wounded by the Arrow of Beauty," 38.
3. *Compendium*, xvii.

Hopefully, these images will guide our meditations both *"ante et post scriptum"*! They certainly have continued to inspire my prayer and reflection since I first encountered them during a Junior Year Abroad sixty years ago.

I. Looking Back . . . and Forward to Vatican II

I begin by "Looking back and forward to Vatican II." But, in doing so, I would like to begin with a note of personal witness.

By the providence of God and the generosity of the Archbishop and people of the Archdiocese of New York, I began my theological studies in Rome in the Fall of 1962—the time of the opening of the Second Vatican Council. Vatican II, of course, remains the indispensable point of reference for Catholic theology and spirituality even after more than fifty years. Indeed, one might legitimately wonder: have we yet received it fully, perhaps even "misremembered" it?[4]

I certainly had some excellent professors at the Gregorian University during the years of the Council—Bernard Lonergan, René Latourelle, Francis Sullivan (to name a few). But, to be honest, most of the real excitement took place in the evenings at lectures by Rahner and Congar, Chenu and Cullman. For a time Rome seemed once again the center of the world. And to experience the gradual opening of a formerly rather closed clerical Rome during that period was marvelous to behold.

November 20, 1962 was a particularly remarkable day. In my memory, I still vividly recall the astonishment we all experienced. On that day, the document "On the Sources of Revelation," prepared by the Theological Commission (headed by Cardinal Ottaviani) was voted on by the Council fathers. There had been considerable discussion of the document in the days preceding the vote, and it had received much criticism for its style—overly scholastic and abstract, insufficiently biblical, historical, and ecumenical—a product of the reigning neo-scholasticism of the time.

When it came time to vote, more than 60 percent of the bishops chose not to accept the draft. But, according to the ground rules of the Council, it required a two-thirds negative vote to remand the document to Committee.

At that point, Pope John XXIII, with blessed common sense, intervened. He ordered that the document be re-composed, and created a new Commission to accomplish the task, joining Ottaviani's Doctrinal Commission with the Secretariat for Christian Unity headed by Cardinal Bea.

---

4. See O'Regan, *Anatomy of Misremembering*, Preface: "Forgetting, Remembering, Misremembering."

The impression created among those of us in Rome was electrifying—and not only among students like me. The great theologian Yves Congar wrote in his diary that evening: "I could scarcely believe it!"[5] We all sensed that we were witnessing a radical new beginning, a veritable revolution.

What emerged from the new joint commission was the epoch-making Dogmatic Constitution on Divine Revelation, *Dei Verbum*. Its more concretely historical, personalist, and pastoral style, helped set the tone for all the documents of the Council.[6]

Vatican II produced sixteen documents of varied length and importance. But in interpreting the Council, in establishing an appropriate "hermeneutic," the four "Constitutions" play a decisive role. They are, of course, *Sacrosanctum concilium*, *Lumen gentium*, *Dei Verbum*, and *Gaudium et spes*. However, in many ways it is the Dogmatic Constitution on Divine Revelation, *Dei Verbum*, which holds a primacy among them.[7]

For if God does not take the initiative to reveal himself, there is no foundation for the Church. It becomes only a human association and organization. And if God has not given himself definitively in Christ, there is no basis for liturgy. It becomes a merely human gathering, like an American legion parade, or the devoted fans at any sporting event.

A truly distinguishing characteristic of *Dei Verbum*'s presentation of revelation is that it is *explicitly Christocentric*. Though it celebrates God's revelation in the course of the history of the people of Israel, it confesses that God's revelation attains its fullness in *the person of Jesus Christ*.[8] It is this Christ-centered understanding of God's revelation and promise that permeates the documents of Vatican II—prominent not only in *Sacrosanctum concilium* and *Lumen gentium*, but also in *Gaudium et spes*.

I call attention to *Gaudium et spes*, §§10, 22, and 45 as prime instances of Vatican II "rekindling the Church's Christic imagination," and this in its "Pastoral Constitution." These crucial paragraphs of *Gaudium et spes* give the lie to any facile separation, much less dichotomy, between "dogmatic" and "pastoral" in Church teaching and practice.[9]

Here, for example, is the astonishing claim of *Gaudium et spes*, §45, which concludes Part One of the Pastoral Constitution:

5. Congar, *My Journal of the Council*, 195.

6. For a magisterial discussion of many aspects of the ecclesial and theological drama of Vatican II, see Wicks, *Investigating Vatican II*.

7. Wicks concurs with this privileging of *Dei Verbum*. See *Investigating Vatican II*, 223–24.

8. *Dei Verbum*, §2.

9. See the fine article by Granados, "The Synergy of Doctrine and Life," drawing upon Irenaeus, Augustine, and Aquinas.

> For the Word of God, through whom all things were made, was made flesh so that as perfectly human he would save all human beings and sum up all things. The Lord is the goal of human history, the point on which the desires of history and civilization turn, the center of the human race, the joy of all hearts and the fulfillment of all desires. He it was whom the Father raised from the dead, exalted and placed at his right hand, making him judge of the living and the dead. It is as given life and united in his Spirit that we make our pilgrimage towards the climax of human history which is in full accord with the designs of his love, "to unite all things in Christ, things in heaven and things on earth" (Eph 1:10).

Now one might understandably object: do you perhaps exaggerate in overstressing the Christocentric nature of Vatican II's understanding of revelation? Did not the Church always confess Christ? Did we not always profess Jesus as Son of God and son of Mary? One divine person in two natures? Certainly, these dogmatic assertions form a lasting part of the Church's deposit of faith.

Yet I contend that Vatican's II's *re-Sourcement* sought to know Christ in a new way: to re-discover the Person of Jesus Christ—not only through propositions *about him*, but by inviting and fostering a personal encounter *with him*—an encounter that leads not merely to an assent of the mind, but also a consent of the heart, and hence to transformation of life. And it sought to bring that renewed sense of Christ's reality and primacy into all facets of the Church's life and its relation to the world. So all the Popes since the Council have explicitly advocated a "new evangelization": a Church in mission to bring the Good News who is Jesus Christ to the world.

Thus, I fully agree with Nicholas Healy who writes: "Before dogma is something the Church formulates, dogma is something Christ himself is; dogma is first and foremost Christ himself as incarnate Word and enfleshed truth."[10]

The historian of Vatican II, John O'Malley, argues that "the universal call to holiness" weaves through the documents of the Council like a golden thread. He suggests that such an emphasis is unique in the history of ecumenical councils. O'Malley writes: "Among the recurring themes of the Council expressive of its spirit, the call to holiness is particularly pervasive and particularly important . . . It is the theme that to a large extent imbued the Council with its finality."[11]

---

10. Healy, "Henri de Lubac on the Development of Dogma," 679.
11. O'Malley, *What Happened at Vatican II*, 310.

What I would add, as essential complement to O'Malley's insight, is that, for the Council, the source and enabler of that call is the holy One himself: Jesus Christ. Indeed, the call to holiness has, in the mind and heart of the Council, a distinctive Christological foundation. For the revelation of the uniqueness of Christ is not primarily a propositional truth for our instruction, but an existential summons to transformation of life according to the image of Christ: being clothed with Christ, taking on the mind of Christ, living the life of Christ.

Thus the Council notably achieved one of the salient goals of the *nouvelle théologie* movement of the 1940s and 50s. In an excellent article Paolo Prosperi writes that for *la nouvelle théologie* "returning to the fathers meant asserting the unity between dogmatic theology and the living experience of Christ in the Church . . . the inseparable bond between mysticism and theology . . . putting back at the center knowledge through syggeneia (con-naturality), which for the fathers was the only real way to access the mystery of God."[12]

Vatican II's dialectic of *ressourcement* and *aggiornamento* is founded upon its bold and creative re-appropriation of the New Testament confession that "Jesus Christ is the same yesterday, today, and forever" (Heb 13:8).[13]

If the great achievement of the Second Vatican Council was this evangelical *re-Sourcement*—a renewed realization of the Christic Source of the Church's life and mission—a fair amount of the post-conciliar confusion and crisis can be attributed to the misremembering[14] or, worse, willful neglect of this achievement. I have elsewhere sought to elucidate further this loss of the Christic Center.[15] In doing so, I have been beholden to the analyses of Joseph Ratzinger himself. But, before taking up Ratzinger's own assessment of the post-conciliar challenges, let us reflect on the theological vision and perspective he brought to the Council.

---

12. Prosperi, "*Sources Chrétiennes* and the Return to the Fathers," 643–44. For the influence of the series, *Sources Chrétiennes*, on the labors of Vatican II, see Ratzinger, "*Sources Chrétiennes* and the One Unique Source," 383–88.

13. Significantly, this verse of the Letter to the Hebrews is quoted in *Gaudium et spes*, §10 at the close of the "Introduction," thus providing the Christological foundation and orientation for the remainder of the Pastoral Constitution.

14. O'Regan has insightful and instructive pages on Hegel's "Christological Derailment" which uncannily foreshadows some of Catholicism's post-conciliar developments and defections. See *The Anatomy of Misremembering*, 185–204.

15. Imbelli, *Rekindling the Christic Imagination*, xv–xviii. See also Levering's important book, *An Introduction to Vatican II*, especially chapter 5: "Vatican II as an Ongoing Theological Event: The Way Forward."

II. Ratzinger on Revelation: The Inextricable Nexus between Theology and Spirituality

The clearly Christocentric understanding of Revelation in *Dei Verbum* laid the foundation for the Christologically saturated teaching of the Council. And a person who helped secure that foundation was the thirty-five year old theologian Joseph Ratzinger.

Joseph Ratzinger, then a young professor at the University of Bonn, had been chosen by Cardinal Frings of Cologne as his theological advisor. Already in his "Inaugural Lecture" at Münster (to which he had moved in 1963) Ratzinger declared: "Revelation means God's whole speech and action with man; it signifies a *reality* which Scripture makes known but which is itself not simply identical with Scripture. Revelation, therefore, is more than Scripture to the extent that reality exceeds information about it."[16] Thus revelation exceeds even the divinely inspired images and propositions of Scripture.

And Ratzinger elucidates further the implications of this statement:

> There can be Scripture without revelation. For revelation always and only becomes a reality where there is faith. The unbeliever remains under the veil of which Paul speaks in 2 Corinthians 3. He can read Scripture and know what it contains. He can even understand, purely conceptually, what is meant and how its statements cohere, yet he has no share in revelation. Revelation is in fact fully present only when, in addition to the material statements which testify to it, its own inner reality is operative in the form of faith. Consequently revelation to some degree includes its recipient, without whom it does not exist. Revelation cannot be pocketed like a book one carries around. It is a living reality which calls for the living person as the location of its presence.[17]

I hold that this conviction, inspired to a large degree by his studies of Augustine and Bonaventure, remains as one of the salient motifs of Ratzinger's theological *itinerarium*.[18] Indeed, it clearly anticipates his later thematic "spiritual Christology."

---

16. Rahner and Ratzinger, *Revelation and Tradition*, 35.

17. Rahner and Ratzinger, *Revelation and Tradition*, 36.

18. Michael Schmaus, one of the two readers of Ratzinger's *Habilitationschrift* (necessary for teaching at the university level), worried that his position smacked of subjectivism and even modernism. For the "drama" of the dissertation's composition, revision, and defense, see Ratzinger, *Milestones*, 106–12.

For Ratzinger, as for Augustine and Bonaventure, there is an intimate, inseparable connection between his theology and his spirituality, between the content of faith (*fides quae*) and its experiential appropriation (*fides quā*). Indeed, like them, these are, for him, but two sides of one coin. And, like them, his theological-spiritual vision is *explicitly and pervasively Christocentric*.[19]

III. *Introduction to Christianity*: Laying the Foundations of a "Spiritual Christology"

In 1983, the now Cardinal Joseph Ratzinger published a book of essays to which he gave the title, *Behold the Pierced One: An Approach to a Spiritual Christology*. In the book's "Preface" he expressed his intention "to consider Christology more from the aspect of its spiritual appropriation" than he had previously done.[20]

I will return to that book in due course. But the major contention that I would like to argue in this part of the presentation is that the foundation for Ratzinger's "spiritual Christology" was already securely laid in his now classic, *Introduction to Christianity*. The book, of course, originated as lectures delivered at Tübingen in summer 1967, published in German in 1968 and in English in 1969. I maintain that what he later came to call his "Spiritual Christology" was already abundantly present in these lectures.

From the very beginning, the book clearly resonated with readers, as it had with its original audience. By 2005, the original German edition had gone through twenty-four reprints, and translations had appeared in seventeen different languages.

In commenting upon the book, permit me to proceed once more by way of personal reminiscence. I think it evokes some of the turmoil of the postconciliar years in which the book appeared.

My doctoral studies took place at Yale from 1967–1970—even before there was a "Yale School"! I was one of the first of a cohort of Catholics to pursue graduate studies in theology at a non-Catholic institution. The years 1967–1970 were not happy ones in either Church or country. I refer to 1968 in particular as my "*annus horribilis*."

I had been ordained barely three years and was living at Saint Thomas More House, the seat of the Catholic chaplaincy at Yale. The talented and well-respected chaplain was on a year's sabbatical. In the event, he never

---

19. See the insightful reflections of Haddad, "Kneeling Theology."
20. Ratzinger, *Behold the Pierced One*, 9.

returned from the sabbatical and went on to leave priestly ministry—unfortunately, a not uncommon occurrence in those turbulent years.

Frenzy for change permeated both Church and society. The political crisis of the Vietnam War spilled over into classroom and chapel, provoking tension-filled meetings of newly-formed liturgical committees. At times this seeped into the celebration of the liturgy itself.

One small, though, to my mind, portentous, incident from those days has remained vividly with me. I was at supper with the acting Chaplain, and we had as a guest the Provincial of a small religious congregation. We recited a quite perfunctory grace before meals. Before we had even seated ourselves, the visitor commented: "Oh, I see you still pray: we have gone from formal prayer to informal prayer to no prayer." He said this not as boast, but with a sense of poignant regret. More than fifty years later, the scene seems a paradigm of the disorientation experienced by so many in the wake of the Council, as a highly institutionalized Church, with a liturgy unchanged for centuries, sought to find its way in a new religious and cultural landscape where familiar markers were obscured.

In the midst of this turmoil, both institutional and personal, there appeared, literally out of the blue, the English translation of a book by a German scholar, with the not very "jazzy" title: *Introduction to Christianity*. It turned out to be an oasis in a parched land. What was it about the book that impressed so deeply?

First was the clear acknowledgement of the theological-spiritual crisis that had erupted in the immediate post-conciliar years. In the "Preface" to the first edition, Ratzinger lamented the "confusion about the real content and meaning of Christian faith" and the consequent "watering down of the demands of faith."[21] He provocatively employs to this end the parable of "Clever Hans" who successively exchanges the gold which he had inherited for items of lesser value until he is left, at last, with a worthless stone which he then discards.

In a similar vein, in 1992, looking back on the situation in 1972 when the new journal *Communio* was launched, Ratzinger spoke of some in the immediate post-conciliar period who made endless appeals to the supposed "spirit" of the Council. He wrote: "They sold goods from the old liberal flea-market as if they were new Catholic theology."[22]

Then, in the "Preface" to the new edition of *Introduction to Christianity* in 2000, Ratzinger specifies (what was already clear in the first edition)

---

21. Ratzinger, *Introduction*, 31.
22. Ratzinger, "*Communio*: A Program," 437.

that the "crisis" in question was—and remains—fundamentally a *Christological crisis*.

He writes:

> If God has truly assumed manhood, and thus is, at the same time, true man and true God in Jesus, then he participates as man in the presence of God, which embraces all ages. Then, and only then, is he, not just something that happened yesterday, but is *present among us, our contemporary in our today*. That is why I am firmly convinced that a renewal of Christology must have the courage to see Christ in all his greatness, as he is presented by the four gospels together, in the many tensions of their unity.[23]

But *Introduction to Christianity* is far from a sustained lament. It presents, rather, a positive vision and proposal. In the original "Preface" he speaks of "understanding faith afresh as making possible true humanity today."[24] Notice Ratzinger in no way opposes authentic "*aggiornamento*": it is intrinsic to his project. What he seeks is theological creativity faithful to the heart of the Church's kerygma and catechesis: the person of Jesus Christ.

Let me select some aspects of *Introduction to Christianity* that advance this constructive vision.

Significantly, Ratzinger sets his entire presentation within the liturgical context of the baptismal profession of faith, articulated in the Apostles' Creed. Clearly for him this is not a polite bow to ritual, a prescribed familiar and familial tradition. Rather, in a phrase that has captivated me since I first read it almost fifty years ago, he declares that faith "is an all-encompassing movement of human existence."[25] It is a radical "turning" marked by existential renunciations and conversions—a personal and person-forming turning to the East, to the risen and ascended Jesus Christ who is ever-coming.

He specifies further: "Christian faith is more than the option in favor of a spiritual ground to the world; its central formula is not 'I believe in something,' but '*I believe in you*.' It is the *encounter* with the man Jesus and in this encounter it experiences the meaning of the world as a person."[26] One recognizes here a clear foreshadowing of Benedict XVI's famous assertion in *Deus Caritas Est*: "Being Christian is not the result of an ethical choice or

---

23. Ratzinger, *Introduction*, 29 (emphasis added).

24. Ratzinger, *Introduction*, 32.

25. Ratzinger, *Introduction*, 88. One recalls the "*moto spiritale*" that marks the Pilgrim's descent and ascent in Dante' *Divina Commedia*.

26. Ratzinger, *Introduction*, 79 (emphasis added).

a lofty idea, but the encounter with an event, a person, who gives life a new horizon and a decisive direction."[27]

And Ratzinger sums up his vision and conviction: "Ultimately, all the reflections contained in this book . . . revolve around the basic form of the confession: 'I believe in you, Jesus of Nazareth, as the meaning (*logos*) of the world and of my life.'"[28] Of course, the further question, inseparably both spiritual and theological, is: who is this man? "Who do you say that I am?"

Ratzinger goes on to devote more than one hundred pages of Part Two of the book to the topic: "Jesus Christ." I offer one quote that is particularly rich and that undergirds his emergent spiritual Christology: "the peculiarity of Jesus' 'I,' of his person . . . lies in the fact that this 'I' is not at all something exclusive and independent, but rather is Being completely derived from the 'Thou' of the Father and lived for the 'You' of men."[29]

Ratzinger's life-long meditation on the person and unique significance, the *novum*, of Jesus Christ, finds expression in his careful exposition of Jesus' relational pattern of existence. For Ratzinger "relationality" is constitutive of who Jesus is. Jesus the Christ is the one who receives all *from* the Father and shares himself fully, his entire person, *for* the sake of men and women in all their historical concreteness.

Thus the image that focuses and animates Ratzinger's spiritual Christology is the Johannine image of the crucified/raised Jesus from whose *pierced side* flow the blood and water of new life. He makes explicit reference to this image in the important section of *Introduction to Christianity* entitled, "Christ, the 'Last Man.'"[30] The "last man" is, of course, Paul's *ho eschatos Adam*, the new man who inaugurates God's new creation. The pierced side reveals Christ as "the completely open man, in whom the dividing walls of existence are torn down, who is entirely '*transitus*' (Passover, 'Pasch')."[31]

This Image provides the title of the book that will further thematize his call for a "spiritual Christology," *Behold the Pierced One*, and will be invoked five times in his inaugural encyclical as Pope, *Deus Caritas Est*.

If we truly behold "the Pierced One," if we enter into the movement of existence, the *transitus*, that he realizes and enables, then, of course, we will undergo transformation. Indeed, "Being a Christian means essentially changing over from being for oneself to being for one another."[32] In a real

---

27. Benedict XVI, *Deus Caritas Est*, §1 (translation slightly modified).
28. Ratzinger, *Introduction*, 80–81.
29. Ratzinger, *Introduction*, 208.
30. Ratzinger, *Introduction*, 240–41.
31. Ratzinger, *Introduction*, 240 (translation slightly modified).
32. Ratzinger, *Introduction*, 252.

sense it is to "pass over" from being merely an individual to becoming in Christ a person: one defined by his or her relationships.

In one of the most suggestive assertions in the book Ratzinger writes: "The Christian sees in man, not an individual, but a person. And it seems to me that this passage from individual to person contains the whole span of transition from antiquity to Christianity, from Platonism to faith."[33]

To my mind the contemporary theologian who shows special kinship with Ratzinger is Rowan Williams. In a profound meditation on the icon of the Transfiguration, Williams writes: "Looking at Jesus seriously changes things. If we do not want to be changed, better not to look too long or too hard."[34] In the writings of both Ratzinger and Williams one is repeatedly struck by the grammar of "*novum*/transformation" that governs and structures their work. In this they are manifestly heirs of the fathers of the Church.[35]

Thus the issue is far deeper than merely "imitating" Christ, by following the path that he indicates. It is rather the *birth of a new self*, on the Way that Jesus has opened through the veil to the Father. Ratzinger's Spiritual Christology is mystagogic. It advocates and guides our entering into the mystery of Christ, a "Christification," that goes beyond mere moralism. In a short, but rich essay, he writes: "The *sequela Christi* has a much higher goal: to be assimilated to Christ, so as to achieve union with God . . . The *sequela Christi* is not a question of morality. It is a 'mysteric' theme: the conjoining of divine action and our human response."[36]

In *Introduction to Christianity* he writes: "Christian existence is put with Christ into the category of relationship."[37] Christians, by baptism, are incorporated into the relational flow of filial existence, *from* the Father, *through* the Son, *in* the communion of the Holy Spirit. And, thus, intrinsic to their identity is to be *for* others. The prepositions are paramount!

Though I won't develop this here at any length, one need not fear that Ratzinger (and the Creed's!) "Christocentrism" risks lapsing into a "Christomonism."[38] Like Augustine and Bonaventure, Ratzinger's Trinitarian

33. Ratzinger, *Introduction*, 160.

34. Williams, *The Dwelling of the Light*, 13.

35. This is abundantly evident in Williams' new book: *Christ: The Heart of Creation*.

36. Ratzinger, "The New Evangelization," 398. An important (though quite neglected) theme of Charles Taylor's monumental *A Secular Age* is that of divinization or *theosis*. I have suggested affinities between the constructive approaches of Ratzinger and Taylor in Imbelli, *Rekindling the Christic Imagination*, xxi–xxviii.

37. Ratzinger, *Introduction*, 186.

38. In light of my previous remarks concerning a post-conciliar loss of the Christic Center, one might plausibly argue that the far greater threat today is that of a

vision is foundational to his theological and pastoral reflection. The prime analogue of the "from/for" rhythm of existence is the very life of the Trinity. Relational existence is constitutive of Trinitarian "personhood." It is this dynamic life that the Eternal Word of God incarnates in Jesus Christ.[39]

One must admit that the "spiritual Christology" limned in *Introduction to Christianity* contains scant reference to the Eucharist. The word does not even appear in the index to the English edition (though, not surprisingly, it is listed in the always more exhaustive German). This is understandable in that Ratzinger's chosen perspective in the book is the baptismal profession of the Creed and the movement of existence it initiates. Certainly, in other writings, both as theologian and Pope, the Eucharist receives sustained consideration in his development of a spiritual Christology—as it must.

However, there are two places in the volume which merit attention in this regard. In the important and rich "Excursus on Christian Structures," Ratzinger articulates what he calls "The Law of Excess [Überflusses]." Here he makes explicit reference to the change of water into wine at Cana and thus to the Eucharist. He speaks of Jesus Christ as "the infinite self-expenditure [one might even 'wastefulness'] of God [*Christus ist die unendliche Selbstverschwendung Gottes*]."[40] That pouring out of Christ finds its supreme sacramental embodiment in the Eucharist.

The other notable reference to the Eucharist occurs in his consideration of "the communion of saints" at the end of the exposition of the Creed. He holds that the *communio sanctorum* refers in first instance to "the holy things" set upon the "Eucharistic table," and derivatively, but inseparably, to the "Eucharistic community" they effect.[41] But it is crucial to affirm the proper order: while the Church, indeed, "confects" the Eucharist, it is the Eucharistic Christ who constitutes the Church in the Spirit. Because

---

"Spiritmonism." Cyril O'Regan suggests that for von Balthasar "Hegel and his epigones have fundamentally reversed the order of reference and made Christ refer to the Spirit, rather than the Spirit to Christ." The result is that "the community divests itself of the concrete particularity of Christ . . . Through pneumatic displacement the community's memory of Christ becomes self-referential" (*Anatomy of Misremembering*, 200). I contend that a similar "misremembering" is by no means absent from the Church today. Indeed, Ratzinger's repeated cautions about a self-referential ecclesial community, especially in its liturgical celebrations, bespeaks just such a concern.

39. In an essay written in 1960, "Christocentrism in Preaching?" the young theologian contends that "Christocentric preaching" is, by its nature, "Trinitarian preaching," "namely the exposition of the way of Christian existence through Christ in the Spirit to the Father." See Ratzinger, *Dogma and Preaching*, 46.

40. Ratzinger, *Introduction*, 261.

41. Ratzinger, *Introduction*, 234.

Ratzinger's spiritual Christology is at its heart Eucharistic, I will return to Eucharist in the final section of the article.

There is one final theme to lift up from *Introduction to Christianity*. This too comes from the section "Excursus on Christian Structures," or as Ratzinger calls it in another place, "Principles of Christian Existence."[42] Principle five concerns "Finality and Hope." Here he addresses again the uniqueness and eschatological reality of God's definitive revelation in Jesus Christ. There is thus *no "Third Age"* of the Spirit, if that is understood as a surpassing of the fullness realized in Christ Jesus. Thus, in company with both Bonaventure and Aquinas, his insistence upon "finality." The end time has truly been initiated in the death, resurrection, and ascension of Jesus Christ.

And yet . . . there remains a "not yet," and, hence, a hope. "The union that has taken place at the one point 'Jesus of Nazareth,' must attain the whole of mankind, the whole one 'Adam,' and transform it into the body of Christ. So long as this totality is not achieved, so long as it remains confined to one point, what has happened in Christ remains simultaneously both end and beginning."[43] We recognize here the Pauline vision of the eschatological achievement of the one "perfected person" (Eph 4:13—*eis andra teleion*), lovingly exegeted by Augustine as the *totus Christus*.

I call attention to one implication of this affirmation of both "finality and hope," which entails serious responsibilities for preaching and teaching. In this very section of his book, Ratzinger maintains that "faith can have final [definitive] statements in which its intrinsic finality is articulated." Dogmatic statements are of crucial import. Still, he continues, "this does not mean that these formulas cannot open further in the course of history and thus be understood in fresh ways, just as the individual must continually learn to understand the faith afresh as a result of his or her own experiences of life."[44] Was this not John XXIII's intention for the Council: not new truths, but new understanding and expression?[45]

Indeed in the essay on "Christocentrism in Preaching" (to which I referred earlier) Ratzinger laments that "perhaps nothing in recent decades has done more harm to preaching [and I would add "teaching"] than the loss of credibility that it incurred by merely handing on formulas that were no longer the living intellectual property of those who were

---

42. Ratzinger, *Introduction*, 269

43. Ratzinger, *Introduction*, 263–64.

44. Ratzinger, *Introduction*, 265.

45. For a nuanced understanding of Pope John's famous opening address to the Council, with its distinction between the content of the faith and its mode of expression, see Guarino, *The Disputed Teaching of Vatican II*, 34–37.

proclaiming them."[46] John Henry Newman castigates these merely rote repetitions as "unreal words!"[47]

IV. Further Delineating "Spiritual Christology"

In this section I will supplement these reflections on *Introduction to Christianity* by turning to *Behold the Pierced One*, the book of essays in which Ratzinger formally announced his intention "to consider Christology more from the aspect of its spiritual appropriation than I had hitherto done."[48]

In the first essay, "Taking Bearings in Christology," he sought to spell out how such spiritual appropriation is "*realized.*" I use that word, so dear to John Henry Newman, advisedly, and will return to it again. Ratzinger proceeds by articulating several theses—the third and fourth of which are particularly relevant to my purpose.

Thesis Three states: "Since the center of the person of Jesus is prayer, it is essential to participate in his prayer if we are to know and understand him."[49] One hears echoes here of Evagrius' well-known dictum: "The theologian is one who prays and one who prays is a theologian."

But one also recalls Newman's famous distinction between "notional" and "real" apprehension. I contend that Ratzinger's "spiritual Christology" is a pastoral-theological call, ever more urgent in this era of the "Nones," to move from a merely notional apprehension, a purely academic Christology if you will, to a *lived, personally appropriated Christology*. To know spiritually is participatory knowing, not distance education. Spiritual exercises are incumbent upon the seeker.

Thus, towards the end of his elaboration of the thesis, he writes: "Real advances in Christology can never come merely as the result of the theology of the schools . . . as important as schools are. It must be complemented by the theology of the saints, which is theology from experience. All real progress in theological understanding has its origin in the eye of love and in its faculty of beholding."[50]

One catches resonances of the famous conclusion to Saint Bonaventure's *Itinerarium* where he exclaims: "If you wish to know how such things come about, consult grace, not doctrine; desire, not understanding; prayerful groaning, not studious reading; the Spouse, not the teacher; God, not

---

46. Ratzinger, *Dogma and Preaching*, 57.
47. Newman, "Unreal Words," 977–87.
48. Ratzinger, *Behold the Pierced One*, 9.
49. Ratzinger, *Behold the Pierced One*, 25.
50. Ratzinger, *Behold the Pierced One*, 27.

man; darkness, not clarity."[51] Neither Bonaventure nor Ratzinger would endorse a dichotomy here. But each, I think, would assign a primacy.

Thesis Four then adds a further important dimension to Ratzinger's understanding of a "Spiritual Christology."

"Sharing in Jesus' praying involves *communion* with all his brethren. Fellowship with the person of Jesus, which proceeds from participation in his prayer, thus constitutes that all-embracing fellowship that Paul calls the 'Body of Christ'. So the Church—the 'Body of Christ'—is the true subject of our knowledge of Jesus."[52]

And Ratzinger professes the conviction that permeates all his pastoral-theological endeavors: "In the Church's memory [*anamnesis*] the past is present because *Christ is present and lives* in her."[53] In his body, the Church, the Christian *encounters Christ*, not merely as the object of exegetical study, but most crucially as the living Lord of the Church, its beloved Spouse. We recognize here the persuasion that inspires Benedict XVI's *Jesus* books.

Clearly related to this theme of Christ's ongoing presence (and greatly deserving of further study) is the critical significance of Christ's Ascension for Ratzinger's spiritual Christology. In general, the Lord's Ascension often languishes as a rather neglected topic in contemporary theology. How often, even among liturgists, is the "Paschal Mystery" truncated to the Lord's death and resurrection without reference to its completion in the Ascension?[54]

Ratzinger, both as theologian and preacher, does not slight the mystery of the Ascension. In the splendid "Epilogue" to *Jesus of Nazareth, Part Two*, he writes: "The departing Jesus does not make his way to some distant star. He enters into communion of power and life with the living God, into God's dominion over space. Hence he has not 'gone away,' but now and forever, by God's own power, he is present with us and for us." Therefore, Ratzinger insists, "[Jesus'] going away is in this sense a coming, a new form of closeness, of continuing presence . . ."[55]

I think it consonant with Ratzinger theological vision to say that Christ's Ascension establishes a new, redeemed order of existence—a reconfiguration of space and time, centered around the person of Jesus Christ, which is the present visible order brought to transfigured fulfillment. Indeed, Ratzinger maintains that the Christian understanding of heaven is

---

51. Saint Bonaventure, "The Journey of the Mind to God," 58.
52. Ratzinger, *Behold the Pierced One*, 27 (emphasis added).
53. Ratzinger, *Behold the Pierced One*, 27 (emphasis added).
54. I have considered the topic more fully in Imbelli, "*Sursum Corda*." See also the fine study by Kelly, *Upward*.
55. Ratzinger/Pope Benedict, *Jesus of Nazareth, Part Two*, 283.

constitutively Christological. Thus, in *Introduction to Christianity*, he writes: "heaven and the Ascension of Christ are indivisibly connected; it is only this connection that makes clear the Christological, personal, history-centered meaning of the Christian tidings of heaven."[56]

This new order of existence, the Pauline "new creation," inseparably comprises three interrelated dimensions. Ratzinger develops this insight in another essay of *Behold the Pierced One*, entitled "Eucharist, Christology, Ecclesiology: the Christological Core." Here he shows how these three are dimensions of *the one mystery of Christ* "in whom the whole fullness [*pleroma*] of deity dwells bodily [*somatikos*]" (Col 2:9). Somatic relationality intimately binds the ascended Lord with his Eucharistic and ecclesial body.

A salient consequence of the absolute uniqueness of Jesus Christ, the new Adam—*ho eschatos Adam* (1 Cor 15:45)—is the depth of the transformation to which disciples are called. A remarkable passage of this essay declares: "The goal of Eucharistic communion is a total recasting of a person's life, breaking up a man's whole 'I' and creating a new 'We'. Communion with Christ is, of necessity, a communion with all those who are his: it means that I myself become part of this new 'bread' which Christ creates by transubstantiating all earthly reality."[57] In the next section of this essay we will further consider the scope of the transformation which the Eucharist sacramentalizes and empowers.

Joseph Ratzinger's spiritual Christology thus exhibits a profoundly challenging theological-pastoral dialectic. To realize concretely the newness of Jesus Christ is to realize that we are summoned by Jesus to a radically transformed way of life. And, as we enter more deeply into that new life (Dante's "*Vita Nuova*"), we are led to a deeper realization of the identity and mission of Jesus, the first-born of creation and first-born of the dead.

Jesus' prayerful attentiveness to the will of the Father and his total dedication to the true good of others—his "pro-existence"—are to be replicated in his disciples who are called to become *filii in Filio*. But this stupendous vocation can only be realized *in Spiritu Sancto*—in the communion of the Spirit which is the Body of Christ.[58]

---

56. Ratzinger, *Introduction*, 313.

57. Ratzinger, *Behold the Pierced One*, 89.

58. See the striking remarks of Congar: "If I were to draw but one conclusion from the whole of my work on the Holy Spirit, I would express it in these words: no Christology without pneumatology and no pneumatology without Christology." Indeed, he insists, "the vigor of a lived pneumatology is to be found in Christology. There is only one body which the Spirit builds up and quickens and that is the body of Christ." See *The Word and the Spirit*, 1 and 6.

The Classics of Spirituality, from Augustine and Bonaventure, through Teresa of Avila and John of the Cross, to Thérèse of Lisieux and Teresa Benedicta of the Cross, "flesh out" the concrete shape of transformation, of what configuration to Christ entails. Hence they are not extracurricular activities; they are integral to the theological curriculum itself. They integral to and indispensable for a truly spiritual Christology.

V. Eucharistic Mysticism and Spirituality

In this final section I want to relate more explicitly Ratzinger's insistence upon encounter with the Living Jesus Christ, and the transformed life to which it calls Christians, to the reality of the Eucharist. Here mystery and mysticism are concentrated and receive paradigmatic expression.

I think Peter John McGregor is exactly right when he says that "the goal of Ratzinger's spiritual Christology is Eucharistic."[59] Some of his fine homilies and meditations from the later seventies have been published in English under the title, *God Is Near Us: The Eucharist the Heart of Life*.[60] Here Ratzinger's Eucharistic vision and spirituality are set forth in a succinct and accessible way. They manifest once more the inseparable nexus of the doctrinal and pastoral.

But I will concentrate in particular upon Benedict XVI's *Sacramentum Caritatis*, the Apostolic Exhortation he wrote following the Synod on the Eucharist (2005). There he evokes once again the figure of the pierced, crucified One and explicitly relates it to the Eucharist. He writes:

> A contemplative gaze "upon him whom they have pierced" (Jn 19:37) leads us to reflect on the causal connection between Christ's sacrifice, the Eucharist, and the Church. . . . *The Eucharist is Christ who gives himself to us and continually builds us up as his Body*. . . . the Church is able to celebrate and adore the mystery of Christ present in the Eucharist precisely because Christ first gave himself to her in the sacrifice of the cross. The Church's ability to "make" the Eucharist is completely rooted in Christ's self-gift to her. . . . We too, at every celebration of the Eucharist, confess the primacy of Christ's gift. . . . it was Christ who loved us "first" (1 Jn 4:19).[61]

Here we see once more the warning against a community's liturgical celebration that becomes self-referential—a theme so prominent in Ratzinger's

---

59. McGregor, *Heart to Heart*, 197.
60. Ratzinger, *God Is Near Us*.
61. Benedict XVI, *The Sacrament of Charity*, §14 (emphasis added).

The Spirit of the Liturgy. It is a warning against what I have called the "decapitated Body," a community which in its liturgical practice is effectively and affectively sundered from its Head. Ratzinger insists that Jesus Christ, the Head of the Body, does not exercise an absent Lordship, but is present, nourishing and building up his body, the Church, through the gift of his body, his Eucharistic self. Jesus' Ascension does not remove him, but establishes a new and lasting presence.[62]

But, if truly united with its Head, the community, whose very identity, whose "subsistence" (whose very "personhood"[63]) is founded in the Eucharist, will cultivate a *"Eucharistic Form of Life."* Thus Part Three of *Sacramentum Caritatis* is entitled: "The Eucharist, A Mystery to Be Lived," and the first section is: "The Eucharistic Form of the Christian Life." Such a Eucharistic form of life entails taking on the heart and mind of Jesus Christ so that Eucharistic spirituality become the measure of our thoughts and actions, and the criterion by which we discern the values and disvalues of a given culture.[64] For the theologian Pope, Romans 12:1–2 serves as ongoing inspiration and imperative: "I appeal to you brethren, by the mercies of God, to present your bodies as a living sacrifice, holy and acceptable to God, your spiritual worship [*logiké latreia*]. Do not be conformed to this world, but be transformed by the renewal of your mind, that you might discern what is the will of God, what is good and acceptable and perfect."

A Eucharistic form of life is not, for Benedict, one of withdrawal into some supposedly uncontaminated spiritual realm.[65] Like the Eucharist itself it is radically material, fruit of the earth and work of human hands, transformed by the power of the Word and the Spirit. Indeed, I would not hesitate to speak of Ratzinger/Benedict's "Eucharistic mysticism."[66] But it is a mysticism rooted in the Eucharist and is, thus, corporeal, communal, and cosmic: in a word, "somatic."[67]

---

62. Griffiths writes: "The principal condition of the possibility of the Eucharist is exactly that Jesus has ascended . . . After the Ascension, his flesh, veiled as bread, and his blood, veiled as wine, can be touched and tasted everywhere and at once, without constraint by the metronome of time or the map grid of space." *Christian Flesh*, 51.

63. Mühlen's pioneering work *Una Mystica Persona* remains a salutary spur to systematic theology.

64. For challenging reflections, see the concluding section, "Eucharistic Passages," in Tück, *A Gift of Presence*, 301–39.

65. The considerations of O'Malley, "Joseph Ratzinger Is Not a Platonist," are apposite.

66. See my audio presentations: Imbelli, *Christic Imagination*, especially lecture nine: "Dwelling in Christ's Transfigured Presence: the Mystic Dimension of Christian Faith."

67. In *On the Way to Jesus Christ*, 124–28, under the heading "The Eucharist as

Benedict contends that "every great reform in the Church has in some way been linked to the rediscovery of belief in the Lord's Eucharistic presence among his people."[68] Karl Rahner once famously claimed that "the Christian of the future will be a mystic—one who has experienced something—or will not be."[69] Joseph Ratzinger is, perhaps, more diffident in employing the term "mystic." Yet, I maintain that his "spiritual Christology" in effect proposes that: "The Christian of the future will be a Eucharistic mystic—one who has experienced Someone, the living Lord—or will not be."

Throughout his long service to Christ's Church, Joseph Ratzinger/Benedict XVI has had as overriding theological-pastoral concern to foster real friendship with Jesus. Exploring his spiritual Christology leads, mystagogically, to the realization that *Jesus Christ's very being is to be Eucharist*. The sacrament of the Eucharist is the privileged locus where friendship with Jesus is nourished and cultivated. To the extent that we become present to his real Presence, our very self becomes Eucharistic: a living out of gratitude to the Father and generosity towards our brothers and sisters.

In Eucharistic celebration and adoration, as nowhere else, the believer can echo Saint Paul's daring and joyful exclamation ("It is no longer I who live, but Christ lives in me. And the life I live now in the flesh, I live by faith in the Son of God who loves me and gives himself for me" [Gal 2:20]), and join Joseph Ratzinger in quoting his beloved *Rule of Saint Benedict*: "*Christo nihil omnino praeponere*"—Cherish Christ above all![70]

Conclusion

Having begun on a personal note, let me end in a similar way. In 1970 when I first began to teach at the New York Archdiocesan Seminary, I chose, as a major text, the newly translated work of Professor Doctor Joseph Ratzinger. I used it in each of my eight years there.

It provided for me and, I hope, for my students, what Henri de Lubac's *Catholicism* had provided the young seminarian Joseph Ratzinger in 1949. Speaking, years later, of de Lubac's classic work, Cardinal Ratzinger called it "an essential milestone on my theological journey." It opened for him, he says, a vivid sense of the "*Catholica*," the "all-embracing": "the inner unity of I and Thou and We," rooted in the Triune God.[71]

---

the Sacrament of Transformations," Ratzinger delineates a five-fold transformation that Christ effects.

68. Benedict XVI, "Sacrament of Charity," §6.

69. Rahner, "Christian Living Formerly and Today," 15.

70. *Rule of Benedict* LXXII, 11. Latin text in Venarde, *The Rule of Saint Benedict*, 226 (my translation).

71. Lubac, *Catholicism*, 11.

And de Lubac achieves this by returning theology to its Christic Center, drawing upon its own deepest resources, its life-giving Source. Yet, Ratzinger insists, de Lubac is not engaged upon an antiquarian exercise. De Lubac is in constant dialogue with his contemporaries and brings their most intimate questions to his task, and thus can offer real, not fabricated answers.

Can one find a more apt characterization of Joseph Ratzinger's own achievement in *Introduction to Christianity*?

Bibliography

Benedict XVI. *The Sacrament of Charity*. Washington DC: USCCB, 2007.

———. *Deus Caritas Est*. December 25, 2005. http://w2.vatican.va/content/benedict-xvi/en/encyclicals/documents/hf_ben-xvi_enc_20051225_deus-caritas-est.html

Bonaventure, "The Journey of the Mind to God." In *The Works of Bonaventure, I: Mystical Opuscula*, translated by José de Vinck, 1–58. Patterson: St. Anthony Guild, 1960.

Compendium to the Catechism of the Catholic Church. Washington, DC: USCCB, 2006.

Congar, Yves, OP. *My Journal of the Council*. Translated by Mary John Ronayne, OP, and Mary Cecily Boulding, OP. Collegeville: Liturgical, 2012.

———. *The Word and the Spirit*. Translated by David Smith. San Francisco: Harper&Row, 1986.

Granados, José. "The Synergy of Doctrine and Life." *Communio* 43 no. 1 (Spring 2016) 104–22.

Griffiths, Paul J. *Christian Flesh*. Stanford: Stanford University Press, 2018.

Guarino, Thomas. *The Disputed Teaching of Vatican II: Continuity and Reversal in Catholic Doctrine*. Grand Rapids: Eerdmans, 2018.

Haddad, Jordan. "Kneeling Theology: Believing in Order to See Scripture." *Church Life Journal* October 17, 2018. http://churchlife.nd.edu/2018/10/17/kneeling-theology-believing-in-order-to-see-scripture/.

Healy, Jr., Nicholas J. "Henri de Lubac on the Development of Dogma." *Communio* 44 no. 4 (Winter 2017) 667–89.

Imbelli, Robert P. "*Sursum Corda*: Ascension Theology and Spirituality." In *Sufficit Gratia Mea: Studi Offerti al Cardinale Angelo Amato*. Vatican City: Libreria Editrice Vaticana, 2019.

———. *Christic Imagination: How Christ Transforms Us*. https://www.nowyouknowmedia.com/christic-imagination-how-christ-transforms-us.html.

———. *Rekindling the Christic Imagination: Theological Meditations for the New Evangelization*. Collegeville: Liturgical, 2014.

Kelly, Anthony. *Upward: Faith, Church, and the Ascension of Christ*. Collegeville: Liturgical, 2014.

Levering, Matthew. *An Introduction to Vatican II as an Ongoing Theological Event*. Washington, DC: The Catholic University of America Press, 2017.

Lubac, Henri de. "Mysticism and Mystery." In *Theological Fragments*, translated by Rebecca Howell Balinski, 35–69. San Francisco: Ignatius, 1989.

---. *Catholicism: Christ and the Common Destiny of Man.* "Foreword" by Joseph Cardinal Ratzinger. Translated by Lancelot C. Sheppard and Sister Elizabeth Englund, OCD. San Francisco: Ignatius, 1988.

McGregor, Peter John. *Heart to Heart: The Spiritual Christology of Joseph Ratzinger.* Eugene: Pickwick, 2016.

Mühlen, Heribert. *Una Mystica Persona: Die Kirche als das Mysterium der Identität des Heiligen Geistes in Christus und den Christen—Eine Person in Vielen Personen.* München: Schöning, 1964.

Newman, John Henry. "Unreal Words." In *Parochial and Plain Sermons*, 977–87. San Francisco: Ignatius, 1997.

O'Malley, John W. *What Happened at Vatican II.* Cambridge: Harvard University Press, 2008.

O'Malley, Timothy. "Joseph Ratzinger Is Not a Platonist." *Church Life Journal.* October 16, 2018. http://churchlife.nd.edu/2018/10/16/joseph-ratzinger-is-not-a-platonist/

O'Regan, Cyril. *The Anatomy of Misremembering: Von Balthasar's Response to Philosophical Modernity*, volume I: Hegel. New York: Crossroad, 2014.

Prosperi, Paolo. "*Sources Chrétiennes* and the Return to the Fathers." *Communio* 39 no. 4 (Winter 2012) 641–62.

Rahner, Karl and Joseph Ratzinger. *Revelation and Tradition.* Translated by W. J. O'Hara. New York: Herder and Herder, 1966.

---. "Christian Living Formerly and Today," in *Theological Investigations*, vol. 7. Translated by David Bourke, 3–24. New York: Herder, 1971.

Ratzinger, Joseph. *Behold the Pierced One: An Approach to a Spiritual Christology.* Translated by Graham Harrison. San Francisco: Ignatius, 1986.

---. "Christocentrism in Preaching?" In *Dogma and Preaching: Applying Christian Doctrine to Daily Life.* Translated by Michael J. Miller and Matthew J. O'Connell, 40–58. San Francisco: Ignatius, 2011.

---. "*Communio*: A Program." *Communio* 29 no. 3 (Fall 1992) 436–49.

---. *God Is Near Us: The Eucharist, the Heart of Life.* Translated by Henry Taylor. San Francisco: Ignatius, 2003.

---. *Introduction to Christianity.* Translated by J. R. Foster and Michael J. Miller. Revised edition with a new preface. San Francisco: Ignatius, 2004.

---. *Milestones: Memoirs 1927–77.* Translated by Erasmo Leiva-Merikakis. San Francisco: Ignatius, 1998.

---. "The New Evangelization." *Communio* 44 no. 2 (Summer 2017) 389–400.

---. "*Sources Chrétiennes* and the One Unique Source." *Communio*, 44 no. 2 (Summer 2017) 383–88.

---. *The Spirit of the Liturgy.* Translated by John Saward. San Francisco: Ignatius, 2000.

---. "Wounded by the Arrow of Beauty: The Cross and the New 'Aesthetics' of Faith." In *On the Way to Jesus Christ*, translated by Michael J. Miller, 32–41. San Francisco: Ignatius, 2005.

---/Pope Benedict XVI. *Jesus of Nazareth, Part Two, Holy Week: From the Entrance into Jerusalem to the Resurrection.* Translated by Philip J. Whitmore. San Francisco: Ignatius, 2011.

Tück, Jan-Heiner. "Eucharistic Passages." In *A Gift of Presence: The Theology and Poetry of the Eucharist in Thomas Aquinas*. Translated by Scott G. Hefelfinger, 301–39. Washington DC: The Catholic University of America Press, 2018.

Venarde, Bruce L., ed. and trans. *The Rule of Saint Benedict*. Dumbarton Oaks Medieval Library 6. Cambridge: Harvard University Press, 2011.

Wick, Jared, SJ. *Investigating Vatican II: Its Theologians, Ecumenical Turn, and Biblical Commitment*. Washington, DC: The Catholic University of America Press, 2018.

Williams, Rowan. *Christ: The Heart of Creation*. London: Bloomsbury Continuum, 2018.

———. *The Dwelling of the Light: Praying with Icons of Christ*. Grand Rapids: Eerdmans, 2004.

11

Touching the Void

Ratzinger's Soteriology

FRANCESCA MURPHY

I. Touching the Void

TOUCHING THE VOID IS a true story and it actually happened. The narrative first appeared as a book, which sold over a million copies and made its way into film.[1] It documents the story of Joe Simpson and Simon Yates, two mountain climbers who attempted to scale a mountain in Peru named Silua Grande. Silua Granda looks to the amateur like a vertical shard of rock, because that's what it is. On the way back down from the peak, Joe Simpson broke his leg so he could not climb. Joe's companion, Simon Yates, tried to lower him on a rope, but Joe slid off the edge, into the abyss. The narrator explains that, in movies, people singlehandedly hoist other men up a hundred yards on ropes. But in real life, he says, it is physically impossible to lift such a weight while hanging onto a rock.

It is a tacit law of the mountaineering community that a climber never cuts off someone who is roped up to him. So Simon tries all night to find a way to haul his brother climber back up. But it cannot be done. In the morning, he cuts the rope. There seems to be nothing else he can do. He continues his climb down, and searches below for the corpse. He cannot find Joe's body, and, in any case, it's a natural presumption that Joe didn't survive the fall. Simon continues back to the base camp. But Joe has actually plunged into a deep abyss and survived his fall. He cannot walk. Worming his way on the ground, Joe finds a narrow corridor leading out. He rolls himself on the snow and ice for several days until he is just outside the base camp.

---

1. The book by Simpson appeared in 1988; the movie *Touching the Void* appeared in 2003.

In the movie, Joe decides to forgive Simon just before he reaches the base camp. He crawls into camp just as Simon is leaving to go home. I don't know if he really forgave Simon then and there, but, unlike many other mountaineers who have heard his story, Joe Simpson has always insisted that Simon had no choice in what he did. He has never criticized him for cutting the rope. It must have been a necessary condition for his emotional survival after the ordeal that he not harbor any anger toward the partner who cut him off. His act of forgiveness is his act of recovering his manhood and dignity after crawling alone for days consigned to a near-subhuman condition. In the same act, of course, he gave Simon back his lost humanity.

I always remember this movie as being called 'Falling into the Abyss,' and I was a bit afraid I'd called my paper that, and there is no movie or book named *Falling into the Abyss*. I begin with this true story movie because it seems to dramatize the condition of 'Sheol' or death as Ratzinger describes it in his *Introduction to Christianity*. I don't mean to draw a deep moral message from *Touching the Void*, and preach that as Christians we must not cut the rope, or explain to you that we are all invisibly but profoundly and spiritually roped up on this Peruvian mountain of life. I don't even want to rub your noses in Joe's act of forgiveness. The movie and its protagonists can be turned into ethical examples, but the appeal of the story lies deeper than that. It shares the magnetism of Arctic adventure stories, and the appeal of several more recent movies about astronauts trapped in outer space, and that attraction lies in the horrifying notion of being all alone.

Joe 'touches the void' when the rope is spliced and he is dropped off the edge of the mountain by himself. The story captures the horror of dropping into dark emptiness, and finding oneself cut off in a howling waste, utterly alone. The story literally enacts the fallen condition as Ratzinger, very traditionally, describes it. For Ratzinger's soteriology likewise homes in on the horror of plummeting alone into a closed and exitless abyss. For Ratzinger, what Christ saves humanity from is a condition of metaphysical alone-ness experienced as pure, whited out loneliness. Ratzinger may say other things about human fallenness in later works, and he may elsewhere give human fallenness a rather more scholastic or moralizing interpretation. But in his *Introduction to Christianity*, the fallen state is described as the phenomenologically accessible condition of pure loneliness.

Ratzinger is always, throughout his life, a thinker who lived through German National Socialism, and the Second World War. The typical German re-thinking of the question of how this civilized nation descended into barbarism is embedded in his conception of Fall and Redemption. In that sense, he's very typical of his generation. For a decade or so, after the Second World War, there's something of a renewal of attention to human falleness and imperfectability. In 1954, the novelist William Golding writes *Lord of the Flies*, about English public school boys devolving into savages when shipwrecked without adults on a tropical Island. In a less-well known novel, *Pincher Martin*, published in 1956, Golding describes the stream of consciousness of a navy officer trying to survive on the narrow slip of rock after his ship has been torpedoed. By the end of the novel, we realize that the eponymous protagonist is drowned and dead. The sailor is clinging by himself to that tooth of a rock because that is who 'Pincher Martin' is: a man who is entirely alone in life and in death. It is this perception of what the Christians call 'postlapsarian humanity' that Ratzinger addresses through the conception of 'salvation' in his *Introduction to Christianity*.

II. Not the Theologian's Theologian

With those opening paragraphs, it's natural to think of Ratzinger's soteriology in this book as 'apologetical' rather than 'dogmatic.' Ratzinger does not seem to write as a 'theologian's theologian' in this book. He doesn't use awkward terms like 'pre-lapsarian' and 'postlapsarian.' He doesn't assume his audience appreciate that they exist in a state of alienation from God, from which Christ heroically rescues them. He doesn't assume they owe God a moral or ontological debt, which Christ conveniently pays off on their behalf. He does not describe Christianity as a debt-forgiveness operation. Even allowing for an increased sense of the imperfectability of human beings in the immediate post-war period, these theological schemes are not readily obvious to anyone who is not fully cognizant of Christian dogmatic theology, or who does not spontaneously interpret their condition as the Catechisms describe it to be.

Though he may speak more irenically elsewhere, in his *Introduction to Christianity* Ratzinger is rather dismissive of Anselm's satisfaction theory. He dismisses not only the Anselmian project of deducing *a priori* the human need for a 'God-man' to make satisfaction for sin to God, but also sprinkles cold water on the wider soteriological project of a 'juridical' atonement.[2] It is hard to repress the sense that Ratzinger wants to sidestep the notion of Christ restoring legal order to the cosmos through his innocent death, and wanting to avoid it because it takes us into 'theological' territory which makes civilian Christians itch and feel uncomfortable, without resonating with their sense of their identity and desires. Anselm's satisfaction theory is theologically satisfying and lovely to teach to the pious folk, but especially for the generation who were Ratzinger's immediate

2. Ratzinger, *Introduction*, 231–34.

audience, such an ethical-based soteriology didn't connect with their 'Sunday-best' sense of identity, let alone with how they actually felt about God and humanity. His audience could readily grasp the horror of loneliness, and the sense of atonement as rescuing them from that, but not so easily grasp that they are sinners who owe God an infinitely valuable Christ-ransom to bail them out of eternal punishment.

It might seem, then, that in this book Ratzinger sets aside a Godward theory of atonement, like the satisfaction theories, and adopts what we may call a 'manward' theory of atonement: the recipient of atonement, in such a typically Patristic and Orthodox understanding, is humanity, rather than God. It might seem that Ratzinger wants to define the condition from which humanity is saved, not so much as 'original sin,' with the Western tradition, but rather more as 'original death,' with the Eastern Orthodox and Byzantine Catholic legacy. And it might seem that Ratzinger does so because the Eastern and Byzantine legacy is more experientially and evidentially accessible. It seems as if he is starting where modern humanity is, and with its own idiosyncratic experience and sense of destiny. We have to add some caveats to this conception, and not only that Ratzinger was no Schleiermacher, setting off from some imagined common human experience and reaching the heights of theology only delicately and politely once he has selected a diplomatic, non-religious language in which to address his audience.

Ratzinger does not give us either an experientially based 'soteriology from below' or a juridical, moralizing and theologically-correct soteriology from 'above.' Even when he wants to tell us what theology is, and how its knowledge of God is grounded in faith, Ratzinger explains that through a modern secular adage, Heisenberg's uncertainty principle according to which the observer is part of what he is observing. Ratzinger is grounding himself in a well-known non-theological principle, a principle of modern physics when he tells his readers that "Even the reality 'God' can only impinge on the vision of him who enters into the experiment with God—the experiment that we call faith."[3] Ratzinger presents his soteriology, not in human experience as compartmentalized off from spiritual and mystical experience, and not in theological dogma, but in some area between the human and the theological, where the believer and the skeptic discover their commonalities. He is wanting the skeptic to find the chink in the armor of the believer, and the believer to find the chink in the armory of skepticism. He is trying to speak from within a position of faith, certainly, but one which is not "sealed-off," "self-sufficient," and cleanly demarcated from skepticism. He is seeking the "secret uncertainty" within both belief and

---

3. Ratzinger, *Introduction*, 176.

unbelief, where the two can converse.[4] Perhaps that is just a poetic way of saying that Ratzinger in this book presents his soteriology as a response to human questions that can appeal equally to St. Thérèse of Lisieux as to an atheist. He's not going to stand on the far side of the abyss and shout into it with a megaphone, but, like St. Thérèse, he plunges into it.

For Ratzinger, the personal, Triune God is a datum of revelation, known through faith. He doesn't think of philosophy, or human reasoning, as being capable of achieving the 'personal' God. He speaks in the *Introduction to Christianity* of the "lonely silence of philosophical questioning."[5] So even though Ratzinger so resoundingly defends philosophy and reason in this book, philosophical questioning is still a *lonely* pursuit, an act of humanity in its deathly, solitary confinement. And yet, what that lonely questioning unknowingly seeks, is the Biblical God, "the God . . . with a face, the personal God."[6] If the fallen human condition is defined as one of loneliness, what such solitude desires above all is a human face. This is why, perhaps, the *Introduction* opts for a non-juridical conception of atonement: some kind of 'objective' satisfaction does not satisfy the need for a *personal* redeemer. As Ratzinger puts it, "Christian faith is more than the option in favor of a spiritual ground to the world; its central formula is not 'I believe in something', but 'I believe in you.' It is the encounter with the man Jesus, and in this encounter it experiences the meaning of the world as a person."[7]

Methodologically, Ratzinger doesn't enter into a phenomenology of human consciousness and decide that loneliness is, after all, a negative experience, nor does he start from a theological conception of what humanity most needs. Rather, he enters into both experiences at once. It was, as he realizes, St. Thérèse who plunged into a loneliness far surpassing that of the modern atheist. The loneliness of abandonment in Sheol is measured by that lonely abandonment of Christ on the Cross. Ratzinger may not be the theologian's theologian. But he does nonetheless write theological theology, which is rather a different notion.

III. Original Sin

The only piece of theological thesaurus writing in the *Introduction* is about Jesus as the 'Last Adam,' who completes the 'hominization' of humanity. Ratzinger looks from the risen Christ back to Adam, and not from Adam

4. Ratzinger, *Introduction*, 41–42.
5. Ratzinger, *Introduction*, 30.
6. Ratzinger, *Introduction*, 135.
7. Ratzinger, *Introduction*, 79.

to Christ. Adam and the fall story have been part of soteriology, one could say loosely, ever since Saint Paul. Paul writes his midrash on Genesis 1–3 in the light of Christ, specifying the meaning of the text in a way that was not obviously attributed to it by the authors of the Old Covenant. Catholic theology has perhaps traditionally preferred looking forward from Adam to Christ than backward. For the Fathers and the Mediaevals, it is the fact that fallen Adam is or was causally 'homoousios with us' that projects down through the generations the falleness that makes Christ's recreation of humanity necessary for salvation. Without fallen *Adam*, there are no fallen individuals. Thus in 1951, insisting on monogenism as against polygenism, Pius XII wrote that

> the faithful cannot embrace that opinion which maintains either that after Adam there existed on this earth true men who did not take their origin through natural generation from him as from the first parent of all or that Adam represents a certain number of first parents. Now it is in no way apparent how such an opinion can be reconciled with that which the sources of revealed truth and the documents of the Teaching Authority of the Church propose with regard to original sin, which proceeds from a sin actually committed by an individual Adam and which through generation is passed on to all and is in everyone as his own.[8]

We need not imagine that the young Ratzinger scorned this paragraph of *Humani Generis*. Just as today we have John Paul II priests, so Ratzinger was a Pius XII Catholic, sharing the pope's aversion to racism and his moral aspiration on behalf of the unity of the human race. In one of his earliest little books, *On Christian Brotherhood,* Ratzinger wrote that "All men, Israelites and Gentiles, ultimately constituted a single humanity because of their single human source and the single creative act of God."[9] But nonetheless, it seems fair to say that, for Ratzinger, the accent is on the creative act of God in forming a single human race, and the emphasis is on Christ, and his eternal election, as constituting the perennially 'future' exemplar of humanity. The *Introduction to Christianity* seems more interested in the future 'teleogenesis' of humanity than its monogenetic origins.

---

8. Pius XII, *Humani Generis*, §37.
9. Ratzinger, *The Meaning of Christian Brotherhood*, 9.

IV. Solidarity is Not Enough

Bringing in or extracting and excising 'Adam' as the fall source of a single, fallen humanity does not help moderns with the 'homoousios with us' which the Chalcedonian formula ascribes to Christ. Moderns have, perhaps, less difficulty with 'homoousios with the Father' than with 'homoousios with us,' because the former looks like a straight datum of Christian faith, and you believe it or not, whereas the 'homoousios with us' looks like it ought to make some kind of sense to us, given that—to all intents and purposes—it is about *us*. It is a hard sell for moderns because of Christianity. The doctrine of the persons of the Trinity, and the doctrine of the two natures in one person in Christ deepened our Western appreciation of the meaning of the word 'person,' so that over the centuries, the West in particular, Christian and less Christian, Protestant and Catholic, developed an appreciation of the idiosyncrasy and uniqueness of the person as such, human or divine. We dignify and respect the uniqueness of the person in a way that the ancients, including the Fathers of the first Five centuries, did not. We appreciate that God is not in a genus and neither is the person, divine or human. This in turn makes it difficult to think of each radical unique person as a chip off the old block of Adam. It makes 'homoousios' harder to conceive, because we know that the unique human person is not a token of a universal type called 'humanity.' And then likewise with Christ: except by a blind act of faith, we find it hard to see how the individual man Jesus shares a single common humanity with each human individual person in history.

This is where Ratzinger's concept of the person as relation becomes essential. His claim in the *Introduction to Christianity* that, whether divine or human, personality only exists in relatedness, is at the core of his soteriology. In this way, Ratzinger combines ancient and modern in a particular way. I can scarcely read those many passages in the *City of God*, for instance, where Augustine seems to speak of the collective 'block' of humanity as superior to the mere individual: here Augustine seems to me to be quite unbaptized in his anthropology. Ratzinger obviously sees the difficulty, but he does not abandon the ancients. Rather, following Henri de Lubac in *Catholicism*, Ratzinger presents us with the paradox that it is because Christianity starts from the 'whole' that it is able more deeply to care for the individual person. If we start from the *isolated individual*, that is, the un-related individual who does not have 'for-ness' written into his DNA, no individual is going to count for much. The isolated individual is the individual as fallen and un-recreated, unhealed. If we start with that individual, we will only ever envisage salvation as every man for himself, rushing for the exits out of the crevasse, and oddly enough, according to

Ratzinger, we will never prize the dignity of the unique individual person. For the same 'modern people' who struggle with the 'homoousios with us' likewise bang their heads over the 'scandal of particularity,' and all salvation hanging from one single, particular individual. Ratzinger thus responds to the two objections together, stating that, because of its

> relation to the whole, Christianity lives from the *individual* and for the individual, because only by the action of the individual can the transformation of history, the destruction of the dictatorship of the milieu come to pass. . . . in Christianity *everything* hangs in the last resort on *one individual*, on the man Jesus of Nazareth, who was crucified by the milieu—public opinion—and who on his Cross broke this very power of the conventional 'everyone,' the power of anonymity, which holds man captive. This power is now confronted by the name of this individual, Jesus Christ, who calls on man to . . . contribute to the renewal of history. . . . Because Christianity wants history as a whole, its challenge is directed . . . at the individual; . . . for this reason it depends on *the* single individual in whom the bursting of the bondage to the forces and powers took place. . . . because Christianity relates to the whole and can only be understood from the idea of community . . . because it does not mean the salvation of the isolated individual but being enlisted in service to the whole, . . . it is committed to the principle of 'the individual' in the most radical form. *Here* lies the . . . necessity of the unheard-of scandal that a single individual, Jesus Christ, is acknowledged as the salvation of the world. The individual is the salvation of the whole, and the whole receives its salvation only from the individual who *truly* is salvation and who . . . for this reason ceases to exist for himself alone.[10]

Every people that has ever lived must have observed that new things happen because individual human beings make them happen. Every people who has lived on earth has the tacit knowledge that it is the actors who make the story, and that the story has no agency without its individual actors. The ancient Greeks knew it, and every people which has carved inscriptions of its kings and warriors going into battle knew at heart the 'great man theory of history.' But they could not articulate their sense, because they prized order and collectivity, the whole 'story,' over freedom and individuality. So only Genesis 1–3, with its vision of what Ratzinger calls 'creative consciousness' or 'creative love,' as the source and origin of human history, enabled us to articulate the principle that historical novelty rides on the back of free

---

10. Ratzinger, *Introduction*, 249–50.

and creative personality. The Jewish and Christian scriptures taught us to articulate the universal experience that free, creative personalities are the ones who make history happen.

To be creative consciousness is to be apt for history. Without creative consciousness at its back, there would be no history, but only the same old—same old, the rotating story. But without such creative freedom, such history, there would be no evil either, Ratzinger observes: " . . . if the *logos* of all being . . . is consciousness, freedom, and love, then it follows . . . that the supreme factor in the world is not cosmic necessity but freedom." This implies that

> "one can only comprehend the world as incomprehensible . . . For if . . . the supreme point in the world's design is a freedom that upholds, wills, knows, and loves the whole world as freedom, then this means that together with freedom the incalculability implicit in it is an essential part of the world. Incalculability is an implication of freedom . . . A world created and willed on the risk of freedom and love is no longer just mathematics. As the arena of love it is also the playground of freedom and also incurs the risk of evil.[11]

V. Loneliness

This little word 'evil' brings us back to loneliness, to the individual isolated in and by his sin. As we said before, this loneliness is a common experience, and Ratzinger knows that pretty well, but he also knows that we learn the very meaning of our human loneliness from Christ, and from his cry of dereliction. Ratzinger claims that this 'cry on the Cross' contains in itself the descent into hell, and thus the fate of humanity as it currently stands: the fate of humanity is to touch the void, to fall into the abyss. What is brought to light, Ratzinger says, by Jesus' cry of dereliction is "simply the abyss of loneliness of man in general, of man who is alone in his innermost being. This loneliness, which is usually thickly overlaid but is nevertheless the true situation of man, is . . . in fundamental contradiction with the nature of man, who cannot exist alone; he needs company."[12] The nature of man is to be 'for,' to be relational, but the "situation" of humanity is to be consigned to hellish solitude.

---

11. Ratzinger, *Introduction*, 159–60.
12. Ratzinger, *Introduction*, 298.

In the next few lines, here, Ratzinger mentions two human experiences which eighteenth and nineteenth century reductionists from David Hume to Herbert Spencer and the early Andrew Lang proposed as primitive causes of religion. One is simply primitive fear, and the other is fear of being alone with a dead body. It's striking that here, in the midst of explaining the meaning of Christ's descent into hell, Ratzinger stops and mentions two emotions which the reductionists laid at the door of belief in god or gods: childish fear, and adult foreboding in the presence of dead bodies. Ratzinger names these fears, saying that

> As soon as he is alone in the darkness, and thus has the experience of utter loneliness, fear arises, the fear peculiar to man, which is not fear of anything in particular but simply fear in itself. Fear of a particular thing is . . . harmless; it can be removed by taking away the thing concerned. . . . where man falls into extreme loneliness he is not afraid of anything definite that could be explained away; . . . he experiences the fear of loneliness, the uneasiness and vulnerability of his own nature . . . If someone has to keep watch alone in a room with a dead person, he will always find his position to be somehow . . . eerie . . . What arises here is . . . fear . . . in being alone with death, the eeriness of loneliness in itself, the exposed nature of existence.[13]

Human existence is exposed and vulnerable, on a knife edge which touches the void on the one side. Ratzinger takes on Hume and Spencer, and says yes, we are frightened because there is indeed something to be afraid of, "the eeriness of loneliness in itself, the exposed nature of existence." There's no denying that sinful, fallen humanity has carved its gods in the hope of keeping that fear in abeyance. But deifying the fear merely scotches the snake, it does not kill it.

The only gesture that can genuinely drive the fear away at its source does not come from us, but from another:

> the child will lose his fear the moment there is a hand to take him and lead him and a voice to talk to him; at the moment therefore at which he experiences the fellowship of a loving human being. Similarly, he who is alone with the corpse will feel the bout of fear recede when there is a human being with him, when he experiences the nearness of a "You." . . . The fear peculiar to man cannot be overcome by reason but only by the presence of someone who loves him.[14]

13. Ratzinger, *Introduction*, 298–99.
14. Ratzinger, *Introduction*, 299–300.

As I loudly hinted at the start, there is a Western, more moralizing soteriology, bent on redeeming us from 'original sin,' and an Eastern soteriology which concerns itself with the overcoming of 'original death,' and, in this work of 'fundamental theology,' Ratzinger works with the latter conception. But he cannot just speak of death as an objective, cosmic fact which Christ has, through his own death, trampled down. Ratzinger wants to take us to that iconic moment, where "the tombs opened and the bodies of the saints were raised."[15] But he wants to lead us there through the personalist phenomenology of death, lest victory over the abyss be cheap, and eternal life an empty pair of words. Death, says Ratzinger, really is "what theology calls 'hell,'" where hell

> denotes a loneliness that the word love can no longer penetrate ... In truth ... there exists a night into whose solitude no voice reaches; there is a door through which we can only walk alone: the door of death.... all the fear in the world is fear of this loneliness.... it is possible to understand why the Old Testament has only one word for hell *and* death, the word *sheol*; it regards them as ultimately identical. Death is absolute loneliness. But the loneliness into which love can no longer advance is—hell.[16]

Christ's descent into hell is the existential meaning of the 'homoousios with us': fallen humanity, humanity fallen into hell, encounters his face and his outstretched hands. Homoousios with our nature, he enters into our fallen human condition in order creatively to change the landscape. In the *Introduction to Christianity*, Ratzinger's Christ does not enter 'hell' or 'sheol' as one damned to loneliness, but in order to take the initiative and give companionship to the lost souls.[17] Ratzinger's Christ enters hell in solidarity

---

15. Ratzinger, *Introduction*, 301.

16. Ratzinger, *Introduction*, 300–1.

17. I have been asked whether I intended to indicate here that Ratzinger's conception of hell diverges from that of Ratzinger's friend, Hans Urs von Balthasar. Ratzinger gave his opinion about von Balthasar's thesis in *The Sabbath of History*. Ratzinger states, "I was asked in the summer of 1956 to review a new book of Hans Urs von Balthasar (*Die Gottesfrage des heutigen Menschen*, Vienna: Herder, 1956) in which the author shifts the article on the descent into hell to the center of Christian faith and life. According to Balthasar, Christ participated himself in hell, in the deepest sense of the word; only in the last level of his descent did redemption penetrate into the deepest abyss, that is to say, hell. At the time I did not want to adopt this thesis that Balthasar later (1969) developed again in a grand and impressive way in his *Theology of the Three Days*. I have to admit that even today, as in 1956 and 1967, I find it difficult fully to concur with the great Swiss theologian with whom I developed a close friendship. I prefer to leave this mysterious sentence, which leads from the historical world into the hiddenness of death, in its mysterious obscurity. A rather banal suggestion of some exegetes seemed to

with the human condition, but enters hell as unfallen, that is, as one capable of entering and overcoming the deathly silence of solitude. By bringing life and love into death, Christ eliminates its hellish character.

Bibliography

Golding, William. *Lord of the Flies*. London: Faber and Faber, 1954.
———. *Pincher Martin*. London: Faber and Faber, 1956.
Pius XII. *Humani Generis*. August 12, 1950. http://w2.vatican.va/content/pius-xii/en/encyclicals/documents/hf_p-xii_enc_12081950_humani-generis.html.
Ratzinger, Joseph. *Introduction to Christianity*. Translated by J. R. Foster. Ignatius, San Francisco: 1990, 2004.
———. *The Meaning of Christian Brotherhood*. London: Sheed and Ward, 1966; Ignatius: San Francisco, 1993.
———. *The Sabbath of History*. Translated by Susan Scott Cesaritti. Washington, DC: William Congdon Foundation, 1998.
Simpson, Joe. *Touching the Void: The Story of One Man's Miraculous Survival*. London: Jonathan Cape, 1988.

---

me already in 1956, and still in 1967 and again today, to indicate a direction that allows the unknowable to remain in the unknowable and yet at the same time in its modesty can take up what seems to be the essential point in Balthasar's thesis. It was said by some theologians (and probably still is said) that what the theologians give of themselves constitutes whatever is over-interpretation. In reality, the '*inferi*' of the Creed, that in German was first translated by *hell* and more recently by *kingdom of death*, is simply the Latin equivalent of the Hebrew word *sheol* which indicates a realm of the dead, that can be imagined as a kind of shadowy existence, existence and non-existence at the same time. It is very similar to the image of *hades* that we have inherited from Homer that coincides rather with the view of the dead of the Ancient East. Accordingly, the word expresses only that Jesus died. Since I always had great respect for the exegetes, I assumed that this statement was as such correct, but saw too that it was not thought through to the end. For what does it mean that someone has 'died'? What is death? How does it stand with someone who from an empirical point of view is dead? What does the 'kingdom of death' consist of . . . ? . . . the solution occurred to me. Yes, Jesus died, he 'descended' into the mysterious depths death leads to. He went to the ultimate solitude where no one can accompany us, for 'being dead' is above all loss of communication. It is isolation where love does not penetrate. In this sense Christ descended 'into hell' whose essence is precisely the loss of love, being cut off from God and man. But, however, wherever he goes, 'hell' ceases to be hell, because he himself is life and love, because he is the bridge which connects man and God and thereby also connects men among themselves. The final solitude no longer exists—except for the one who wants it, who rejects love from within and from its foundation, because he seeks only himself, wants to be from and for himself." Ratzinger *The Sabbath of History*, 21–22.

12

The Homelessness of Pneumatology

Ratzinger on the Spirit and the Church in the Modern World

Patrick X. Gardner

I. Introduction

THE MOST STRIKING FEATURE about Joseph Ratzinger's treatment of the Holy Spirit in the *Introduction to Christianity* is its brevity. Falling within his broader discussion of "The Intrinsic Unity of the Last Statements of the Creed," his exposition on the Spirit spans only seven pages.[1] His treatment of the Church fairs little better (extending the count by only ten pages). Why so few words on topics of such import? Practical constraints were no doubt a factor: the 1967 summer term at Tübingen was drawing to a close, and time did not afford Ratzinger the luxury of expounding a whole pneumatology.[2] We might also forgive Ratzinger for writing so few words when the Apostles' Creed itself spares hardly any for the Spirit or the Church. Ratzinger even suggests that there may even be something fitting about this reticence. Speaking about the Holy Spirit, he says, is an especially difficult, even dangerous prospect.[3] There is an elusive quality to the Spirit and a poverty unique to our language about him. Perhaps then it is foolish to expect more than a few pages of any pneumatology faithful to its subject.

It is more likely, however, that Ratzinger offers no treatise on pneumatology because he never intended the *Introduction to Christianity* to be a standard work of dogmatics. While it originated with his Tübingen lectures, Ratzinger describes the book's purpose by invoking the aims of the Second Vatican Council: to rediscover the Church's "voice," to make it

---

1. Ratzinger, *Introduction*, 331.
2. Voderholzer, "Integral Faith Formation."
3. Ratzinger, "The Holy Spirit as Communio," 324.

comprehensible in a new age, and to "endow Christianity once more with the power to shape history."[4] He was not writing systematic theology in a vacuum, but attempting to "understand the faith afresh as something that makes possible true humanity in the world of today . . . "[5] And fulfilling this purpose requires him to engage in tasks that differ from those we would expect of someone composing a textbook on Catholic doctrine. First, he must diagnose the obstacles preventing modern men and women from understanding the Christian faith; and, second, he must present the tenets of that faith in a way that makes their significance for human life clear and compelling. What Ratzinger *does* say about the Holy Spirit and the Church, then, is not primarily a matter of getting the doctrine right for its own sake. His main concern is with the credibility of the Creed's third section—how to think and speak about these articles of faith so that what is credible about them can overcome the obstacles to belief we are most familiar with.

In this chapter, I address the question: what, according to Ratzinger, makes for a credible interpretation of the Creed's statements on the Spirit and the Church? I begin by examining Ratzinger's definition of belief and what this entails about the credibility of the Creed's articles. I then discuss what he says about those features of modern thought that most obscure the credibility of the Creed's claims. Here I focus on the misinterpretation that Ratzinger suggests is behind some of our distinctively modern misunderstandings about the Spirit and the Church: a pneumatology he describes as "homeless."[6] Finally, I defend the claim that Ratzinger's alternative pneumatology—one that prioritizes the Spirit's presence and activity in the Church—is more credible, because it can show how the Creed speaks to the very meaning of our lives.

II. Belief, Credibility, and Meaning

Ratzinger's first step in determining what makes the Creed credible is to return to a definition of "belief" that is more faithful to the context of the Creed's composition. As it was defined at the First Vatican Council, belief or the act of faith is described as an act of the intellect. It is to assent to propositions that, while not based on direct evidence, nonetheless attain a certainty akin to knowledge.[7] Ratzinger agrees that belief involves the intellect and is concerned with truth. But he insists that when early Christians pronounced

---

4. Ratzinger, *Introduction*, 12–13.
5. Ratzinger, *Introduction*, 32.
6. Ratzinger, *Introduction*, 333.
7. First Vatican Council, *Constitutio dogmatica de fide catholica* (*Dei Filius*), 804–11.

credo at their baptism, that act was irreducible to and incommensurate with knowledge.[8] His concern is that belief has become overly intellectualized. When we define it exclusively as an act of the intellect, we risk confusing it with an incomplete and imprecise kind of knowledge.[9] Alternatively, belief in the biblical sense meant a holistic act of trusting or a commitment of one's whole self. It was and remains, he says, a decision at the very core of our human existence. Moreover, it is defined by what one is committing to or deciding for. It is the attitude one takes toward the "ground" of one's being— "holding firm" and "taking a stand" upon it.[10] And because this "ground" or organizing principle will exceed what is tangible, belief retains the sense of a "leap"—a commitment to the invisible.[11] It is, he concludes, the act of "taking up a stand in the totality of reality."[12]

Belief is thus existential rather than epistemological. More than with truth, goodness, or beauty, belief is concerned with meaning. Meaning, Ratzinger says, is that "ground" on which our being depends: the principle or intention that explains why we exist and that imbues our lives with direction and purpose. It points to a reason—a *logos*—that upholds our lives and our world, making them intelligible.[13] Ratzinger notes that there is a desire for this meaning at the heart of our being, since it is that without which we could not live and act (not even in the pursuit of our most mundane ends). It is, he says, the "bread" on which the most human part of us subsists, and its absence would render our existence absurd: "the totality of man would remain homeless."[14] So belief then is fundamentally an existential decision: a determination of our whole selves or an act of trust in something invisible—something beyond and before what we can know, which renders us and everything we can know intelligible. It requires "entrusting oneself to the meaning that upholds me and the world; taking it as the firm ground on which I can stand fearlessly."[15]

Belief in this sense, however, is at odds with the dominant attitude of our time. As Ratzinger notes, it has become increasingly difficult for us to identify the "I" of our present situation with the "I" in the Creed's "I

---

8. Ratzinger, *Introduction*, 72.
9. Ratzinger, *Introduction*, 76, 69.
10. Ratzinger, *Introduction*, 69.
11. Ratzinger, *Introduction*, 50–51.
12. Ratzinger, *Introduction*, 72.
13. Ratzinger, *Introduction*, 73.
14. Ratzinger, *Introduction*, 72–73.
15. Ratzinger, *Introduction*, 73.

believe."[16] Surprisingly, Ratzinger suggests this is not because unbelief is more prevalent now than in ages past. Doubt is, after all, a perennial companion to the believer in all ages. It is rather because the great ideology of our day is one of *techne*. Its attitude toward reality prizes most the goods that humans realize through ingenuity and creative power. Such goods have come to count as all we can truly know and even all that is truly real for us. According to Ratzinger, *techne* has come to shape our view of the world because of unfortunate missteps in our intellectual history. With figures like Giambattista Vico (1668–1744), what we can know is reduced to what we ourselves have made (*verum quia factum*).[17] Soon this judgment extends not merely to what we've made or accomplished (the "facts" of history), but to what is *makeable*—to what we are capable of achieving (*verum quia faciendum*).[18] Belief, then, runs counter to this ideology. To the extent that it is about something more than our making, belief itself hardly appears believable to us.

The real problem with an attitude of this kind is that it cannot account for the "ground" or meaning that belief aspires to. According to Ratzinger, *techne* can only value and explain what originates from us (the visible, tangible products of our making). But meaning—what gives intelligibility to our existence in the first place—is not something we can manufacture or make. To try to account for meaning in this way, Ratzinger says, would be as absurd as pulling oneself out of a bog by one's hair. "Meaning that is self-made is in the last analysis no meaning."[19] Only something that precedes our power to make can qualify as meaning: something that is not visible and tangible, but invisible and intangible—more real than our making. Ratzinger concludes that "the ground on which our existence as a totality can stand and live, cannot be made but only received."[20] If our dominant attitude dispenses with belief and seeks meaning only in what we can produce, then modernity leaves us in a state of existential "homelessness."

If *techne* fails to account for our meaning, what *can* account for it? According to Ratzinger the only sufficient answer is God. For Christians, the word "God" signifies a reality that infinitely exceeds the range of our technical prowess. It is a personal reality that creates and maintains all things in their existence. Moreover, Ratzinger insists that fundamental to the Christian confession of God is what he calls the "primacy" of *logos* to the understanding of

16. Ratzinger, *Introduction*, 49.
17. Ratzinger, *Introduction*, 58–63.
18. Ratzinger, *Introduction*, 63–66.
19. Ratzinger, *Introduction*, 73.
20. Ratzinger, *Introduction*, 73.

God.[21] As *logos*, God is "pure intellect"—Truth, Reason, Meaning—who creates through an act of meaning (i.e., thinking).[22] He is thereby able to imbue being itself with intelligibility. We have direction, truth, and purpose because we are always already thought, before we ourselves engage in any making or thinking.[23] In this sense, God *is* our meaning and "ground" (our *logos*). And belief—as an act that has God as its object—is meaningful. Unlike with technical knowledge, the content of belief can in principle express something about the truth and purpose of our existence.

Because it is an attitude toward God, then, belief can be meaningful in a way that *techne* cannot. Yet Ratzinger suggests that a generic God alone isn't sufficient for belief to be meaningful. Christian belief in the truest sense is not concerned merely with an "entirely Other" or a God "completely outside the world and time."[24] The structure of belief also involves what Ratzinger calls the "scandal" of particularity: the "positivism" of a God who enters into relationship with us. The original confession of belief at baptism was always a response to a God who creates us with purpose—who reveals himself to us and comes to face us in the midst of our history. Christian faith has a personal character. It is not trusting in an abstract spiritual ground ("I believe in something"), but trusting in a someone ("I believe in *you*"). It is, Ratzinger says, to experience "the meaning of the world as a person." "The meaning of the world is present before us; it vouchsafes itself to us as love and loves even me and makes life worth living . . . "[25] So belief that is only about a God "in himself" and that doesn't encompass his "being-with-us" doesn't amount to true belief. It cannot explain how God is *our* meaning, *for us*. It would only be the acknowledgment of an impersonal and objective fact: "[God] retreats into an immeasurable distance, and if God is no longer a God-with-us, then he is plainly an absent God and thus no God at all . . . "[26]

For Ratzinger, then, the technical mastery and existential absurdity of Western Europe in the 1960s provides Christians with an opportunity. It is an opportunity to demonstrate *techne*'s inability to ground the meaning of our lives, as well as an opportunity to demonstrate how Christian beliefs can succeed where *techne* fails. The claims of the Creed appear more credible in this context not because their truth can be demonstrated, but because they are in principle more meaningful than the expressions of knowledge

21. Ratzinger, *Introduction*, 151–58.
22. Ratzinger, *Introduction*, 59.
23. Ratzinger, *Introduction*, 29, 151–53.
24. Ratzinger, *Introduction*, 54.
25. Ratzinger, *Introduction*, 79.
26. Ratzinger, *Introduction*, 28.

or *techne*. Ratzinger's approach is thus to reveal how the Creed's language is, first, language *about God*—about the *logos*, Reason, and meaning of our world; and, second, language *about us*, i.e., language that does not refer only to this God "in himself," but encompasses God's relationship with us. Ratzinger can therefore expose the credibility of each section of the Creed by showing how its articles meet these two criteria.

III. Stumbling Blocks and a Homeless Spirit

If the credibility of the Christian faith is a matter of explaining how the Creed speaks to the meaning of our existence, there remains the question of demonstrating this in the case of each particular claim that the Creed makes. How does each statement following the "I believe . . . " convey something about God as the *logos* or meaning who renders all things intelligible? Moreover, how does it convey something about God as the ground and meaning of *our* existence, and not merely a set of propositions about God in himself? Ratzinger suggests that there are "stumbling blocks" peculiar to each claim contained in the Creed, making it difficult to interpret them as meaningful.[27] His task in the chapters of the *Introduction* is to address these "stumbling blocks" and clear them from the path of our understanding.

For many today, Ratzinger notes, "the main obstacle to belief" is not the lure of atheistic arguments or the prevalence of skepticism, but the Church itself.[28] The Creed states, for instance, that the Church is "holy." But according to Ratzinger, we are now especially prone to doubt this claim because the sinfulness of Christians is abundantly more evident to us. How, we might ask, could anyone seriously believe that the Church is "holy" when the many centuries of its history read like a catalog of human failures, testifying against it? How could these words make sense to us, especially today when Catholics are still reeling from a decades-long and worldwide sex abuse crisis, exposing so many of the Church's leaders as wolves rather than shepherds? As Ratzinger says, we can understand—an even sympathize with—Dante's depiction of the Church as the Whore of Babylon in Canto 19 of the *Inferno*.[29] In effect, the *unholiness* of Christians makes it difficult to recognize in the creedal claim anything about a reality that supplies our lives with meaning, direction, or intelligibility. It does not register as the kind of proposition that could serve as the object of a total commitment on our part.

---

27. Ratzinger, *Introduction*, 339.
28. Ratzinger, *Introduction*, 340.
29. Ratzinger, *Introduction*, 339.

The same point holds for the Creed's profession that the Church is "catholic," and a "communion of saints." Ratzinger notes that the visible disunity of Christians undermines the credibility of these claims. The Body of Christ today often resembles a dismembered corpse more than it does a vital and unified organism. In spite of our best ecumenical efforts, we are arguably more familiar than ever before with Christian *dis*unity. After all, what meaning can the words "communion" and "catholic" have when the garment of the Church seems so torn by disputing parties more loyal to their doctrinal tribes than to the Mystical Body they share? Even within the ranks of a given denomination, discord seems everywhere present, as race, class, and political ideologies segregate a community that, according to Paul, ought to transcend such loyalties. Once more, what appears most evident to us about the Church belies what the Creed claims about it.[30]

For Ratzinger, the real obstacle in both of these cases is an underlying problem of interpretation. The fact that the unholiness and disunity of Christians appear as good reasons to doubt the Creed suggests a prior failure to take its words as referring to something more than human making. If one interprets these claims to mean "the Church's members and institutions are themselves holy" or "Christians have joined themselves together," then they do not appear to us as credible. We do not recognize them as propositions about something that could, even in principle, supply our lives with meaning. This is to understand the Creed in keeping with what Ratzinger has already identified as the existential spirit of our age. If *techne* or what is makeable is the highest value informing our vision of reality, it will subtly constrain what we imagine our words can refer to. If all we mean by "holy" is the moral purity attained by the Church's members, or the proper functioning of its human structures, the Church's *un*holiness will shine through. Similarly, if all we mean by "catholicity" and "communion" is the unity that its members maintain through their own efforts, then we simply won't find that among Christians (certainly not enough to vindicate the Creed's claim about it). Ratzinger suggests, then, that the ideology of *techne* keeps us from seeing in the Creed's claim anything about God, and thus anything about our meaning. Modern men and women "can no longer see in [the Church] anything but the human struggle for power, the petty spectacle of those who, with their claim to administer official Christianity, seem to stand most in the way of the true Spirit of Christianity."[31]

One solution to this problem—readily available in the tradition—is to show that the Creed's claims about the Church bear some reference

---

30. Ratzinger, *Introduction*, 340.
31. Ratzinger, *Introduction*, 340.

to the Holy Spirit. Ecclesiological beliefs would say something about the meaning and ground of our being if they could be construed as claims "about" the divine Spirit active through the Church. Yet according to Ratzinger the "stumbling block" facing the Creed's claims about the Spirit makes this difficult. The only words in the Creed that speak of the Holy Spirit directly are "I believe in [the] Holy Spirit." In this case the words are "about" God, and thus about the source of meaning in the world. But the Creed's concision here is potentially troubling. The words about the Spirit seem to have no real reference to us. If they seem meaningless to modern men and women, it is because they seem to speak of the Spirit only "in himself," rather than of a "God facing outward," in relationship with us and as the meaning of *our* lives.[32]

In this case, the underlying problem is not technical thinking or an ideological bias for human making. It is instead, Ratzinger suggests, a deficient pneumatology on the part of believers. Christians are approaching the Creed with an impoverished understanding of what language about the Holy Spirit means. There has been, he says, a separation in Christian thought and practice between two ways of understanding the Spirit: the Spirit understood as a person within the Godhead (what theologians call the "immanent" Trinity), and the Spirit understood as the power of God active in history. Ratzinger is clear that this distinction is a natural part of Christian reflection. Even when the Creed was first composed, there was a fruitful tension between the events of salvation history and the trinitarian conclusions we infer from them. The problem, however, arises when this tension is progressively forgotten—when this distinction is interpreted as an opposition. According to Ratzinger, the result is that the Spirit becomes "homeless." He is relegated to the Godhead and no longer thought to "dwell in" or operate through the Church. Our speech or discourse about the Spirit, then, becomes detached from anything having to do with the purpose of our existence. It is "absorbed" into our general speculations about the Trinity, and "for all practical purposes," he says, the Spirit has no meaning and "no function for the Christian consciousness."[33]

It is likely that for Ratzinger the correlation of these problems is no coincidence. He seems to suggest that the one is an enabling condition for the other. When Christians even inadvertently relegate their speech about the Spirit to the abstraction of trinitarian discourse, this homeless pneumatology abandons our speech about the Church to be thought exclusively in terms of human making. Taking the Spirit out of history and

---

32. Ratzinger, *Introduction*, 332.
33. Ratzinger, *Introduction*, 333.

ecclesiology ensures that our speech about the Church will not even in principle refer to anything divine. It will instead simply reflect the dominant ideology of our time, rushing in to fill the vacuum in what we deem to be possible or credible. The Church, Ratzinger notes, is then no longer understood charismatically, beginning from pneumatology, but rather "as something all too earthbound and finally explained entirely on the basis of the power categories of worldly thinking."[34] We are left, then, with a hermeneutic of the Creed's articles that can never be truly credible or meaningful. The words about the Spirit bear no meaning for us, and the words about the Church, like all products of human ingenuity, bear no relation to the meaning and ground of our being.

The baptized Christian—and more importantly, the potential catechumen—ought to be able to recognize in the Creed's third section a fitting object for her act of belief—a true ground and meaning for her life upon which she can take a stand. Yet as Ratzinger has shown, there are interpretive judgments we bring to the Creed that frustrate this recognition and that limit the range of meanings that our words about the Spirit and Church can have. What then are the conditions for overcoming these "stumbling blocks" and recovering the credibility of these beliefs? Ratzinger's chapter on the "intrinsic unity" of the Creed's final section develops an alternative hermeneutic. It involves an approach to pneumatology that encompasses more than abstract trinitarian discourse. It articulates instead a Spirit active in history—a God "with us"—and thus one meaningfully related to our lives. It thereby makes possible an approach to the Church that encompasses more than the products of human ingenuity—one that articulates ecclesiological language as claims about God (about the Spirit) and thus claims about our meaning.

IV. Meaningful Pneumatology

In place of a "homeless" pneumatology, then, Ratzinger argues that a more credible interpretation calls for a more economic pneumatology. A pneumatology of this kind takes the Spirit's activity in history (in the "economy") as the guiding norm of its language and reasoning. It does not deny what the Church affirms about the Spirit's status in the Trinity's inner life, but it does deny that our understanding of the Spirit is sufficient if our speech is restricted in this way. Ratzinger therefore affirms that we must return perpetually to the Spirit's presence among us as the enduring source and justification of our doctrinal beliefs. He attempts to recover as a priority

---

34. Ratzinger, *Introduction*, 333.

of our reasoning something of the original sense that the first version of the Creed possessed: the notion that the Spirit is the power through which the world is sanctified and the risen Christ is made present. He proposes a pneumatology that sees the Spirit "at home" in his mission—in his relations with us—and especially in the Church.[35]

If we take this recommendation seriously, the effect it can have on Christian discourse is significant. It follows on Ratzinger's view that a pneumatology of this sort leaves us with little to say that *directly* and *exclusively* refers to the Spirit. Paradoxically, a pneumatology focused on the Spirit's relations and activities in salvation history gives us fewer words that are just about the Spirit. The Spirit suddenly seems to vanish as an object of our belief. He is phenomenologically impoverished, we might say: somehow more elusive for us the more we reflect on his nearness to us. Ratzinger suggests that this is what we should expect, since it reflects the peculiarly self-effacing character of the Spirit as a divine person. As Christ says in the Farewell Discourse of John's Gospel, the Spirit will speak of Christ, but will give us no new words about himself (John 15:26—16:15).[36] Our claims about the Spirit in a discourse more faithful to the original context of the Creed's composition appear deferred or indirect. We speak of the Spirit only by speaking about something else.

Yet it follows for Ratzinger that we do and indeed must have a great deal to say about the Spirit in this way. The implication is that if we only speak about the Spirit when speaking of other things more immediately related to us, then our speech about these other things is in fact pneumatological. Ratzinger argues that this holds true for the whole third section. We can only understand the remaining articles of faith when we interpret them as claims about the Spirit. He proposes that the statements on the forgiveness of sins, the resurrection of the body, and life everlasting do nothing more than unpack what is implicit in the words, "I believe in the Holy Spirit." These statements are then so many "elaborations" on those words, since they are in the fullest sense "descriptions of the ways in which the Spirit works in history."[37] When one professes faith in them, one is professing faith in a divine person.

Ratzinger finds support for this approach in Augustine's writings on the Church. In his 1974 essay, "The Holy Spirit as Communio: Concerning the Relationship of Pneumatology and Spirituality in Augustine," he argues that our speech about the Spirit must take its departure from the economy

---

35. Ratzinger, *Introduction*, 331–33.
36. Ratzinger, *Introduction*, 331.
37. Ratzinger, *Introduction*, 334.

of salvation, that is, from where we find the Spirit operative in history and in relation to us. In order "to speak meaningfully, reliably, and defensibly about the Holy Spirit," he writes, our pneumatology cannot be purely theoretical and theological (in the sense of a discourse concerned only with God). It "must touch an experienced reality" that we've interpreted, communicated, and tested.[38] Similarly, when we adopt this perspective, the Spirit seems to disappear as an exclusive object of our language and thought. "He withdraws from us into mystery even more than Christ," and his mode of being is characterized precisely "by not speaking on his own."[39] At the same time, however, our discourse about *ourselves* suddenly makes the Spirit accessible to us in a new way. "The Holy Spirit is recognizable in the way in which he forms human life . . . He makes himself recognizable by gaining a new center for human life. Speaking about the Holy Spirit includes looking at him in man, to whom he has given himself."[40]

In the *Introduction to Christianity*, looking at the Holy Spirit "in man" means looking at him given especially in the Church. Our doctrine about the Church, Ratzinger concludes, must take its departure from our doctrine about the Holy Spirit.[41] This conclusion may at first seem out of character for Ratzinger. As Bradford Hinze notes, Ratzinger developed a reputation for championing a christocentric, incarnational model "as the source and norm of the sacramental, hierarchical, and clerical character of the Church."[42] He was also well-known for criticizing overly "pneumatic" and charismatic ecclesiologies, viewing these as an enduring threat to the Church's institutional structure.[43] His concern in the *Introduction*, however, appears to be the opposite danger: a Church that is not pneumatic enough. He holds that an authentic understanding of the Creed sees the Church "in terms of the Holy Spirit, as the center of the Spirit's activity in the world."[44] The Church is, then, "the house of the Spirit," and, "when she truly exists as Church," she "is a creation of the Spirit."[45] It follows for Ratzinger that we must take key terms in the creedal confessions about the Church as primarily referring to the Holy Spirit.

38. Ratzinger, "The Holy Spirit as Communio," 325.
39. Ratzinger, "The Holy Spirit as Communio," 324–25.
40. Ratzinger, "The Holy Spirit as Communio," 324.
41. Ratzinger, *Introduction*, 373.
42. Hinze, "Releasing the Power of the Spirit," 364.
43. Hinze, "Releasing the Power of the Spirit," 365. See also the comparisons between the theology of St. Bonaventure and the pneumaticism of Joachim of Fiore in Ratzinger, *The Theology of History in St. Bonaventure*.
44. Ratzinger, *Introduction*, 335.
45. Ratzinger, *Introduction*, 334, 325.

How then does a pneumatology of this kind correct our understanding of the Church's holiness? On this view, the holiness of the Church does not consist in the moral rectitude or sinlessnesss of its members. According to Ratzinger, the Creed is not directing us to recognize the Church in the most virtuous group of humans one can find. Its holiness does not refer to a product of human making or effort. Instead, the term "holiness" refers to a divine person. The Holy Spirit just is the Church's holiness: he is the *power* to affect forgiveness, conversion, and penance, rather than the tangible fruits of sanctity that individual Christians have merited. As we've seen, if the Creed were speaking only of such fruits, its credibility would falter before the actual sinfulness in the great *corpus permixtum* that we find the Body of Christ to be. It would amount to an expression of belief in something wholly eschatological—never realized in history when wheat and tares grow together. While it is true that holiness will be part of the Church's eschatological destiny, Ratzinger interprets the Creed as speaking of a holiness the Church possesses even now. This "holiness" of the Church is something it receives in spite of its sins, not something it achieves. It is a profession of belief that the Spirt is the power by which holiness is realized and sin overcome, and that this power is given in or through the Church: "it is really and truly the holiness of the Lord that becomes present in her."[46]

Similarly, this more economic pneumatology corrects our understanding of the Church's unity and catholicity. Here the true unity of the Church does not consist in any visible organization and consensus—not even that provided by the pope and bishops. "Communion" and "catholicity" refer, once more, to the Spirit. With Augustine, Ratzinger notes that the *communio* of the *communio sanctorum* just is the Spirit's name: "becoming a Christian means becoming *communio* and thereby entering into the mode of being of the Holy Spirit."[47] As with holiness, we ought not expect the Church's unity to be something fully embodied among us during our earthly pilgrimage, like perfect agreement among its members. Nor should we take this simply as a belief that the Church *will be* fully one, someday perhaps after Christ's return. The Creed is referring instead to the Spirit as the power of unification—something we first and foremost receive and cooperate with in varying degrees *in via*. To the extent that it is manifest among us, it appears as an "abiding love": a "bearing with one another" in spite of our manifold disagreements and divisions.[48]

---

46. Ratzinger, *Introduction*, 341.

47. Ratzinger, "The Holy Spirit as Communio," 326–27. See also Nichols, *The Thought of Pope Benedict XVI*, 28–29.

48. Ratzinger, "The Holy Spirit as Communio," 332. See also Ratzinger, "The Theological Locus of Ecclesial Movements," 482–91.

Yet wouldn't it be true to say that the Church is "holy" and "catholic" even now because of Mary and the saints, and not because the Church receives the Spirit as a power to sanctify and unify? After all, Catholics profess Mary's Immaculate Conception, and thus her freedom even from original sin, as something already realized. The saints too, though not immaculately conceived, embody the holiness of Christ through their deeds so fully that they merit eternal life. To the extent that Mary and the saints are true members of Christ's Body—the Church Triumphant—isn't it possible to understand the creedal confession as an expression of belief in *their* holiness and unity? Ratzinger's reading suggests that Mary and the saints are sufficient to make the Creed's claims true. But they aren't necessary to do so. Ratzinger suggests that it is more accurate, and arguably more fundamental, to interpret the third section of the Creed pneumatologically—as claims about the Spirit. For the Church to be holy and catholic, it is enough to express faith in the Church as the community that possesses the Spirit as the power to sanctify and unify. And arguably the holiness and unity found among Mary and the saints testify to this. Even for them, holiness and unity are not merely the products of their own efforts—not merely things they've achieved or merited. It is only through the holiness of the Holy Spirit—and by sharing in the unity that he *is*—that the communion of saints becomes a holy communion at all.

It also follows that the Creed is not locating the Church's holiness and catholicity in its institution. The rest of what we can say about the visible Church—its ministers, offices, structures, and laws—are for Ratzinger only the instruments of this holiness and unity. They are the varied *means* by which the power of sanctification and unity are given and received. The real essence of the Church derives from what the Spirit is "for" the Church: "as forgiveness, conversion, penance, eucharistic communion, and hence plurality and unity . . . "[49] We thus encounter this essence primarily in the sacraments. Unity or catholicity, for instance, is "first and foremost the unity of Word and sacrament: the Church is one through the one Word and the one bread."[50] Ratzinger affirms that, in a real sense, the visible and institutional dimensions of the Church have their whole *raison d'être* in being a means of facilitating this sacramental activity. Even the papacy and the episcopal organization—important as these are—are simply a means of mediating the Spirit's *communio*.[51] In a "pneumatological ecclesiology," the Church cannot

---

49. Ratzinger, *Introduction*, 346.
50. Ratzinger, *Introduction*, 346.
51. Ratzinger, *Introduction*, 346.

be deduced from its organization; its organization must be deduced from what the Church more originally is.[52]

Ratzinger's brief discussion of this alternative approach to pneumatology is therefore intended to show how the claims expressed in the third section of the Creed are proper objects of belief, i.e., those that (in principle) can be truly meaningful. It presents the listener not with a Spirit in the abstract (and thus with a God only considered "in itself"), but with one meaningfully related to us (as the power of our conversion, sanctification, communion, etc.)—a meaning we can recognize as our own. Secondly, this interpretation enables us to read the Creed's claims about the Church as claims about the Spirit, and thus claims about the meaning or *logos* of our existence—claims about more than the products of our making. It allows for a truly "theocentric" conception of the Church, and, for Ratzinger, only a theocentric Church is in the end "entirely human."[53] It alone allows us to grasp what happens in and through the Church as our "about-turn into real humanity."[54] It appears as something that "turns man around toward a new being that he cannot give to himself . . . "—something that "raises men up" and "gives them a home."[55]

V. Conclusion

Ratzinger's concern in the *Introduction*, as we've seen, is with the credibility of Christian doctrine or the profession of the Apostles' Creed in our day: "What is the meaning and significance of the Christian profession 'I believe' *today*, in the context of our present existence and our present attitude to reality as a whole?"[56] Ratzinger defines belief in existential terms, and so, unlike the products of *techne*, the content of the Creed is credible because it is about something that in principle supplies the meaning and ground of our existence. It has God as its subject matter (the *logos* that imbues us and the world with meaning and intelligibility), and it articulates God's relation to us. Moreover, as we've seen, part of Ratzinger's task requires him to diagnose the "stumbling blocks" that make it difficult to interpret the claims of the Creed as meaningful in this way.

The Church for Ratzinger is arguably the greatest such "stumbling block." Its sinfulness and disunity seem to contradict what the Creed calls

52. Ratzinger, "The Holy Spirit as Communio," 333; Ratzinger, *Introduction*, 346.
53. Ratzinger, *Introduction*, 336.
54. Ratzinger, *Introduction*, 335.
55. Ratzinger, *Introduction*, 334–35.
56. Ratzinger, *Introduction*, 47.

us to believe about it. Yet Ratzinger implies that this judgment is rooted in a prior tendency to interpret the Creed's claims only in terms of human efforts, not in terms of our meaning. This condition is made possible by a particular pneumatology that restricts claims about the Holy Spirit to abstract trinitarian theology (a discourse with no immediate relation to us). In response, then, Ratzinger proposes a more original and more economic pneumatology. It is a discourse that prioritizes speaking about the Spirit indirectly and in relation to us—as the power we receive for our sanctification and unification. This approach, finally, allows for a meaningful ecclesiology. The Creed's claims about the Church can now be understood as claims about the Spirit (and thus about God, the source of meaning and purpose in our lives).

If anything, the obstacles to belief that Ratzinger identified in 1968 are even more prevalent today. We are perhaps more likely to think of reality as the ephemeral products of our making, with no inherent connection to what makes our lives meaningful. And this seems especially true of the Church. We cultured despisers of the post-industrial West are more prone to see the Church as a purely human institution—something that cannot transcend the vanity and brokenness of human *techne*, and thus something that cannot sustain the complete, existential commitment of our act of belief. Recent polling shows that those in the U.S. identifying as "spiritual but not religious" are growing steadily in number.[57] We might be tempted to take this as a sign that, while the institutional Church is in the midst of a credibility crisis, perhaps belief in the Spirit is undergoing something of a renewal. Yet there's good reason to think that such appeals to the Spirit and spirituality, unmoored from the institution, are no more meaningful than the words of the pneumatology Ratzinger criticizes. As Henri de Lubac warned, any Spirit glorified in opposition to the institutional Church courts a similar kind of "homelessness." One's pneumatology risks becoming a cipher for the dominant ideologies of our day: "detached from Christ" and his Church, "the Spirit can become almost anything."[58]

So Ratzinger affirms that wrestling with these "stumbling blocks" will be an enduring task for theologians, catechists, and apologists. In some sense the greatest apologetic we have with regard to the Church and the Spirit is not to have the Spirit always on our lips—after all, the Spirit does not even speak up for himself. It is rather to live "in" the Spirit. There is perhaps no more credible witness to what Christians believe about the Spirit and the Church than a community that cooperates with the Spirit's power; that actually becomes holier and more unified; that, like Mary and the saints, makes

---

57. Lipka and Gecewicz, "More Americans Now Say."
58. Lubac, *La postérité spirituelle*, 439.

the "about-turn into true humanity" which the Spirit enables.[59] Yet here Ratzinger cautions us. We need to resist the urge to moralize and to scandalize nonbelievers by giving the impression that the Spirit and the Church are only where the most moral human efforts are found. What Ratzinger models for us in the *Introduction* is vigilance: vigilance about how we present and understand our beliefs about the Spirit and the Church, so their true meaning can shine through, and so our confession does not simply mirror the meaningless dogmas of our technocratic age. At the very least, it seems, it will be our task and our vocation to show others what it means to give the Spirit, and humanity as a whole, a proper "home."

Bibliography

First Vatican Council. *Constitutio dogmatica de fide catholica (Dei Filius)*. In *Decrees of the Ecumenical Councils*, vol. 2, edited by Norman P. Tanner, 804–11. London: Sheed & Ward, 1990.

Hinze, Bradford E. "Releasing the Power of the Spirit in a Trinitarian Ecclesiology." In *Advents of the Spirit: An Introduction to the Current Study of Pneumatology*, edited by Bradford E. Hinze and D. Lyle Dabney, 347–81. Milwaukee: Marquette University Press, 2001.

Lipka, Michael and Gecewicz, Claire. "More Americans Now Say They're Spiritual but Not Religious." http://www.pewresearch.org/fact-tank/2017/09/06/more-americans-now-say-theyre-spiritual-but-not-religious/.

Lubac, Henri de. *La postérité spirituelle de Joachim de Flore, tome II: de Saint-Simon à nos jours*. Le Sycomore Serie Horizon 8. Paris: Éditions Lethielleux, 1981.

Nichols, Aidan, OP. *The Thought of Pope Benedict XVI: An Introduction to the Theology of Joseph Ratzinger*. London: Burns & Oates, 2007.

Ratzinger, Joseph. "The Holy Spirit as Communio: Concerning the Relationship of Pneumatology and Spirituality in Augustine." *International Catholic Review: Communio* 25 (1998) 324–37.

———. *Introduction to Christianity*. Translated by J. R. Foster and Michael J. Miller. San Francisco: Ignatius, 2004.

———. "The Theological Locus of Ecclesial Movements." *International Catholic Review: Communio* 25 (1998) 480–504.

———. *The Theology of History in St. Bonaventure*. Translated by Zachary Hayes. Chicago: Franciscan Herald, 1989.

Voderholzer, Rudolf. "Integral Faith Formation in the Spirit of the Second Vatican Council." Presentation, *Introduction to Christianity* at 50 from the McGrath Institute for Church Life. Notre Dame, IN, November 5, 2018.

---

59. Ratzinger, *Introduction*, 335.

13

Hide and Seek

The Eschatology of *Introduction to Christianity*

LEONARD J. DELORENZO

> *Seek his face always* (Ps 105:4)

IT IS NOT THE point of Christianity to "get into Heaven." It is not so much that this is the wrong aim as it is the wrong way of aiming. Imagine, if you will, a teenager breaking in to a water park in the middle of the night with his friends, where they have free reign of a place that has become to them a veritable paradise. Christian hope has nothing to do with that—and not only because of the illegality of the endeavor. Even if this teenager waited till morning, paid his dues, and walked through the turnstiles, getting in to this water park would still have nothing to do with the way of Christian hope. That is because the idea of "getting in" objectifies the place and depersonalizes both the end and the means. This is really an example of a destination obsession.[1]

Bad eschatology often displays various forms of this destination obsession, but the point of departure for that errant way of aiming is found much earlier; it has to do with a pathology of *hiding*. When projected outwards to its furthest limits, the pathogen manifests itself in an image of Heaven as *place*—vast, yet measurable—from which we are now exiled but into which we may one day walk, *where* others reside, *where* God dwells. God is the God of that *place*, or so some might think. That is the wrong way of imagining. As seen from the end, the saints do not go to Heaven; they go to Christ: their communion in him *is* Heaven.

---

1. The question of whether or not there is or is not any autobiographical aspect to this particular example for the author exceeds the scope of the present essay.

In my reading of Joseph Ratzinger's *Introduction to Christianity*, we find both this diagnosis regarding the destination obsession of bad eschatology, and the correction from Revelation regarding the thoroughly personalizing eschatology of the saints in Christ. What I intend to argue is that in Ratzinger's seminal work, his eschatology is not so much about what is seen, what is achieved, or what is desired as a destination. Rather, his eschatology is more like a way of seeing, and indeed it is a seeing as from the end.

In this essay, I intend to dialogue with Ratzinger's text, tracing the sight line that opens from the end all the way to the beginning, by which I mean his articulation of the beginning of Christian faith. In doing so, I will describe more fully what I mentioned above about the "pathology of hiding." From there, I will focus on how he presents the revelation of the personal God as the definitive overcoming of our obsession with the objectification of space. I will then move to identify the way in which redemption is personalizing, even to the point of death. From that low point, so to speak, I will then take Ratzinger's lead to the high point, by which I mean the vision of Heaven opened up in the Ascension. From that end, my concluding remarks will focus on the response to an ultimate question that Ratzinger himself poses: whether Christianity has the power to shape history after all.

Terms of Estrangement: Don't Blame the Trees

Creation begins with a command, but redemption begins with a question. This question is the first one the Lord God asks in all of Scripture, and God addresses the question to his creature, the one he fashioned out of earth stuff, into whom he breathed his own breath, from and for whom he created a companion. The Lord God *asks*, "Where are you?" (Gen 3:9).

We know where man is: he is hiding. He has covered his intimate parts with uncomfortable fig leaves and now he is hiding behind the trees. We should notice what God's question does: it draws the man out. Yes, he comes out with his lame excuses and his penchant for blame rooted in shame, but, nevertheless, out he comes. This is the beginning of the emergence of man—redeemed man. It is a beginning founded in the word that the Lord God speaks, which man hears because he is the one addressed, and which, in the end, will culminate in man's complete unveiling.

What does it mean to hide behind tress and cover intimate parts? These trees have become *things*. They were not initially *things*: they were initially images of the Lord God's providential care: delightful to look at and good for food, given freely for the creature to enjoy (Gen 2:9, 16–17; cf. 3:6). They were instruments of reference that communicate the care of the Creator to the creature and direct the creature back to his Creator. In Augustine's terms, the trees were to be "signs," which "are used in order to signify something else."[2] In the second creation account, the trees signify God's providential care—they express and represent his care, and in that way should facilitate encounter and indeed communion.

But the man who wishes to hide himself objectifies these would-be signs, draining the trees of their given meaning for him and constructing his own meaning with them. They serve *his* purpose; they stand in place of intimacy. To hide behind the trees is to reverse the trees' given significance. Those things which were meant to point to the Creator as expressions of His care are now made to obstruct the gaze of the Creator, to keep the creature hidden and, presumably, inaccessible. By hiding, the trees are inordinately "enjoyed" in terms of "clinging to something lovingly for its own sake" instead of "referring what has come your way to what your love aims at."[3] Man clings to the trees—his defenses—and not to God. He is now estranged in his own land, standing at a distance from the one with whom he is created to walk intimately, together with his companion.[4]

The Lord God closes the distance and speaks his question right through the trees. He speaks *to* man: "Where are *you*?" With that question, the Lord God both locates his creature by his address and stirs up a sense of initial recognition in his creature.

This picture serves us well for appreciating Ratzinger's presentation of the Christian faith. As he observes, Christian faith begins in a word given, which invites a response that will grow in volume and confidence: "It becomes evident that belief is not the result of lonely meditation in which the 'I', freed from all ties and reflecting alone on truth, thinks something out for itself; on the contrary it is the result of a dialogue, the expression of hearing,

---

2. Augustine, *De Doctrina Christiana*, 307 (I.2.2).

3. Augustine, *De Doctrina Christiana*, 307 (I.2.2). Following Augustine here, Bonaventure says that "In relation to our position in creation, the universe itself is a ladder by which we can ascend into God," but "the mirror presented by the external world is of little or no value unless the mirror of our soul has been cleaned and polished" (Bonaventure, "The Soul's Journey to God," 60 [I.2], 56 [Prologue.4]). In terms of "hiding behind the trees," it is not the trees themselves that have become something they are not, but rather the intention with which the creature invests them. It is from the mirror of his soul that the mirror of the external world is obscured.

4. Resonances with Martin Buber's classic work certainly abound here, though a thorough engagement with his thought would be required to employ him in service of this reading. It is at least interesting—and perhaps even more than interesting—that Buber's first extended example or exercise in "I and Thou" concerns the contemplation of a tree (see Buber, *I and Thou*, 56–57).

receiving, and answering that guides man through the exchanges of 'I' and 'You' to the 'We' of those who all believe in the same way."[5]

That "same way" of belief is the way of being addressed personally and of responding personally—that is to say, of becoming and being a person. This way of belief drives out the procedures of depersonalization, behind which man hides in the "closed and inward looking self," as Ratzinger puts it elsewhere.[6] Or, as he explains it a few pages earlier in *Introduction to Christianity*, "This means that faith is located in the act of conversion, in the turn of one's being from worship of the visible and practicable to trust in the invisible . . . [faith] signifies an 'about-turn' by the whole person that from then on constantly structures one's existence."[7]

Ratzinger describes this dynamic of being drawn out and identified in the act of faith as the "anthropological shape of belief."[8] The man behind the trees steps forward in response to the Lord God's question and says "*I* was afraid . . . *I* was naked . . . *I* hid myself" (Gen 3:10). And just so, the one about to be drawn through the baptismal waters says, "*I* renounce . . . *I* renounce . . . *I* renounce" so as to be able to say "*I* believe . . . *I* believe . . . *I* believe" just before the content of his profession restructures his very existence.[9]

It is precisely in that lost garden of self-imposed alienation that the Lord God addresses man with a question, and that question locates man. Man's expulsion from the garden is the divine judgment on the sick obsession with setting the terms, with hiding, with avoiding intimacy, with recasting the garden in one's own image, by one's own preferences. The return to the garden is no mere admission through a turnstile, but rather the redeemed willingness and the blessed capacity to be revealed—intimately—and to be made capable of personal encounter. The garden is not a place for hiding but for being present and seeking presence, so that the price of admission is becoming and being a *person*.

Liberating God from This-Place-and-That

When that procedure of hiding was instituted something else happened, and its lingering effects are momentous. Man has fabricated an idea of space

---

5. Ratzinger, *Introduction*, 90; see also Ratzinger, *Truth and Tolerance*, 89.

6. Benedict XVI, *Deus Caritas Est*, §6. See also Benedict XVI, *Caritas in Veritate*, §66; Benedict XVI, *Jesus of Nazareth I*, 141; and Ratzinger, *Introduction*, 289.

7. Ratzinger, *Introduction*, 88.

8. Ratzinger, *Introduction*, 90.

9. This threefold renunciation followed by the threefold profession of faith occurs immediately before the Baptism, proper (see Padrini, "Rite for the Baptism of One Child," §§94–95).

measured by separation, as if to say: "You, Lord God, are the one on the other side of the trees. My 'space' is over here, on this side."

Even as man steps out in response to the Word of God, this idea of space lingers. It structures the imagination. The gates of the garden from which he is expelled become, for man, the ultimate image of this spatial obsession. There are sacred places and profane places; places of encounter and places of privacy; places of communion and places of autonomy; places where God is and places where God is *not*. The idea of Heaven as a place is the final projection of the pathology of hiding: Heaven is God's *place*.

Earlier in the Genesis account, the trees were reconceived in the initial question of the serpent: "Did God really say: You shall not eat of any tree of the garden?" (Gen 3:1 JPS). This is a loaded question, one that carries within it an entire worldview. The initial commandment was, of course, almost completely the opposite in its tone, as the Lord God granted to the man permission to eat of *every* tree in the garden, save this one. The trees and indeed the entire garden speak overwhelmingly of an economy of gift, but the serpent's question stipulates rivalry, as if everything in this garden were a twisted sign of God's possessiveness. The questions within the serpent's question are therefore something like, "Will you allow God to claim these trees as his own, or will you take them as yours? Are they His property or your property? Is this His place or your place?" The focus on the trees and the shift in their meaning is the beginning of the boundary between God's place and the creature's, as the creature comes to see it. It is the creature, therefore, who defines his Creator as a local deity—over there, separate from me—and the act of hiding behind the trees and the expulsion from the garden are manifestations of reality as man has chosen to see it.

In *Introduction to Christianity*, Ratzinger comments on the liberation of God from this-place-and-that. This has to do with Israel's choice for the personal God over the local god, the *numen personale* over *numen locale*. In contrast to "the locally defined and limited deity," Ratzinger writes,

> the 'God of our fathers' expresses a completely different approach. He is not the god of a place but the god of men: the God of Abraham, Isaac, and Jacob. He is therefore not bound to one spot but is present and powerful wherever man is. . . . God is seen on the plane of I and You, not on the plane of the *spatial*. . . . He is not anywhere in particular; he is to be found at any place where man is and where man lets himself be found by him.[10]

Of course, man's history is in large part our sluggishness in allowing ourselves to be found by God. The misuse of the trees is still so enticing—it

---

10. Ratzinger, *Introduction*, 123, emphasis added.

seems safer. With an appeal to Ratzinger's liturgical theology, we might thus say that life in the Church is where that addiction to the spatiality of separation is healed, and it is healed through the practice and rhythm of allowing the mediated encounter with the personal God to be translated from liturgical practice to daily life. God is thus liberated from this-place-and-that as the Christian becomes liturgical: moving from ritual observation to charitable service, all as one complete act of worship.[11]

Those who enter into Christ do not enjoy their own simultaneous private experiences. In him they meet "the many"—Christ is the space in whom all who share in him share in one another. This speaks to the eschatological horizon of the Eucharistic life: the Christian is oriented to the discovery of his neighbor in the discovery of God, within the Body of Christ, so that, as we read in *Deus Caritas Est*, "the Eucharist that does not pass over into the concrete practice of love is intrinsically fragmented."[12] The whole point is to dispel the illusion of spatial separation, and charity is the remedy for that spell. Those who partake of the Eucharistic communion practice saying what the saints rejoice in saying: not "I am here," but rather, "I am for you."

The beauty of this passing-over from ritual to service is not expressed in an idea but is given in *person*. The personal God redeems the man obsessed with hiding in the *person* of Jesus Christ; he *is* the revolution of space. The space of encounter is not any particular site; the space of encounter is his very person.[13] His work is the personalization of man in union with the personal God, and who-he-is is inseparable from his work. As Ratzinger writes,

> The 'servant' aspect is no longer explained as a deed, behind which the person of Jesus remains aloof; it is made to embrace the whole existence of Jesus, so that his *being* itself is service. And precisely because this being, as a totality, is nothing but service, it is sonship. To that extent it is not until this point that the Christian revaluation of values reaches its final goal; only here does it become fully clear that he who surrenders himself completely to service for others, to complete selflessness and self-emptying, literally *becomes* these things—that this very

---

11. See Benedict XVI, *Deus Caritas Est*, especially §12–18; Ratzinger, *Introduction*, 289; Ratzinger, *The Feast of Faith*, 27–29; Ratzinger, *The Spirit of the Liturgy*, especially 18–23; and Ratzinger, *Pilgrim Fellowship of Faith*, especially 111–20.

12. Benedict XVI, *Deus Caritas Est*, §14.

13. "[W]hat underlies the Eucharist: the sacrifice of Jesus, who sheds his blood for us, and in so doing steps out of himself, so to speak, pours himself out, and gives himself to us" (Benedict XVI, *Jesus of Nazareth I*, 269). See also Ratzinger, *The God of Jesus Christ*, 34.

person is the true man, the man of the future, the coinciding of man and God.[14]

This is not the anthropomorphizing of God, but, in Ratzinger's words, "the logicizing of man."[15] The point, therefore, is not that God is to found here-or-there, but that man himself has become and is to become the place for the dwelling of God. God encounters man where he is and in the whole of who he is. You cannot project *that* idea of space outwards. It turns out that the boundary of encounter is one's own willingness to become hospitable to the dwelling of God. That hospitality is inseparable from partaking in the mission of Christ, in whom the sacrifice made for us reconstitutes us. This is the anthropological fruit of the liturgy:

> The liturgy is not about the sacrificing of animals, of a "something" that is ultimately alien to me. This liturgy is founded on the Passion endured by a man who with his "I" reaches into the mystery of the living God himself, by the man who is the Son. So it can never be a mere *actio liturgica*. Its origin also bears within it its future in the sense that representation, vicarious sacrifice, takes up into itself those whom it represents; it is not external to them, but a shaping influence on them. Becoming contemporary with the Pasch of Christ in the liturgy of the Church is also, in fact, an anthropological reality.[16]

Space in Christ, through Death

The saints are the ones refashioned in Christ, the ones who have traversed the boundary. Not the boundary into the amusement park of Heaven as through a turnstile; no, they have crossed the boundary that they themselves constructed, as one-time participants in the fallen man, where they kept themselves at a distance from the intimacy of encounter. The saints do not go to Heaven, they go to Christ; their communion in him *is* Heaven.

Indeed, we may and perhaps ought to imagine that man's search for the holy site of God has been thwarted and overturned by God's search for man. In the person of Christ, the "Where are you?" of Genesis 3 has penetrated all the way to the depths of man's hiding. In Christ, the whole man has been found.

---

14. Ratzinger, *Introduction*, 226 (see also 185); and Ratzinger, *The God of Jesus Christ*, 82–83.
15. Ratzinger, "The Relationship of the Liturgy to Time and Space."
16. Ratzinger, "The Relationship of the Liturgy to Time and Space."

To speak ever so briefly about the last barrier behind which man hides, we may allow Ratzinger to teach us that it is the fear-of-isolation itself that we hide behind, and always have. The pathogen that induced the hiding in the first place is this very fear. It is the fear that, perhaps, God is not for me; perhaps I must make my own way; perhaps in the end I am really alone. That tremor of fear opens up the vast chasms of separation with which man surrounds himself. "In the last analysis," Ratzinger writes, "all fear in the world is fear of this loneliness"[17] and "it is something that cannot be overcome by rational means."[18]

It is right there, in and through that very fear, that the Word of God finds man; this is the utter depth into which the "Where are you?" from Genesis reaches. "I am hiding," man says, "in the place where you are *not*, O Lord, where I have created what I fear: a place where I am alone. How could anyone will to enter into my pitiable state?"

To this the Lord God says, "I do will it"—and that Word is spoken in *person*, in the flesh. The literally *unthinkable* happens: the Word, who is all personal address, who is all communication, who is the measure of communion, enters into the solitariness, the loneliness, the alienation of man who hides. Death has been *imagined* as the space of alienation and isolation par excellence, but the Word that addresses man revolutionizes even that space. "*No!*" God says, "I will not accept these terms of yours. I will not be the God of that place, over there. I am *your* God, and I, the personal God, join you, in your isolation, in *person*."[19]

The consistency of Ratzinger's thought breaks through here. In the beginning, he stresses that the nature of Revelation is not the Word in isolation but rather the *encounter* with the Word. Revelation is relational. The restructuring of the space of worship according to a redeemed anthropology—again, "the logicizing of man"—is the priority of encounter running all the way to the end, right into the end of man in death. Death itself is restructured as a space of encounter, in Christ.

---

17. Ratzinger, *Introduction*, 301.

18. Ratzinger, *Introduction*, 299.

19. In one succinct passage that is representative of Ratzinger's "Theology of Death," he writes, "In the descent of Jesus, God himself descends into Sheol. At that moment, death ceases to be the God-forsaken land of darkness, a realm of unpitying distance from God. In Christ, God himself entered that realm of death, transforming the space of noncommunication into the place of his own presence" (Ratzinger, *Eschatology*, 93). Compare this to Balthasar's biblically constructed comment on the descent of Christ into solitariness in *Mysterium Paschale*, 162–63. For Balthasar's complementary and pertinent treatment of Paul's "En Christoi," see *Theo-Drama III*, 245–50. I treat Ratzinger's and Balthasar's respective theologies of death in tandem in my *Work of Love*, 74–95.

The "space of death" is swallowed up by the personal God. Death itself is personalized—at the extreme limit where loneliness and alienation become final, "the fear peculiar to man [is] overcome [not] by reason but only by the presence of someone who loves him."[20] Hell, in Ratzinger's description, is "now only deliberate self-enclosure."[21] This tragic state is laid bare as nothing more and nothing less than man's pathological preference for hiding. But the Word of God crosses that boundary so that it is really kind of impossible to imagine a deliberateness so strong as to resist that communion—thus: the contradiction of hell.[22]

Face-to-Face, By Christ's Ascension

The real upshot, of course, is not in the revolution of the idea of death or even of hell, but indeed in the reality of Heaven. In Christ, our spatial obsessions have themselves been obliterated, revealed for the sham that they are. As Ratzinger writes,

> [H]eaven was not a place that, before Christ's Ascension, was barred off by a positive, punitive decree of God's, to be opened up one day in just as positive a way. On the contrary, the reality of heaven only comes into existence through the confluence of God and man. Heaven is to be defined as the contact of the being 'man' with the being 'God'; this confluence of God and man took place once and for all in Christ when he went beyond *bios* through death to new life.[23]

The introduction of the mystery of the Ascension is instructive here. As the descending act of the Incarnation is the Word of God personally addressing man who is hiding (all the way to the descent into hell), the Ascension is this same Word-made-flesh blazing the path unto everlasting communion with God. The whole drama is orchestrated in Christ—that is to say, personally, in and as his *person*. Towards the beginning of *Introduction to Christianity*, Ratzinger writes that "the most fundamental feature of Christian faith [is]

---

20. Ratzinger, *Introduction*, 299–300.

21. Ratzinger, *Introduction*, 301. Elsewhere, Ratzinger writes that the "self-assertion" of man's perverse desire for "self-sufficient totality ... is at root a refusal of communication, which issues in a misjudgment about reality at large and the truth of man's existence in particular" (Ratzinger, *Eschatology*, 99).

22. "Heaven reposes upon freedom, and so leaves the damned the right to will their own damnation" (Ratzinger, *Eschatology*, 216). See also Ratzinger, *Introduction*, 311–13.

23. Ratzinger, *Introduction*, 313.

its personal character," and, in like fashion, that Jesus "is the presence of the eternal itself in the world."[24] He continues in the same section writing that,

> Christian faith lives on the discovery that not only is there such a thing as objective meaning but that this meaning knows me and loves me, that I can entrust myself to it like the child who knows that everything he may be wondering about is safe in the "you" of his mother. Thus in the last analysis believing, trusting, and loving are one, and all the theses around which belief revolves are only concrete expressions of the all-embracing about-turn, of the assertion "I believe in you"—of the discovery of God in the countenance of the man Jesus of Nazareth.[25]

By his Ascension, all of these discoveries in Jesus are united to the full discovery of who he is: the Son of God. What he became is thereby united to what he is, eternally. The saints are the ones who make this journey in him, so that their communion in him is united to his communion with the Father: *ut unum sint*.

To read the beginning of Ratzinger's presentation of the Christian faith in light of his presentation of the Ascension and Heaven, one may detect, I believe, a profoundly Augustinian insight in his work. This insight concerns Christ as both *the* sign pointing to God and the one who shares equality with the Father. By heeding Christ as he is given and as he is seen "here," we are being gathered up into his Sonship. The Ascension is the movement where the one who has taken the form of a servant is completely revealed as the one who is always in the form of God.

In Book I of *De Trinitate*, Augustine teaches the necessity of this movement in the divine plan. He came *in human likeness* so that we could see him in history, but not so that he would be exhausted in history. As Augustine writes,

> [I]t was necessary for the form of a servant to be removed from their sight, since as long as they could observe it they would think that Christ was this only which they had before their eyes. . . . It also explains that other text, *Do not touch me, for I have not yet ascended to the Father* (Jn 20:17). Touching concludes as it were the process of getting acquainted. He did not want this heart, so eagerly reaching out to him, to stop at thinking that he was only what could be seen and touched. His ascension to the

---

24. Ratzinger, *Introduction*, 79.
25. Ratzinger, *Introduction*, 80.

Father signified his being seen in his equality with the Father, that being the ultimate vision which suffices us.[26]

This is the whole mission of Christ: to bring those who "live by faith" in him to share in his sonship as the one who is equal with the Father: "to the *face to face* vision, as the apostle calls it (1 Cor 13:12)."[27] The mission of Christ and the identity of Christ are inseparable. Commenting on this dynamic in *De Trinitate*, Khaled Anatolios offers the following:

> [As Augustine understands,] God and creation are radically different; what mediates between them are the signs and symbols, the *similitudines*, provided by God to refer humanity to the full vision and contemplation of his being. . . . The person of Christ ultimately represents both the supreme historical sighting (*visum*) that orients faith and the ultimate eschatological object of the vision of contemplation. . . . Using the *kenōsis* hymn of Philippians 2, [Augustine] provides an account of both the human/divine difference as well as the personal unity of Christ in terms of this epistemological framework. In the form of God (*forma dei*), Christ is the object of eschatological vision in his unity with the Father and the Spirit; in the form of the servant (*forma servi*), he is the object of seeing by faith. Because of the unity of his person, Christ is the secure and perfectly efficacious link between the vision of faith and the eschatological vision.[28]

For Christ to be both the historical sighting and the eschatological object of contemplation means that he is the reality become the sign. He restores all other signs: all signs are read through him. Bonaventure follows Augustine in developing this insight. To Bonaventure, the Son is the "Eternal Art which is the form that not only produces all things but also conserves and distinguishes all things, as the being which sustains the form in all things and the rule which directs all things. Through it our mind judges all things that enter it through our senses."[29] The Son is the act of representation

---

26. Augustine, *The Trinity*, I.18. While meditating on another of Christ's mysteries—the finding of Jesus in the Temple at age twelve—Balthasar offers an illuminating comment that resonates with Augustine's own comment here: "We find him definitively only in the place of the Father, in heaven, which is to say when finding no longer implies containing God within our space, but rather when it means that we have been found by God, that we have entered into his space, then we are 'known by God' (1 Cor 13:12)" (*The Threefold Garland*, 60).

27. Augustine, *The Trinity*, I.16.

28. Anatolios, *Retrieving Nicaea: The Development and Meaning of Trinitarian Doctrine*, 248.

29. Bonaventure, "The Soul's Journey to God," II.9.

par excellence, eternally begotten of the Father. He is the very principle of representation. Who he is refers to the Father eternally. In light of Philippians 2, when the Son takes the form of the servant to appear in human likeness, he becomes, at one and the same time, someone to be seen in the flesh and the one who makes present the unseen Father. His humanity is the sign of his divine sonship, and the sign does not pass away but is permanently united with what it represents. The trees, which fallen man misuses, were meant to point to God's providential care. The Son of God who is the Son of Mary is that providential care, in person. "For God who said, *Let light shine out of darkness*, has shone in our hearts to bring to light the knowledge of the glory of God on the face of Jesus Christ" (2 Cor 3:6 NAB). Our vision is healed by gazing upon his face.

Ratzinger seems to evoke in his brevity what Augustine and later Bonaventure spent many words to explain. Ratzinger says that Christ in his Ascension permits "human existence to find its geometrical place, so to speak, inside God's own being."[30] His Ascension turns our gaze to Heaven, but what is to be seen in this heavenly vision is a place that is no place. The highest point of contemplation is the communion in God into which Christ gathers his disciples, and that can only be seen through participation and not from the safe distance of some *other* place. To see the face of Jesus is to see the face of God that we are to seek always. The poles of existence become determined according to the person of Christ: by his descent all the way to hell he responds to the "loneliness and rejected love" of God's creature hiding in self-alienation, and by his Ascension he points us to the opposite end as "fulfilled love . . . granted to man."[31]

The wondrous questioning of the psalmist is thus answered in Christ: "Where can I hide from your spirit? From your presence, where I can flee?" Christ is the reason the psalmist can rejoice in truth that, "If I ascend to the Heavens, you are there. If I make my bed in Sheol, you are there" (Ps 139:7–8).[32]

Making History

In Christian eschatology, anthropology stretches to the dimensions of Christology. If we take the perspective from behind the trees as normative, we misperceive the whole thing. The practice of the Christian life is seeing

---

30. Ratzinger, *Introduction*, 312.
31. See Ratzinger, *Introduction*, 311–13 (quote from 313).
32. See Ratzinger, *The God of Jesus Christ*, 28–35; cf. Augustine, *The Confessions*, IV.19.

the whole thing as from the end: from what we shall be to what we are not yet (1 John 3:2). The consequences of this reorientation are definitive; it even yields an eschatological statement about history.

In the preface to the year 2000 edition of the *Introduction to Christianity*, Ratzinger begins by posing a crucial and sobering question: Does Christianity have the power to shape history? He arrives at the answer to that question at the beginning of the final paragraph of the entire text, where he writes that, "The goal of the Christian is not private bliss but the whole. He believes in Christ, and for that reason he believes in the future of the world, not just in his own future. He knows that this future is more than he himself can create."[33]

The Christian dares to hope well beyond himself; indeed, he hopes for himself only within the whole, with the others. The hope for Heaven is not at all about admission to a place; it is about the life of charity shared among the saints, in Christ. As Ratzinger writes about the elect at the end of his *Eschatology*, "in their being together as the one Christ, they *are* heaven."[34] Heaven is determined Christologically and therefore anthropology is likewise determined Christologically, for the destiny to which man is called is one of sharing in who Christ is: the Son of God in whom the many are gathered.

History is measured according to this end: in denial and rebellion from this reality—hiding from it even—all is subject to judgment; ordered to and seeking this end, history is true. Christianity has the power to shape history, Ratzinger contends, because it reveals what man is and what man is to become. All forms of alienation and isolation—from God and between human beings—is antithetical to life in God, outside of whom there is no life.

The Word of God who does not cease to cry out "Where are you?" is the perpetual occasion for man's examination of conscience. That question is the beginning of the movement of salvation, but it is a movement that demands a response. Any response is a start; the only tragedy is to keep hiding. Being found by God means also being found with and for others— to seek the wellbeing of others in the world is inseparable from seeking the face of God. "[O]n the 'Last Day', at the end of history, and in the company of all mankind indicates the communal character of human immortality, which is related to the whole of mankind, from which, toward which, and with which the individual has lived and finds salvation or loses it."[35] This is the rule of history.

33. Ratzinger, *Introduction*, 358.
34. Ratzinger, *Eschatology*, 238 (emphasis in text).
35. Ratzinger, *Introduction*, 351.

Selected Bibliography

Anatolios, Khaled. *Retrieving Nicaea: The Development and Meaning of Trinitarian Doctrine*. Grand Rapids: Baker Academic, 2011.

Augustine. *The Confessions*. Translated by Maria Boulding. New York: Vintage, 1998.

———. *Teaching Christianity: De Doctrina Christiana*. Translated by Edmund Hill. Hyde Park: New City, 1996.

Benedict XVI. *Caritas in Veritate*. June 29, 2009. http://w2.vatican.va/content/benedictxvi/en/encyclicals/documents/hf_ben-xvi_enc_20090629_caritas-in-veritate.html.

———. *Deus Caritas Est: God Is Love*. Boston: Pauline, 2006.

Bonaventure. "The Soul's Journey to God." In *Bonaventure*, translated by Ewert Cousins, 51–116. The Classics of Western Spirituality. Mahwah: Paulist, 1978.

Buber, Martin. *I and Thou*. Translated by Walter Kaufman. New York: Touchstone, 1996.

DeLorenzo, Leonard J. *A God Who Questions*. Huntington: Our Sunday Visitor, 2019.

———. *Work of Love: A Theological Reconstruction of the Communion of Saints*. Notre Dame: University of Notre Dame Press, 2017.

Padrini, Paolo. "Rite for the Baptism of One Child." iBreviary. Accessed June 7, 2019. http://www.ibreviary.com/m/preghiere.php?tipo=Rito&id=103.

Ratzinger, Joseph. *Eschatology: Death and Eternal Life*. 2nd ed. Edited by Aidan Nichols. Translated by Michael Waldstein. Washington, DC: Catholic University of America Press, 2007.

———. *The Feast of Faith: Approaches to a Theology of the Liturgy*. San Francisco: Ignatius, 1986.

———. *The God of Jesus Christ: Meditations on the Triune God*. Translated by Brian McNeil. San Francisco: Ignatius, 2008.

———. *Introduction to Christianity*. 2nd ed. San Francisco: Ignatius, 2004.

———. *Pilgrim Fellowship of Faith: The Church as Communion*. 1st ed. Edited by Stephan Otto Horn and Vinzenz Pfnur. Translated by Henry Taylor. San Francisco: Ignatius, 2005.

———. "The Relationship of the Liturgy to Time and Space." Church Life Journal. November 2, 2018. http://churchlife.nd.edu/2018/11/02/the-relationship-of-the-liturgy-to-time-and-space/.

———. "Salvation: More Than a Cliché?" Church Life Journal. October 23, 2018. https://churchlife.nd.edu/2018/10/23/salvation-more-than-a-cliche/.

———. *The Spirit of the Liturgy*. San Francisco: Ignatius, 2000.

———. *Truth and Tolerance: Christian Belief and World Religions*. San Francisco: Ignatius, 2004.

Tairako, Tomonaga. "Reification–Thingification and Alienation–Basic Concepts of Marx's Critique of Political Economy and Practical Materialism." *Hitotsubashi Journal of Social Studies* 49 no. 1 (2018): 1–28.

14

The Liturgical Metaphysics of Gift in *Introduction to Christianity*

Timothy P. O'Malley

The thought of Louis-Marie Chauvet, specifically in his two works *Symbol and Sacrament: A Sacramental Reinterpretation of Christian Existence* and *The Sacraments: The Word of God at the Mercy of the Body*, dominates American sacramental theology. In both works, Chauvet offers a critique of premodern sacramental grammar, what he calls the objectivist scheme, in which "the insistence on the objective efficacy of the sacraments is done at the expense of the concrete existential subjects."[1] Chauvet proposes a reconfiguration of sacramental theology according to the categories of symbol and language. This revolution allows the Church to pass beyond a sacramental metaphysics dominated by instrumental causality and a perceived neo-Platonic division between *signum* and *res*. The sacraments do not operate in the order of efficacious signification but instead pertain to "a symbolic representation of the Other, where [the sacraments] are appreciated as language acts making possible the unending transformation of subjects into believing subjects . . ."[2] The efficacy of the sacraments is understood as a linguistic event that is formative of the subject.

The stress in Chauvet's sacramental economy is on the symbolic world made possible through the ritual laws of the sacraments. Such a world creates and recreates Christian identity through "the discursive logic of the sign, the identifying challenge of the symbol, [and] the world-transforming power of the *praxis*."[3] Through this sacramental reinterpretation of Christian existence, the Church learns anew that grace is "less a value-object to be received than a symbolic receiving of oneself: receiving oneself from God in Christ, through

---

1. Chauvet, *The Sacraments*, xv.
2. Chauvet, *Symbol and Sacrament*, 45.
3. Chauvet, *Symbol and Sacrament*, 180.

the work of the Spirit, as daughters and sons, as sisters and brothers."[4] The anthropological and theological task of each person is to receive and to create a world through participation in the sacramental economy. There is no beyond in the sacraments, no eternal order of divine love separate from the linguistic and ritual event of mediation. The Christian must set "aside the will to master its subject and secure identity, pursuing instead the never-ending and in-securing way of faith seeking understanding in the concrete, material mediations of our Christian existence."[5]

There are benefits to Chauvet's account of sacramental theology, in particular his careful attention to the liturgical act, as integral to sacramental efficacy. His sacramental reading of the Eucharist does not focus exclusively on the transformation of the elements of bread and wine into Body and Blood as a philosophical or theological dilemma to be overcome through theory. Divine presence for Chauvet is mediated through the very ritual activity of saying the words of the Institution narrative, of breaking and giving the elements.[6] One cannot describe Eucharistic presence without attention to the concrete celebration of the liturgy, the embodied act of Eucharistic worship.[7]

Still, such an approach to sacramental grace—one that eliminates entirely the categories of *signum* and *res*—comes with significant problems. Jean-Yves Lacoste has properly argued that this entrance into divine presence within the Eucharist is not reducible to the ritual or language acts that constitute the liturgical celebration. When the believer adores the Eucharistic species, bending the knee before the tabernacle, the believer is not symbolically receiving oneself in the mode of ritual symbolization. Instead, the believer is encountering an eschatological reality through sacramental signification. The believer is worshipping. Lacoste writes, "This conclusive gesture is exposed in the world of faith; and in the world of faith, if such a field of experience merits the name of world, the thing-reality (*chose-res*) of the sacrament, given inseparably with the sacrament, returns inevitably to the background *sacramentum tantum*."[8] The reality of divine presence, of total self-giving love made present in the sacrament, is mediated through the *sacramentum tantum*. But, there is always a surplus, something more available to the Christian, through the mediation of the *sacramentum tantum*. The doctrine of transubstantiation, supposedly a fruit of metaphysical speculation dominated

---

4. Chauvet, *The Sacraments*, 95.
5. Boeve, "Theology in a Postmodern Context," 23.
6. Chauvet, "The Broken Bread as Theological Figure," 255.
7. Mitchell, "Rituality and the Retrieval of Sacrament," 208.
8. Lacoste, *L'intuition sacramentelle et autres essais*, 94–95.

by technocratic instrumentality, preserves the mystery of the Eucharist as a sacrament of faith in which the believer both adores and feasts upon the presence of the sacramental, Eucharistic Christ.[9]

Traditional sacramental metaphysics is not reducible thus to technical instrumentality. It instead focuses on a presence, on an original act of divine donation, to which the human person can attune oneself through the liturgical proclamation, "*Mon Seigneur et mon Dieu.*" A sacramental metaphysics depends on the capacity of the Christian "to be present himself at the event of the gift," a gift that transcends the particular ritual, historical, or social celebrations of that rite.[10] The sacraments redeem through enabling human beings to participate in divine love, a love that is not transcribed exclusively within the cultural and ritual body of the Church.

Joseph Ratzinger's liturgical metaphysics operates more within the sacramental intuition of Jean-Yves Lacoste than the symbolic formation of identity discernable in Chauvet. Ratzinger's liturgical metaphysics is not (as Lieve Boeve contends) an example of a pre-modern return to the pre-existing *Logos*, a world of meaning that is more Platonic than Christian.[11] Instead, Ratzinger's liturgical thought is oriented by a metaphysics of donation, one in which the human person first receives divine love before he or she makes or constructs a self.[12] Through this act of reception, the Christian enters into an embodied way of self-giving love, the very *Logos* made flesh. Such an embodied entrance into that which is not reducible to the visible and tangible transfigures the Christian's whole approach to existence. The Christian is guided by an open identity characterized not by narrative ambiguity but sacrificial love. The only self to be formed is the one constantly discovered in increasing desire for union with Christ.[13]

The Liturgical Metaphysics of *Introduction to Christianity*

Ratzinger's *Introduction to Christianity* is not the most obvious text to analyze for insight into his liturgical metaphysics. *Introduction* rarely mentions liturgical celebrations or sacraments, in contrast to Ratzinger's better known works on the topic, including his *The Spirit of the Liturgy*, *Feast of*

---

9. Tück, *A Gift of Presence*, 74–75.
10. Lacoste, "Presence et affection," 220.
11. Boeve, "Thinking Sacramental Presence in a Postmodern Context," 8.
12. O'Malley, "Liturgical Memory and Liquid Modernity," 129.
13. "If we have a self, it is one that is eternally stigmatized and thus eternally becoming as it learns ever-more fully of its own true significance, its own true reference, its own true identity, in the love of Christ" (Cavadini, "The Darkest Enigma," 149).

Faith, and *The Eucharist—Heart of the Church*.[14] Yet, a closer reading of *Introduction* reveals Ratzinger as a thinker who situates metaphysics in the domain of divine donation rather than abstract, eternal forms. Metaphysics is completed in doxology.

From the beginning of the *Introduction*, as Ratzinger establishes what constitutes belief, he highlights the dynamic, self-diffusive quality to a metaphysics oriented toward a non-visible meaning. For Ratzinger, the human person has not been made simply for technical or calculative thought. He dismisses a reduction of the human person to an instrument for *teche* alone: "By thinking only of the practicable, of what can be made, [the human person] is in danger of forgetting to reflect on himself and on the meaning of his existence."[15] Already, the concern with metaphysics is not the ascertaining of eternal principles as much as grasping the meaning of existence.

For Ratzinger, the human person is made to seek out meaning, to discover the donative dimension of existence. As Ratzinger writes, "Meaning is the bread on which man, in the intrinsically human part of his being, subsists. Without the word, without meaning, without love he falls into the situation of no longer being able to live . . . "[16] Much of this meaning is not immediately tangible to the human person. That which is measurable, quantifiable, and observable are not the sole measure of what constitutes reality.[17] A couple who marries one another does not operate exclusively according to the visible or tangible. The couple lives out of the act of consent, the promise of love made by husband and wife, a transcendent promise that comes to define their existence. It is the bond of commitment that becomes the horizon of meaning for the couple, an act of faith or belief whereby the couple commits to one another until the separation forced by death.[18]

This account of belief is defining of what it means to be a human being. Every human being must choose an orientation toward reality. The scientific nihilist proclaims that there is no meaning in the world except the vibration of quarks, of tangible physical reality. The politician proclaims that the only thing that matters in the world is the use of power. Such professions of faith are not actually scientific statements. They become a philosophy, an orientation toward the world that observation alone cannot discern. The tree does not say, "There is no meaning." Human anatomy does not say, "There is no

---

14. For Ratzinger's entire corpus of liturgical and sacramental texts, see Ratzinger, *Theology of the Liturgy*.
15. Ratzinger, *Introduction*, 71.
16. Ratzinger, *Introduction*, 73.
17. Ratzinger, *Introduction*, 51.
18. Blondel, *Action*, 242–48.

meaning." The human person does not say, "Might beats right." The nihilist and political power player has taken a non-tangible, non-physical stance toward existence. Every human being must eventually believe in something, even if that belief is in nothing. And this act of belief always bypasses pure physicalism or positivism.

Belief is not a matter of empirical analysis—of measuring and quantifying what is perceived. Belief is first a posture of openness to reality, a response to the *logos* or meaning that is already given within the created order. Such a *logos*, an understanding of the meaning of the world, is not immediately evident to the human person insofar as it is unseen and invisible. Further, since it is not created by the human person, a mere construct of mind, belief presumes that reality is characterized by a gift given even before the human person was capable of receiving it.

The fundamental posture of the Christian is to recognize that the world is oriented toward a specific meaning, a *logos* that is given to the human person. Yet, this *logos* is not available simply as a Platonic form, floating in the ether of an eternal world. This meaning is made available through both a concrete world (creation) and a concrete person, Jesus Christ. At the center of Ratzinger's liturgical metaphysics of gift is the person of Jesus as given for the renewal of the entire created order: "Christian faith lives on the discovery that not only is there such a thing as objective meaning but that this meaning knows me and loves me, that I can entrust myself to it like the child who knows that everything he may be wondering about is safe and in the 'you' of his mother . . . "[19] This is not a metaphysics of totalizing, instrumental presence. Instead, it is a presence of relationality, a recognition that the meaning of the cosmos is available in a God that exists *for us*. It is a metaphysics of love.

Here, Ratzinger concludes the opening chapter of the *Introduction* with a theme that will appear throughout the text. The meaning that precedes the making is the enfleshment of the divine *Logos* in history. Jesus Christ is erotic and agapic truth made flesh. As Ratzinger argues in his description of Jesus Christ in the *Introduction*:

> For the peculiarity of Jesus' 'I,' of his person . . . lies in the fact that this 'I' is not at all something exclusive and independent but rather is Being completely derived from the 'Thou' of the Father and lived for the 'You' of men. It is identity of *logos* (truth) and love and thus makes love into the *logos*, the truth of human existence. The essence of faith demanded by a

19. Ratzinger, *Introduction*, 80.

> Christology so understood ... is entry into the universal openness of unconditional love.[20]

Jesus Christ is the presence of the truth. This is a truth that is revealed not through an abstract metaphysics but a logos-centered offering of love. In the end, the gift that precedes the making is a sacrifice of divine love that no human person could have constructed on one's own. This fundamental relationality defines both what it means to be divine (the three persons of the Trinity) and to be a human being created in the image and likeness of God.[21]

It is within this context in the *Introduction* that Ratzinger connects this metaphysics of gift, of sacrificial and divine love, to the Christian orientation to worship. The cross, for Ratzinger, is the revelation of the totality of divine and human love in a visible, tangible act by the God-man. The mystery of the cross, the shedding of blood unto the end, is "an embodiment of the fact that he offers no more and no less than himself."[22] This offering is a revelation to the human person of what it means to say "God" and "man" alike. To be God, to live as a human being created in the image and likeness of God, is to be oriented fundamentally toward self-gift. Christian worship is that concrete process whereby the Church receives such love, assuming a posture of radical reception and not self-creation:

> Christian worship consists in the absoluteness of love, as it could only be poured out by the one in whom God's own love had become human love; and it consists in the new form of representation included in this love, namely, that he stood for us and that we let ourselves be taken over by him. So it means that we can put aside our attempts at justification ... accept the gift of love of Jesus Christ, who 'stands in' for us, allow ourselves to be united in it, and thus become worshippers with him and in him.[23]

The sacramental economy of the Church allows the human person to enter into the self-giving love of Jesus Christ through the mode of receptivity. The Christian discovers a technology of the self that does not require an eternal union with God apart from that which is visible or tangible, including human history. Instead, one is led into a more radical entrance into history, made possible because the *Logos* outside of all time and space became flesh, revealing to humanity that the meaning of existence is the gift

---

20. Ratzinger, *Introduction*, 208.
21. Ratzinger, "Concerning the Notion of the Person in Theology," 447.
22. Ratzinger, *Introduction*, 287.
23. Ratzinger, *Introduction*, 287–88.

of love. Liturgical worship for Ratzinger is not reducible to the construction of a group's self-identity through ritual and language. Rather, there is always a surplus, a "more" to the act of worship, insofar as the giver of the gift is capable of an infinite gift of love.

The Liturgical Metaphysics of Gift as Challenge to Chauvet

Ratzinger's later liturgical works are a development of the original insight related to the liturgical metaphysics of the gift. The goal of Christian worship is not escaping into some eternal world of forms or an instrumentalization of the sacraments into techniques intended to force God into the bestowal of grace. But he is optimistic that God's self-revelation in Jesus Christ, the entrance into history, is in fact accessible to the human person through material signs. Such a presence certainly exceeds the signifying capacity of the signs, but it is the divine presence, the *logos* made available to the human person through the created order. As Ratzinger notes in his account of creation, "Christian belief in God means that things are the being-thought of a creative consciousness, of a creative freedom, and that the creative consciousness that bears up all things has released what has been thought into the freedom of its own, independent existence."[24] It is possible to make sense of the world, to read creation, as expressing something about the goodness of the Creator. As human creatures, we are free to discover this goodness, to search for it, and to live as creatures made for freedom.

It is perhaps here where Ratzinger offers a definitive counter to Chauvet's proposal of a postmodern sacramental theology—one that places the emphasis on the creation of a subject who must succumb to the presence of the absence of God rather than on participation in a donative, erotic, *logos* made available through the senses. Chauvet underlines throughout his argument that sacramental theology must give itself over to a presence of an absence. He writes in his *Symbol and Sacrament*:

> This amounts to the slow work of apprenticeship in the art of 'un-mastery,' a permanent work of *mourning* where, free of *resentment*, a 'serene' consent to the '*presence of the absence*' takes place within us little by little. In gospel terms, this is a work of conversion to the presence of the absence of a God who 'crosses himself out' in the crushed humanity of this crucified One

---

24. Ratzinger, *Introduction*, 157.

whom humans have reduced to less than nothing and yet where, in a paradoxical light, faith confesses the glory of God.[25]

Note the difference between Ratzinger and Chauvet relative to the cross. For Ratzinger, the cross is the dazzling revelation of divine love, an ecstatic presencing of love made available through contemplation of the crucified and risen Lord. For Chauvet, there is no visible glory in the crucified one. God is crossed out. God is made absent except in the image of crushed and destroyed humanity. If the Christian is to come to terms with this truth, with the presence of the absence, then the Christian must recognize that God is now available only through the seeming poverty of the human body. Chauvet notes that the presence of the absence depends on a more radical assent to sacramental mediation, " . . . mediation, *by way of the senses*, of an institution, a formula, a gesture, a material thing—as the (eschatological) place of God's advent."[26] There is no reality beyond the rite itself, beyond the act of mediation, beyond what is perceived and interpreted by the human being.

It is within the Eucharist in particular that Chauvet describes the most fundamental presencing of this absence. He writes:

> the Eucharist seems to us the *paradigmatic* figure of this presence-of-the-absence of God outside of which the faith would no longer be the faith, which holds us upright, watchful, in hope and exacts that we live in love in order to give God this body of humanity and of world for which God has made us responsible . . . The 'here' of the Eucharistic presence, in its signifying, empirical materiality, refers us to the 'here' of the faith, duly instituted and duly inscribed *somewhere*. It refers us back to the body—that is, to the historical, social, economic, and cultural determinations, even to the most individual determinations of our desire—as the place where the truth of our faith will come about.[27]

In the fracturing of what looks like bread, in the outpouring of the cup, there is no evidence of a divine presence. The body perceives what looks like broken bread, what seems like poured out wine. This presence of the absence brings the Christian back to the body of culture and history, the only place where the absent God may be searched for. For only here may God be sort of found, kind of discovered, in the ethical task that becomes gift for each Christian: "The liturgy is *powerful pedagogy where we learn to*

---

25. Chauvet, *Symbol and Sacrament*, 74.
26. Chauvet, *Symbol and Sacrament*, 83.
27. Chauvet, *Symbol and Sacrament*, 405.

consent to the presence of the absence of God, who obliges us to give him a body in the world . . . "[28] The constant undertaking is to give oneself over to the consent of this absence, to let Eucharistic worship continue in the world as an eschatological activity. It is the return-gift of ethical action. The regular celebration of the liturgy becomes a symbolic performance whereby the Christian participates in the "*'work' of plowing, of turning, of 'converting' to the gospel the symbolic field that Christians are.*"[29]

Yet, one returns again to the original critique levied implicitly against Chauvet by Lacoste. Christians do not participate in the liturgy as if it is exclusively about a consent to the presence of the absence. They kneel before the Blessed Sacrament. They kiss a book of the Gospels. They incense objects and build churches full of stained glass as acts of love. They reverence those places where God has been adored. They compose music to glorify God and worshipfully create iconography that makes accessible the image of God adored by the kissing worshipper. For most Christians, worship is related to the assent to a presence, to a meaning that must be received by the human person coming from Christ, as mediated through the material act of worship. Are most Christians wrong, sad saps who have been influenced by an onto-theology emerging from the supposed defects of ancient philosophy and a clericalized medieval Catholicism?

In the end, Chauvet's account fails because there is insufficient attention to love within the sacramental economy. For example, in his account of symbolic exchange Chauvet describes grace as related to an anthropology of gift-giving. Gift-giving does not operate according to an economic model where object "x" has value "y." Rather, gift-giving is always an exchange of the subjects themselves. In the bestowal of this wedding ring, husband and wife give themselves. The offer of the gift is bestowed so that subjects may enter into relationship with one another: "what gives us the possibility of becoming and living as subjects in this process . . . of gift-reception-return-gift that structures every significant relationship . . . every 'human' relationship, between partners . . . "[30]

The model of the gift is itself a kind of heuristic for understanding the bestowal of divine grace. God is the original giver, the one who created human beings as oriented toward the act of gift. Divine grace is not an "object" to be received as much as the process of gift and return gift that orients the entire sacramental economy. Grace "effects" the human person through the symbolic labor of the return-gift. Chauvet writes, "This truth

28. Chauvet, *Symbol and Sacrament*, 265.
29. Chauvet, *The Sacraments*, 94.
30. Chauvet, *Symbol and Sacrament*, 107.

[the truth of its relationship with God] [is] effected, not by 'amassing' spiritual values, but by a symbolic work whose process is nothing other than that of *symbolic exchange* or of verbal communication between subjects."[31] It is this return-gift, the capacity of the human person to offer one's own subjectivity back to God through ethical action within the Church that is the very essence of divine love for Chauvet.

Such an account of divine love, though, too quickly bypasses the incommensurate gift of love offered by the sacrifice of the Word made flesh and the return-gift of the human person back to God. Sacrifice, for Chauvet, cannot be a matter of divine redemption or expiation since this understanding of sacrifice would operate once more in the order of exchange. It places too much emphasis, according to Chauvet, on God's activity rather than the return-gift that the human person is capacitated to perform through the Eucharist. Eucharistic sacrifice in the Christian mode is in fact an anti-sacrifice, one that moves the human person away from a servile attitude toward a filial attitude:

> One sees what is at stake in what we call the *anti-sacrificial*: not the negation of the sacrificial or a part of it (its dimension of reconciliation), but *the task to convert all the sacrificial to the gospel in order to live it, not in a servile, but in a filial (and hence in a brotherly and sisterly) manner*. This is precisely why the realization of this intimate association, based on our common filiation, by the ethical practice of reconciliation between human beings, constitutes the premier place of *our* 'sacrifice.' That is what the anti-sacrifice of the Eucharist shows us and enjoins us to do.[32]

The memory of Christ is celebrated in the Eucharist, is given as gift, so that we might become a Eucharistic people made for this filial activity of reconciliation within the world.[33] There is no "value" to this gift, only the constant labor of the Spirit's work of transforming men and women into sons and daughters of God and thus brothers and sisters with one another.[34]

Chauvet is not wrong to emphasize the ethical demands of the Eucharist. But his situating of divine love in the process of symbolic exchange, in the anthropological act of gift-giving, is unnecessarily reductive. Not all gift-giving, not all acts of love, are occasions of symbolic exchange. The mother who gazes into the eyes of her child is not doing so out of the expectation that there *will* be a return gift of love—even if such a return-gift

31. Chauvet, *Symbol and Sacrament*, 109.
32. Chauvet, *Symbol and Sacrament*, 311.
33. Chauvet, *Symbol and Sacrament*, 313.
34. Chauvet, *Symbol and Sacrament*, 545.

of the smile may come.³⁵ Instead, the mother delights in the presence of the child. The mother cares for the child whether or not there will be a return gift of love because the act of parenting is oriented toward a self-less gift. One often loves simply to love. Further, the child in encountering the love of the parent is immersed into a world of gift, a world of love that is not dependent on his or her actions. The child does not need to reason about this love, to understand the "obligation" that the love requires. This moment of love comes radically from the outside, meeting an exigency that the child is not even aware is present.³⁶ In fact such love comes even as a gift to the mother or father, who in encountering one's child discovers a *logos* to existence that was previously unperceived. There is a contemplative dimension to this kind of love, a desire to simply dwell in the presence of the beloved. The return-gift is not immediately required, for the first act is delight, adoration, awareness of the gift of love that has indeed become present. Symbolic exchange risks becoming a monstrosity, where there is no presence of communion except the impetus to further action. There are some gifts that are bestowed to which there is no appropriate action except presence, the gift of the self before the beloved. The task is to become a lover rather actor, a dweller rather than a doer.

Likely, Chauvet goes awry because he assumes (though never proves) that traditional sacramental theology was driven by a technocratic, onto-theological rationality that instrumentalized the sacramental encounter—an assumption that has been thoroughly critiqued.³⁷ His account of medieval sacramental theology, as well as grace, pays no attention to Hugh of St. Victor's reflection of the Church's sacramental life as a series of bridal gifts to adorn the Church and the soul of each believer with the mysteries of love before eternal consummation in the beatific vision.³⁸ He bypasses Hildegard of Bingen's account of the Eucharist as a dowry bestowed by Christ to the Church, as well as a nuptial encounter in which the Christian and Christ enter into the deepest of unions.³⁹ Symbolic exchange brackets out divine *eros*, the manner in which God's love in the Eucharist is a reality that is supererogatory, supersaturated, a gift of love so penetrating that contemplative wonder is the first response.

---

35. Balthasar, *Unless You Become Like This Child*, 17–18.
36. Cavalletti, *The Religious Potential of the Child*, 44.
37. Chauvet has been severely critiqued for his misreading of Augustine, Hugh of St. Victor, and Thomas Aquinas on sacramental causality. See Blankenhorn, "The Instrumental Causality."
38. Hugh of St. Victor, "Soliloquy on the Betrothal-Gift of the Soul" 57 and 58.
39. Hildegard of Bingen, *Scivias*, II.6.1, 4, 11.

Ratzinger's account of the liturgy, as the immersion of the human person into the sacrificial love of God made available in the Church, offers an alternative approach to sacramental theology that avoids Chauvet's exaggerated apophatic sacramental theology drawn more from Martin Heidegger than St. Thomas.[40] Here, it will be worthwhile to examine but three facets of Ratzinger's liturgical and sacramental theology that he develops from his original insight of the donative dimension of creation and redemption in the *Introduction*: the centrality of sacrifice within the cosmos, the relationship between creation and history, and the nature of liturgical action as formative of human desire.

Ratzinger's liturgical theology is grounded in an account of sacrifice as closely linked to the cosmos. Worship is not something that God offers to the human person only after the fall. Rather, creation itself is oriented from the beginning toward worship: "If creation is meant to be a space for the covenant, the place where God and man meet one another, then it must be thought of as a space for worship."[41] Creation is a gift to the human person, an invitation to enter into relationship with God. The history of salvation encompasses both creation and covenant. For Ratzinger, creation is not even reducible to a particular act of love. Rather, it is the very possibility of love to begin with: "He created it so that love could exist."[42] Creation is that moment in which God makes possible the freedom of the created order, existing apart from God. Love becomes possible in this moment of creation insofar as there is a distance between Creator and creature.

The covenant, including the Laws governing worship, is the very completion of creation. In this way, one must recognize that the original donation that made possible creation, the primordial act of freeing love, is the origin of the act of worship. Therefore, worship involves sacrifice, a return gift of love back to God. Sacrifice, for Ratzinger, is an occasion of surrender. But it's not a surrender marked by pain, an understanding of redemption as a commercial exchange between God and the human person. Sacrifice is "the *civitas Dei*, that is, love-transformed mankind, the divinization of creation and the surrender of all things to God: God all in all (cf. 1 Cor 15:28). That is the purpose of the world. That is the essence of sacrifice and worship."[43] Sacrifice reveals the underlying metaphysics of all

---

40. There is an appropriate apophaticism in St. Thomas Aquinas around the Eucharist. See Vernard, *A Poetic Christ*, 399–402; Tück, *A Gift of Presence*, 316–19.
41. Ratzinger, *The Spirit of the Liturgy*, 14.
42. Ratzinger, *'In the Beginning . . . ,'* 30.
43. Ratzinger, *The Spirit of the Liturgy*, 15.

creation. Human beings were created for gift, and in sacrificial love, they resume this doxological vocation.

It is here that Ratzinger introduces a model of sacrifice drawn from the early Church. He speaks of sacrifice not as a form of symbolic exchange but as *exitus* and *reditus*. He recognizes the philosophical grounding of these terms in Plotinus. But he quickly moves beyond Plotinus since a Christian *reditus* or return does not mean an escape from the created order. Instead, the *exitus* is the act of divine creation when human beings were formed by God in the image and likeness of the Creator. But human beings abused this gift. They did not love in return, instead underscoring their own dependence apart from God. An abuse of freedom becomes a rejection of God, a refusal of true freedom and thus cult alike.

The divine sacrifice of the cross is a restoration of this freedom through the obedience of the Son who loved unto the end. As Ratzinger writes, "The Son becomes man and in his body bears the whole of humanity back to God. Only the incarnate Word, whose love is fulfilled on the Cross, is perfect obedience ... his incarnate obedience is the new sacrifice, and in this obedience he draws us all with him and at the same time wipes away all our disobedience through love."[44] This traditional approach to redemption does not erase the human condition, turning the human person into a servile creature dependent on an economic exchange, as Chauvet charges. Instead, it redeems because the act of love upon the cross is a divine and human act beyond what any fallen creature could perform. It is the perfect act, revealing the reality of what human love can actually be when offered back to the Father through Christ. Christ bestows to the human family what the human family itself could not give.

This is the sacrifice, the *exitus* of God that is made available in the liturgy. Sacrifice is the meaning of existence, the proper orientation of the cosmos. Ratzinger writes relative to sacrificial cult:

> If 'sacrifice' in its essence is simply returning to love and therefore divinization, worship now has a new aspect: the healing of wounded freedom, atonement, purification, deliverance from estrangement. The essence of worship, of sacrifice—the process of assimilation, of growth in love, and thus the way into freedom—remains unchanged. But now it assumes the aspect of healing, the loving transformation of broken freedom, of painful expiation. Worship is directed to the Other in himself, to his all-sufficiency, but now it refers itself to the Other who alone can

---

44. Ratzinger, *Jesus of Nazareth, Part Two*, 235.

extricate me from the knot that I cannot untie. Redemption now needs the Redeemer.[45]

Worship is the moment in which the human person recognizes that his or her freedom may only flourish, be given full expression, in that return-gift of love offered back to the Father through Christ.

The acts of love are not identical insofar as divine love, the sacrifice of the Word made flesh, exceeds what any human could offer. The Word made flesh resurrected from the dead offers a gift to the human person, to the Church that could not have been given before. It is a gift that is available in the interior life of God, bestowed in creation, offered in the covenant, given anew in the redemption provided by Christ now memorialized in liturgical celebration. It is now the Church who stands before God in gratitude in light of this supererogatory love. Worship becomes participation in the sacrifice of Christ, the "logificiation" of the human person.

Every dimension of human life has a place in this sacramental economy—creation and salvation history are one in the same. Ratzinger does not speak about a divine grace descending from above, one that exists entirely apart from the natural religiosity of the human person. If the meaning of existence is a *logos* of love, then natural religion already points toward the meaning of life as a donative event, a return act of gratitude to God.

Here, he is able to affirm the importance of the human *bios*, of ritual action and cultural expression, without ridding the Church of a metaphysics that grounds the sacramental economy. Natural sacraments exist within the world because the *logos* has provided a reasonable order for the world. The world is symbolic, not simply functional—in this, Ratzinger agrees with Chauvet. But to affirm the symbolic dimension of the world does not mean that one must evacuate the created order of metaphysics, of a first philosophy that exists beyond the physical. The world has a meaning that offers itself to the human person. And this meaning is discerned in a non-physical manner, through the act of understanding.

For example, creation sacraments "develop at the important junctures ... [of] birth and death, a meal, and sexual relations."[46] A meal is ultimately never just a meal, the filling of the body with sustenance. A meal, celebrated in the company of other persons, becomes a kind of sacrament of what it means to be a human being. He writes, "In a meal man discovers that he is not the founder of his own being but lives his existence in receptivity. He experiences himself as someone who has been endowed, who lives on the unmerited gift

---

45. Ratzinger, *The Spirit of the Liturgy*, 19.
46. Ratzinger, "The Sacramental Foundation of Christian Existence," 156.

of a fruitfulness that seems always to be waiting for him, as it were."[47] The biological act of eating in common within the human family becomes a "type" of the communion to which the creature finds flourishing.

The Christian sacramental economy does not destroy the creation sacraments. Such creation sacraments are elevated through immersion into salvation history. Ratzinger writes, "the Christian sacraments mean not only insertion into the God-permeated cosmos . . . they mean at the same time insertion into the history that originates in Christ."[48] Through the sacraments that always involve created material, one enters into the divine history. It is precisely through the concreteness of the human condition that the sacraments renew the Christian person. The materiality mediates the history of Christ, and the history of Christ provides a new horizon for the materiality.

This is not a neo-Platonic account of sacramental grace. But it is an account that recognizes that a supererogatory divine love is made present through the sacramental economy, one that transcends the material itself. God uses matter as an instrument for the salvation of the person, renewing matter in the process. It is Ratzinger's exegesis of Christ's own Eucharistic offering in the Last Supper that incarnates this union of creation and history. In describing the Last Supper, Ratzinger comments:

> The breaking of bread for all is in the first instance a function of the head of the family, who by this action in some sense represents God the Father, who gives us everything, through the earth's bounty, that we need for life. It is also a gesture of hospitality, through which the stranger is given a share in what is one's own; he is welcomed into table fellowship. Breaking and distributing: it is the act of distributing that creates community. This archetypally human gesture of giving, sharing, and uniting acquires an entirely new depth in Jesus' Last Supper through his gift of himself. God's bountiful distribution of gifts takes on a radical quality when the Son communicates and distributes himself in the form of bread . . . In this sacrament we enjoy the hospitality of God, who gives himself to us in Jesus Christ, crucified and risen.[49]

Divine hospitality reveals the very meaning of eating and drinking. The act of the Church celebrating this sacrament ritually matters in all of its particularity. The act of breaking and giving, of eating and drinking, becomes

47. Ratzinger, "The Sacramental Foundation of Christian Existence," 157.
48. Ratzinger, "The Sacramental Foundation of Christian Existence," 162.
49. Ratzinger, *Jesus of Nazareth: Part 2*, 129.

the very space whereby God "saves" the human person. This salvation is divine history working within the Church. The goal of worship is not the fostering of a subject but participation in a divine history that does not obliterate creation. One experiences in the Eucharist the simultaneous recognition of total sacrificial self, at the same time that one's very body participates in this love through eating and drinking.

Every action that the body performs in the act of worship is linked to this immersion of the created body into salvation history in love. God seeks to bring the human person—body and soul—into union with Christ. Chauvet's sacramental theology is almost entirely focused on the words of the Eucharistic Prayer, along with but a few gestures. Apart from the fracturing rite, he attends little to the concrete body involved in worship. There is the body of history, the social body, and the cultural body. But too often, the physical body is absent. Ratzinger avoids this temptation precisely because he knows that the human body is a divine gift already. The body was made for liturgical action, for that *actio* of sacrifice that God seeks to perform in the Church.

Standing, kneeling, and sitting are therefore not merely practical dimensions of the liturgy—ones incidentally never mentioned by Chauvet. Instead, they are the very manner in which the Christian comes to participate in the sacrifice of Christ as embodied creatures. Kneeling, of course, is an act of obedience. It is a performance of the body whereby one gives the entirety of the will over to another. But, Christians don't kneel before just any power. This is not a purely natural gesture, one of subservience rather than filial friendship. The act of kneeling is an embodied performance of worship that brings one into communion with Christ: "Through him, through the Crucified, the bold promise of the Old Testament is now fulfilled: all bend the knee before Jesus, the One who descended, and bow to him precisely as the one true God above all gods . . . The Christian liturgy is a cosmic liturgy precisely because it bends the knee before the crucified and exalted Lord."[50] Kneeling takes on a performative dimension for the Christian, one where the cosmic and the historical meet. A natural posture is subsumed into adoration of the resurrected Christ, the one who reveals the meaning of existence in sacrificial love.

These three dimensions of Ratzinger's liturgical and sacramental thought reveal that one need not give up metaphysics in order to develop an existentially meaningful sacramental theology. Chauvet's characterization of pre-modern sacramental theology as concerned merely with technique, instrumentality, causality, and the quantification of grace is just that—a characterization. Surely, pre-modern sacramental theology might have dealt more sufficiently with the liturgical act, with the natural religiosity that concerns

50. Ratzinger, *The Spirit of the Liturgy*, 121.

the human being. But Ratzinger's approach—grounded in a metaphysics of donation—demonstrates that one need not get rid of sign and reality, of the visible and the invisible, to develop an existentially meaningful sacramental theory. Instead, through a proper understanding of the metaphysics of creation, of the orientation of all existence to sacrifice, the sacraments become the fullest expression of a truly human life.

Conclusion

It is time for American theologians to offer more serious challenges to Chauvet's insufficient explanation of sacramental theology, including his account of theological history, as well as his use of ritual theory. The theory of symbolic exchange in the sacraments is reductive, failing to recognize that not all "love" can be understood according to the model of human gift-giving. Such a narrative ignores the manner in which love is inscribed in the very sacramental economy, within theories of instrumental causality.

Ratzinger establishes that creation is oriented toward gift, but a very different type of gift—a gift of love that is beyond what the human being can accomplish on one's one. There is a meaning, a divine act of love, that orders the entirety of creation. The filial identity of the human person is achieved not by denying metaphysics, the separation of Creator and creature. Instead, only by sufficiently recognizing this separation, underlining the totality of love made available through the sacramental economy, can one develop a sacramental theology that attends to an existentially meaningful efficacy. Ratzinger gets far closer to articulating this kind of sacramental theology, beginning with his *Introduction to Christianity*, than Chauvet.

Bibliography

Balthasar, Hans urs von. *Unless You Become Like This Child*. Translated by Erasmo Leiva-Merikakis. San Francisco: Ignatius, 1991.

Blankenhorn, Bernard. "The Instrumental Causality of the Sacraments: Thomas Aquinas and Louis-Marie Chauvet. *Nova et Vetera* 4 no. 2 (2006) 255–94.

Blondel, Maurice. *Action (1893): Essay on a Critique of Life and a Science of Practice*. Translated by Oliva Blanchette. Notre Dame: University of Notre Dame Press, 1984.

Boeve, Lieven. "Theology in a Postmodern Context and the Hermeneutical Project of Louis-Marie Chauvet." In *Sacraments: Revelation of the Humanity of God— Engaging the Fundamental Theology of Louis-Marie Chauvet*, edited by Philippe Bordeyne and Bruce T. Morrill, 5–24. Collegeville: Liturgical, 2008.

———. "Thinking Sacramental Presence in a Postmodern Context: A Playground for Theological Renewal." In *Sacramental Presence in a Postmodern Context*, edited by L. Boeve and L. Leijssen, 3–38. Leuven: Leuven University Press, 2001.

Cavadini, John C. "The Darkest Enigma: Reconsidering the Self in Augustine's Thought." In *Visioning Augustine*, 138–55. Hoboken: Wiley Blackwell, 2019.

Cavalletti, Sofia. *The Religious Potential of the Child: Experiencing Scripture and Liturgy with Young Children*. Translated by Patricia M. Coulter and Julie M. Coulter. Chicago: Liturgy Training, 1992.

Chauvet, Louis-Marie. *The Sacraments: The Word of God at the Mercy of the God*. Translated by Madeleine Beaumont. Collegeville: Liturgical, 2001.

———. *Symbol and Sacrament: A Sacramental Reinterpretation of Christian Existence*. Translated by Patrick Madigan, SJ, and Madeleine Beaumont. Collegeville: Liturgical, 1995.

Hildegard of Bingen. *Scivias*. Translated by Mother Columba Hart and Jane Bishop. New York: Paulist, 1990.

Hugh of St. Victor. *Soliloquy on The Betrothal-Gift of the Soul*. In *On Love: A Selection of Works of Hugh, Adam, Achard, Richard, and Godfrey of St. Victor*, edited by Hugh Feiss, OSB, 185–232. New York: New City, 2012.

Lacoste, Jean-Yves. *L'intuition sacramentelle et autres essais*. Paris: Ad Solem, 2015.

———. "Présence et affection." In *Sacramental Presence in a Postmodern Context*, edited by L. Boeve and L. Leijssen, 212–31. Leuven: Leuven University Press, 2001.

Mitchell, Nathan. "Rituality and the Retrieval of Sacrament as 'Language Event.'" In *Sacraments: Revelation of the Humanity of God—Engaging the Fundamental Theology of Louis-Marie Chauvet*, edited by Philippe Bordeyne and Bruce T. Morrill, 207–24. Collegeville: Liturgical, 2008.

Ratzinger, Joseph. "Concerning the Notion of Person in Theology." *Communio* 17 (1990) 439–54.

———. *'In the Beginning...': A Catholic Understanding of the Story of Creation and the Fall*. Translated by Boniface Ramsey, OP. Grand Rapids: Eerdmans, 1990.

———. *Introduction to Christianity*. Translated by J. R. Foster. San Francisco: Ignatius, 2004.

———. *Jesus of Nazareth, Part 2—Holy Week: From the Entrance Into Jerusalem to the Resurrection*. Translated by the Vatican Secretariat of State. San Francisco: Ignatius, 2011.

———. "The Sacramental Foundation of Christian Existence." In *Theology of the Liturgy: The Sacramental Foundation of Christian Existence*. The Complete Works of Joseph Ratzinger Volume 11, 153–68. Translated by Kenneth Baker, SJ and Michael J. Miller. San Francisco: Ignatius, 2014.

———. "The Spirit of the Liturgy." In *Collected Works, vol. II: Theology of the Liturgy: The Sacramental Foundation of Christian Existence*, translated by John Saward, 3–152.

O'Malley, Timothy P. "Liturgical Memory and Liquid Modernity." *Antiphon* 22 no. 2 (2018) 121–37.

Tück, Jan-Heiner. *A Gift of Presence: The Theology and Poetry of the Eucharist in Thomas Aquinas*. Translated by Scott G. Hefelfinger. Washington DC: Catholic University of America Press, 2018.

Vernard, Olivier-Thomas. "The Eucharist: The Exercise of Adoration—Glosses on 'Adoro Te.'" In *A Poetic Christ: Thomist Reflections on Scripture, Language, and Reality*. Translated by Kenneth Oakes and Francesca Aran Murphy, 392–418. New York: T&T Clark, 2019.

V. Spiritual Theology

15

On Christian Structures

CLEMENS SEDMAK

Introduction

IN HIS REVIEW OF the English translation of Joseph Ratzinger's *Introduction to Christianity*, Keith Ward identifies relationality and "being for" as the key points of Ratzinger's book:

> His underlying theme is that substance-philosophy is not adequate to Christian truth, and what is needed is a relation-philosophy, for which relation is 'a primordial form of being' (p. 131). Thus a person 'is the pure relation of being related, nothing else', and man's personhood consists in complete open-ness, losing one's individuality in a total being from and being-for others. God in his Trinitarian being is pure relation; and Jesus, as the completely open man, is one with God. In this, he is also the forerunner of a new humanity, to which Christian faith points. Christian faith is basically 'changing over from being for oneself to being for one another' (p. 190) and from the infinite love.[1]

Even if one were not prepared to agree with that reading of the *Introduction*, it cannot be denied that the "being-for" is of central importance to the book. Ratzinger has explicitly drawn attention to "the principle of 'For'" in an excursus of the book, entitled "Christian Structures." I will pay special attention to this excursus which is offered in the book in part Two, the part on Jesus Christ. I want to explore the idea of Christian structures in conversation with Ratzinger's *Introduction to Christianity*. I take the liberty of moving from structures in a more Heideggerian sense ("the structures of existence") to a social ethics-approach of exploring institutions and social structures. The principle of "For," identified as a hermeneutical key point

---

1. Ward, Review, 86–87.

of reference by Keith Ward, is relevant for the idea of Christian structures since a) structures need to express this principle themselves, b) structures need to support an individual's honest attempt to live out this for-dimension in his or her life. My point of departure is Joseph Ratzinger's question: "Does God dwell in institutions?" and his reply: "To this we must first of all simply say 'yes.'"[2]

What do we do with the claim that God dwells in institutions?

I will proceed in three steps: I will make some remarks about institutional ethics and the ethics of institutions, and will point to the limits of institutional ethics; I will then sketch a spirituality of institutions in conversation with Ratzinger's insights into structures; finally, I will illustrate the point of a spirituality of institutions by making use of one particular biblical passage, 1 Kgs 8:10–11.

1. Structures, Institutional Ethics, and Its limits

Structures are generally the result of processes of building; Latin *structure* is connected to *struo*, a building activity. The term has been semantically expanded from the structure of buildings to the structure of sentences, the structure of organisms, the structure of the universe, the structure of human existence, social structures. A structure is the result but also the framework of human action, established by actions and enabling actions at the same time.[3] Structures make certain actions possible that would not be possible without structures, and they make certain actions undesirable and more difficult.

Structures enable institutions; an institution generates contexts within which certain types of actions can be repeated because of rule-based standardization. These rules structure the sphere of action in a way that allowed and prohibited, prescribed and supererogatory actions can be distinguished. Agency has lost neutrality and "value-freedom," and a system of consequences of actions has to be established in order to build institutional capacity.[4] The concept of structure on the behavioral level is linked to the concept of habit, thus: to patterns and repetition. It is in this context of agency and interactions that institutional ethics arises. I want to distinguish two dimensions from institutions that play a key role in the ethics of institutions: institutional experience and institutional agency.

---

2. Ratzinger, *Introduction*, 183.

3. Giddens, *New Rules of Sociological Method*, 121.

4. That is why Jon Elster argues that formal sanctions, such as punishment, are a necessary feature of institutions. See *Nuts and Bolts for the Social Sciences*, chap. 15.

Institutional experience is shaped, more often than not, by social markers. Oscar Lewis' influential (and controversial) studies on "the culture of poverty" suggested mistrust in institutions based on negative experiences as a sign of a way of life shaped by poverty.[5] Jill Leovy in her account of gang violence in Los Angeles confirms the experience of institutional suspicion: "He was afraid to deal with police for fear of exposure or being sent to prison."[6] She also observes that the institutions were not investing in the area, which adds to the building up of mistrust: "The poor people down here never get anything, and they need good detectives."[7] One key aspect of institutional experience is "visibility" and "recognition"; the experience of being invisible is the fate of persons who are socially excluded. Being seen through, being treated as if not being present, is a way of humiliating a person. If we define "respect" as "being recognized as a source of normative claims," we can see the connection between invisibility, lack of respect, and a negative institutional experience. Which are the patterns of recognition within an institution? Where can we identify entry points for humiliation or patterns and practices of humiliating in institutional settings? These are important ethical questions to ask.

A second aspect of institutional ethics is institutional agency. Institutions establish patterns of institutional agency where the individual person appears as an institutional agent fulfilling role expectations: an institution can be defined "as an interlocking double-structure of persons-as-role-holders or office-bearers and the like, and of social practices involving both expressive and practical aims and outcomes."[8] Institutional agency is complex because it involves other players, and because the individual action is embedded in a wider framework. The central concept in the teleological account of social institutions is that of *joint action*.[9] The involvement of

---

5. See Lewis, *La Vida*, and Lewis, *Anthropological Essays*.

6. *Ghettoside*, 78. She observed that there was a prohibition to work with the police (81) and a shadow legal system was established (79). Institutions failed to establish trust: "They were shooting each other but still seemed to think the police were the problem . . . 'You don't care because he's a black man!' someone yelled" (18). The institutions also had good reasons to work with a hermeneutics of suspicion: "the security guard explained that the hospital had problems with gang rivals trying to enter the trauma center 'and finish it'" (115).

7. Leovy, *Ghettoside*, 52.

8. Harré, *Social Being*, 98.

9. Miller, *Social Action: A Teleological Account*, chap. 2. These joint actions involve not only different agents, but also show patterns of dependence and interwovenness. As Parson observed: "actions do not take place separately each with a separate, discrete end in relation to the situation, but in long complicated 'chains' . . . [and] the total complex of means-end relationships is not to be thought of as similar to a large number

different stake holders constitutes the challenge of coordination: An institution is based on and the creator of collaborative action situations. Collaborative action situations require coordination and require the coordinated effort of different players in order to be successful. There are a number of challenges to the successful dealing with collaborative action situations. Let me mention three: There are public good problems ("free riding") and common pool resources problems ("Tragedy of the Commons"), there is the challenge of layered agency (principal-agent)-problems (hierarchies). Institutional ethics deals with the challenge of safeguarding proper coordination in collaborative action situations. A key point to consider in these situations is the question of incentives. What is the incentive structure of an institution? Have "perverse incentives" been encouraged?[10] These are important ethical questions.

The Limits of Ethics

Institutional ethics with a twofold focus on institutional experiences and institutional agency leaves us with questions of recognition, humiliation, coordination, and incentives as key questions of an ethics of social structures. As a project of "ethics," an ethics of institutions will focus on the general (in a Kantian tradition: on an impersonal standpoint), on the systematic (listing aspects and arguments), on "the positional" (with the ambition of ethics to offer and develop a position), on the proper justification of claims with the specific role of arguments. Furthermore, as a project of ethics, institutional ethics will subscribe to a primacy of action and agency as the key domain of ethics.

From a theological point of view, however, it is important and interesting to see the limits of ethics; there are limits to what ethics can "do" for us. There are, to mention a few, the well-established limits of motivation (why act ethically?), there are the limits of language (expressed, for example, in Adorno's reflections on poetry after Auschwitz or George Steiner's essays in *Language and Silence*), there are the limits of arguments in the light of the power of narratives and experiences; there are the limits of agency with the finality of unresolvable suffering. A striking example of these limits of ethics can be found in the struggle of Rabbi Kalonymus Kalmish Shapiro (1889–1943), who led the Jewish community in the Warsaw ghetto. Rabbi Shapiro

---

of parallel threads, but as a complicated web (if not a tangle)" (*The Structure of Social Action*, 229).

10. This question has been prominent in the work of Elinor Ostrom. See e.g. Ostom, Schroeder, and Wynne, *Institutional Incentives and Sustainable Development*.

had to ask the question of whether God was with the Jewish community, with the institution of the synagogue. Looking at the institution of the secret synagogue that he ran in the ghetto, he too asked Joseph Ratzinger's question: "Does God dwell in institutions?" And with Ratzinger the Rabbi's reply was: "To this we must first of all simply say 'yes.'"[11] But Rabbi Shapiro could not obtain the answer from ethics. He had to make use of other, deeper, more painful, more personal, more paradoxical resources: his faith. Before his death, Rabbi Shapiro buried a manuscript entitled *Esh Kodesh* (Holy Fire).[12] As spiritual head of his flock, Shapiro is here concerned with the sufferings of the Jewish people. In a lecture given in February 1942, Rabbi Shapiro cites Isa 63:9, which describes God's pity for his people, and argues that because God is eternal, his pity must also be eternal.[13] Divine pity as something infinite and endless goes beyond anything we as humans can imagine, and even transcends anything in this world since everything here is finite, has an end. God keeps his suffering and pity to himself; there is no outward display, as can be read in Jeremiah: "But if you will not listen, my soul will weep in secret for your pride" (Jer 13:17). The Rabbi invites his people to be with God, to assist God in God's weeping. What does it mean to believe in a God who weeps in secret? What does it mean to believe that God is present in the institution of the holy house, in the midst of suffering and despair? We would not expect ethics to provide an answer to this question.

There are limits to the ethics of institutions; there are limits as to what concepts like "incentives" and "institutional agency" can do. These limits allow space for theology, and could be read to call for a two-fold transformation: a) the transformation of technological problems of institutional management into ethical questions; and b) the transformation of ethical questions into spiritual challenges. The question whether God lives in institutions is not a question of ethics.

2. A Spirituality of Institutions and Structures

"Does God dwell in institutions?" Ratzinger's reply: "To this we must first of all simply say 'yes.'"[14] What do we do with the claim that God dwells in institutions?

I want to reconstruct Joseph Ratzinger's contribution to a spirituality of institutions. I want to reconstruct his indirect contribution to a theology

11. Ratzinger, *Introduction*, 183.
12. Cf. Polen, "Divine Weeping."
13. Polen, "Divine Weeping," 255.
14. Ratzinger, *Introduction*, 183.

and spirituality of institutions and structures—"indirect" because his project was clearly not located in the context of Catholic Social Teaching; Catholic Social Teaching does not play an explicit role in the *Introduction*. But I hope to be able to show that the *Introduction* has a lot to offer with regard to social ethics in a Catholic tradition. I want to distinguish four dimensions of a spirituality of institutions: the principle of "for," the unity of love and truth, the material dimension, the vertical dimension.

2.1 The Principle of "For"

Being a Christian means to be a social being; we are persons because we are encountered in second-person-situations.[15] We are called to community and called by a community. "Being a Christian is in its first aim not an individual but a social charisma,"[16] "being a Christian means essentially changing from being for oneself to being for one another."[17] Christians live lives that are not their own; the life of a Christian is a life committed to God and the community. "The goal of the Christian is not private bliss but the whole."[18] The anthropological insight into our "for-ness" has to be translated into structures and social systems if they are to do justice to who we are as persons. This concern with "our being for others" needs to be translated into proper structures to minimize arbitrariness, enable coordination, and provide stability. The principle of "for"—being for the other, being for another—reminds us that structures are not self-serving; they are not ends in themselves. They serve a purpose and are instruments, means to an end. They need to be characterized by a will to a proper exodus: "the *being* of Christ ("incarnation" theology!) is *actualitas*, stepping beyond and out of oneself, the exodus of departure from self; it is not a being that rests in itself, but the act of being sent, of being son, of serving. Conversely, this 'doing' is not just 'doing' but 'being'; it reaches down into the depths of being and coincides with it. This being is exodus, transformation."[19]

Structures and institutions follow the "for"-principle: "It is not hard to see that in spite of all the philosophical and juridical terminology employed, the guiding thread remains that truth which the Bible expresses in the little

---

15. In the words of Rowan Williams: "I'm a person because I am spoken to, I'm attended to, and I'm spoken and attended and loved into actual existence" (*The Person and the Individual*, 19).

16. Ratzinger, *Introduction*, 187.

17. Ratzinger, *Introduction*, 190.

18. Ratzinger, *Introduction*, 277.

19. Ratzinger, *Introduction*, 171.

word 'For', in which it makes clear that we as men live not only directly from God but from one another, and in the last analysis from the One who lived for all."[20] There is a tendency in institutions to go against the "for-principle." Let me mention three: (i) There is a tendency in institutions to produce self-preserving and self-aggrandizing patterns of institutional agency; institutional agency has a tendency to prioritize the status of the institution over the well-being of individuals who are drawn into institutional acting.[21] Individual agents "represent" the institution and act "on behalf" of the institution and within their institutionally assigned role which shapes the agency. This diminishes "the human factor" and gives rise to institutional sub-cultures. (ii) There is the phenomenon of self-referential actions: institutions (often for legal and accountability reasons) prescribe actions that are not considered meaningful by the people involved, but serve the purpose of "being able to say that we did it." One example: I took a group of students to another country, and the University organized a risk management session that covered highly unlikely events like a terrorist attack. When I commented on the improbability of this happening, I was told: "We know that; but we must be able to say that we have conducted the session in case of a law suit." These actions, in the final analysis, then become self-referential and do not serve a purpose beyond the institution. (iii) There is the phenomenon of legal over-development with "too many rules" and "too many guidelines." There is a paradox here: legal instruments should generate clarity and legal security; if these instruments and the rules are multiplied, they create confusion and decrease a sense of clarity and security. More often than not, dynamics and pressures of accountability lead to a multiplication of rules and guidelines which, in turn, undermines trust, as observed by Onora O'Neill with particular reference to the British Health Service NHS.[22]

In order to curb these in-built anti-kenotic tendencies of structures and institutions, we have to remind ourselves of the for-principle, and we have to remind ourselves of the reality of the Cross in institutions—being a person for others is to be a person of the Cross:

> [H]ow little it really has to do with the cheerful romanticism of progress. For to be the man for others, the man who is open and thereby opens up a new beginning, means being the man in the sacrifice, sacrificed man. The future of man hangs on the cross— the redemption of man is the cross. And he can only come to himself by letting the walls of his existence be broken down, by

---

20. Ratzinger, *Introduction*, 174.
21. Cf. Hubig, "Probleme einer Ethik institutionellen Handelns."
22. See O'Neill, *A Question of Trust*.

looking on him who has been pierced (Jn 19:37), and by following him who as the pierced and opened one has opened the path into the future.[23]

Structures need to be prepared to "die," to sacrifice, to accept the reality of kenosis.

2.2 The Unity of Love and Truth

A belief in Christ limits the arbitrariness of structures; structures have to be truth-based if they want to be Christian: "Christianity thus put itself resolutely on the side of truth and turned its back on a conception of religion satisfied to be mere outward ceremonial which in the end can be interpreted to mean anything once fancies."[24] The truth is a person, not a body of teaching: "Jesus did not leave behind him ... a body of teaching that could be separated from his 'I', as one can collect and evaluate the ideas of great thinkers without going into the personalities of the thinkers themselves."[25] The Creed offers no teachings of Jesus. What does it mean to have structures based on a person?

It may be something like the ability to be surprised and disrupted. When reflecting on the historian's work on Auschwitz, the German historian Christian Meier remarked that there had to be the ability to be horrified ever again in a fresh way. There has to be sober historical analysis and professional historiographic treatment. But we should not treat Auschwitz as one topic of history as others.[26] We could articulate the same idea with regard to institutions. We do what we do in our institutions, but there have to be these moments of personal truth: "It is the Lord!" (John 21:7).

It is against this background that structures express a relationship and that we are called to build structures of love, structures that reflect discernment and decisions of loving persons, and structures that make it easy for persons to become loving persons. Ratzinger comments on the relationship between love and faith, and makes the claim that "faith which is not love is not really *Christian* faith."[27] In a footnote he rejects Luther's allocation of love to the outward life, thus to the worldly and the secular and the profane.[28]

23. Ratzinger, *Introduction*, 181.
24. Ratzinger, *Introduction*, 97.
25. Ratzinger, *Introduction*, 149.
26. Meier, *Von Athen bis Auschwitz*, 152.
27. Ratzinger, *Introduction*, 154.
28. Ratzinger, *Introduction*, 154, n. 12.

This makes a difference for a reflection on structures; love can then serve as a bridge to help us see the heaven opened in the Here and Now.

Love leads to excess, to abundance—an important feature of Christian life in general and structures in particular, according to Ratzinger. Abundance is a feature of Christian structures since the "excess" of God is one of the defining features of understanding what it means to be Christian:[29] "Only the lover can understand the folly of a love to which prodigality is a law and excess alone sufficient."[30] The idea of abundance is strangely at odds with the idea of efficiency as the highest good of an institution. The idea of abundance means "do not maximize." The idea of abundance is an invitation to a culture of gift and giving: "love can only be received as a gift."[31] This brings us to the role of gratuitousness.

Pope Benedict XVI has invited us to explore this dimension of gratuitousness more deeply and explicitly in his 2009 encyclical *Caritas in Veritate*. In §24 Pope Benedict talks about the role of gift: "*Charity in truth* places man before the astonishing experience of gift. Gratuitousness is present in our lives in many different forms, which often go unrecognized because of a purely consumerist and utilitarian view of life. The human being is made for gift, which expresses and makes present his transcendent dimension." And in §36 he discusses some of the challenges:

> The great challenge before us, accentuated by the problems of development in this global era and made even more urgent by the economic and financial crisis, is to demonstrate, in thinking and behaviour, not only that traditional principles of social ethics like transparency, honesty and responsibility cannot be ignored or attenuated, but also that in *commercial relationships* the *principle of gratuitousness* and the logic of gift as an expression of fraternity can and must *find their place within normal economic activity*. This is a human demand at the present time, but it is also demanded by economic logic. It is a demand both of charity and of truth.

Here we have crossed the bridge from ethics to spirituality. It is an invitation to the project that "shape and structure be given to those types of economic initiative which, without rejecting profit, aim at a higher goal than the mere logic of the exchange of equivalents, of profit as an end in itself."[32] A spirituality of institutions will be committed to establishing structures that reflect

---

29. Ratzinger, *Introduction*, 193–98.
30. Ratzinger, *Introduction*, 198.
31. Ratzinger, *Introduction*, 202.
32. Benedict XVI, *Caritas in Veritate*, §38.

this gratuitousness. Ethics cannot save us here—it is so hard to overcome the utilitarian default position since the utilitarian position is so persuasive with its promise of "doing the best." There may be a difference between "doing the best thing" and "doing the right thing."

I see this as the main challenge to any institution: overcoming utilitarianism with its sense of "can do"-agency. A very important clarification about the non-utilitarian element in the Christian vocation can be found in Ratzinger's *Introduction to Christianity*:

> [H]e who tries to reckon where duty ends and where he can gain a little extra merit by an *opus supererogatorium* (work of supererogation) is a Pharisee, not a Christian. Being a Christian does not mean duly making a certain obligatory contribution and perhaps, as a specially perfect person, even going a little further than is required for the fulfilment of the obligation. On the contrary, a Christian is someone who knows that apart from all this he lives first and foremost as the beneficiary of a bounty . . . The calculatingly righteous man, who thinks he can keep his own shirt-front white and build himself up inside it, is the unrighteous man. Human righteousness can only be attained by abandoning one's own claims and being generous to man and to God.[33]

Ethics gets us to Phariseeism in the best sense, but not beyond that position and attitude; this is where we cross the bridge towards spirituality. A Catholic common good commitment with its promise that "no one be left behind" is in tension with a rationally calculating utilitarian approach. The unity of "love" and "truth" cannot be measured in the language of economic success.

2.3 The Material Reality

Ignatius of Loyola once dealt with a confrère who complained about the burden of responsibilities for *temporalia*. Manuel Godinho had been appointed treasurer of the college in Coimbra, and complained that his state of being immersed in financial matters was an obstacle to his growth in perfection. Ignatius replied in a letter, date January 31, 1552, by underlining the importance of temporal and material realities: "Though the charge of temporal affairs seems to be and is distracting, I have no doubt that by your good and upright intention you turn everything you do to something spiritual for God's glory."[34] There is a historicity and materiality in the human condition, dignified by the incarnation, which cannot be denied without theological loss.

---

33. Ratzinger, *Introduction*, 196.
34. Ignatius of Loyola, "Letter To Father Manuel Godinho."

Taking the material reality seriously in the right spirit is an expression of spiritually appropriate humility. Ratzinger, in reflecting on the article on the virgin birth, warns in a footnote—rejecting Schoonenberg's approach to the matter—against a merely symbolic interpretation of dogma: "the attempt to make even the symbola capable of merely 'spiritual' interpretation would be enveloping the history of dogma in a smoke-screen."[35]

We have all heard about the debates concerning the relationship between Ratzinger's thought and Platonism. It may be worthwhile pointing out that the *Introduction* in the excursus on Christian structures gives us a clear idea that we as humans are embodied beings:

> [T]he principle of 'body' and 'corporality' by which man is governed means two things: on the one hand the body separates men from one another, makes them impenetrable to each other . . . . at the same time existence in a corporal form necessarily also embraces history and community . . . human beings live and depend in a very real and at the same time very complex sense on one another.[36]

We are not atomized individuals. Ratzinger quotes Baader's formula "cogitor ergo sum."[37] Understanding our embodied nature means recognizing our human vulnerability. Based on a theology of incarnation and the dignity of history that comes with it, we can recognize that there is finality in history,[38] a finality in the material world.

Taking material and carnal reality seriously is an important aspect of institutional ethics. One way of humiliating a person according to Avishai Margalit is to make a person lose control over her/his bodily functions.[39] It is part of an ethics, but even more so of a spirituality of institutions, to recognize vulnerability. Vulnerability is the condition "to be susceptible to harm, injury, failure, or misuse."[40] We can be damaged; we live lives of risk. Our bodies can be disfigured; pain can be imposed on a person. Our human condition as "embodied beings" creates a sense of dependence on external circumstances that institutions have to take seriously. The concentration camps are probably the most disturbing examples of institutional settings that systematically undermined the respect for bodily needs and material realities. Persons were deprived of their personhood and reduced to the

---

35. Ratzinger, *Introduction*, 212, n. 52.
36. Ratzinger, *Introduction*, 184.
37. Ratzinger, *Introduction*, 185.
38. Ratzinger, *Introduction*, 199.
39. Margalit, *The Decent Society*, 115.
40. Formosa, "The Role of Vulnerability in Kantian Ethics," 89.

toxic stress of exposed vulnerability. Vulnerability, in this setting, meant utter dependence on the arbitrariness of others. Theologically, vulnerability can be understood as dependence, ultimately as dependence on God; this is a final word about the human condition.

A spirituality of institutions will call for a proper way to respect the bodily reality of the person. Let me end with one example: in September 2018, *The Washington Post* published an article about Chamseddine Marzoug, a former Tunisian fisherman, who gives dignity to migrants who perish on their journeys to Europe by digging graves for the bodies he finds on the beaches of the Tunisian town of Zarzis.[41] He buries them at the "Cemetery of the Unknown." This is just one example of a spiritually sensitive way of respecting the material and bodily reality of the human person beyond considerations of "efficiency" or "utility." Accepting the material aspect of our human condition means taking the vulnerability of the human person seriously, not as a deficit, but as a defining feature.

2.4 The Vertical Dimension

Structures need to provide stability. The idea of institutionalization of procedures and concerns by way of structures is linked to a commitment to preservation: "institutions by definition are the more enduring features of social life," as Anthony Giddens observed.[42] However, ultimate stability does not come from structures. Whenever we deal with political, social, institutional issues we can ask the question: "Where do we speak from?" We do not expect perfection from what we can build ourselves. We do not expect heaven on earth as in some utopian literature. The Christian "believes in Christ, and for that reason he believes in the future of the world, not just his own future. He knows that the future is more than he himself can create. He knows that there is a meaning which he is quite incapable of destroying."[43]

We do not expect lasting stability from structures. If they claim to provide this, if they lose their instrumental and serving character, they have lost it—there is only one God, and this leaves no space for idols. In reflecting on Exod 3:14 and the self-revelation of God, Ratzinger points out: "In this simple 'I am' the God of Israel confronts the gods and identifies himself as him who *is*, in contrast to those who have been toppled over and pass away."[44] Ultimate stability can be found in the first and final

41. Raghavan, "A Tunisian gravedigger."
42. Giddens, *The Constitution of Society*, 24.
43. Ratzinger, *Introduction*, 277–78.
44. Ratzinger, *Introduction*, 89.

and lasting word, in the *logos*. Joseph Ratzinger highlights this point about faith as the ultimate foundation with reference to Isa 7:9 ("If you do not believe, then you do not abide," or in another translation: "If you do not believe then you will have not hold"). Faith means holding firm: "faith in God appears as a holding on to God through which man gains a firm hold for his life. Faith is thereby defined as taking up a position, as taking a stand trustfully on the ground of the word of God."[45]

This faith-dimension as a vertical dimension does not allow for a reduction of our lives to a horizontal perspective:

> In view of the New Testament's message of love, there is more and more of a tendency today to resolve the Christian religion completely into brotherly love, 'fellowship', and not to admit any direct love of God or adoration of God: only the horizontal is recognized; the vertical of immediate relationship to God is denied. It is not difficult to see . . . how this at first sight very attractive conception fails to grasp not only the substance of Christianity but also that of true humanity.[46]

And this again contributes to the firmness of our foundation.

An important dimension of the vertical dimension of institutions is what could be called the intangible infrastructure. The "intangible infrastructure" consists of ideas, values, knowledge, and spirituality. In his homily at Manger's Square, Bethlehem, during his pilgrimage to the Holy Land in May 2009, Pope Benedict exhorted the assembly to cultivate a new spiritual infrastructure: "Your homeland needs not only new economic and community structures, but most importantly, we might say, a new 'spiritual' infrastructure; capable of galvanizing the energies of all men and women of good will in the service of education, development and the promotion of the common good."[47] This passage is quite significant. Pope Benedict's approach towards the Holy Land can be seen as a project of encouraging a new 'spiritual infrastructure.' His speeches during his pilgrimage in May 2009 reflect the intention of motivating a sense of this need for a new spiritual infrastructure. The Pope has not come to the Holy Land in order to make politics. He has not come as a politician, but as a pilgrim—and his message is not about tangible and visible infrastructure, but about intangible and spiritual infrastructure. He does not encourage political changes, or make political suggestions, but refers to the 'invisible,' 'the moral,' and 'the

---

45. Ratzinger, *Introduction*, 39.

46. Ratzinger, *Introduction*, 219.

47. Benedict XVI, "Homily of His Holiness Benedict XVI. Manger's Square - Bethlehem."

religious' dimension of human existence. In his address during the welcoming ceremony, the Pope mentioned the fact that the Holy See and the State of Israel have many shared values and commitments. He mentions the shared commitment to memory, the special status of Jerusalem, and the honoring of the victims of past atrocities. Benedict mentions (in the address to the President during his courtesy visit to the presidential residence on 11 May 2009) trust as a key element of this spiritual infrastructure.

The spiritual infrastructure shapes and informs the tangible one: "Christian belief . . . means opting for the view that what cannot be seen is more real than what can be seen. It is an avowal of the primacy of the invisible as the truly real, which bears us up and hence enables us to face the visible in a calm and relaxed way—knowing that we are responsible before the invisible as the true ground of things."[48]

We are living in a hope that cannot be taken away: "A salvation of the world does exist—that is the confidence which supports the Christian and which still makes it rewarding even today to be a Christian."[49] We are committed to a "classification of human activity as only of penultimate importance"; this classification "gives it at the same time an inner liberation: man's activity can now be carried on in the tranquility, detachment and freedom appropriate to the penultimate."[50]

A spirituality of structures and institutions will strive for this intangible, this spiritual infrastructure.

2.5 Summary

I have tried to make use of Ratzinger's theology in the *Introduction* to sketch a spirituality of institutions based on four pillars, namely: the principle of "for," the unity of love and truth, the material dimension, the vertical dimension. I have translated these pillars into a language of curbing structural overdevelopment, of pursuing a principle of gratuitousness, of honoring vulnerability and the human body, and of striving for a spiritual infrastructure.

3. God's Way of Dwelling in Institutions

"Does God dwell in institutions?" Ratzinger's reply: "To this we must first of all simply say 'yes.'"[51]

48. Ratzinger, *Introduction*, 43.
49. Ratzinger, *Introduction*, 278.
50. Ratzinger, *Introduction*, 202.
51. Ratzinger, *Introduction*, 183.

But how does God dwell in institutions? Some points of reference can be found in the moving scene where the ark is brought into the temple in chapter 8 of the First Book of Kings. The passage reads as follows:

> ¹ Then Solomon assembled the elders of Israel and all the heads of the tribes, the leaders of the ancestral houses of the Israelites, before King Solomon in Jerusalem, to bring up the ark of the covenant of the Lord out of the city of David, which is Zion. ² All the people of Israel assembled to King Solomon at the festival in the month Ethanim, which is the seventh month. ³ And all the elders of Israel came, and the priests carried the ark. ⁴ So they brought up the ark of the Lord, the tent of meeting, and all the holy vessels that were in the tent; the priests and the Levites brought them up. ⁵ King Solomon and all the congregation of Israel, who had assembled before him, were with him before the ark, sacrificing so many sheep and oxen that they could not be counted or numbered. ⁶ Then the priests brought the ark of the covenant of the Lord to its place, in the inner sanctuary of the house, in the most holy place, underneath the wings of the cherubim. ⁷ For the cherubim spread out their wings over the place of the ark, so that the cherubim made a covering above the ark and its poles. ⁸ The poles were so long that the ends of the poles were seen from the holy place in front of the inner sanctuary; but they could not be seen from outside; they are there to this day. ⁹ There was nothing in the ark except the two tablets of stone that Moses had placed there at Horeb, where the Lord made a covenant with the Israelites, when they came out of the land of Egypt. ¹⁰ And when the priests came out of the holy place, a cloud filled the house of the Lord, ¹¹ so that the priests could not stand to minister because of the cloud; for the glory of the Lord filled the house of the Lord (1 Kgs 8:1–11 NRSV-CE).

In their "handling" of the Ark—in the widest meaning of the word—the priests experience a fullness. They are in the most holy of holy places, the place where they are to carry out their ministry. Paradoxically, however, they are prevented from doing so exactly because they are in that most holy of places, made so by God's actual fullness of presence—a presence which the priests see and feel.

The Ark as sanctuary has hitherto lead a nomadic existence but will now settle; it is given a permanent home in the house—Temple—of God. The Ark becomes the centrepiece—the heart—of the Temple. We sense here a shift in the power structure: it is no longer God as presence guiding his people along a path; it is a space, a place built in which he now resides—making it that most holy of places. A structure has been established. This no longer a life of transition, with the main aim of moving ever closer to some destination, but life, as it is, as it happens every day. It could therefore seem to be less God as being who provides stability, an anchor point for this nomadic race, than the house built among his people which provides a spatial home and a structure for God.

God takes ownership of the Temple which has been built for this one purpose. At the same time, this holy space should not be interpreted as a move to limit or localize God. Quite the reverse is the case. In the tenth volume of the *City of God*, St. Augustine discusses this seemingly fixed placement, anchoring down of the covenant in the ark ("the ark of testimony") as follows: "By this name it is sufficiently indicated, not that God, who was worshipped by all those rites, was shut up and enclosed in that place, though His responses emanated from it along with signs appreciable by the senses, but that His will was declared from that throne."[52]

God communicates his abiding presence, felt by the fullness of his glory, in this special space. Those present can but submit themselves to the "thick darkness" dwelling here, and bow down before those doing service here: thus this house becomes holy, becomes a temple of God. A temple is a space separated from the outside world; it is a shelter, a safe place. Thus we may ask, does the space become the house of the Lord through what a priest does or by the presence of God's divine glory? There is no simple answer to this question, and it certainly cannot be solved by a simple "both" as 1 Kgs 8:11b suggests, since the ministry his servants carry out is incommensurate with his glory. We might at this point consider the duality of meaning in "house of the Lord": this house is built *for* the Lord and it is a house *from* the Lord: a space he possesses. 1 Kgs 8:10–12 suggests a transfer of one meaning to the other, from the former to the latter. In dwelling in the temple, God fills it with his presence—a presence so full and so strong that the priests "could not stand," thus rendering them incapable of performing their service. This is both paradoxical and logical at the same time: paradoxical because God's presence precludes the power of sacred works and priestly services, and yet logical because the very point of the temple is something beyond what a human construction can ever attain or express.

God takes possession of "the house of the Lord" in a way that reveals the primacy of the intangible over the tangible, breath over stone, the divine over human, limitlessness over limited. For only when God has taken possession of the temple, only when he has "moved in," does the temple find fulfilment. In the book of Ezekiel we read: "Then the glory of the Lord rose

---

52. Augustine, *City of God* X, 17 (p. 191 of the English translation).

up from the cherub to the threshold of the house; the house was filled with the cloud, and the court was full of the brightness of the glory of the Lord" (Ezek 10:4 NRSV-CE). God appropriates this space on the strength of a two-way relationship and not due to some single one-sided deed. In the second book of Chronicles we find out the "reason" or "cause" of this cloud, namely the human act of worship, liturgical praise to God:

> It was the duty of the trumpeters and singers to make themselves heard in unison in praise and thanksgiving to the Lord, and when the song was raised, with trumpets and cymbals and other musical instruments, in praise to the Lord, 'For he is good, for his steadfast love endures forever,' the house, the house of the Lord, was filled with a cloud, so that the priests could not stand to minister because of the cloud; for the glory of the Lord filled the house of God (2 Chr 5:13–14 NRSV-CE).

This appropriation is a communicative act which transforms the room into a sacred space. Built as a house for the Lord, it becomes a house of the Lord.

The cloud of the Lord fills the temple in a way that leaves no space empty; the cloud takes possession of this property in a way that nothing else can. It is incompatible and irreconcilable with all men, even the priests and the services they perform. In filling the temple of the Lord in 1 Kgs 8:10, the action of filling is at the same time the fulfilment of "the Glory of the Lord" in the next verse, 1 Kgs 8:11. This transition from "cloud" to "Glory" marks a transition, too, from initial fear of an unknown experience to a gentle assurance and indeed guarantee—from 1 Kgs 8:11a to 1 Kgs 8:11b. It is because the glory of God absorbs and consumes all available space that the priests are rendered incapable of doing their priestly duties, which are clearly an important aspect of the meaning and understanding of the words "House of the Lord." In other words, it represents a house in which particular things take place and come about. This is a statement about structures.

Structures that invite divine agency disrupt human agency. Making space for God implies the readiness to be disrupted by God. There is no room then for structural complacency and self-righteousness. "Semper reformanda" means being always called to an ever new kenosis.

Conclusion: Inhabited Structures

Institutional experience and institutional agency have been identified as key challenges of institutional ethics. Following Ratzinger's insights in the *Introduction*, I would like to respond to these challenges by a spirituality of institutions based on four pillars, namely: the principle of "for," the unity of love and truth, the material dimension, the vertical dimension. I have translated these pillars into a language of curbing structural overdevelopment, pursuing a principle of gratuitousness, honoring vulnerability and the human body, and striving for a spiritual infrastructure. The main pillar, however, is the recognition of institutional dependence on divine agency.

A spirituality of institutions allows the institution to be disrupted by God in the very way the priests have been disrupted in their ministry in the first book of Kings. A disruption of structures can only happen if there is the proper spiritual infrastructure with its kenosis, its silence, its willingness to listen to God, its minimizing the Ego of human agents in the spirit of John 12:24: "Very truly, I tell you, unless a grain of wheat falls into the earth and dies, it remains just a single grain; but if it dies, it bears much fruit" (NRSV-CE).

The German thinker Aleida Assman has distinguished between inhabited and non-inhabited memory.[53] Inhabited memory consists of memories that are talked about, cared about—memories that shape the way we live our lives. Non-inhabited memories are archival material and matters of museums—nice to have and to look at, but of no relevance for our lives. We need to inhabit the structures we build by the appropriate spiritual infrastructure. And by doing so, paradoxically, we leave space for God to inhabit the structures. Once God inhabits our structures and institutions, we cannot act as if the institution was more than a means to an end. In other words: we have to inhabit our structures by way of an exodus, by way of inviting God to abide.

Bibliography

Assmann, Aleida. "Funktionsgedächtnis und Speichergedächtnis." In *Generation und Gedächtnis*, edited by Kristin Platt and Mihran Dabag, 169–85. Opladen: Leske & Budrich, 1995.

Augustine. *City of God*. In *Nicene and Post-Nicene Fathers, First Series*, Vol. 2. Translated by Marcus Dods. Edited by Philip Schaff, 1–511. Buffalo: Christian Literature, 1887.

Benedict XVI. *Caritas in Veritate*. June 29, 2009. http://w2.vatican.va/content/benedict-xvi/en/encyclicals/documents/hf_ben-xvi_enc_20090629_caritas-in-veritate.html.

———. "Homily of His Holiness Benedict XVI. Manger's Square - Bethlehem. Wednesday, 13 May 2009." https://w2.vatican.va/content/benedict-xvi/en/homilies/2009/documents/hf_ben-xvi_hom_20090513_mangiatoia.html.

Elster, Jon. *Nuts and Bolts for the Social Sciences*. Cambridge: Cambridge University Press, 2015.

---

53. See Assmann, "Funktionsgedächtnis und Speichergedächtnis," 182–83.

Formosa, Paul. "The Role of Vulnerability in Kantian Ethics." In *Vulnerability*, edited by C. Mackenzie et al., 88–109. Oxford: Oxford University Press, 2014.

Giddens, Anthony. *The Constitution of Society: Outline of the Theory of Structuration*. Cambridge: Polity, 1984.

———. *New Rules of Sociological Method*. London: Hutchinson, 1976.

Harré, Rom. *Social Being*. Oxford: Blackwell, 1979.

Raghavan, Sudarsan. "A Tunisian gravedigger gives migrants what they were deprived of in life: Dignity." *The Washington Post*, September 10, 2018. https://www.washingtonpost.com/world/a-tunisian-gravedigger-gives-migrants-what-they-were-deprived-of-in-life-dignity/2018/09/10/8b77e72a-a6f5-11e8-ad6f-080770dcddc2_story.html?utm_term=.68d1bfde1a54.

Hubig, Christolph. "Probleme einer Ethik institutionellen Handelns." In *Ethik institutionellen Handelns*, edited by Christolph Hubig, 11–27. Frankfurt/Main: Campus, 1982.

Ignatius of Loyola. "Letter To Father Manuel Godinho: On Necessary Temporal Occupations (January 31, 1552)." https://www.library.georgetown.edu/woodstock/ignatius-letters/letter19.

Leovy, Jill. *Ghettoside: A True Story of Murder in America*. New York: Spiegel & Grau, 2015.

Lewis, Oscar. *Anthropological Essays*. New York: Random House, 1970.

———. *La Vida: A Puerto Rican Family in the Culture of Poverty*. New York: Random House, 1966.

Margalit, Avishai. *The Decent Society*. Cambridge: Harvard University Press, 1996.

Meier, Christian. *Von Athen bis Auschwitz*. Munich: C.H. Beck, 2002.

Miller, Seumas. *Social Action: A Teleological Account*. New York: Cambridge University Press, 2001.

O'Neill, Onora. *A Question of Trust*. Cambridge: Cambridge University Press, 2002.

Ostrom, Elinor, Larry Schroeder, and Susan Wynne. *Institutional Incentives and Sustainable Development: Infrastructure Policies in Perspective*. Boulder: Westview, 1993.

Parson, Talcott. *The Structure of Social Action*. New York: Free, 1968.

Polen, Nehemia. "Divine Weeping: Rabbi Kalonymos Shapiro's Theology of Catastrophe in the Warsaw Ghetto." *Modern Judaism* 7 no. 3 (1987) 253–69.

Ratzinger, Joseph. *Introduction to Christianity*. New York: Herder and Herder, 1970

Rowans, William. *The Person and the Individual: Human Dignity, Human Relationships and Human Limits*. London: Theos, 2012.

Ward, Keith. Review (Shorter Notice) of *Introduction to Christianity* by Joseph Ratzinger. *Theology* 74 no. 608 (February 1971) 86–87.

16

On the Absenting of Christ

Cruciform Beauty in Ratzinger's *Introduction to Christianity*

JENNIFER NEWSOME MARTIN

I. Introduction

THOMISTIC AESTHETICS SUGGESTS IN Question 39 of the *Summa* that the three fundamental conditions of beauty are *integritas* (wholeness, perfection), *consonantia* (proportionality, harmony), and *claritas* (radiance, luminosity, clarity or brightness).[1] Two points are especially notable here: first, the most proximate context of the question is not an independent treatise on beauty and aesthetics as such, but rather Thomas's consideration of the Trinity, specifically with respect to the question of how the hypostatic relations relate to divine substance; article 8 interrogates whether or not the traditional manner in which the essential attributes are appropriated to each of the personal relations is fitting. For Aquinas, the appropriation of beauty to the Son as wholeness, proportion, and clarity is entirely appropriate: wholeness because the Son is wholly and truly of the same nature as the Father, proportionality because the Son is the Father's perfectly representative image, and radiance because the Son as Logos illumines the intellect. That Aquinas offers these specific features of beauty in a trinitarian, and more specifically, a Christological context, is instructive for considering the phenomenon of beauty both of and in Ratzinger's magisterial text, *Introduction to Christianity*. In Ratzinger, beauty appears never in an exclusively aesthetic or aestheticized register, but is always calibrated theologically, to Christ,

---

1. "Species or beauty has a likeness to the property of the Son. For beauty includes three conditions, 'integrity' or 'perfection,' since those things which are impaired are by the very fact ugly; due 'proportion' or 'harmony'; and lastly, 'brightness' or 'clarity,' whence things are called beautiful which have a bright color" (Thomas Aquinas, *Summa Theologica*, Prima Pars, Question 39 [8c]).

the "image" or "icon" of the invisible God (Col 1:15). Moreover, Ratzinger's book maximizes the dialectic of presence and absence in his account of the revelation of God in Christ, which is already something of an aesthetic consideration. All images, in fact, signify by a somewhat peculiar, paradoxical structure of presence-in-absence: the significance of any given image rests almost entirely on the non-identity between the image itself and the invisible, hidden content which is expressed in it.

Secondly, that Aquinas appeals so heavily to Augustine's *De Trinitate* in this particular section of the *Summa* provides an invitation, if not an absolute injunction, to draw out Ratzinger's own relative privileging of Augustine over Thomas.[2] Though Aquinas does quote prodigiously from *De Trinitate* throughout this question, he most certainly does not replicate it in terms of style. Aquinas maintains a scholastic approach (and for good reason), while Augustine's *De Trinitate* is a marvelously rambling, jumbled, and polyphonic catalogue of spectacular (if deliberate) failure of images and analogues, whose net effect could be experienced as one of disintegration, but whose failures reintegrate ultimately into a final prayer for transformation, for the refiguring or repatterning of the human being according to its divine prototype. In his return to Augustine and the Platonic aesthetic tradition which stretches out before him, especially in the *Symposium*, Ratzinger does not subvert but rather aspirates the more propositional nature of Thomistic aesthetics, or at least interpretations of such which would identify classical art and aesthetics as theology's most fitting conversation partner. This Augustinian turn in Ratzinger, mediated heavily by Hans Urs von Balthasar (1905–1988), complicates and might even in some instances invert conventional Thomistic readings of wholeness, proportion, and radiance.

Ratzinger's famous 2002 address at the annual Communion and Liberation meeting in Rimini ratifies the generally Augustinian tenor of his aesthetic sensibility. In this address Ratzinger marvels at a striking juxtaposition of antiphons which introduce Psalm 44 on the Monday of the Second Week of the Psalter, one during Lent and the other during Holy Week. During Lent, the antiphon is from Ps 45:2: "You are the most handsome of men; grace is poured upon your lips; therefore God has blessed you forever" (NRSV). During Holy Week, however, the antiphon comes from Isa 53:2: "He had no form or majesty that we should look at him, nothing in his appearance that we should desire him" (NRSV). The apparent tension fixed in these Vespers prayers—on the one hand a superlative beauty and a lavish outpouring of grace, and on the other the stark absence of beauty and grace

---

2. Cf. Ratzinger, *Volk und Haus Gottes*.

to such a degree that it even provokes repulsion—is palpable. Ratzinger references Augustine's early text *De pulchro et apto*, which, he writes,

> had a keen appreciation of this paradox and realized that in this regard, the great Greek philosophy of the beautiful was not simply rejected but rather, *dramatically called into question what the beautiful might be, what beauty might mean* . . . Referring to the paradox contained in these texts, he spoke of the contrasting blasts of "two trumpets", produced by the same breath, the same Spirit. He knew that a paradox is contrast and not contradiction. Both quotes come from the same Spirit who inspires all Scripture, but sounds different notes in it. It is in this way that he sets us before the totality of true Beauty, of Truth itself.[3]

For this chapter, I take a cue from Ratzinger's gloss of Augustine in order to interrogate precisely "what beauty might mean," not only for Ratzinger himself, specifically as intimated in his *Introduction to Christianity*, but also more generally for Christian art, which must account for the doubled mode—abjection/absence and glory/presence—in which Christ appears. I will suggest that Ratzinger's cruciform concept of beauty in *Introduction to Christianity*, informed by his Holy Week meditations written in 1967 but published much later alongside the art of American abstract expressionist William Congdon,[4] allows for the possibility of the full gamut of revelatory disclosures of God, including in hiddenness, silence, interruption, distance, contradiction, paradox, formlessness, pain, the mystery of death, vulnerability, abjection, poverty, woundedness, and a commingling of light and darkness, joy and grief. To the end of arguing for the inclusion of what we might call a "darkened" aesthetics[5] which will allow counter-intuitive interpretations of *integritas*, *consonantia*, and *claritas*, this chapter marshals and provides an interpretation of the theological aesthetics of Hans Urs von Balthasar, whom Ratzinger admired as a friend, colleague, and formative theological influence.[6] Despite the fact that Balthasar has sometimes

---

3. Ratzinger, "The Feeling of Things, The Contemplation of Beauty," italics added.
4. See Ratzinger and Congdon, *The Sabbath of History*.
5. Cf. Drahos, "Dark Beauty: Toward a Catholic Theological Aesthetics."
6. Cf. Ratzinger's preface to *Behold the Pierced One*, 9–10; Ratzinger "Homily at the Funeral Liturgy for Hans Urs von Balthasar"; and Ratzinger, *Milestones*, esp. 98, 143–44. In his memoir Ratzinger acknowledges the influence of the "great figure" of Balthasar, reporting that "meeting Balthasar [in Bonn] was for me the beginning of a lifelong friendship I can only be thankful for. Never again have I found anyone with such a comprehensive theological and humanistic education as Balthasar and de Lubac, and I cannot even begin to say how much I owe to my encounter with them" (*Milestones*, 143). In the same passage, Ratzinger details the conditions under which

been caricatured as advocating for an aesthetic that leans more toward the classical and anti-modern, or, with its resolute emphasis on wholeness, proportion, and beauty, criticized for not accounting sufficiently for suffering, ugliness, darkness, or the fragmentary nature of human existence, I will suggest that the case is otherwise. On my view, the notion of beauty and revelation in the *Introduction* and in those Holy Week meditations which inform it permits and, put even more strongly, even requires the inclusion of non-figural or post-representational art that prescinds from form. I will suggest in particular that the work of Congdon (1912–1998), who was affiliated closely with the Action Painting movement associated perhaps most recognizably with Jackson Pollack, provides a concrete visual analogue for Ratzinger's relational personalism that stipulates the radically porous boundaries of the person, equally applicable to trinitarian thought, Christology, and theological anthropology. Indeed, as it is for Ratzinger, it is also so for Balthasar and Congdon. In their respective theological and artistic modes, the governing understanding of the person is fundamentally relational and communal, received in its full dignity as gift, dynamic, and ecstatic or eccentric such that the center and meaning of the person literally "stands outside" of the self, primarily in God and secondarily in other people and in the gathered community of the Church.

II. "Brightness/Darkness": Meditations on Holy Week

In the summer of 1967, the same time that Ratzinger was writing and delivering the lectures at the University of Tübingen that were soon to be published as *Introduction to Christianity*, he was also composing a set of "Meditations on Holy Week." These theretofore unpublished meditations were eventually published some thirty years later alongside a selection of paintings from Catholic artist William Congdon in a book called *The Sabbath of History*, a so-called "involuntary dialogue," labeled such because the images and the text developed independently of one another. Ratzinger's meditations published in this art book not only cross-pollinate with his 1967 "Introduction

---

Balthasar, along with de Lubac, Bouyer, Le Guillou, and Medina and others, launched the publication of *Communio*, which was designed to be "an international journal whose work would both be done out of the heart of communion in sacrament and faith and also lead to its enhancement" (144). This point is significant for the connections this chapter draws between the aesthetics of Balthasar and William Congdon, not least because in this context Ratzinger suggests that *Communio* had a particular provenance in Italy: this was due specifically to Balthasar's having become acquainted with Msgr. Luigi Giussani, the founder of the Communion and Liberation movement, to which Congdon belonged since the early 1960s.

to Christianity" lectures thematically, but also reference them explicitly. In his retrospective look at the origins of the reflections thirty years removed, Ratzinger notes that these Holy Week meditations functioned as a kind of imaginative seedbed for the *Introduction to Christianity* lectures. He writes, moreover, that it was clear "that Christology had to form the heart of these lectures and that the theology of the Paschal Mystery should in turn occupy a central place in them . . . The lectures should surpass, to be sure, the boundaries of academic theology."[7]

It is fitting that just as proportionate space is allotted to Christology in the Apostles' Creed upon which Ratzinger modeled the structure of *Introduction to Christianity*, so too is the same proportion given over to Christology in the lectures, and within Christology the requisitely proportional emphasis on the Paschal Mystery. Likewise, the tonal shift he mentions as a *desideratum* from an exclusive reliance upon the conventions of academia to the inclusion of questions of existential import, and the way in which Ratzinger managed to pitch the lectures to a popular audience without in the least compromising their intellectual rigor, is less a pragmatic choice than an aesthetic one. It is clear even from a cursory reading of the *Introduction* that Ratzinger indeed accomplished his desired end of opening the lectures up beyond the borders of academic theology. Think, perhaps, of the marvelously compelling ways in which he represents the universal phenomenon of doubt, or the fearful loneliness of hell which is an existential space, even a "dimension of human nature" that all human beings have experienced to some degree.[8] He does not condemn doubt or even seem to muster much interest in the propositional claims of atheism, but instead draws out the precisely *aesthetic* quality of these experiences and positions by representing the utter pathos of the universally experienced "exposed nature of [human] existence."[9] Stylistically, too, the *Introduction* liberally employs images and narrative that texturize and concretize the theological claims he will make: readers can vividly imagine and remember, for instance, the shipwrecked Jesuit from Paul Claudel's *Satin Slipper* choking on salt water and clinging to his broken plank, Kierkegaard's hapless clown trying ineffectively to warn the people of the burning village, the trembling child walking alone through the woods in the dark, or Martin Buber's resounding gong of the "terrible perhaps" of Rabbi Levi Yitschak's answer to the Enlightenment scholar.

I turn briefly now to the text of Ratzinger's Holy Week meditations in *The Sabbath of History* before considering some of Congdon's visual

---

7. Ratzinger, *Sabbath*, 17.
8. Ratzinger, *Introduction*, 312.
9. Ratzinger, *Introduction*, 299.

images that accompany them. These meditations are significant not only because they informed the content of *Introduction to Christianity* heavily, but also because the text has an aesthetic texture independent of its juxtaposition with the art. Ratzinger employs the painterly vocabulary of *chiaroscuro*, which refers to the artistic technique of depicting strong contrasts between light and dark in one composition, recognizable most famously in the work of Caravaggio. Reflecting on his own birth and baptism on Holy Saturday of 1927, Ratzinger wrote that his "life from its beginning seemed oriented to his strange chiaroscuro of pain and hope, of divine hiddenness and presence" that characterizes Holy Week, the grief of Good Friday, the inarticulable abjection of Holy Saturday, and the unexpected, all-surpassing joy of the Easter miracle. Ratzinger likewise speaks of the phenomenon in the Holy Week liturgy of the tension of "brightness/darkness" that marks all of Christian existence, recalling again Augustine's interpretation of the liturgically juxtaposed scriptural passages of beauty and wretchedness as two distinct trumpet calls that nevertheless proceed from the same breath of the Holy Spirit.

For this man who came into the world in the fragile interlude space of a Holy Saturday, it is no surprise that his writings mark the day's deep theological and existential significance. On Ratzinger's account, both in the Holy Week meditations and in his treatment of Christ's descent into hell in the *Introduction*, the twentieth century itself was a long Holy Saturday; it is this century that marks the "day that expresses the unparalleled experience of our age, anticipating the fact that God is simply absent, that the grave hides him, that he no longer awakes, no longer speaks, so that one no longer needs to gainsay him but can simply overlook him."[10] Here is the out-Nietzsche-ing of Nietzsche, as Ratzinger adopts without compunction the phrase that "God is dead" into "the tradition of Christian Passiontide piety."[11] In a certain sense, Holy Saturday might then become the ultimate legitimation of aesthetic formlessness, though not a formlessness that sublimates itself into nihilism or pure banality, since, for both Ratzinger and Balthasar upon whom he depends, the Johannine kenosis *is*

---

10. Ratzinger, *Introduction*, 294. Cf. the profoundly similar wording of Ratzinger's Holy Week meditations: "Holy Saturday, day of the burial of God—is that not in an uncanny way our day? Does our century not begin to become one large Holy Saturday, a day of God's absence, a day when an icy emptiness grows even in the hearts of the disciples so that they prepare for the way home with shame and fear and on their Emmaus journey, gloomy and disturbed, sink into hopelessness, failing to notice that the one thought to be dead is in their midst? God is dead and we killed him. Did we actually notice that this statement was taken almost literally from the language of Christian tradition . . . ?" (Ratzinger, *Sabbath*, 38–39).

11. Ratzinger, *Introduction*, 294.

the glory. For both Ratzinger and Balthasar, the hiddenness and the silence of Holy Saturday is not the absence of revelation but the very form of the disclosure of Trinitarian love.[12]

III. A Balthasarian Aesthetics of Formlessness, Abstraction, and the Non-Figural

In this section, I offer an account of what I take to be Balthasar's native affinity with an aesthetics that can and even must include post-representational and non-figural art.

Skeptics may well take issue with this defense of artistic abstraction by rightly pointing to Balthasar's insistence upon *Gestalt*, or the "form." The formlessness and often contingency of abstract expressionist, modern, and non-figural works might seem clearly to elude or even to surpass his thoroughly Catholic aesthetic. It is certainly true that Balthasar did express caution about the potential perils of abstraction in art, especially in works of sacred art whose fundamental goal is praise and proclamation: in his untranslated 1965 essay, "*Christliche Kunst und Verkündigung*," for instance, Balthasar worries about whether some abstract art over-emphasizes immanence or is vulnerable to an uncoupling from the objective data of revelation of which Jesus Christ is the perfect and concrete form. In the same essay, however, Balthasar writes that, in a *theological* sense, abstract art is not at first equivalent to the non-figural as such, but rather art deliberately detached from or hostile to the "single concrete supernatural goal" of humanity; this is art, he says, that has "fallen into God-forgetting immanence."[13] So Balthasar's embargo here is not against immanence as such but only modes of immanence that are "God-forgetting." Abstraction as Balthasar seems to understand it, then, is not abstraction from the figural but rather abstraction from the *religious* (and therefore the full human) experience.

Moreover, he quotes approvingly from Vatican II's 1963 constitution *Sacrosanctum Concilium*, which notes that the Church has never identified any privileged or normative artistic style with itself, but has allowed historically for a full range of artistic expression, which should "be given free scope in the Church, provided that it adorns the sacred buildings and holy rites with due reverence and honor" (§123). Balthasar encourages the freedom of artistic license, which models the freedom of the Holy Spirit,

---

12. As Ratzinger put it so simply in the Holy Week meditations in *The Sabbath of History*, "I knew that the silence of Holy Saturday is filled with the mystery of hope" (23).

13. Balthasar, "Christliche Kunst und Verkündigung," 720.

only accompanied by the given assurance that modern works do not undermine the spirit of Christian piety. Indeed, Balthasar's pressing commitment to beauty's radical freedom—which, much like the Spirit, blows where it will—seems to include the possibility of the non-figural. In the first volume of his *Theo-Logic*, Balthasar writes:

> Beauty can enter into every partial aspect and element, *even into those apparently contrary to one another*... For this reason, beauty can seem, from one point of view, to consist entirely in measure, in proportion, in delimited form, as if the image, understood as the appearance of the essence, were its true home. *But in the twinkling of an eye, beauty can also appear to consist essentially in movement, in the rhythm of communication itself, or in the eternal movement of yearning for what lies beyond all delimited forms and images. At one moment it can look like perfect formality, at other like sheer formlessness, but both modes of appearance*—one can call them the classical and the romantic, the linear and the painterly, the Apollonian and the Dionysian—are in reality only manifestations of the same mysterious ground of beauty.[14]

This text provides at least a minimal threshold for measuring Balthasar's hospitality to non-figural art that allows for beauty's radically free disclosure even in formlessness.

Furthermore, some of Balthasar's ontological commitments suggest a possible affinity with abstraction and formlessness: namely, his commitment to the plurality of being and appearing phenomena as symbolic and self-expressive, the salutary persistence of mystery, and his radical kenoticism. First, for Balthasar, being is structurally plural and symbolic; it moves toward the self-expression of infinity to finitude, interiority to exteriority, essence to appearance, invisibility to manifestation. For Balthasar both "form" and "splendor" are required for theological aesthetics; neither can be surpassed or abandoned, since truth and beauty emerge in their dynamic and organic interplay in what Balthasar elsewhere calls the "floating middle between the appearance and the thing that appears."[15] For Balthasar, "both natural and artistic form has an exterior which appears and an interior depth, both of which, however, are not separable in the form itself. The content (*Gehalt*) does not lie behind the form (*Gestalt*), but within it."[16] Importantly, for Balthasar even those artistic constructions which

---

14. Balthasar, *Theo-Logic Vol. I*, 223–24; italics added. Hereafter abbreviated as *TL I*.
15. Balthasar, *TL I*, 138.
16. Balthasar, *The Glory of the Lord Vol. I*, 151. Hereafter abbreviated as *GL I*.

> reduce the dimension of depth to a minimum by attempting to express everything at the horizontal level of surface, color, and rhythm [abstraction] . . . may be seen in a thousand different ways by the eye, that by virtue of its own power is able to perceive the relationships of form in one of many different ways. This shows that even here there comes into play phenomena of interior subjective expression, for instance, phenomena of intentionality (what the artist 'wanted to say') and of simple subjective disposition. One can seek in various ways to come to know the intention and disposition of someone who expresses himself on a surface: through objective information concerning what he meant to say, through subjective empathy, which proceeds from the data of the work itself, or finally through a loving comprehension of the artist's whole person.[17]

We might extrapolate from this excerpt from *The Glory of the Lord* that artistic abstraction might be especially good for cultivating in those who patiently view it the virtue and the practice of empathy. To pause before a work of non-figural, non-representational art presses upon the perceiver the aesthetic and even ethical responsibility not to dismiss it as simplistic or impenetrable nonsense, but rather to attend to it with care as a donating phenomenon expressive of an interior, subjective invisibility. How can we look upon the work not only with a hermeneutic of charity but even, as Balthasar puts it, through the eyes of "loving comprehension" to see something true of the artist who made it? And how else does any phenomenon—or more importantly, any other human person—appear in our field of vision besides as a phenomenon of inscrutable mystery who could be as easily dismissed or caricatured because we think we know all there is to know about it? Here there is a clear link between personalist aesthetics and personalist ethics: what is encountered in non-representational art presents itself to the gaze of the perceiver phenomenologically; it gives itself over as it appears, creating obligation and responsibility in the one who sees it to look upon it with understanding, patience, and empathy.

Second, for Balthasar, being is marked by mystery as a permanent, persistent phenomenon even in the most mundane manifestations of being in the world. The gratuity and grace of these ordinary expressions of being in the world is, Balthasar thinks, "a daily renewed, perennially inexhaustible wonder."[18] That anything at all should exist and give itself to human perception is astonishing; we must look at everything as if awaiting this mysterious disclosure. Encountering works of art, particularly post-representational

17. Balthasar, *GL I*, 442.
18. Balthasar, *TL I*, 142–43.

ones, distills this experience into concentrated form, encouraging a receptive vision that awaits further and further disclosures of their inner mystery, and chastening the closure of conceptual mastery. In Balthasar's epistemology, incomprehensible mystery is a feature of knowledge, not a jeopardizing detriment to it;[19] mystery is a "permanent, immanent property" of being.[20] Being reveals itself far in excess of what can be grasped conceptually: every phenomenon, particularly works of art, signifies an "eternal more" that resists full analysis or closure.[21]

Third, for Balthasar, Being is impressed with the self-effacing and silent dereliction of Holy Saturday, which instantiates concretely that eternal and infinite distance between the Father and the Son in the Trinitarian relations, into which all lesser distances (of sin, suffering, pain, and so on) can be taken. This "distance" of love is made manifest for Balthasar most perspicuously on Holy Saturday, where it, in Balthasar's provocative description in his lyrical text *Heart of the World*, "could gape wide as the distance between heaven and hell, from whose pit the Son groans his 'I thirst,' *the Spirit now no longer anything but the huge, separating and impassable chaos.*"[22] For Balthasar, God "hides" God's Self under counter-intuitive forms and anti-forms: a vulnerable divine heart planted at the center of the world, the silence of Holy Saturday, the agony of the cross, Jesus' sense of abandonment by the Father. But for Balthasar, as for Ratzinger, this hiddenness and the silence of Holy Saturday is not the absence of revelation but the very form of the disclosure of Trinitarian love. The radical distance of the immanent Trinitarian relations is fully revealed between Father and Son at the abjection and forsakenness of the Son.[23] These sites of darkness, which might otherwise be excluded from classical aesthetic considerations, are rather for Balthasar and Ratzinger indications of love and glory.

These thinkers draw out well the dialectical structure of revelation as simultaneously concealing even as it reveals.[24] This (aesthetic) phenomenon of presence-absence is what Ratzinger in the *Introduction* calls Christianity's structural "law of disguise," wherein God reveals God's Self in a doubled mode: certainly Ratzinger the Bonaventurean affirms that the "radiance" and brilliance of God "shimmer[s] through the world and its

19. Balthasar, *TL I*, 143.
20. Balthasar, *TL I*, 131
21. Balthasar, *TL I*, 142-3.
22. Balthasar, *Heart of the World*, 54.
23. Balthasar, *Theo-Drama Vol. IV: The Action*, 320, 323. Hereafter abbreviated as *TD IV*.
24. For Balthasar, cf. especially the section "Dialectic of Sensory Manifestation," in *The Glory of the Lord Volume VI*, 31-50.

intelligible structure," but God appears also and perhaps even more fittingly as "the Omega, the last letter in the alphabet of creation, as the lowliest creature in it," whose countenance has no form of beauty to attract our eyes; under the "sign of the lowly... [as] actually a pure nothing."[25] This is the dialectic of presence and absence in another idiom wherein "the hidden quality of God... assumes the scandalous form of his palpability and visibility as the Crucified One."[26] True beauty, that is, divine/Christological beauty, thus includes a series of gradual diminutions and disappearances, a radically kenotic pouring out of God in

> the series Earth—Israel—Nazareth—Cross—Church, in which God seems to keep disappearing more and more and, precisely in this way, becomes more and more manifest as himself. First there is the Earth, a mere nothing in the cosmos, which was to be the point of divine activity in the cosmos. Then comes Israel, a cipher among the powers, which was to be the point of his appearing in the world. Then comes Nazareth, again a cipher within Israel, which was to be the point of his definitive arrival. Then at the end there is the Cross, on which a man was to hang, a man whose life had been a failure; yet this was to be the point at which one can actually touch God. Finally there is the Church, the questionable shape of our history, which claims to be the abiding site of his revelation. We know today only too well how little, even in her, the hiddenness of the divine presence is abolished... Thus what is small by a cosmic or even worldly scale represents the real sign of God wherein the entirely Other shows itself... The cosmic Nothing is the true All, because 'for' is the really divine thing.[27]

As we will see, these theological diminutions are repeated artistically in William Congdon's gradual absenting of Christ's body from the picture plane in preference to drastically post-representational portrayals of the suffering Christ.

IV. "Behold the Pierced One": The Porosity of Personhood and the Aesthetic Imperative

As in Aquinas and Ratzinger, Balthasar's theological aesthetics is likewise situated against and inseparable from the horizon of his trinitarian theology

---

25. Ratzinger, *Introduction*, 255–56.
26. Ratzinger, *Introduction*, 255.
27. Ratzinger, *Introduction*, 256–57.

and Christology, both of which assume a Christian personalism which understands "person" as a category that is thoroughly open to the O/other. In Balthasar's trinitarian thought, the eternal relations ("persons") of the Trinity are radically kenotic, marked by a self-emptying surrender which anticipates, is continuous with, and permits the kenotic acts in the economy of creation, and the incarnation, the passion of Christ, the descent into hell, and the silence of Holy Saturday. The eternal generation of the Son as consubstantial Other by the Father is an eternal kenotic act which constitutes rather than jeopardizes the Father's personhood. This self-renunciation (which the Father both is and does) is inclusive of all analogical distance and worldly Godforsakenness, because the Father's act and substance of self-renunciation manifests what Balthasar calls provocatively "a (divine) Godlessness (of love, of course). The latter must not be confused with the godlessness that is found within the world, *although it undergirds it, renders it possible and goes beyond it.*"[28] The Trinitarian relations of identity in (infinite) difference thus are the kenotic drama which envelops all of creation, such that being and all appearing phenomena bear its mark.

Ratzinger's reflections on the Trinity in *Introduction to Christianity* do not repeat but are fundamentally simpatico with Balthasar's. The way that Ratzinger treats the language of "Fatherhood" and "Sonship" in Trinitarian discourse is similarly decisive for understanding that the "persons" of the immanent Trinity are not separate modern personalities, but rather indications of pure relatedness. Ratzinger suggests that "'Father' is purely a concept of relationship. Only in being for the other is he Father; in his own being in himself he is simply God. Person is the pure relation of being related, nothing else. Relationship is not something extra added to the person, as it is with us; it only exists at all in relatedness."[29] Similarly, in the case of Sonship, Ratzinger draws out beautifully the Gospel of John's commitment to depicting the absolute simultaneity and relation of Father and Son (found in statements from Jesus in John like, "The Father and I are one" [10:30] and "Whoever has seen me has seen the Father" [14:9]). The being of Jesus as the incarnation of the eternal Son is thus the fullest actualization of genuine human personhood because his personhood is perfectly relational, received, and ecstatic; it is marked by a perfect surrender and openness to God and to others, and invites Christian believers to do the same. Here I quote Ratzinger at some length:

> The Son . . . does not proceed in any way from himself and so is completely one with the Father; since he is nothing beside him,

28. Balthasar, *TD IV*, 324.
29. Ratzinger, *Introduction*, 183.

claims no special position of his own, confronts the Father with nothing belonging only to him, makes no reservations for what is specifically his own, therefore he is completely equal to the Father. The logic is compelling: If there is nothing in which he is just he, no kind of fenced-off private ground, then he coincides with the Father, is 'one' with him. It is precisely this totality of interplay that the word 'Son' aims at expressing. To John, 'Son' means being from another; thus, with the word he defines the being of this man as being from another and for others, *as a being that is completely open on both sides*, knows no reserved area of the mere 'I.' When it thus becomes clear that the being of Jesus as Christ is a completely open being, a being 'from' and 'toward', which nowhere clings to itself and nowhere stands on its own, then it is also clear at the same time that this being is pure relation (not substantiality) and, as pure relation, pure unity . . . To John, being a Christian means being like the Son, becoming a son; that is, not standing on one's own and in oneself, but living completely open in the 'from' and 'toward.'[30]

Thus, what marks divine Sonship for Ratzinger is precisely the Johannine principle of "being-for," a radical openness, transparency, and porosity of the borders of the self. What it means to be a person, whether human or divine, is therefore to exist in radical transparency, both by and for the other, to allow oneself to enter into an experience of radical communion. When human beings cultivate the theological virtue of genuine love—which is a self-giving and a surrender that does not exhaust or evacuate the self but rather brings it toward its eventual fulfillment and perfection—human beings not only image but also truly participate in the Trinitarian nature of God.

For Ratzinger, this principle of openness and the privileging of relation is utterly consistent in both its immanent and economic registers, that is, in the hypostases of the divine persons as well as in the corporeality of the incarnate Jesus. Corporeality signifies doubly for Ratzinger; it is at the same time a "bridge" to others and to history, and also that which signifies "the limit that divides us, closes us off within the barriers of our ego."[31] In both 1967 texts under consideration, Ratzinger draws attention to the outflow of blood and water which pours from the side of Christ opened by the soldier's lance in John's Gospel (19:33–34). With this act, which recalls symbolically the opened side of Adam in Genesis from which the rib is taken for Eve's creation, the radical relationality and porosity of theological persons is made evident. "The limit of the body," Ratzinger suggests,

30. Ratzinger, *Introduction*, 187; italics added.
31. Ratzinger, *Sabbath*, 33; cf. *Introduction*, 245–56.

"no longer binds him . . . as the risen one, he is the open space which calls us all."³² Out of the side of Christ comes the Church and her sacraments of baptism and Eucharist, the site *par excellence* where Christ's body is broken "for the many, for you."³³

For Ratzinger, "the opened side of the crucified, the mortal wound of the new Adam, is the point of departure of true human existence: they will look on him whom they have pierced."³⁴ This allusion to Zechariah in John ("I will pour out on the house of David and on the inhabitants of Jerusalem a spirit of mercy and supplication, so that when they look on him who they have thrust through, they will mourn for him as one mourns for an only child, and they will grieve for him as one grieves over a firstborn" [12:10 NAB]) sharpens the sense that John is offering to us an aesthetic imperative. We must look upon Jesus, "the completely open man, in whom the dividing walls of existence are torn down, [he] is entirely 'transition,'" a person who "knows no . . . firm boundaries but is essentially openness . . . "³⁵ On Ratzinger's reading of this prophetic quote, herein lies *in nuce* the full meaning of the Gospel of John. The aesthetic imperative to *look* is echoed in the Good Friday liturgy, "Behold, behold the wood of the cross," and in Pilate's words from Jn 19, the same chapter in which we see the outpouring of the blood and water: "Behold the man!" For Ratzinger it is precisely by *looking* upon the one who has been pierced (John 19:37) that we can see Beauty itself and the only means by which we can come to ourselves.

In his own context as a Catholic artist, Congdon too advocated for a kind of radically relational personalism. In the mid 1980s, for instance, he lamented contemporary culture's complicity in the "disintegration" of the human person and her "alienation" from community.³⁶ What he meant by community, however, exceeds by an order of magnitude merely sociological, political, or institutional structures in preference for a more ontological—even Augustinian—participation in the trinitarian God who dwells in the deepest interior of the self. "Only Christian communion," he writes, "is a communion of being, that is, of the true love of God."³⁷ As with both Balthasar and Ratzinger, Congdon too is deeply Johannine: "'I am,' and we are insofar as we are grafted onto his 'am.' In the depths of myself is the Christian communion. The more Christian the communion I live, the

32. Ratzinger, *Sabbath*, 34.
33. Ratzinger, *Introduction*, 251; cf. *Sabbath* 29–33.
34. Ratzinger, *Sabbath*, 31. Cf. Ratzinger, *Behold the Pierced One*.
35. Ratzinger, *Introduction*, 240.
36. Congdon, "An Artist," 174.
37. Congdon, "An Artist," 174.

more I am in the depths of myself, and the more I am myself . . . "[38] Following Jacques Maritain, though at some distance,[39] Congdon was convinced that this hidden, mysterious communion planted within every Christian believer was the condition of the possibility for creative intuition and the creation of a genuinely religious work of art. The Christian artist perceives the created order not as over against an autonomous subject of perception, but rather as continuous with herself. "I recognize myself," Congdon reflects, "in 'that' stone because it bears the physiognomy of my life; it is a sign, it is marked by my entire history. When taking a walk, I recognize 'myself,' I bend over, I pick up 'myself,' and carry 'myself' home because it is 'I.' Just as the picture that comes to be born in me is 'I,' so too the stone that is uncovered in me is 'I.' I recognize myself equally in both."[40] To glimpse reality from this place of non-monadic, non-egoistic, communal perception is thus in a way to borrow the "eyes" of God.

V. "'For' is the really divine thing": Congdon's Disappearing Christ

Again, the structural principle of "being for"—which Christ reveals perspicuously both in his divinity and in the truest form of humanity—is for Ratzinger that which is truly divine and that which is truly beautiful. William Congdon's art marks lucidly this trajectory of the diminution of God that Ratzinger elaborates both in *Introduction to Christianity* and in the Holy Week meditations of *The Sabbath of History* as a companion text to a selection of Congdon's paintings. In post-representational art, particularly in the movement of abstract expressionism of which Congdon was a master, physical materials are brought more nearly to the surface of perception; brushstrokes and smudges in the texture of the paint become significant; they are meant to be noticed and not invisibly "seen through" to the so-called "real" content or subject of the painting, that is, what it purports to represent. Abstract expressionism in general and Congdon in particular deliberately endeavored to bring art down to earth, into the materiality, phenomenality, and tactility of lived human experience. This kind of art welcomes what would have in classical art been adulterations, like the cigarette butts, tacks, buttons, keys, coins, nails, and other paraphernalia nearly drowned in the thick paint of Jackson Pollack's 1947 work *Full Fathom Five*. Indeed, Congdon preferred to use a palette knife, awl, or a

---

38. Congdon, "An Artist," 175.

39. It is noteworthy that Maritain composed the foreword to another of Congdon's books of art, called *In My Disc of Gold: Itinerary to Christ of William Congdon*.

40. Congdon, "An Artist," 178–79.

spatula to manipulate layers of his paint rather than a brush, believing that art must be constructed or "built," since for him the revealed texture of the paint itself was as, if not more, important than the realism of the content depicted. Written in the margins of one of Congdon's sketchbooks is the following self-directive: art "is building—use knife—construct it—don't (brush) to make *look* like it."[41] Even as the form of the body of Christ is gradually "disfigured," the persistent materiality and even corporeality of the paint continually asserts itself.[42]

Apart from quick and startling sketches of faces of the dying during wartime like *Morgen Tod*, drawn at Belsen in 1945 (the piece that Rodolfo Balzarotti has called Congdon's "certificate of birth as a painter"[43]), Congdon generally avoided depicting the human figure until after his conversion to Roman Catholicism in 1959, when he set on what can rightly be called an obsessive fixation upon painting crucifixions, painting no less than 180 of them.[44] It is possible to track a general trajectory toward a declining realism and a steady "absenting" of the form of the human body from the visual field. Over the course of time the crucifixions Congdon painted begin to look less and less like a human figure. This attenuation of realism in the human form is observable in at least two ways: first, some of the crucifixions began to be nearly indistinguishable from landscapes; and second, the nearly formless, larval figurations of human suffering depicted during and after two mid-1970s trips to India become superimposed deliberately on the later crucifixions, in which the form of the body was no longer recognizable as such. Rodolfo Balzarotti describes these crucifixions as bearing the theme of Holy Saturday—though simultaneously intimating resurrection in the energetic gestures evident in the dynamic movement of the paint—as they gradually underwent "metamorphosis and consummation. The human figure becomes disfigured: under the pressure of the flesh . . . or like a 'bone' or rigid bar suspended on the black background . . . "[45] Congdon's "*Crucifixion no. 2*" is recognizable as a cruciform image but departs from traditional iconography, especially given the isolation of the corpus.

41. Congdon, B2A 1949, f XXIX r.

42. Rodolfo Balzarotti reflects beautifully on the "carnality" and even woundedness of the "flesh" of Congdon's paintings in "William Congdon: Action Painting," 716.

43. Balzarotti, "William Congdom: Action Painting," 713.

44. In 1960 Congdon did a series of other paintings with recognizable religious content—depictions of the annunciation, the nativity, the transfiguration, the garden of Gethsemane, and so on—but he eventually distanced himself from them, accusing himself during that time of convert zeal as being overly 'moralistic' and therefore not truly "free" (Balzarotti, "William Congdom: Action Painting," 695–96).

45. Balzarotti, "William Congdom: Action Painting," 718.

William Congdon
Crocefisso No. 2 (1960)
oil on masonite—35x23 in
© The William G. Congdon Foundation, Milan

There is no gesture toward other historical figures like Saint John, the Blessed Virgin Mary, or Mary Magdalene. There are no feet or hands in the frame, but rather the strong presence of the intersection of horizontal and vertical lines, which were repeated in the landscapes of his later Bassa Milanese period. In *Crocefisso no. 46*, painted nine years later, Congdon constricts the frame even further, scraping and cutting the paint with his knife to evoke, though not to represent realistically, the slumped, downcast head of the dead Christ. The figuration of the human form of Christ is in this piece only gestural.

William Congdon
Crocefisso No. 46 (1969)
oil on panel—23 7/8 x 19 3/4 in
© The William G. Congdon Foundation, Milan

After visiting Bombay in 1973, Congdon paints *Bombay* no. 19, in which the masses of suffering human figures he saw in India are presented in the road shorn of their limbs and faces.

William Congdon
Bombay No. 19 (1973)
oil on panel—23 5/8 x 19 3/4 in
© The William G. Congdon Foundation, Milan

His notebook jottings and sketches corroborate that there is a deliberate juxtaposition between the formlessness and poverty of the human condition in Bombay and in paintings like *Crocefisso no. 90* and *no. 91*.

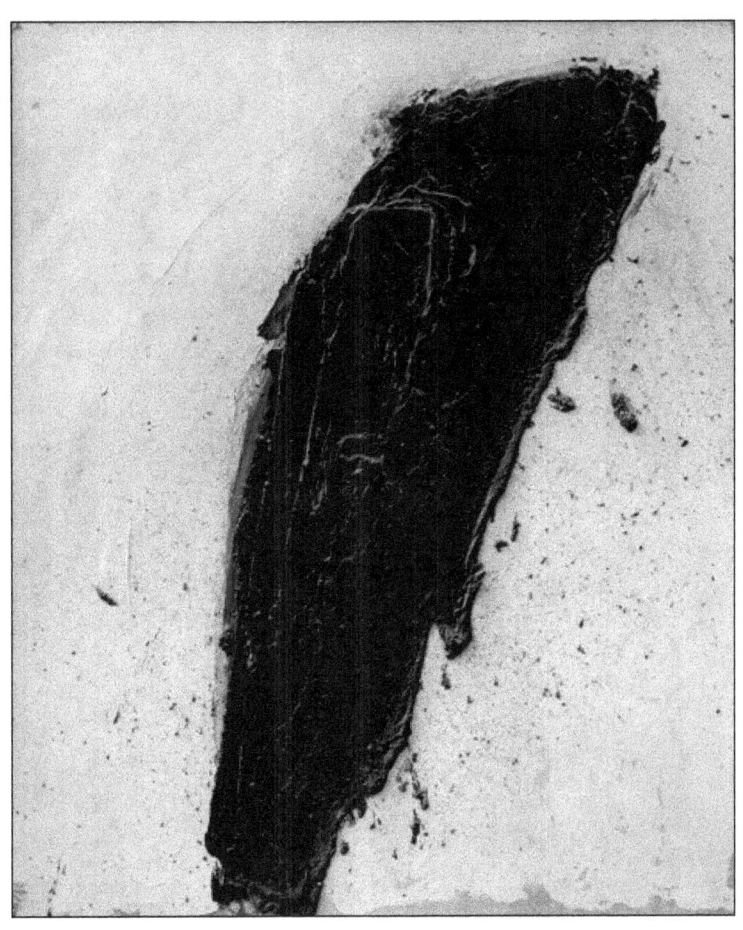

William Congdon
Crocefisso No. 90 (1974)
oil on panel—47 1/4 x 39 3/8 in
© The William G. Congdon Foundation, Milan

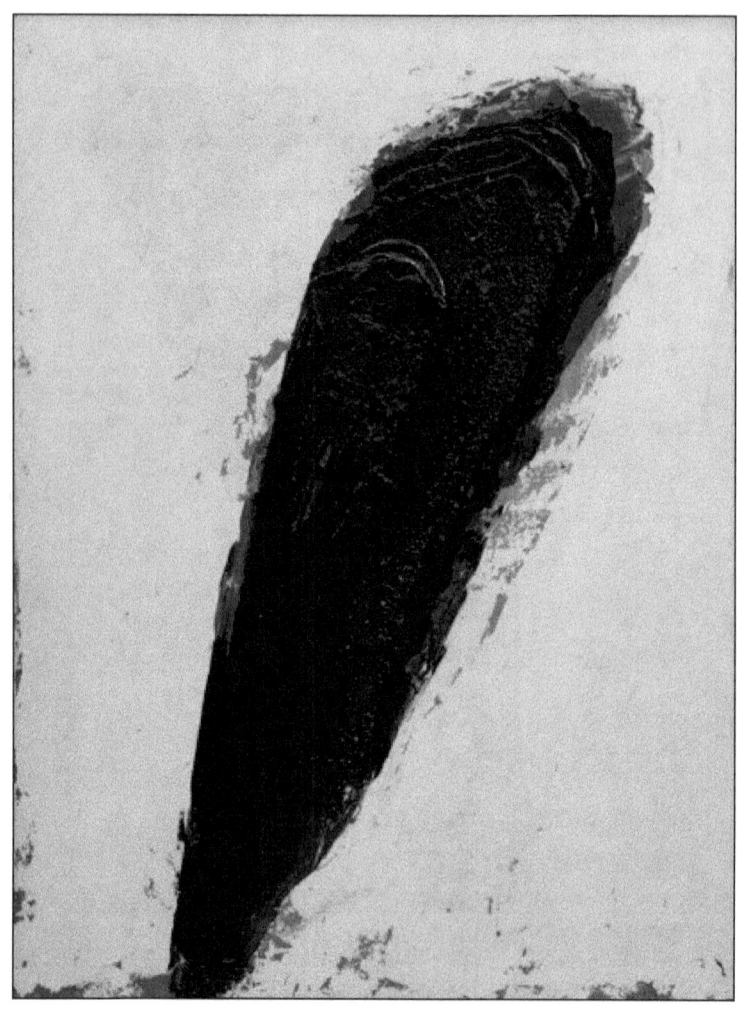

William Congdon
Crocefisso No. 91 (1974)
oil on panel—41 x 31 1/2 in
© The William G. Congdon Foundation, Milan

These India trips thus inaugurate Congdon's increasing diminution of the figure of Christ to *only* a gestural torso; we can clearly see a level of deliberate self-quotation between the Bombay paintings and the crucifixions. For Congdon, resonant of Ratzinger's theological reflections in *Introduction* and the Holy Week meditations, depictions of the circumscribed borders of the body of Christ must dissolve—not at all in order to denigrate the body as such, but rather by this expropriation to demonstrate radical solidarity with the suffering poor. In a 1973 diary entry, Congdon describes *Crucifix* 90 provocatively as

> a flat squashed dry lava flow, but trampled as if the traffic of 'sin' had crossed over it for or since all eternity, until the body, what was body, became a stain. It is the road of Bombay, it is the world that continually tramples Christ under. The tar of the road became Christ who became tar in order to let himself be flattened until he flowed, in the fire of love, beyond any boundary. He flows everywhere, and even more in the splinters of the ashes like a bombardment of hate.[46]

This image resonates beautifully with a similar one from Book One of Augustine's *De Doctrina Christiana*, where Christ is depicted as the one who in his incarnation and Passion lays himself down, transforming himself into the very pavement of the road by which sinners can return home. Congdon here prescinds from symbolic or realistic representation in order that those who engage his art can truly see, albeit under the law of disguise, the figure of Christ poured out in the Passion as a smudge of tar, a pure nothing, entirely transition; yet because and not in spite of this absenting, He is the most beautiful thing there is or has ever been.

Conclusion

This chapter has aimed to demonstrate that Ratzinger's *Introduction to Christianity* witnesses to an account of beauty and revelation that is broadly Augustinian and Johannine, informed by (a certain reading of) Balthasarian aesthetics, and expressed concretely in the paintings of William Congdon, with which Ratzinger's 1967 Holy Week meditations have been provocatively paired. Thomas's conditions of wholeness, proportionality, and radiance may well persist in Ratzinger's aesthetics, but generally appear under a different, counter-intuitive sign: the integral, immediately intelligible symbolic form reveals itself most truly in the utter dissolution of itself in kenotic formlessness; proportion looks like excessive disproportionality, a "holy folly," or "staggering lavishness" of the love of a God who would spend God's Self fully without remainder;[47] radiance is obscured under the signs of the lowly, wherein the Alpha is hidden in the Omega, and the suffering

---

46. William Congdon, Diary entry, 2 February 1973; quoted in *The Sabbath of History*, 99.
47. Ratzinger, *Sabbath*, 48.

Christ, the pierced one, makes himself in Augustine's words "the pavement under our feet along which we could return home."[48]

Bibliography

Aquinas, Thomas. *St. Thomas Aquinas: Summa Theologica, Vol. I–V*. Translated by the Fathers of the English Dominican Province. Notre Dame: Ave Maria Press, 1948.

Augustine. *Teaching Christianity*. Translated by Edmund Hill, OP. The Works of Saint Augustine: A Translation for the 21st Century I/11. Hyde Park, New City: 1996.

Balthasar, Hans Urs von. "Christliche Kunst und Verkündigung." In *Mysterium Salutis, Vol. I*, edited J. Feiner and M. Löhrer, 708–26. Einsiedeln and Cologne, 1965.

———. *Heart of the World*. San Francisco: Ignatius, 1979.

———. *The Glory of the Lord: A Theological Aesthetics, Vol. I: Seeing the Form*. Translated by Erasmo Leiva-Merikakis. San Francisco: Ignatius, 1982.

———. *The Glory of the Lord: Volume VI: Theology: The Old Covenant*. Translated by Brian McNeil, CRV, and Erasmo Leiva-Merikakis. San Francisco: Ignatius, 1991.

———. *Theo-Drama: Theological Dramatic Theory, Vol. IV: The Action*. San Francisco: Ignatius Press, 1994.

———. *Theo-Logic: Theological Logical Theory: The Truth of the World, Vol. I*. Translated by Adrian J. Walker. San Francisco: Ignatius, 2001.

Balzarotti, Rodolfo. "William Congdon: Action Painting and the Impossible Iconography of the Christian Mystery." *Communio* 36 (Winter 2009) 694–720.

Congdon, William. "An Artist, His Art, and the Christian Community." *Communio* 13 no. 2 (Spring 1986) 170–88.

———. *In My Disc of Gold: Itinerary to Christ of William Congdon*. New York: Reynal and Company, 1960.

Drahos, Kristen. "Dark Beauty: Toward a Catholic Theological Aesthetics." PhD diss., University of Notre Dame, 2016.

Ratzinger, Joseph. "Homily at the Funeral Liturgy for Hans Urs von Balthasar." *Communio* 15 no. 4 (Winter 1988) 512–16.

———. "The Feeling of Things, The Contemplation of Beauty," Message to the Communion and Liberation (CL) Meeting at Rimini. August 24-30, 2002. http://www.vatican.va/roman_curia/congregations/cfaith/documents/rc_con_cfaith_doc_20020824_ratzinger-cl-rimini_en.html.

———. *Behold the Pierced One: An Approach to a Spiritual Christology*. San Francisco: Ignatius, 1986.

———. *Introduction to Christianity*. 2ND ed. San Francisco: Ignatius, 2004.

———. *Milestones: Memoirs 1927-1977*. San Francisco: Ignatius, 1998.

——— and William Congdon. *The Sabbath of History*. Milan: The William G. Congdon Foundation, 2000.

———. *Volk und Haus Gottes in Augustins Lehre von der Kirche*. Munich: Karl Zink, 1954; reprint St. Ottilien: EOS, 1992.

Thomas Aquinas, *Summa Theologica*. Translated by the Fathers of the English Dominican Province. Second and Revised Edition, 1920.

---

48. Augustine, *De Doctrina Christiana*, 1.17.16. English translation in *Teaching Christianity*, 114.

Epilogue

The Pedagogy of Introducing

JOHN C. CAVADINI

"A SALVATION OF THE world does exist—that is the confidence that supports the Christian and that still makes it rewarding even today to be a Christian."[1] That is the closing sentence of Ratzinger's *Introduction to Christianity*. I have cited it here because it may be that it has some major clues about what the pedagogy of introducing Christianity presupposes. If this closing sentence is indicative in any way of what Ratzinger hopes to have achieved, one could conclude that, in introducing Christianity, it is essential to communicate "the confidence that supports the Christian" and that "makes it rewarding ... to be a Christian." This distinguishes Ratzinger's version of introducing Christianity from a predominantly descriptive introduction to a cultural phenomenon named "Christianity," even as that cultural reality coincides with the religion of the same name. This is not therefore primarily an historical introduction—a work of social or cultural history.

And yet, the *Introduction* is styled (even within the text and not just on the title page) as an introduction to *Christianity*, and not to Christian faith, or Catholicism. When he says, in the Preface to the New Edition, that, if he "had this *Introduction to Christianity* to write over again today [= April 2000],"[2] he would have made certain changes, he does not include a change in title. Furthermore, as he opens Chapter 1 of Part Two on "Jesus Christ," he notes: "It is only in the second section of the Creed that we come up against the real difficulty—already considered briefly in the introduction—about *Christianity* [my emphasis]."[3] Again, he uses the word "Christianity" and

1. Ratzinger, *Introduction*, 359.
2. Ratzinger, *Introduction*, 29.
3. Ratzinger, *Introduction*, 193.

not "Christian faith" or "Christian belief" or some other substitute. Finally, in the Preface to the New Edition, he notes that "With these considerations [about Christ and God] we have reached the point from which an 'introduction to Christianity' must set out today,"[4] placing the crucial phrase in scare quotes to indicate that he chose it specifically.

Ratzinger does sometimes speak as though Christian faith or Christian belief or Catholicism were the actual subject of the introducing. In Chapter 5 of Part 1, he notes that "Our previous reflections have brought us to the point at which the *Christian profession of faith* in the one God passes over by a kind of inner necessity to the profession of faith in the triune God,"[5] while, in the Preface to the 1968 edition, Ratzinger says that he intends to accomplish "what Karl Adam accomplished almost half a century ago [the same distance as we are today from the first publication of the *Introduction*] at the same university [of Tübingen] in such a masterly fashion with his *Spirit of Catholicism*."[6] Just earlier in this Preface, he had noted: "Let us return to the question about God and about Christ as the centerpiece of an introduction to the Christian faith."[7] These kinds of statements are echoed throughout the text. And it would be splitting hairs to hold out for the significance of an introduction to Christianity specifically *over against* an introduction to Christian faith and belief, especially since we won't communicate the "confidence" that makes it "rewarding" to be a Christian without a thorough examination of what Christian faith is and what it means to believe. In fact, most of what the book is taken up with *is*, in fact, a brilliant theological introduction to Christian faith and what it means. Sometimes he seems to collapse "Christianity" and "Christian belief" together completely, such that it would seem that introducing Christianity means the same thing as introducing the Christian faith. For example: "At the same time it becomes evident that the idea of freedom is the characteristic mark of the Christian belief in God as opposed to any kind of monism. At the beginning of all being it puts not just some kind of consciousness but a creative freedom that creates further freedom. To this extent one could very well describe Christianity as a philosophy of freedom."[8]

But let us return to the closing sentence of the book to see if there are any further clues there to the project of introducing Christianity, specifically with an eye to discerning what pedagogy it is that we need to emulate if we

4. Ratzinger, *Introduction*, 24.
5. Ratzinger, *Introduction*, 162 (my emphasis).
6. Ratzinger, *Introduction*, 32.
7. Ratzinger, *Introduction*, 25.
8. Ratzinger, *Introduction*, 157–58.

are going to "introduce" in Ratzinger's spirit. "A salvation of the world does exist—that is the confidence that supports the Christian and that still makes it rewarding even today to be a Christian." Here we can notice not just the desire to communicate to the reader the confidence that makes it rewarding to be a Christian, but that this confidence "*still*" makes it worthwhile, "*even today*." So the issue is not just that it is plausible that it had at one time been worthwhile to be a Christian, but that it still is, and the telltale "even" in "even today" shows that the task of communicating why it is worthwhile and rewarding to be a Christian is undertaken against a kind of negative expectation—namely, that it is a surprise, almost, that it should be so, and that those for whom the book is written, if convinced, might even be surprised that in fact they were convinced. The "*still*" and the "*even today*" of the last sentence of the book offer us perhaps the most crucial clue as to the pedagogy of introducing, as Ratzinger sees it, for an *Introduction* could have presented *Christianity* as something—an historical reality, which was at one time (perhaps for many centuries) "rewarding" to the Christian, and the "confidence that support[ed] the Christian" could be excavated and brought into view for the cultured person by a kind of cultural archaeology and by a bridging act of sympathetic historical imagination, but it would have been clear to all that the only leap of faith involved was to imagine, based on the *Introduction* given, that this was true.

It is true that Ratzinger is interested in producing an account of what could be equally at home in an intellectual archaeological treatise, namely, what *distinguishes* Christian faith (apart from issues of relevance, but analytically and objectively) from other options that have existed or do exist. For example, again in his chapter on "Faith in God Today," he comments, "Thus the specific features of the Christian faith as opposed to other intellectual choices of the human mind now [after the foregoing reflections] stand out in clear relief."[9] And this is after having declared not merely "Christian faith," but "Christianity" itself, as a "philosophy of freedom" (as already indicated). But these analytical moves to unearth the objective meaning of the Christian faith are all aimed at persuading the reader that *because* these analyses of objective content are true accounts, it still makes sense, it is still rewarding, or *would be* still rewarding to be a Christian, *even today*. These feats of intellectual analysis are all in effect invitations or (we could say) temptations, to look again, to take a second look, to reconsider—occasions of sin perhaps if one of the greatest intellectual offenses imaginable today would be to take this cultural artifact, Christianity, and its concomitant baggage, the Christian faith, *seriously*. Well, who *wouldn't*

9. Ratzinger, *Introduction*, 158.

be tempted by a "philosophy of freedom," by an "intellectual choice" which consists in "the option for the primacy of freedom as against the primacy of some cosmic necessity of natural law"?[10] What? I—the cultured modern reader—thought that was *my* position, *my* intellectual choice—I don't like natural law and I like freedom! In spite of myself, I am feeling tempted to committing a not so venial intellectual sin . . .

Ratzinger doesn't help (far from it) as he continually stokes this temptation as he works through the project of "introducing." He keeps raising the doubts that might—that do—haunt the would-be modern believer from the start, even the very doubt that it may not be possible to erase doubt from the mind of the believer, and that in fact one thing both believer and non-believer may treasure as an experience that connects them is, precisely, doubt. Far from seeming to have "confidence," the believer seems like a clown trying to explain his or her point of view to non-believers, and it is more than insinuated that, if he is honest with himself, he can perhaps feel like a clown even trying to explain it to him or herself: " . . . if he who seeks to preach the faith is sufficiently self-critical, he . . . who takes his calling seriously will clearly recognize not only the difficulty of the task of interpretation but also the insecurity of his own faith, the oppressive power of unbelief in the midst of his own will to believe."[11] The "introducing" envisioned as corresponding to this situation is thus just as much ordered towards believers as to unbelievers, especially towards those who wish to preach (and we can add, to teach) the Christian faith. Such a person should be self-aware and not be embarrassed to be in the same boat as others who do not believe, as though faith were a credential that made one culturally respectable—and yet unbelievers are asked for the same kind of self-examination or self-awareness: if I am honest, these characterizations of the Christian faith that Ratzinger offers *are*, in some sense, *me*—and I am tempted to unbelief in my unbelief. Perhaps I feel my heart quicken a little . . . "it might be true!"[12]

And with every doctrine that Ratzinger examines, there are questions, and questions within questions, asking whether this or that doctrine can still be believed, asking the reader not only these questions in particular, but, both believer and non-believer, to be honest with themselves, to know themselves. And so the question is inflected slightly differently for each: "Can I *still* believe, if I am honest with myself?" (for the believer) and "*Can I believe? Even today?*" (for the non-believer). The series of questions starts with maybe the most basic question: "What in fact is 'God,' really? In other

---

10. Ratzinger, *Introduction*, 158.
11. Ratzinger, *Introduction*, 41.
12. See Ratzinger, *Introduction*, 46.

ages this question may have seemed quite clear and unproblematical [but was it? It's implied]; for us [be honest, believers and unbelievers] it has become a genuine inquiry again. What can this word 'God' signify?"[13] Then there are questions within the question, to make sure the scope of the honesty, or the temptation, either to belief or unbelief, is utterly clear: "Where does this idea of 'God' really come from? From what roots does it grow? How is it that what is apparently the most superfluous, and, from an earthly point of view, most useless, subject in history has at the same time remained the most insistent one? And why does this subject appear in such fundamentally different forms?"[14] "Yeah," the non-believing believer, or the believing non-believer, might be tempted to say, "Why?" Oops—we said it together! *If* we were honest, even with our different inflections: "How *can* I *still* believe in something so useless?" or, "Why *is* it that something so useless remains so insistent *even today*?"

We get to ground zero of doubt, so to speak, at the beginning of the first chapter in the second part, on Jesus:

> It is only in the second section of the Creed that we come up against the real difficulty—already considered briefly in the introduction—about Christianity: the profession of faith that the man Jesus, an individual executed in Palestine round about the year 30, the *Christus* (anointed, chosen) of God, indeed God's own Son, is the central and decisive point of all human history. It seems both presumptuous and foolish to assert that one single figure who is bound to disappear farther and farther into the mists of the past is the authoritative center of all history.[15]

"Yeah, that's right!" we, both believing unbelievers and unbelieving believers, say together—if we are honest. And perhaps we hear ourselves saying (even before Ratzinger says it) that indeed, not to put too fine a point on it, "The birth of Jesus from a virgin of whom things like these [recounted in St. Luke's text] has long been a thorn in the flesh of rationalizers of every kind."[16] Of *every* kind ... hmmmm ..., believer or unbeliever, I wasn't going to exactly say it this way ... am I a 'rationalizer'—if I'm honest? "Distinguishing various sources is supposed to minimize the New Testament testimony"—well, doesn't it?—"references to the unhistorical thinking of the ancients are supposed to remove the event to the realm of the symbolical"— well, that *would* help both my belief and my unbelief—"and insertion to the

13. Ratzinger, *Introduction*, 103.
14. Ratzinger, *Introduction*, 103.
15. Ratzinger, *Introduction*, 193.
16. Ratzinger, *Introduction*, 273.

context of the history of religions is supposed to show that it is a variant of a myth"—yes, that's what I was worrying about, *or that's what I was banking on*![17] One more example can come from the third article of the Creed (not to leave it out) on the resurrection of the body, that is, of individuals, not (in this context) that of Jesus. After issuing a series of questions, one after the other, and questions within questions, he notes that nevertheless "We have still not reached the end of our questions. If this is the position [that is, that Christianity is essentially concerned with the resurrection neither of 'soul' nor 'flesh' considered in themselves, but of the person], is there really such a thing as a resurrected body, or can the whole thing be reduced to a mere symbol for the immortality of the person?"[18] And again, a little later: "Has, then, the resurrection no relation at all to matter? And does this make the 'Last Day' completely pointless in comparison with the life that always comes from the call of the Lord?"[19]

It is true, then, that for Ratzinger the pedagogy of introducing is very heavily focused on the interpretation of Christian belief, on the Christian faith, and on temptations simultaneously to belief and unbelief. The brilliant clarifications of what Christians believe, the analysis of what is *still* true and what is true *even today*, even in the midst of all of our questions, addressing our temptations as believers to give up and agree that relativism is the only modern option, or prompting the temptation of unbelievers to think that maybe, after all, it isn't—is essential to the "introducing," which appears much less from this point of view as a first introduction from no knowledge whatsoever, as a kind of second look at something one is tempted on the grounds of modernity to give up—or, alternatively, something one had given up or not entertained as a serious option and, upon looking again, be tempted to go farther.

Nevertheless, this does not explain why the book is entitled *Introduction to Christianity* rather than *Introduction to Christian Faith* or the like. I'd like to suggest in this regard that, though I made the grandiose claim that we had come to "ground zero" in the article on Christ, that is actually a deflection away from the real occasion of strife. Just as the mystery of the Church is a secondary mystery relative to the mystery of Christ and reflects that mystery (as the Fathers liked to say) as the moon reflects the sun, so in reverse the difficulties with the mystery of Christ are a deflection of the difficulties with the third article of the Creed, on the Church:

---

17. Ratzinger, *Introduction*, 273.

18. Ratzinger, *Introduction*, 356.

19. Ratzinger, *Introduction*, 358. Ratzinger continues the questions right until the penultimate page of the book (in the English translation).

> For us men of today [the "today" of "even today" from the last sentence] the *basic stumbling block of Christianity* [NB] lies first of all simply in the superficiality to which the religious element seems to have settled down. It irritates us that God should have to be mediated through outward forms: through Church, sacrament, dogma, or even just through the Gospel (kerygma), to which people like to withdraw to reduce the irritation and which is nevertheless itself something external.[20]

To amplify the irritation even further (and as we might expect), a question is asked: "Does God dwell in institutions, events or words? As the eternal Being, does he not make contact with each of us from within?"[21] Uncharacteristically, this question is answered immediately: "To this we must first of all simply say Yes and then go on to say that if there were only God and a collection of individuals, Christianity [NB] would be unnecessary."[22]

As it is, Ratzinger explains (in keeping, I would add, with virtually *any* good faith reading of Vatican II) that, for the salvation merely of individuals, there would be "no need of either a Church or a history of salvation, an Incarnation or a Passion of God in this world." But "Christian faith [NB] is not based on the atomized individual but comes from the knowledge that there is no such thing as the mere individual, that, on the contrary, man is himself only when he is fitted into the whole."[23] Although bodily existence on the one hand separates individuals from each other, on the other hand "existence in a corporal form necessarily also embraces history and community,"[24] involving physical descent and dependence, the reception of language itself from a distant past, and all of the relationships to which these give rise (summarized under the name "Adam"), and this "body" (and the cosmos in which it is inextricably located) are themselves the subject of salvation. There is no such thing, to use C. S. Lewis's phrase, as "mere Christianity," that is, a set of doctrines or dogmas more or less held in common by Christians to which "Christianity" may be reduced by a process of abstraction.

C. S. Lewis's book, *Mere Christianity*, a very popular text for courses that strive to "introduce" the Christian faith in a way intelligible to contemporaries, actually implies a pedagogy aggressively opposed to the abstracting strategy of C. S. Lewis's text which, in effect, responds to the scandal caused

---

20. Ratzinger, *Introduction*, 244 (my emphasis).
21. Ratzinger, *Introduction*, 244–45.
22. Ratzinger, *Introduction*, 245.
23. Ratzinger, *Introduction*, 245.
24. Ratzinger, *Introduction*, 245.

by disagreement among Christian communions to abstracting from all of them to a least common denominator with its own distinctive "smell."[25] But this pedagogy seems very much a pedagogy of the atomized individual—a pedagogy addressing the intellectual issues of an apologetics for the Christian faith in our day, whereas Ratzinger's *Introduction* eschews accomplishing this by leaving "Christianity" behind as an abstraction which is, in fact, no one's actual religion. I believe this is why it is popular among Evangelical and non-denominational Christians, and with Christian analytic philosophers who, often quite brilliantly, use the text in class and invoke its insights.

"Christianity," as opposed simply to "Christian faith" or "Christian belief," is constitutively an external affair, a reality that has visible continuity in history, and is the mark of the presence of the Church, as herself a constitutively visible, corporate reality, in the world. There is no "Christian faith" without "Christianity," but there is no "Christianity" without the Church, and therefore an apologetic for the Church is at the center (not the periphery) of an *Introduction to Christianity*. And, "if we are honest with ourselves"—that call for self-knowledge once again—"we are tempted to say . . . that the Church is neither holy nor Catholic."[26] Therefore, "for many people today the Church has become the main obstacle to belief. They can no longer see in her anything but the human struggle for power, the petty spectacle of those who, with their claim to administer official Christianity [*NB*, not 'the Christian faith'], seem to stand most in the way of the true spirit of Christianity [*NB*, not 'Catholicism']."[27] Ratzinger rather poignantly concedes (perhaps only here in the whole of the *Introduction*) that such ideas cannot be compellingly refuted by mere reason because the damage is partly in the affective part of a person, where love is disappointed and disillusionment creates the bitterness of destroyed hopes.

And yet one has to start somewhere, from the "objective elements" that reason may discern regarding the contours and coordinates of a mystery that is, like all the truths of revelation, ultimately beyond reason. Can one evoke a love this way? Only if at first reason is used to throw cold water on the illusions that have no part in the mystery and yet seem so attached to it such that, when they are destroyed, the mystery seems to be lost as well. For example, the reason the Church is called "holy" in the Creed is not "because her members, collectively and individually, are holy sinless men—this dream, which appears afresh in every century, has no place in the waking world of our text, however movingly it may express a human longing that

25. See C. S. Lewis, "Introduction," 6.
26. Ratzinger, *Introduction*, 339.
27. Ratzinger, *Introduction*, 340.

man will never abandon until a new heaven and a new earth really grant him what this age will never give him."[28] In other words, the "confidence" involved in being a Christian is not a confidence in a group constitutively bound by human virtue. Reason can help dissipate this "rationalized" view of the Church in favor of the true mystery, and perhaps in a way that evokes the "understanding" necessary to love. Love of the Church is love of Christ working in the Church: "But it is really and truly the holiness of the *Lord* that becomes present in [the Church] and that chooses again and again as the vessel of its presence—with a paradoxical love—the dirty hands of men. It is holiness that radiates as the holiness of Christ from the midst of the Church's sin."[29] Christ did not disdain mixed company in his lifetime, and he still does not turn up his nose: if He did, whose personal holiness would be enough to merit being His vessel? Where then would we find Him in this world, as opposed to simply in the inner world of the heart which (in any event) is equally dubious if it is human? "One could actually say that precisely in her paradoxical combination of holiness and unholiness, the Church is in fact the shape taken by grace in this world."[30] Ratzinger's description of the unholy holiness of the Church, which follows, is the best and most moving I have ever come across, though it is too long to quote here.

If we take our pedagogical cue from Ratzinger at this point, it will mean that the main project, in a sense, is ultimately aimed at elucidating and clarifying the mystery of the Church—and not just at the point the Church is covered in the third article of the Creed, but, in a sense, all along, so that, when it comes time to treat the mystery of the Church, it will appear as a recapitulation of the exposition of everything foregoing, instead of a kind of optional add-on for the obsessive or the tough minded. C. S. Lewis has the image of the apologetic enterprise as one in which one defends "mere Christianity" as in a hallway, and then, if one wishes, one goes off into one of the rooms off of the hallway, that is, a particular denomination. I can't think of a strategy less likely to work, unless one means by "Christianity" simply a set of dogmatic propositions to which one gives assent. Instead, the pedagogical aim of the *Introduction to Christianity* must be, in the last analysis, to teach love of the Church—not as itself the central mystery, but as the mystery which teaches us most about how Christ loves us, how he loves the world in which we live, and how he loves the whole universe of creatures that came forth from His hand in the first place. Only then will we see the full extent of salvation and be able to agree: "A salvation of the world does

28. Ratzinger, *Introduction*, 340–41.
29. Ratzinger, *Introduction*, 341.
30. Ratzinger, *Introduction*, 342.

exist—that is the confidence that supports the Christian and that still makes it rewarding even today to be a Christian." Thank You.

Bibliography

Lewis, C. S. "Introduction." In *St. Athanasius, On the Incarnation,* translated and edited by a Religious of C.S.M.V. Crestwood: St. Vladimir's Seminary Press, 1994.
Ratzinger, Joseph. *Introduction to Christianity*. With a New Preface. Translated by J. R. Foster and Michael J. Miller. San Francisco: Ignatius, 2004.

Index

Abraham, 36, 136, 178, 245
Aquinas, Thomas. *See* Thomas Aquinas.
Aristotle, xviii, 13, 28, 38-40, 152-54, 158

baptism (or baptismal), xx, 11, 60, 70-71, 73, 80, 93, 122, 144-48, 174, 185, 199, 201-2, 227, 229, 244, 299, 307
beauty, 173, 191, 227, 246, 294-301, 304, 307, 315
Bible, 54, 71-73, 121, 125, 280
Body of Christ, xxxi, 122, 145, 203, 205-6, 231, 236, 246, 309, 314
Bonaventure, xxiv, 8, 12, 28, 78, 133, 147, 152-58, 189, 196-97, 201, 203-5, 207, 243n, 251-52, 303
Buber, Martin, 13, 33, 134, 243n, 298

Catholicism, 67, 76-79, 82-83, 157, 160-61, 168n, 181, 195n, 263, 309, 317-18, 324
child (or children, childhood), xix, 18, 44, 48, 52, 144, 222, 244n, 250, 259, 264-65, 298, 307
confession (or confessional), xvi, xx, xxiii, xxv, xxvii, 9, 69-70, 74, 76, 80-85, 106, 129, 132, 138, 145, 171-72, 195, 200, 228-29, 235, 237, 240
conscience, 33, 61n, 158, 253

consciousness, 21, 45, 55, 104, 154, 176, 184, 215, 217, 220-21, 232, 261, 318
contemplation, 120, 123, 243n, 251-52, 262
conversation (or conversations), xxix, 13, 41, 52, 83-84, 109-10, 113-15, 117, 275-76, 295
conversion, xxv, 25, 56, 73-74, 93, 97, 99, 105, 144-45, 149, 169n, 170, 174, 183, 185, 199, 236-38, 244, 261, 309
Creator, xxix, 32, 36-37, 58, 95, 176, 243, 245, 261, 266-67, 271
credibility, xxvi, 33, 203, 226, 230-31, 233, 236, 238-39
culture (or cultures, cultured), xix, xxvii, xxx, 37, 50, 60, 68n, 75, 85, 103, 158, 168-69, 182-83, 185, 191, 208, 239, 262, 281, 283, 307, 319, 320

De Lubac, Henri, 4n, 20-21, 62, 68n, 69, 72-73, 77-81, 86, 145-46, 152n, 154n, 175, 189, 194n, 209-10, 219, 239, 296n, 297n
dialectic (or dialectical, dialectics), xxiv, 20, 50, 59, 148, 154n, 155, 157, 160-61, 195, 206, 295, 303-4
Dionysius the Areopagite, 158
discipleship, 182

ecclesiology, xviii, 5–6, 18, 20–21, 47, 49–50, 90, 99–100, 102–3, 233, 237, 239
ecumenical, xx, xxvii, 21, 25, 32, 36, 40n, 44, 73, 76, 82–84, 87, 130, 160, 192, 194, 231
ecumenism, 29–30, 69–70, 76, 82–87
empathy, xxiv, 157, 181, 302
Enlightenment, 33, 59, 85, 89–91, 93–94, 99, 101–4, 298
epistemology, 14, 74, 146, 153, 171, 303
eschatology, xxvii–xxviii, 30, 145, 149, 155n, 241–42, 252–53
ethics, xxix–xxx, 61, 101, 275–80, 283–85, 291, 302
evangelization, xix, xxiv, 60, 152, 156–57, 194
evil (or evils), 9, 62, 144, 221

Francis, Pope, xix, xxvi, 159n
freedom, 38, 41, 53, 92, 138, 144, 168n, 176, 184, 220–21, 237, 249n, 261, 266–68, 276, 288, 300–301, 318–20
fundamentalism, 155, 157–61

glory, 252, 262, 284, 289–91, 296, 300, 303
goodness, 134, 148, 227, 261
Gospel (or Gospels), xix, xxiv, xxxi, 7, 15–16, 33, 53, 111, 114, 116–17, 122–23, 127, 156, 159n, 160n, 169, 181–83, 191, 199, 234, 261, 263–64, 305–7, 323
grace (or graces), xxix, 18, 20, 28, 44–45, 54, 58, 62, 99n, 102, 104, 137, 146, 154n, 184, 198, 204, 255–56, 261, 263, 265, 268–70, 295, 302, 325

Habermas, Jürgen, 39, 173n, 182
Hegel, G. W. F., xix, 51, 53, 57, 59, 62, 91–92, 95, 150, 169, 172, 180–81, 195n, 202n

hell (or hellish, hells), xxvi, 17, 20, 47, 180, 221–24, 249, 252, 298–99, 303, 305
heresy, 58, 161
Holy Spirit, xxiv–xxvii, 11, 19, 28, 67, 76, 81, 111–12, 115, 122, 146, 161, 189, 201, 206n, 225–26, 232, 234–39, 299–300
hope, xix, 18, 30, 36, 52, 115–16, 122, 132, 157, 175, 203, 241, 253, 262, 288, 299, 300, 324

ideology, 148, 155, 159, 228, 231, 233
incarnation (or incarnational), xxi, 15–17, 44, 46, 49, 51, 56, 89–90, 92–93, 98, 106, 119, 124, 133, 137–38, 156, 175n, 184, 235, 249, 280, 284–85, 305, 315, 323
infinite (or infinitely), 17, 20, 94, 104, 175, 202, 216, 228, 261, 275, 279, 303, 305
intellect (or intellectual, intellectualize, intellectually), xvi, xxiii, 3, 9n, 13, 15–16, 22, 44–45, 48, 55, 57, 73, 75, 90, 92, 94n, 95, 98–99, 101, 104, 109, 115, 117–18, 127, 133–34, 137, 147n, 149, 155, 159, 173, 182, 203, 226–29, 294, 298, 319–20, 324
interreligious dialogue, 11, 70, 83–85, 87

Jesuit (or Jesuits), xxiv, 34, 93, 103, 134, 161, 298
Jewish (or Jews), xxi, 16, 90, 221, 278–79
John XXIII, Pope, 9, 130, 132, 152, 192, 203
John of Ruusbroec, 158
John of the Cross, 158, 207
John Paul II, Pope, 86, 156, 218

Kant, Immanuel, 45, 59, 91–92, 95, 102, 146, 150, 173–74, 177, 278
Kasper, Walter, xviii–xix, 10, 29–30, 46, 49–55, 57, 60–61, 94n, 156
kerygma, 199, 323

Levinas, Emmanuel, 174n
liturgical (or liturgically), xxviii, 30, 52, 105, 144, 148, 183, 198–99, 202n, 207–8, 246, 255–71, 291, 299
liturgy, xxviii, 11, 21, 30–31, 71, 73, 80, 121, 157, 160–61, 177n, 184, 193, 198, 247, 256–58, 262–63, 266–68, 270, 299, 307
Lonergan, Bernard, 146n, 157, 192
Luther, Martin, 20–21, 59, 67n, 69n, 71, 146, 172, 282

Marion, Jean-Luc, 148n, 151n, 156, 159n
Marx, Karl, xix–xx, 27, 44, 52, 55 59–61, 89, 148–49, 159
Mary of Nazareth, xxii, 18, 109–18, 125–27, 194, 237, 239, 252, 311
Metz, Johann Baptist, 29, 41, 60
Moses, 36, 135–36, 289
metaphysics, xxviii, 34, 59–60, 137, 144, 149–50, 152–53, 156–60, 162, 175, 180, 255–71
ministry, 6–7, 17, 198, 289–90, 292

Neo-Platonists (or Neo-platonic, Neo-Platonism), xxix, 93, 97–100, 106, 255, 269
Neo-Thomism (or Neo-Thomist), xxiv, 147, 152, 158
Nietzsche, Friedrich, xxx–xxxi, 39, 44, 299
nouvelle théologie, 20, 71, 73, 106, 144, 147, 152, 154n, 156, 158, 195

paschal mystery, 148, 205, 298
Paul VI, Pope, 46n, 86
pedagogy, xxxi–xxxii, 262, 317–19, 322–24
phenomenology, 144, 152, 156–57, 160, 170–71, 174, 217, 223
Pius, XII, Pope, 100n, 218
pneumatology, xviii, 19, 49–50, 206n, 225–39

politics (or political, politician), xxiv, 5, 25, 28–29, 32, 34, 36–39, 41, 45–46, 50, 53, 59–60, 72n, 83, 94, 96, 100–101, 105–6, 147, 149, 168–70, 181–82, 198, 231, 258–59, 286–87, 307
praxis (or orthopraxis), xix, 22, 30, 52–55, 58–61, 149n, 255
priest (or priesthood, priests, priestly), 3, 55, 172, 198, 218, 289–92
Protestant (or Protestantism), 22, 49, 67n, 72–73, 76, 82, 172, 219

Rahner, Karl, xxi, 3–4, 6–7, 10, 27–29, 53–54, 60n, 73, 90, 101, 103–5, 146n, 152n, 156, 192, 196n, 209
reconciliation, 106, 181, 264
relativism, xviii, xx, xxiv, 27, 61, 85, 157–58, 160–61, 181, 322
renunciation, 136, 143–51, 157, 199, 244n, 305
resurrection, 15, 28, 69, 121, 148, 203, 205, 234, 309, 322
revolution (or revolutionaries, revolutionary, revolutionize), 13, 14, 28, 59–60, 94, 101–2, 193, 246, 248–49, 255
Ricoeur, Paul, xviii, 38–40

science (or sciences), 31, 50, 59, 89
scripture (or scriptures), xvii, xxi–xxiii, 7–10, 14–16, 28, 31, 71–73, 76, 82, 91–92, 106, 121–22, 129–38, 196, 221, 242, 296
Second Vatican Council. *See* Vatican II.
soteriology, xxvi, 17, 213–19, 223
soul (or souls), xvii, 9, 61n, 99, 109, 223, 243n, 265, 270, 279, 322
Stein, Edith (or Teresa Benedicta of the Cross), 156, 207
suffering, xxiv, 83n, 133, 181, 278–79, 297, 303–4, 309, 315
supernatural (or supernaturalism, supernaturalist, supernaturalised), 98, 100, 147n, 158–59, 300

synod (or synodal), 57, 111, 154, 207

Teresa of Ávila, 207
Thérèse of Lisieux, 207, 217
Thomas Aquinas, xxiv, 36–38, 96, 134, 146, 152–54, 158, 160, 197, 265n, 266, 294–95, 315
transcendence, xxiv, 4, 145, 171, 181, 191
Trinity, xxvii, xxx, 4, 11, 13–14, 72, 132, 137, 175, 202, 219, 232–33, 260, 294, 305

universal (or universalism, universalist, universality, universally), xx, xxi, xxiv, xxx, 31, 37, 55, 61, 92–93, 98, 101–4, 148, 151, 169, 181–82, 194, 219, 221, 260, 298

Vatican II, xvii, xxii, xxv, 3, 5–7, 10, 15–16, 19–20, 24, 26, 40n, 54, 68n, 73, 76–78, 84, 86, 103, 110–11, 129, 152, 160, 189, 192–95, 225, 300, 323
vocation (or vocational), 3, 148, 151, 206, 240, 267, 284

www.ingramcontent.com/pod-product-compliance
Lightning Source LLC
Chambersburg PA
CBHW071150300426
44113CB00009B/1149